A TERRIBLE LIAR

A TERRIBLE LIAR

HUME CRONYN

A MEMOIR

"Memory can be a judicious editor, omitting trial and tribulation. It can also be a terrible liar. . . ."

WILLIAM MORROW
AND COMPANY, INC.
New York

The author gratefully acknowledges the following for permission to use material in this book:

Excerpt from *A New Theatre* by Tony Guthrie, copyright © 1963. Used with permission of McGraw-Hill, Inc.

"First Fig" by Edna St. Vincent Millay. From *Collected Poems,* Harper & Row, copyright © 1922, 1950 by Edna St. Vincent Millay. Reprinted by permission of Elizabeth Barnett, Literary Executor.

"Come to the Edge" by Christopher Logue. From *New Numbers,* Jonathan Cape Ltd., copyright © 1969 by Christopher Logue. Reprinted by permission.

Excerpts from *Letters from an Actor* by William Redfield, copyright © 1967 by William Redfield. Used with permission of Limelight Editions, Proscenium Publishers Inc.

Excerpt from *Life Among the Playwrights* by John Wharton, copyright © 1974 by John Wharton. Used by permission of Random House, Inc.

Excerpts from *My Life with Cleopatra* by Walter Wanger and Joe Hyams, copyright © 1963. Used by permission.

Still photographs from *Cleopatra,* courtesy of Twentieth Century Fox Film Corporation.

Still photograph from *The Cross of Lorraine,* copyright © 1943 by Loew's Inc., ren. 1970, Metro-Goldwyn-Mayer, Inc.

Still photograph from *The Seventh Cross,* copyright © 1944 by Loew's Inc., ren. 1971, Metro-Goldwyn-Mayer, Inc.

Still photograph from *The Green Years,* copyright © 1946 by Loew's Inc., ren. 1973, Metro-Goldwyn-Mayer, Inc.

It is the policy of William Morrow and Company, Inc., and its imprints and affiliates, recognizing the importance of preserving what has been written, to print the books we publish on acid-free paper, and we exert our best efforts to that end.

Library of Congress Cataloging-in-Publication Data

Cronyn, Hume.
    A terrible liar: a memoir / by Hume Cronyn.
       p.   cm.
    ISBN 0-688-10080-5
    1. Cronyn, Hume. 2. Actors—Canada—Biography. I. Title.
PN2287.C682A3 1991
792'.028'092—dc20   91-7936
                                                         CIP

Printed in the United States of America

First Edition

1 2 3 4 5 6 7 8 9 10

BOOK DESIGN BY BERNARD SCHLEIFER

For Jessica and our children:
Susan, Chris and Tandy

And for my fellow compulsive,
Harvey Ginsberg,
who never meddled and never fumed,
who encouraged and restrained and who
I am proud to call my editor

FOREWORD

SUSAN COOPER is responsible for this book. So, of course, whatever its failings, they are her fault. No, she didn't write it, I did, but over the years she badgered and nagged, cajoled and bullied, until overcome by exhaustion, age and lack of more honest employment, I turned on her, snarling: "Very well, I'll write you some letters. I may be able to write letters. Give me a list of things you want me to write about." She did. I promptly lost it. However, I remembered some of the items: "Your family; school; your first theater jobs; meeting Jessie; working in Hollywood; Alfred Hitchcock . . ."

I wrote Susan four letters of about twenty pages each. I rather enjoyed that. Perhaps, I thought, I might find a publisher for a slim volume entitled *Letters to Susan*. I stuck them into a manila envelope marked "L.2.S." and mailed them off to her in Cambridge, Massachusetts. I received a prompt cold shower by telephone.

"These won't do at all."

"Why the hell not?"

"You keep talking to me in them. . . . We didn't even meet till 1974. . . . You have to write a *book*."

"Look, damn it, I undertook to write you some letters . . ."

7

I sulked for a couple of weeks, then started over. That was in 1987. My writing was sporadic—sometimes put aside to work with Susan herself. We have collaborated on a play (*Foxfire*), a teleplay (*The Dollmaker*, for Jane Fonda) and a screenplay based on Anne Tyler's lovely novel *Dinner at the Homesick Restaurant*. Then there were other plays and films which my wife, Jessica Tandy, and I acted in together. All of which gave me a wonderful excuse not to return to this . . . memoir? I suppose that's what it is: a book made of memories. A letter to a friend, which grew.

As I say on my title page, memory can be a terrible liar. Try as you may to recapture with total accuracy an incident or emotion from the past, you can't find those details your memory decided not to keep. Without consulting you, it edited them out long ago; like an overofficious filing clerk, it decided what should survive and what should be thrown away. What's left is at best a subjective truth. But within the limits of memory, I've tried to tell the truth. I'd be unconvincing if I did anything else, for in the other sense of the title, I really am a terrible liar.

Otherwise, I've had only one resolution in mind: to avoid boring recitations of "and then I played . . ." or "and then I slept with . . ."

I wish I had been able to make Jessica Tandy and our three children more of a presence in this book, but it's my story, not theirs. They have their own. Despite an extraordinarily intimate partnership of fifty years, Jessica and I have discovered that you can only share the pain and occasional glory of one another's efforts. You cannot really experience them, live them, or write about them for the other. As she is fond of saying, "He cannot play my parts nor I his."

On the other hand, I could never have got through this memoir—foreshortened though it may be—without Jessica's infinite patience and support, nor without the dedication and persistence of Sylvia Brooks, my friend and secretary of twenty-five years, who had to unravel my tangled longhand, and of course not without the loving scourge of the aforementioned Ms. Cooper. Pax.

A TERRIBLE LIAR

ONE

A CATERPILLAR FLOATED down from the japonica tree. We were sitting in the front garden having tea: my mother, my two older brothers and I. It was a ritual, as so much of my early life was, a ritual exercised in benign surroundings. The japonica was in bloom, an occasional petal would flutter down onto the table—and now the caterpillar. Dick picked it up and drowned it in the dregs of his teacup. Verse held his cup chest high, his elbows propped on the arms of his chair, staring at me like a basilisk. I felt like the caterpillar.

Things weren't going well. I had no business precipitating such tension into an otherwise sunny afternoon. The peaceful gardens of the big house called Woodfield were more accustomed to the sentiments carved into the cement lip of the goldfish pool:

> The kiss of the sun for pardon,
> The song of the birds for mirth,—
> One is nearer God's heart in a garden
> Than anywhere else on earth.

That was both credo and promise—and here was I planting weeds.

"What are we going to do about Junior?"

11

*   *   *

I never much cared for the name, but it didn't really matter; I was called so many things during my growing-up years: "Peewee," "the Runt," and "Jay"—for Junior. Sometimes it was "Fatso." Until I was about ten, I looked rather like a small Toby jug—jug-eared, widemouthed, huge head, short legs, and the whole gently rounded. The mirror was not reassuring.

Now, at nineteen, sitting under the japonica tree, I was thinner but still "Junior," and I had said my piece. I wanted to become an actor. I wanted to abandon my supposed studies at McGill and any thought of an eventual law degree, and go to a professional drama school. Nominally of course the decision would be up to my father, but my mother's judgment would prevail. She was just over five feet in height, my father, six feet two; authority had become a matter of inverse ratio. He was very ill, a wasting sickness that had brought God low. We all knew where He was. He would be there, stretched out on his sofa, possibly sleeping but more likely just "resting"— and chewing. He was trying to substitute Chiclets for smoking. His jaws would move in dreadful, slow deliberation, his mind flickering back to some old triumph never to be mentioned— or more grimly forward to some inevitable but equally unmentionable future. Watching him was like watching a slow-motion erosion of Mount Rushmore. I asked him once what he was thinking and he said softly, "The long, long thoughts," and went back to his cud.

So, we sat in the garden, my brothers—sixteen and eighteen years my senior—surrogates for my father. I can't say that there was a lull in the conversation, only a series of ominous silences. During one of them William appeared to remove the untouched sandwiches: cucumber, tomato and watercress. My mother put her hand on the tea cozy to indicate that we'd keep that. The business proceeded in dumb show.

William wore a short white coat with a mandarin collar, the buttons straining against a generous "corporation." He was a big man with thinning, sandy hair and a formidable rush of teeth to the front. His infrequent utterances carried an unmistakable Scottish burr. My cousins used to mock him, imitating the sibilance with which he offered "White wine, sir?" He was never referred to as a butler, which would have been ostentatious; he was the houseman, doubling when occasion demanded as chauffeur. Then the white coat would be traded for a gray uniform, a cap with a shiny black peak, and black gloves. He took my mother calling: this was nearly sixty years ago, when people still "left cards." They accumulated on a little silver tray in the front hall: *Minnie dear, sorry to have missed you—George is much better and sends his respects.*

The tea was finished, but no resolution had been found; nothing but that pervasive silence. It was getting late; shadows reached across the lawn, there was the smell of nicotiana and the sound of nighthawks. They found good hunting about our garden and would drop from the sky, beaks agape, making a sound like a tuning fork.

To this day I cannot catch the whiff of tobacco plant in bloom or hear a nighthawk without being transported back to the Woodfield garden. On bad days, when rehearsals have taken a giant step backwards, or the reviews are terrible, and despair knots the gut, I may even remember this particular afternoon.

Verse took a final swallow. The cup clinked into its saucer and with awful deliberation he leaned back, arms folded. Dick, looking like a bemused Buddha, twisted his signet ring. Of us all, my mother was the most composed—perhaps because she had by far the greatest anxieties. She sat easily, the fingers of one hand resting against her cheek. How could three people to whom I was devoted seem so ominous? It was Verse who shattered the silence.

"How many years do you think you can afford to waste?"

I did not know the answer and didn't bother to reply. I pushed back my chair and stalked away. I think perhaps I heard my mother say, "Hume?" It was not a command, no more than a gentle inquiry, but I walked on, past the rose bed on my left, the opium poppies and hollyhocks on my right, along the brick path that ran under the pergola and led to the north gate. The gate was on a spring and banged behind me. I had left Woodfield.

Or had I? Probably not. "Lucky is the man who can outlive his inheritance." It surrounded me then, it still haunts me now.

Woodfield had been built by my great-grandfather, the Rt. Rev. Benjamin Cronyn, an Irish cleric and divinity prizeman from Trinity College, Dublin. Legend has it that as a very small boy my grandfather had watched *his* father (the future bishop) haul stone out of the river behind a team of oxen. The stone was for Woodfield, and my grandfather worried about how his father was going to pay for it. How indeed?—unless there was money in some deep sock brought from Kilkenny or Galway, which seems most unlikely. Legend also has it that my great-grandfather came out "to minister to the souls of the Blakes," a family in York, later Toronto. Why then did he settle instead at "The Forks," later London, Ontario? That the two families eventually made contact is obvious enough, because three Blake children and three Cronyn children of my grandfather's generation married one another, leaving me with a gaggle of descendant cousins so complex that I never have sorted it out.

I hardly knew my much older Blake cousins, but became heartily sick of hearing about their parents and grandparents, who were a formidable crew. My great-uncle, Edward Blake, was premier of Ontario and somehow or other managed to hold down seats in both the Canadian and British Houses of Commons. The adjectives "brilliant," "moody," "Puritan" and "humorless" were frequently applied to the Blakes, as was the name Hume, which seems to have been bestowed with careless abandon on both sexes.

At any rate, the stone came out of the river and Woodfield got built. My grandfather grew up there, my father was born there, my brothers and sisters and I were born there. I came along thirteen years after the first four—an obvious error. *"What are we going to do about Junior?"*

Outside the north gate and the bounds of Woodfield, I stood on Queens Avenue, hurt, angry and bewildered. Across the street were the Victorian piles built or inhabited by relatives. At the corner of Adelaide was the mansion built by a great-uncle, Ben Cronyn (yet another Ben), who with questionable taste—conspicuous consumption being a sin only slightly less heinous than adultery, theft, suicide and popery— had had his initials "B.C." carved into the cornerstone. The

present owner was a Mrs. Leonard, who was at pains to explain that the initials did *not* mean "before Christ." She was a
garrulous lady who, I was told, had swallowed a dictionary—
an image which fascinated me when I was young enough to
take the expression literally. I visualized a greedy pelican stuck
with an oversized fish.

When, during the first world war, Mrs. Leonard's sons were
mired in the frontline trenches of France, some friend com-
miserating on their discomfort was reassured with the following: "The dear boys have adjuncts within themselves that render
them impervious to extraneous circumstance." I always loved
that one. One of the dear boys was killed, of course. A wooden
Flanders field cross hung in the Cronyn Memorial Church—
to my left now, at the corner of Queens Avenue and William
Street. Beneath the cross was a brass plaque. I even remember
the inscription. I ought to. I sat beneath it in the family pew
on every Sunday that I was home from school.

In loving Memory of

Lt. Col. Edwin Woodman Leonard, D.S.O.

3rd Brig. Canadian Field Artillery

Died of wounds, Vimy Ridge, France

April 9th, 1917. Aged 33.

"I am finished. Take over and carry on."

Opposite the church stood the residence of my uncle,
Frederick Pimlott Betts. He'd married my father's eldest sister,
Aunty Bloss. Blossom was very much a Blake, but with a difference—she had a sense of humor. Thank God I never saw
her angry; one sensed that this would be cataclysmic. Fortunately her handsome but stern features, her hawklike nose,
were belied by a twinkle. It was something she shared with
Uncle Fred. He always seemed to me to be enormously tall,
perhaps because he had such long legs. These were frequently
encased in striped trousers, morning trousers; above them a
black waistcoat, a watch chain, a short black Oxford coat, a
wing collar and bow tie, a spade beard. Very formal, very much
the proper barrister—but with a twinkle.

One Christmas I'd been given ("from Santa Claus") a pocket watch, a gleaming metal turnip. I rushed from Woodfield to show it to Aunt Bloss; through the snow, down the path, clutching my prize, through the gate, across Queens Avenue—where I stumbled at the curb and saw the watch disappear through a grating that covered the street sewer. Gone, quite gone and irretrievable.

Desolate, I recounted this tragedy in the Betts' house.

Uncle Fred was warming his bum before the coal fire. He had the deepest voice of any man I've ever known. He looked down on me, rocking gently from heel to toe, his hands clasped behind him. "But surely, my dear Hume, you are familiar with the perversity of inanimate objects. It's a law. Absolute. Drop a thing—a collar stud, say—and it never falls where you can pick it up but always contrives to roll under something. Sheer perversity. Don't be upset. It's the way life is."

Rock, rock, twinkle, twinkle.

Between the Betts' house on one corner and the "B.C." house on the other was Endiang. This was my maternal grandfather's house, built by his father, John Kinder Labatt, who founded the brewery that bears his name. Again, legend has it that my mother, Frances Amelia Labatt, looked down on Queens Avenue from an upstairs window and watched my father, cane swinging, stride downtown to his office. "I pity the woman who marries Hume Cronyn," she said. I wonder what quality she had in mind? Well, she had over forty years in which to confirm or deny her prejudice.

My grandfather Labatt looked a little like Edward VII and had the same jollity. When the brewery once trembled on the edge of bankruptcy, as it apparently did on several occasions, his lawyers came to explain the seriousness of the situation, and in the middle of this tale of woe Grandad fell asleep. Perhaps he'd had a hard night. "Well," said the lawyer huffily, "if John Labatt isn't worried about his business, I don't know why I should be." And he left. The Labatts were unquestionably a more relaxed tribe than the Cronyns.

All these relatives . . . their shades surrounded me there on Queens Avenue that evening.

I started to walk, nursing "long, long thoughts" of my own. This whole "What shall we do about Junior?" crisis had been precipitated by my leaving university—unannounced and immediately prior to my final freshman examinations—to grab a job in a stock company in Washington, D.C. Predictably, I ran out of money and had to telegraph home. Dick, as the senior active male in the family during my father's illness, had been deputized to write back, special delivery. There was one sentence in his letter I'm not likely to forget: "If you've decided to make the theatre your profession, you may have been wise to seize the bull by the horns and grasp at this opportunity. However, let me tell you that you've gone about it in the most damnably stupid fashion imaginable."

But he enclosed a cashier's check for fifty dollars.

So much for Dick. But my mother? I knew she'd been under pressure. Junior was spoiled (and he most certainly was). Junior's associations were in questionable taste. I had after all brought an actor, a real live professional actor, home with me for the weekend. He was a young Englishman, with polished hair and a languid manner, and he wore suede shoes. My brother-in-law referred to the shoes contemptuously as "brothel creepers."

I had caught snatches of conversation between my mother and her close friend Georgie Gates, an imperious lady who used a lorgnette and spoke in a mellifluous but rather fruity voice. There was nothing malicious about "Cousin Georgie," but her mountain top allowed only a limited view.

"But isn't it odd?"

"What, dear?"

"About Junior. Such a nice boy but . . ." (she struggled for the right adjective) ". . . odd. What does Cousin Hume say?" She was referring to my father.

"Very little. I think he feels that Junior must choose and that we must help him."

"Of course. Of course. But Minnie dear, you do indulge him—that car, that coat, that *actor!* I do feel for you." The car referred to was my green Franklin Roadster, and the coat, raccoon. I'd been sent off to McGill in both, to the outrage of the entire family—save for my parents.

So my mother had critical voices to contend with. What would she say?

I walked a long way, and I got home late. The light was

still on in my mother's room and she called to me. She spoke softly because my father was asleep on the porch outside.

"You must not be angry with them," she said. "They are only thinking of your own good." She paused. "I will make a bargain with you. Go back to the university for one more year, and if at the end of that time you still wish to go into the theater, I will see to it that you go to the Royal Academy of Dramatic Arts in London, or to the American Academy in New York—as you choose."

How had she even heard of such institutions? I kissed her joyfully and ran downstairs, outside onto the broad Woodfield veranda. In one of its bays sat an enormous king-sized divan, where my father would sometimes lie and read aloud. He read most beautifully, creating worlds that quite eclipsed London, Ontario. Is that perhaps what I wanted to do too? Maybe. But for the moment I only wanted to enjoy my euphoria. I sprawled between the cushions and listened to the dark. The night-hawks were gone but the tobacco plant was still there, and crickets and tree frogs. They made for a terrible stillness and change of mood; from euphoria to something *triste*, from security to—what?

> That is the land of lost content,
> I see it shining plain,
> The happy highways where I went
> And cannot come again.

I had already left home.

TWO

A DOZEN YEARS EARLIER, on November 11th, 1918, I had been given a very large flag and allowed to go out onto Dundas Street and wave at the Armistice Day parade. Finally, the war was over. My mother would roll no more bandages, send no more boxes jam-packed with cigarettes, chocolate, potted meats and socks she'd knitted herself. My brothers would come home—but eighteen other members of the family connection would not. You were never allowed to forget that, or the poppies and the rows of crosses in Flanders fields. Names like Ypres, Vimy Ridge, and Verdun had a lasting resonance for adults, on this day marking the end of the "war to end all wars." But for me, it was just a day with a flag and a parade: military bands, veterans, the garrison from Wolseley barracks, contingents from the police and fire departments, even some cavalry. The horse droppings steamed in the chill November air.

I was seven years old and the next memorable event in my life was whooping cough. I'd been put to bed upstairs in the old day nursery, where I lay in bed and between whoops watched the firelight. It danced in glorious patterns, gave off secret messages and threw wonderful, if slightly ominous, shadows across photographs, books, and prints crowded on

19

the walls. During some of those whooping-cough days I spent time at Mookejewun—Indian for "hill of many springs." This was my grandfather's farm about five miles outside the city; it was a small boy's paradise—and an adult's too, more an oasis than a working facility. I doubt that it supported itself. There *was* a farmer, who tolerated my poking about the barn and diving into the hayloft. There were magnificent trees and ice-cold springs; there were fields of oats and barley that rippled in the wind so that you could watch a breeze travel, crest and fall like an ocean wave. Best of all, there were the trout ponds.

Fifty years onward, in the seventies, I was taken back to the Farm by my sister K (short for Katherine). It had changed. The careful ponds were filled with weed, the trimmed paths overgrown; there was no farmer, and worst of all the course of the river that bordered the property had found new channels. I staggered through the brush, across fallen trees, through briars and bogs, hunting a familiar landmark. Finally my sister asked rather plaintively, "Hume, can you tell me exactly what we're hunting for?" Jessie, in the rear, was fairly terse. "His lost youth," she growled. I plowed on—but it was gone.

As a small boy I'd been told, wryly, that the bottom of the ponds on the Farm were paved with gold. It was some time before I understood that this was a reference to the expense involved in creating them. But gold was dross compared to the magic of those blue-green holes among weed beds, where the springs bubbled and where, if you hunkered down and crept— oh, so carefully—to the bank edge, you could see the trout lazily finning.

Fly-fishing was one more family ritual, and it was at the Farm that my Uncle Will schooled me in its mysteries and magic. I was given my own fly rod, a tubular steel affair (split bamboo came only upon graduation) and five flies: a Parmachene Belle, a Silver Doctor, a Montreal, a Black Gnat, and a Dusty Miller. No allowance was made for inexpert casting, for endless hang-ups, or bird's nests of line or leader so complex that there was no resolving them except with a knife. "The perversity of inanimate objects." I wish I could say it taught me patience. It didn't.

On one black whooping-cough day when the whoops were

particularly bad and I'd dropped my rod for the umpteenth time to throw up in the bushes behind me, I came back, winded and hacking, to find that a trout had taken my sunken fly and wound it around a stump. ("Never leave a fly on the water, Junior, unless you have control of the rod!") It was my last fly and it was gone. First I broke the leader; then I danced hysterically up and down on the rod until there was nothing recognizable left but the reel and a mass of mangled metal. Then I bawled.

I buried the remains and had my diseased tonsils removed, in that order. Was the panic of anaesthesia worse than the shameful aftermath of the tantrum? I think so. I suppose everyone has occasional fantasies of death and may speculate on which form is the most dreadful. I do, and the vote is easy: suffocation. Suffocation in any form whatever; choking to death, drowning, garroting, being buried alive. So when it came to the tonsillectomy and they slapped an inverted sieve over my face and doused it with ether, I gave the doctor and nurses one hell of a battle. *"Let me out, let me out!"*

It may have been the only time I shouted that aloud, but I was to feel it often enough in years to come.

When I was seven, I was sent to boarding school. To be honest, I don't remember being unhappy there—that was to come later, when I was ten and packed off to a *real* boarding school. This first school, Elmwood in Ottawa, was unusual in that for some time I was its only boarder. Later I was joined by another boy, a second stray, but his tenure was short and I remember little about him except that he was pleasant, and that I sometimes joined him in bed for bouts of simulated copulation that were highly inconclusive. I don't believe these instinctive fumblings provoked a sexual ambivalence in either one of us. At any rate, they provided my sole excursion into homosexuality—and were a total loss educationally.

The school gymnasium–cum–assembly hall at Elmwood was deserted and lonely after school hours, but became my private kingdom in the evenings. It was there that I could play wild, imaginative games, there that I became Mowgli or Tarzan, or both the cowboys and the Indians and frequently the horses as well. I led what psychologists refer to as a "rich fantasy life" and made a great deal of noise, galloping around the near-naked room and rearranging the chairs that stood along the walls (all to be carefully replaced later) into forts, stockades or impenetrable jungles.

Where was everyone? A headmaster and his wife were in residence somewhere above the schoolrooms. First there were a Mr. and Mrs. Philpott, later a Mr. and Mrs. Buck. Their images are blurred. Mr. Buck caught me stealing chocolates and I remember his wrath without remembering the punishment. It all seemed a bit unfair, as they were *my* chocolates. Someone had sent me a box, but they had been removed to the head's study for safekeeping and a judicious doling out of one each evening. Was I punished for theft or for trespass? And again where *was* everyone? Where and with whom did I have meals? It's odd not to remember a single meal. From eight in the morning to three in the afternoon Elmwood was abustle with boys and girls from seven to twelve in age. When they went home there was silence. I learned to skate by pushing a chair across the frozen pond. In the spring I would roam about the marsh below it, reeking of citronella, which was specified against mosquitoes. Was it my smell or my crashing about in the pussywillows that discouraged an otherwise constant chorus of spring peepers?

On weekends—some weekends, when the House of Commons, of which my father was a member, was in session—I spent time with my parents. They were living in a small flat in the center of Ottawa. These visits were a bit difficult and bleak, not through any lack of mutual affection but because of the capital's blue laws. Nothing was open except the hotel dining room. My father would take me for long walks beside the Ottawa River. On one of these, in 1920, we encountered a distinguished-looking gentleman enjoying his "constitutional." My father spoke first.

"Good morning, sir."

"Good morning . . . Cronyn of London isn't it? Congratulations."

"Thank you, sir." And we passed on.

"Who was that?"

"The Duke of Devonshire. Governor-General." My father's manner was not exactly brusque, but he didn't believe in wasting words. I never did discover what the "Congratulations" meant. Possibly, they referred to a speech my father had just made in the House of Commons, where he had been the member of the House chosen to reply to the "Speech from the Throne." This was the first such ceremony in the magnificent new Dominion parliament buildings and was an occasion with a capital *O*. The throne speech was made by the governor-general on behalf of His Majesty, King George V—roughly equivalent to an American president's State of the Union Address.

I sat with my mother, Verse and my darling sister Katherine—the latter two, for ceremony's sake, still in World War I uniform—in the visitors' gallery. My father rose to speak and there was a sudden, palpable hush. I don't remember what he said, of course, only that I was terrified he might not remember the words. He'd left the text of his speech in a taxi cab.

My father had only six more years of unafflicted life left to him. After that he was seriously ill for eight years, until he died in 1933. No one every really knew what the trouble was. He developed attacks—"fits," to use an ugly word—in which he would black out and suffer strange muscular spasms. When recovered, he would have no memory whatever of the attack, simply that some little piece of life had been lost to him; had become a blank, a hiatus, something immediately and forever forgotten. I heard such terms as "aphasia," "*le petit mal*," "epilepsy" and "cerebral sclerosis," but after all those conferences with doctors on either side of the Atlantic, what was really wrong?

Mr. Glass was our local druggist. I'd been sent to fill a prescription.

"How is your father?"

"Not very well, thank you."

"Well, you can't expect to burn the candle at both ends and not pay for it."

It was many years later than I read Edna St. Vincent Millay's hymn to candle burning:

> My candle burns at both ends,
> It will not last the night;

But ah, my foes, and oh, my friends—
It gives a lovely light.

And indeed it did. At least, to this occasional but worshipful son it did.

There was one terrifying, poignant moment in my teens that is etched on my memory. We were washing our hands before lunch in my father's bathroom. He turned off the tap, but instead of reaching for the towel, his wet hands fell on my shoulders.

"Oh Hume, I've been such a bad father to you," he said, and he started to cry. It was terrible, horrifying. God didn't cry, God was above such petty, emotional storms—and besides, it wasn't true, he wasn't a bad father, it wasn't true! It was the sickness. I held God's wrists and tried to reassure him.

Typically, I was told nothing of my father's illness until it was well advanced. Since I was away at school, it was felt there was no need for me to know. It was only when we were together, my mother, father and I—at the Tate Gallery in London, England, looking at a picture—that I first noticed my father's face twitch. I was given at that time to "making faces," to fiddling with my knife and fork at the dinner table—in short, to the fidgets. My father rarely rebuked me, but sometimes, with my fingers drumming on the table cloth, or fiddling with the silver, I'd turn to discover his face not a foot from my hand, watching the fiddle with dreadful concentration. My hand would be rapidly withdrawn into my lap where it belonged. Or if I was grimacing, he would imitate me, though it was a gentle mockery followed by a smile. These were object lessons in repose. So, we looked at the picture and, glancing at him, I saw the twitch.

"I'm sorry," I said. "Was I doing that?" My father didn't hear me. I felt my mother's hand on my arm.

"It's all right. Don't say anything." It was obvious that my father hadn't heard her either.

Back at the hotel apartment, my father retired for a "kip"; my mother and I went through the ritual of tea before the fire. She told me then.

The sickness began with spasms and ended, years later, with dreadful falls. Suddenly, from his immense height, he would pitch onto his face: in the drawing room, in the garden, on the golf course. Whenever someone in the house dropped a tray or a flowerpot, my mother would leave the floor in fright. Gradually, my father could find no golf partners, and no bridge partners either. Little wonder. Bridge was an evening ritual, but my father had trouble remembering the trumps, so a little wire gadget stood on the table and once the suit was declared, the gadget would be spun until a miniature card stood upright proclaiming the trump suite. When an attack struck him, and his cards would fly every which way, they would be collected by one of us, sorted out and laid carefully, face down, in front of his inert hands. Once the labored breathing had stopped, he would very tentatively pick up his hand, glance at the gadget and continue the game.

After I left Woodfield I never again played bridge or golf.

Over a period of eight years my father's illness grew inexorably more severe. I was away most of the time: at school, university, the academy, but when I came home on holidays I was aware of the tension, and when the holiday was over, would escape back to wherever I'd come from with a contradictory sense of relief and guilt. Day after day, after week, after month and year, how did my mother stand it?

I remember one occasion when we were having lunch. My mother, my father, his companion-secretary Edward Whitall, one of my visiting sisters and I were eating "Golden Buck" (scrambled eggs with anchovies, I think), and my father had one of his attacks. His fork went spinning, his spine stiffened and arched, and his arms went into uncontrollable spastic movements. No one moved. There was nothing to be done until his right hand came down, *splat,* into the steaming eggs. William, who was serving, came forward, lifted my father's hand from the plate, wiped it clean with a napkin, replaced the fork and stood aside. Not a word had been spoken—a macabre dumb show. After a little the color began to return to my father's face, his breathing became less labored and one of us forced some general conversation. Lunch appeared to continue normally. He picked up his fork rather tentatively, only to put it down at once. His hand hurt. Frowning in perplexity, he alternately splayed and clenched his fingers. Surreptitiously he looked from one to the other of us, seeking some clue, then back to his reddened hand. Finally, he gave up and resigned himself to the mystery.

He turned to my mother. "Jo," he said—he always called her Jo, after the character in *Little Women*—"Jo dear, have we any raspberries?"

Coward that I am, I asked to be excused from the table. It wasn't the attack or the burned hand that did me in, but that unforgettable look of pained bewilderment.

Thirty years later, in the early fifties, I directed my first Broadway play, an adaptation of Ludwig Bemelmans's *Now I Lay Me Down to Sleep,* in which Fredric March and Florence Eldridge were the stars. Freddy played General Leonidas Erosa, an epileptic. He was fascinated with his character's epileptic attacks, and was one of those blessed actors who is not offended by a director's demonstration. My skin crawling, I showed him what I remembered. "You ought to be playing this part," he'd say. Bemmy would look at me sideways: "How do you know it so well?" I rather doubt that I ever told him.

THREE

AT THE PEAK of his career my father was not only a member of the Canadian government but president of the Huron and Erie Mortgage Corporation, president of the Canada Trust Company, president of the Mutual Life Assurance Company; a director of Bell Telephone, of John Labatt, Ltd., of the National Research Council; a governor of the University of Western Ontario; and much more. The candle did indeed burn at both ends.

I give these facts not to impress but to try to define what I was up against. Added to everything else, he was, physically, so damn big, as were my brothers, my uncles, and many of my cousins. Perhaps I tried to make up for a lack of height with a precocious assertiveness. There were few tentative opinions held among our family. Many years after leaving Elmwood, I ran into a man who'd been there with me. He shook my hand, grinned, and said "I remember you. You were the kid who always wanted to stand on the top of the snow pile."

It doesn't sound like an attractive trait and I'm sure it wasn't, but if it gives the lie to the possible impression that I was always a cowed, miserable small boy, the contradiction is overdue. Also, if, unwittingly, I've suggested that my parents were unfeeling and too busy to bother about me, that's wrong too.

Busy they were; unfeeling, never. My father traveled constantly and my mother was rarely left behind. There were four
other children, Woodfield, public service, and business to attend to. My first appearance had been ill-timed. My mother
was forty-five when I was born. Besides all that, there was the
matter of tradition. Children, if it could be afforded, were sent
off to boarding school as a matter of course. There was scarcely
any discussion of where you were to be sent, or at least none
that reached the child's ear. You went where your brothers or
uncles or perhaps even your grandfather had gone. Tough
luck and good-bye.

For me, it was Bishop Ridley College. Ridley is a good school,
perhaps even a great one, but I had a decided love-hate relationship with it. I spent nine years there, with occasional peaks
and miserable valleys, with terror, boredom and dogged routine. Nine years of discipline, of Cadet Corps, regimented and
compulsory games, some laughter—thank God—and almost
total aesthetic poverty.

Of course the school has changed now. For one thing there
are *girls!* What dust must be generated in what number of
spinning graves!

On arrival at Ridley I was taken in tow by an honorary
cousin, Bill Gates, the younger son of Cousin Georgie. He had
the same fruity voice. Bill was an Upper School prefect, a per-
sonage, and a good eight years older than I. He wafted down
from the rarefied atmosphere of the Upper School, across the
playing fields, to the far more humble Lower School. He was
performing a duty, the giraffe acknowledging the mouse. I
was shown the gymnasium; Bill pointed to the light above its
door. "Your brother Dick did that—first electric light around
this place." I wasn't surprised. Dick was always messing around
with electricity.

We carefully skirted a cricket pitch. "This is where Verse
caught it." I knew what he was referring to: a batsman had hit
a leg ball for six and Verse had stopped it with his head. The
result had been a trepanning operation, a metal plate, chorea,
and the end of Verse's school days. When he recovered, he
joined the air force, though how that was even remotely possible I'll never understand. I suppose that after his hair grew

back and he'd stopped shaking and recovered his speech, he felt it was unnecessary to mention the event.

Both my brothers had served with distinction in the R.A.F. during World War I. Verse—the brother who was to worry about my wasted years—saw service first over the Western Front, then India, then back again to the Western Front. In India, he'd incurred the wrath of G.H.Q. and his commanding officer by flying his plane through the Khyber Pass (a highly dangerous exercise), thus violating neutral territory.

His C.O. had him on the mat. "Goddamn it, Cronyn, what are you after?" When Verse explained that he wanted to rejoin his old squadron in England and the Western Front patrols, the C.O. said, "Very well. I'll endorse your application for transfer—and you'll be dead within thirty days."

It didn't happen quite that way, but Verse was to be shot down seven times by enemy fire and to walk away from six of the crashes. On the seventh, he was helped out of his cockpit—speechless. The chorea, St. Vitus' dance, had come back. I have a copy of his cable to my father.

SEPTEMBER 30TH, 1917

WELL. POSTED HOME ESTABLISHMENT. NERVES.

All things considered, Verse could be forgiven for his anxiety over my "play acting."

Bill Gates and I walked on. Bill had a curious, rather regal gait; he held himself very erect, and his legs swung deliberately from the hips, his buttocks tightly compressed. "Tell him to get that rusty quarter out of his ass," said a caustic observer much later, and I was startled by such a graphic impertinence.

Bill must have felt self-conscious ushering around a Lower School boy—the very smallest in the whole school as it turned out. I was aware of curious looks, but no matter; kindly and bravely, Bill stalked on; past the headmaster's house, past Gooderham House, through the arch to the old Dean's House and back again to School House, the library with its plaster busts of Caesar and Cicero, and finally into the old chapel, now an assembly hall. High on those walls hung large black tablets inscribed with the names of the Blake gold medalist winners and of the past head boys. My great-uncle, the Hon. Edward Blake, had established the medal given for academic excellence, and the very first name on the roll of head boys was W. H. Cronyn—the same Uncle Will who had taught me fly-fishing. It was depressing. The spooks of tradition were hovering again.

Back in the Lower School where I belonged, I explored. The basement rambled like a medieval dungeon, smelling of damp and disinfectant. The surround of the urinals was wet with careless pee. Drunken steel lockers leaned against the unpainted cement walls for support. The only other furnishings were scarred wooden benches: scarred from years of ice skates and the carving instinct of small, bored boys. In one empty room I found nothing but an enormous snapping turtle, very much alive and very peevish. It had been caught by a boy named Gooderham Major in a muddy backwater of the Old Welland Canal. When I asked how he managed it, his answer was laconic. "You wade around barefoot, until you feel the shell." Miraculously, Gooderham still had all his toes, and equally miraculous was the fact that he hadn't been caught "breaking bounds" or smuggling this hideous trophy into the school.

Upstairs were the schoolrooms, the dining hall, the small locker room (books and precious possessions) and the blessed sanctuary of the library, with its deal tables and strict rules of silence and minimal motion. Above these were the dormitories. I was in number five, for the very smallest boys. It was directly above the library and sometimes, when the school cat was in heat, she'd take possession of that sacred space in the small hours and yowl inconsolably, raising the hackles on my neck.

Woodfield, where are you?

Mr. Finch was the first master that I met. He wore a gown and had the trick of pulling his nose like Rex Harrison.

"What interests you?" he asked.

"Books," I said.

He gave me one, and a peppermint humbug as well, and I was dismissed.

But I wasn't really bookish. If my end-of-term reading list was double that of anyone else, it was less a tribute to my affinity for the library than to my terror of the more dangerous corridors, where I could be assaulted by McGoohey and Madox Minor.

McGoohey was tall, thin and blond and had a silly, foxlike face. Madox Minor was short, square and powerful. He would sit on my chest, pinioning my arms with his knees, and try to feed me worms. These two were my scourges. The varieties of hilarious torture were infinite. One of the most successful played on my suffocation phobia: I was locked in the map closet. This space was about eighteen inches wide and perhaps ten inches deep—a perfect vertical tomb. More formally, it was used for storing large rolled maps that would be hung before the blackboard during geography and history lessons. The closet door opened from the outside only. How well I knew. Once I was buried alive, my resultant panic—rather like dropping a match into a box of fireworks—was everything my tormentors could hope for. Terrified, screaming in the dark, I would try to kick the door down. When the map closet was unavailable, there were the rough stucco walls of the classrooms. Madox would hold me while McGoohey rubbed the backs of my hands up and down on the stucco. It hurt and I cried, which was of course the whole object.

I had an occasional protector in James Carrington Harvey III, who would break up these star-chamber proceedings, then go on his way. Harvey had both humor and a stoic courage. I remember that once, during the slingshot season (a variety of crazes would overtake the school at different times of the year), Jim intervened in a target practice where I was the bull's-eye, thus drawing the fire on himself. We wore gray flannel shorts and long black stockings. The slingshots were strictly forbidden and fairly sophisticated, made from twisted wire, long thin rubber bands and a small leather pouch that held BB shot. If you were hit, it hurt like hell. Jim stood facing me with his back to my tormentors, replacing a new elastic in his own sling. The BBs bounced off his stockinged legs. I could see his teeth bite into his lower lip, but he refused to acknowledge the hits. This spoiled the fun, and the marksmen gave up in search of a more vulnerable object. It's a wonder that no one ever lost an eye.

McGoohey was big for his age and not very bright. He was

also a bit queer. He had latched onto some of the steamier passages in the Bible and would read them aloud with an inane high-pitched giggle; passages from the Psalms and the Song of Solomon; anything that had to do with "fornication" and Sheba's breasts. The latter would drive him into a paroxysm of excitement. He would clutch at his bony chest with both hands, kneading his nipples and, when a climax had been reached, his mouth would sag, his head tilt toward one shoulder, and both hands would fly out and shake violently. I think of McGoohey sometimes when I'm faced with one of those perverse hot-air hand dryers in a public men's room and find myself waving my hands about to get them dry.

These were mad performances by McGoohey—mad and rather frightening. They never developed into anything as overt as fondling, masturbation or exposure. They were entirely self-contained but required an audience. They seemed to satisfy McGoohey, reduced Madox to fits of laughter that had him rolling on the floor, and left me puzzled and alarmed. I'd never even heard of orgasm.

I accepted the persecutions of McGoohey and Madox for nearly a year, until the tide turned. My emancipation was brought about almost entirely by an extraordinary man named Sergeant Alexander.

I used to haunt the gym. It was Upper School turf, but I was fascinated by "Cap" Iggulden, Sergeant Alexander, and their works. Both were ex–British Army. Both had been sergeant majors and had the bellow and presence to prove it. Cap had won his commission in the field—no mean feat in those days of a class-conscious officer caste. He was the emperor of gymnastics, rigidly fit, every muscle of his torso outlined by his singlet; a fierce kind man who brooked no nonsense, accepted no excuses. Performance was his only criterion. I watched him one Sports Day administer to my friend Harvey, who was a sprinter. Harvey had to run a number of heats before achieving the finals, but unfortunately he had a severe case of hemorrhoids. Cap had him kneeling on a table between races and, using Vaseline, was tucking the piles back into Harvey's rectum. Harvey won.

Cap was also our principal sex educator. The course was

unscheduled and totally informal. The "lectures" generally followed some inadequate physical performance on our part and dwelt solely on masturbation. "It's despicable, lad, despicable! Self-abuse, despicable!" The walls would tremble with his roaring outbursts on the evils of "self-abuse"; sex was never discussed. It was a touchy subject. I suspect that the school left it to parents, and parents to school. The result was an abysmal ignorance or, at best, a shadowed education based on sniggery jokes and the largely fantasized experience of others.

The gym boasted a swimming pool which was called, accurately enough, "the tank": a small, square, cement pit that held very cold water for about half the year. There was no shallow end. It was here that Cap tried to teach us to swim. The instruction delayed my learning for at least a year. The nonswimmers would stand in a shivering, naked line waiting their turn to have a broad canvas belt put over their heads and passed under the armpits. The belt was attached to a long pole and on the other end of the pole was Cap. You were required to jump, which was terrifying; you sank, came up spluttering, and were commanded to "swim, damn you, swim!" Cap would walk along the edge of the tank dragging you through the water, shouting breast-stroke instructions and intermittently dropping the tip of the pole to test your flotation capacity. These were agonizing moments and the method was a complete failure as far as I was concerned. I learned to swim later, during summer holidays, when, to start with at least, I could put a foot on the bottom.

During the winter months, the tank was empty and used as an exercise area. Mats were put down for gymnasts and wrestlers. Boxers skipped rope, sparred, or shadowboxed in the corners under the eye of Sergeant Alexander.

Alexander was a square man with massive shoulders and fur on his chest; he was remarkably light on his feet. He wore some sort of championship belt, had a pleasant smile, and said very little. I'd watch him sparring with the older boys. He never seemed to get hit—never. That impressed me. He never seemed to back away either. He'd duck, feint, weave and sideslip; throw an occasional light punch, but more as a reminder to his opponent to keep his guard up than to score a point. Sometimes,

in frustration, the boy would come at him with a wild flurry
of blows, but these would either land where he wasn't or slide
harmlessly off his gloves or elbows. There was something bal-
letic about it but vaguely dangerous too. What would happen
if the sergeant got mad? He never did; his opponents did, but
he was impervious. I watched for a long time.

One day, following a sparring bout, Alexander came toward
me holding out a pair of sweaty gloves. "Put 'em on."

That was how it began. He was incredibly patient, and now
he talked. He talked about "the art of self-defense;" about the
body's musculature, about balance and footwork, about the ef-
ficacy of a straight left and how it traveled diagonally from the
right toes, through the leg, torso, shoulders and into the punch;
about attack and defense, about timing and how to measure
an opponent's strengths and weaknesses, about seizing the
moment, about rest and waiting, about intelligence. Above all,
he taught me how to exercise. I spent hours in that tank skipping, shadowboxing, punching a bag, trying to develop a set
of nonexistent muscles.

Then McGoohey cornered me one day in the corridor and
the worm turned. I hit him. He put his hand to his nose and
it came away showing a trace of blood. He couldn't believe it.
There was a fractional pause of outraged surprise, then he
came at me, arms flailing, and ran straight into one of my
Sergeant Alexander straight lefts. He was a lot taller than I
and must have outreached me by at least six inches, but this
time his nose bled profusely. Another minute pause and almost by reflex, I stepped in and hit him in the solar plexus.
The wind came out of him with a grunt, then he folded slowly
forward and sat, heavily, making a sound like water running
out of a clogged drain.

The satellite Madox had watched all this with curious de-
tachment. He'd made no move to interfere. Now he turned to
me and grinned, then back to his friend: "You got a snot rag?
There's blood on your collar."

I won my first boxing shield a year later. It reads: "Ridley
College, 75 lb. Championship. H. Cronyn, 1925." And in every
year after, through 1930, I won another one—six in all. By
that time, I was a featherweight (127 pounds).

"Let me out, let me out!" Don't bother. I was free.

FOUR

My first House in the Upper School was the old deanery. Even then, it was a tired building; its floors sagged, its stairs creaked and the windows fitted so ill that in winter you froze. You couldn't pile on enough blankets. A wet dream was a disaster of discomfort.

The House was presided over by "Twa" Thomas. Why "Twa" I have no idea, but, in mockery, the nickname was usually extended into a sort of prolonged bleat—"Twaaa"— perhaps because he was a great believer in pear-shaped tones, with a heavy reliance on the vowels. This seemed to suit his physical appearance: he was a large, smooth, rotund man with a small moustache, who always wore his master's gown. I wondered if he slept in it. I was to know Twa rather better than most because he ran the school's Dramatic Society. (Yes, there was one.) Under Twa's direction, I appeared in *Cox and Box* and some sort of potted amalgam of *The Pickwick Papers*, in which I played a judge, and wore a court wig so long that it made me look rather like a beach umbrella dug too far into the sand, or perhaps a mushroom.

The mathematics master was Ernie Powell ("Ern") who had trouble with phlegm and swallowed a lot. His prominent Adam's apple would run up and down his stringy throat like a busy robin. He had rather full lips, and they would purse before a pronouncement. Was he about to spit or say something? "The square of the hypotenuse—" (swallow and purse) "—of a right-angled triangle equals the sum of the squares—" (swallow and purse) "—on the other two sides" (swallow).

Ern was also the assistant headmaster. He had two sons, Ernest Jr. and George, who unfortunately for them were pupils at the school. George, who was the younger, had been with me in the Lower School and, happily, excelled at games. Ernest was a more studious type and lived up to his name. His father was given to pontificating: "Now George, George is the athlete, but Ern, Ern is the brains of the family." This quotation was repeated over and over again with appropriate swallows and lip-pursings by the school's mimics.

Directly above the mathematics classroom was Little Hell, a fourth-form dormitory noted for its raffish occupants, of which I was proud to be one. Adjoining the eight beds of the dorm was a washroom with four basins and one overworked toilet. The plumbing for this toilet ran down through the classroom below, and the plaster ceiling surrounding the pipes was badly discolored. As the year progressed the stain spread alarmingly, and the plaster threatened to fall. The hurried piss was to blame. Finally the blemish got on Ern's nerves; he marched the inhabitants of Little Hell upstairs, through the dorm, into the washroom, and marshaled us about the offensive convenience. Stabbing an accusatory finger, he said: "If my young son George couldn't urinate straighter than that—" (swallow and purse) "—I'd thrash him!" For years afterward, boys asked the unfortunate George to give demonstrations. I don't think I ever asked him. I liked George. I liked his father as well, except for one occasion when I returned to the school from New York, and he asked me why I hadn't visited the school more often. I mumbled something about being busy, and Ern said: "Ah . . . your *work*," in a tone that implied "harlotry player."

My final housemaster was a wonderful man named Crawford Grier, familiarly known as "Wylie," after his father, a respected Canadian painter. Wylie too was a maverick; he had inherited much of his father's talent and interest, and shared these with the boys of Gooderham House. His was an angel's voice in what to me was a sterile wilderness.

I suspect there was something of the actor in Wylie. Like my father, he read aloud beautifully, but it was more than that; something jaunty in the cock of his hat and the swing of his tightly rolled umbrella. He had a gifted actor's "presence," the unforced smile and relaxed posture. Wylie was on show. He initiated a house newspaper called *The Banderlog,* for which I wrote some very bad derivative poetry. He taught us about meter, scansion and rhyme. He held extracurricular classes in drawing and photography. He gave us a darkroom. He also taught ancient history, with humor and a sense of the theatrical. The only reason I remember Alcibiades to this day is that his name went up on Wylie's blackboard as "Mr. Al. C. Biades."

Taken all in all, I believe the masters at Ridley were a pretty good bunch. There were no sadistic bastards, no perverts, no fools. There were a considerable number who were totally dedicated, some who were sympathetic and prepared to be kind; some, like Wylie, who gave far beyond anything that might be expected of them as a professional obligation. I liked most of them, some liked me and some found me a pain in the ass; but I was never in rebellion against the masters, only against the system as it then existed.

I can see some of them still. I can see "Grunt" McComber, hurrying along wearing his gown. It was untidy and too large for him, so the effect was that of a bedraggled crow who has come late to the pickings. Grunt had a curious accent which inserted the letter *r* into words that could have done without it—he spoke of "Canader," "Americer" and "Australier," and his daughter's name, Dorothy, came out as "Dorfy." Dorothy certainly didn't attend Ridley, but she came to see her parents occasionally and frequently got mislaid. The casement windows of Grunt's apartment would be thrown wide, and you'd hear him call "Dorfy? Yoo-hooer, you-hooer, Dorfy?" It was remarkable what assistance Grunt would get in these searches. Other windows would be flung open and echo Grunt's anxiety. You'd hear the boys' concerned voices joining in a chorus of "Dorfy? Yoo-hooer! You hooer Dorfy?" That good old English word *whore* is of course often mispronounced "hooer."

Poor Dorfy. It was the grossest of libels.

"Twink" Coburn and "Hurphy" Ashburner taught French and algebra, respectively. The former had been an army officer. He was ramrod straight and meticulous in everything. He wore two wristwatches, one on each wrist, and would consult both whenever time was critical. "Gating," a punishment that not only restricted the offender to the school grounds, but also required reporting to the duty master every half hour of one's free time, was one such instance.

"Cronyn reporting, sir." Twink would check both watches with great care, enter my name on his clipboard, nod, and I was at liberty again for another precise thirty minutes. To be gated for two weeks, the usual sentence, was a terrible nuisance, but perhaps I owe my compulsive punctuality at rehearsals to my gating experience.

Hurphy was blind in one eye, which didn't impair his marksmanship. He was a dead shot with a piece of chalk. He could whirl from the blackboard and bounce the chalk off some inattentive or talkative head, all in one beautifully coordinated movement. If that head was yours, you were required to return the chalk. Hurphy would go back to his equations without comment.

Masters were encouraged to join in the school games, either as active participants in practice sessions, or at least as coaches or referees. Hurphy played cricket, and looking back, having lost one eye myself, I wonder how he did it. To hit a ball with impaired depth perception is difficult, but Hurphy did it well.

Twink was a model referee, sprinting around the field, whistle at the ready, wristwatches flashing, running games with military precision. Wylie, a Renaissance man, could play everything, but of them all it was the Upper School headmaster, Dr. Griffith, who was the most impressive. Besides being a scholar, he had a national reputation as a football coach, and for years Ridley owed its primacy in football to his skills and indefatigable energy. Behind his back he was known as "Red" and his hair was still rusty even when I knew him. He was a small man, with a quiet voice and indisputable authority. I saw him once face down the entire school in the midst of a protest march. I don't remember what it was we were protesting, but

I have a vivid memory of the school, some two or three hundred strong, marching across the campus in the dim light of evening, and of seeing the small implacable figure of Red coming out to meet us. It was a collision course but no contest. The march wavered, stopped; Red said a few quiet words and the protesters broke ranks and simply faded away.

Being a master, let alone a headmaster, at a school like Ridley was no treat. It was a repressive school and repression breeds rebellion. Some masters were simply unequipped to handle it. One such was an Englishman, Mr. White: a gentle soul who wrote poetry, some of which was published in the school magazine, *Acta.* I remember only fragments.

> . . . sang Sirmio, lovely o'er the golden lake,
> Where waves tilt eager faces to the sun
> And laugh to welcome you from wayfaring.

And another, which may or may not be from the same poem.

> And you, my sweet Penelope,
> Somewhere out there you wait for me,
> With buds of roses in your hair
> And kisses on your mouth.

This was pretty heady stuff. I particularly liked those laughing waves, to say nothing of the kisses.

One night Mr. White was taking evening study; that period between supper and "lights out" when you were supposed to do "homework" (only there was no home). I don't know how the conspiracy began, but early in the period, an effigy of Mr. White was set afire and lowered from the dormitory above, where it burned brightly outside the study-room window. There was a great show of flinging windows open, putting out the fire, and clearing the room of smoke. Eventually, a kind of ominous calm was restored. It was temporary. I noticed something odd: reference books were piled in a neat, uncharacteristic column on nearly every desk. What was to come? I swear I didn't know; perhaps my sympathies for Mr. White were recognized, perhaps I wasn't trusted. I was not yet a member of the House in which the study took place. I did know that it was possible to short circuit the lighting of any House by removing a fuse and inserting a penny between the fuse and its contact. This was what was done. There was a sudden blackout and in the darkness, every book from every desk was hurled in Mr. White's direction.

It took a long time to get the lights on again. The fuses weren't marked, so every fuse in the box had to be removed to find where the trouble lay. Once the lights were restored, a battered and gibbering Mr. White let go with a tirade against the "barbarians" and "miserable colonial cads"—a phrase I particularly remember—responsible for such unsporting behavior. It was the worst possible kind of response, but was cut short by the arrival of the headmaster. The piles of books had to be picked up, the names of their owners, appearing on the flyleaves, were duly recorded, and inevitably, punishment followed. It was severe. I believe it involved a number of canings for the ringleaders. This wasn't of much help to the unfortunate Mr. White, who returned almost immediately to less barbarian climes.

Considering my inadequacy at team games, my pint size and sharp tongue, it's odd that so many of my friends at Ridley were among the school elite, the "jocks"; first-team members of not just one sport, but sometimes all three; friends like Harris and Curry, Skey and Fletcher. Then there were the mavericks, who were always in trouble. These had a special attraction for me: free, iconoclastic souls who cocked a snook at authority and didn't give a damn.

One such was Trigger. I loved him. He came from Barbados, where, reputedly, his family owned vast plantations. My most vivid memory of him is with blue hair. Actually, he was a sun-bleached blond, almost white-haired, but someone had crept up behind him as he was taking a bath and dumped a large bottle of Waterman's blue-black ink into the tub. This delighted him and he ducked under a number of times to give himself a near-permanent rinse. Soap got the ink off his skin but not out of his hair.

Trigger, or "Thwigger" as he was affectionately known, had a speech impediment. It gave him trouble with his *rs*; *raspber-*

ries became "wasbewwies," *Ridley* was "Widley," and so on. This defect did nothing to slow Trigger down. He was a wild, laughing, quite uncontrollable boy who received far too much pocket money from home and never seemed to have any left. He simply gave it away. In one of his broke periods I bought a beautiful cashmere suit from him for five dollars; a deal that shocked my parents and must have appalled his—if they ever knew about it, which I doubt.

Thwigger was always in trouble, always unrepentant, and always bouncing back for more. He laughed away "detention," strappings, even canings. He was a beautiful swimmer and an acrobatic diver, so his service stripes got full display. Thwigger would accept these punishments with amused contempt and go on to his next caper: slipping out of a window after lights out; smoking in the dorm; rolling marbles down the chapel aisle while on his knees in the middle of prayers; breaking a stink bomb in the chemistry lab, hoping it might be considered an experiment gone wrong. Vain hope: but it did empty the lab, giving us all a free period.

I suppose expulsion was inevitable; Thwigger's relentless pursuit of such exercises ensured that. Twenty years later I was to see him expelled a second time, but that was after he had started to drink. Jessie and I were in Reno. Thwigger was there with his second wife-to-be, both of them getting divorces. They'd met at one of those "drying out" establishments but the "cures" hadn't stuck. We all had dinner together and the future wife got very drunk and very loud. I could see that Thwigger was kicking her under the table, trying to shut her up. She would segue from laughter to tears, then start up all over again. It was painful. In the end, their hotel asked them to find other accommodation, and that would be the end of the story except for a newspaper account that appeared, I think, in the late forties.

The account was of an inquest into an event that had taken place on the observation roof of one of New York's highest buildings. A man and his female companion, said the newspaper, had been enjoying a beautiful starlit night and the vast panorama of colored lights below them, when, quite deliberately, the man began to undress. According to shocked witnesses, the girl watched, laughing, until the man climbed onto the parapet, executed a perfect half gainer and disappeared into the void.

It was one caper from which Thwigger couldn't bounce back.

Thwigger was the most colorful of my maverick friends (and the most tragic), but there were others. As a result, the school chaplain called me into his study one day and gave me a lecture on the undesirable qualities of my friends. I was furious, and sought revenge.

The chaplain, we knew, was a bridge player. Cards were strictly forbidden to the boys. We took a couple of contraband packs and laid a paper trail from the chaplain's door to the door of our housemaster's quarters. The message was clear. All hell broke loose, with threats of mass punishment for the entire House, unless the perpetrators confessed. It became necessary to admit to the crime and I got strapped. Six on each. The strap was cut from machine-belt fiber, about three inches wide and a couple of feet long. The victim held out his hands, palm up, at about shoulder level. First one and then the other, while the administering master brought the strap down hard. It hurt. The trick was to let your hand fall immediately on impact, to offer minimal resistance, and once it was over, to run to the nearest washroom and hold your pulsing hands under the hot-water tap.

Strapping was a relatively casual punishment. It was quickly over, better than losing a half holiday or suffering two hours of detention. The latter meant running around the gym under the tyrannical eye of Cap, or being confined to a classroom and Latin conjugations for two hours, a proceeding of infinite tedium for both culprit and duty master. If a transgressor found a sympathetic master, it was sometimes possible to plea-bargain, to get detention "strapped off," trading a boring penalty for a painful but far shorter one. I became pretty good at this and developed calloused hands.

Caning was the prerogative solely of the headmaster; sometimes, unofficially, of the prefects. It was reserved for major breaches of discipline: smoking, stealing, cheating, breaking a gating—which meant that you were ignoring the punishment for one crime and compounding it with another. It was the last offense that brought me into intimate contact with Red.

I'd been gated for some forgotten breach of rules and, somehow or other, managed to evade the reporting procedure. I went to the movies. Coming back from town, across the high-level bridge, I ran smack into my housemaster, Wylie Grier. He greeted me affably.

"Good afternoon, Cronyn."

"Afternoon, sir."

"And where have you been?"

"In town, sir."

"Doing what?"

"Seeing a film, sir."

"Uh-huh. A good one?"

"Pretty good, sir."

There was a pause. "I believe you're gated, aren't you?"

Wearily, "Yes, sir."

"What a pity."

"Yes, sir."

"You know I'll have to report you to the Head. You really must learn to obey the rules."

"Yes, sir."

"Get along back then. I'm sorry—and good luck."

It was all cut-and-dried. There were exact rules and exact punishments. Everyone knew both. There were few extenuating circumstances, and going to the movies was certainly not one of them. You weighed the possibilities and took your chances. I'd miscalculated.

Waiting for the ax to fall, or more accurately the cane, was the worst part. It was never immediate. There was always plenty of time to contemplate what you might get. Six? Eight? Ten? You went to bed every night in the interim waiting for the call. It always came after lights out, when you were in pajamas. A prefect would stick his head in the door and say, "Cronyn—Head wants you." And that would be the summons. On slippers, on bathrobe, down the stairs, through the library, a knock on the connecting door to the Head's study, a quiet "Enter" in reply, and then you were for it.

I knew what to expect. I knew it would be painful. I'd seen boys in "the tank" who'd been caned. They had blue ladders down their bottoms, looking like eccentric tattoos. These lasted for some time but were considered honorable scars and viewed with respect.

I stood in front of Dr. Griffith's desk while he reviewed the dates and details of my misdeeds. I acknowledged them. We agreed between us that I had been stupid, then I was invited to remove my bathrobe, take a firm grip on the arms of a chair and bend over. I never got a good look at the cane but I heard it whistle.

It would have been humiliating to have made a sound, but even though I was sixteen at the time, I did not feel humiliated by the proceeding. It was too ceremonial, too calm, too inevitable and, surprisingly, impersonal. Whatever my complaints about the school, they had absolutely nothing to do with corporal punishment. It went with the territory. I never saw punishment administered in a passion, or felt that it gave anyone pleasure. I never saw it administered unfairly—if you accepted the rules that provoked it. This is not a defense of something abhorrent to many people, but just setting the record straight. I don't think the strappings and canings affected me one bit. The tyrannies of tedium, regimentation, snobbery, bullying and homesickness were far, far more serious.

But there was one sanctuary at Ridley, and that was the chapel. It played a large part in our lives. We saw it twice a day, for morning and evening prayers. It was a beautiful building, pure Gothic. The sun streamed in through stained-glass windows and their colors dappled the bleached-oak pews beneath. On either side of the altar was the stone reredos, carved with the many names of old boys killed in the first world war. At the annual memorial service the names would be read off, slowly, solemnly, one following another like the muffled roll of a deadmarch. I can still hear some of them now, the names carefully enunciated and separated.

"John . . . Labatt . . . Scatcherd."

"Alan . . . Ferrier . . . Gates."

"Van Renselear . . . Van Tassel . . . Schuyler . . . Irvine."

The magnificence of that last name was brought to earth by the fact that he was called "Mickey"—he had been engaged to my elder sister.

On occasion we were required to make "church parades," and go off to services at St. Thomas's Church in St. Catharines; this meant getting into uniforms, forming ranks and marching behind the Cadet Corps band (where I played a snare drum). A little of this went a long way. The choir at the church was largely female and I used to pass the time through tedious sermons mentally undressing the choir ladies.

There were no such diversions in the Ridley Chapel, but there were other compensations. The choir was eager and better trained, and there was a lot of part singing, with the whole school thundering out the choruses with the organ until the air seemed to tremble in praise of life. Christmas carols were a particular joy, although it was always slightly bemusing to hear a boy soprano singing the role of one of the Wise Men.

The chapel, when full, could be a celebration; it fairly shouted the school motto, *"Terrar dum prosim,"* which, loosely translated, means, "May I be consumed in service." Bishop Ridley, consumed by martyr's flames in the sixteenth century, might well have been proud of it.

The chapel, empty, spoke quite differently to me. It seemed vast and still, waiting. Waiting for what? For whatever I might care to bring to it: the serenity of Woodfield, my sunlit days at Mookejewun (that "hill of many springs"), the smell of balsam, the sound of rippling water, a cathedral of trees, the stillness of wilderness, which is never truly still but speaks with such a gentle voice. These were the elements of my holidays with my parents, things to which they introduced me and which would far outlast the influence of Ridley.

Nevertheless, I would be glad to see the Ridley Chapel again.

FIVE

Of all the holidays at Woodfield, Christmas was the most spectacular. It had a Dickensian atmosphere: very festive, very crowded, and exhausting.

Christmas Day began while it was still dark, in pajamas and dressing gown, having early-morning tea before the wood fire in the old nursery. This was followed by the opening of stockings in my parents' bedroom, where there was another crackling fire. The stockings were attached to the foot rails of the twin four-poster beds. My mother and father stayed in bed—they pretty well had to, as the floor space was totally occupied by children, grandchildren and the all-too-lavish piles of presents.

Preparations for this event had gone on for weeks beforehand: endless lists to be crossed out or amended, piles of colored tissue paper, spools of ribbon, secret wrappings; cards to be written; a tree to be decorated; and all to culminate by Christmas Eve. The one sublime interruption in the evening's chaos was the arrival of the Salvation Army band, which would appear in the driveway and play carols. I would be sent out through the snow to hand a discreet envelope to the captain and then rush back to the business of stuffing stockings—all but my own of course, which hung limp and depressing on the bedpost nearest the fireplace.

The suspense between the early morning tea and my mother's call, "You can come in now," was almost unbearable. But then there was the magic of that firelit room, with its piles of gaily wrapped presents, the laughter, the sound of early-service church bells, the snow outside and the family embrace within.

Breakfast was always late, and the warning bell from the Cronyn Memorial Church always caught me only half-dressed. However, the walk to the eleven o'clock service was only a couple of hundred yards. The church would be overflowing, the Christmas sermon blessedly short, and the collection (perhaps in gratitude) larger than usual. My mother would sing every word of every verse of every hymn, and my father, towering above her, would sing only some of them. He'd start with a will, then give up. As he had a booming baritone voice, these sudden quittings had a startling effect on the surrounding pews. I was aware of the eyes swiveling in his direction. What was wrong? Nothing at all, really. He'd just grown tired or disenchanted. Mother was a far more dedicated churchgoer than he was. I suspect he believed in the form of religious observance, while having grave reservations about the content. He could handle the Lord's Prayer without a qualm, but the creed and all that business about "life everlasting" gave him pause. I'm guessing. I don't know. We never discussed it.

My mother started every day of her life with tea and a little volume called *Prayers, Ancient and Modern*. Both gave her strength to face what was to come. She could be at Woodfield or in the bush, in a hotel or under canvas, aboard ship or in a desert; there was always her prayer book—plus a small traveling kettle, the tea, and a can of Sterno. I still have her prayer book (it threatens to fall apart from her devoted usage) and the leaves are badly scorched and indented because, one morning, she put it down too close to the lighted Sterno.

One of her favorite prayers was by George Dawson, and includes a line which has always haunted me. "Almighty God, we beseech Thee [to help us] to catch the music to which this world is set by Thee."

When in 1942 I married Jessica Tandy, I had the inside of her wedding ring inscribed: "You are the music to which my world is set." And if I didn't quite know what it meant then, Jessie soon taught me.

After church, lunch would be served in the library. The dining room was undergoing a metamorphosis in preparation for Christmas dinner. This involved setting up long tables to be covered with white cloths that were crisscrossed with broad red ribbons and strategically placed bunches of holly. There were silver candelabra and masses of flowers; bowls of paper-white narcissi and forced tulips; the whole house in fact became a winter conservatory. The center hall had been decorated for weeks with fat ropes of twisted evergreen that hung in swags from the picture rails. I don't know whether these were made of balsam or tamarack, but whatever they were, they made all Woodfield smell wonderful.

After lunch there would be a lull—the calm before the storm. People would retire to their rooms to collapse. I would go to my room in the attic, with its lovely dormer windows, to gloat over my stocking loot, or to dip into the most promising of my Christmas books.

At four o'clock the youngest of my cousins, nieces and nephews would arrive for the Christmas tree (more presents) and the appearance of Santa Claus. Finding an acceptable, let alone a willing Santa Claus from among the male members of the family was never easy. Once out of school and "in the theater," I became an obvious candidate, but always managed to avoid it. There was something vaguely embarrassing about so much hearty "Ho-ho-ho" and so many effortful jokes. Besides, the Santa suit—smelling strongly of mothballs—was far too large. It was one occasion when my size was happily convenient. However, some larger family member would eventually be shanghaied into the job and, fortified by a couple of stiff drinks and sweating profusely, he would come galumphing down from the attic to face the ordeal. Invariably, one of the smaller children would burst into tears on his appearance.

Between the Christmas tree ceremony and dinner there was barely time to dress. Evening gowns, white tie and tails . . . I can hardly believe it now. But this was not only another time but a different world. A world in which my father—my *father*, not grandfather—had fought Indians (in the Northwest Rebellion of 1884); a world of ceremony and admired imperialism, a world in which the word *nuclear* might have stumped the most erudite crossword puzzler.

Anyway, the ebb of the Christmas tree party met the flow of dinner guests—some thirty or forty of them, ranging in age from about eight to eighty. Among the eldest were my Aunt Kitty and Aunt Blossom, the latter very matriarchal, holding a silver-topped cane, the former dressed like Chekhov's Masha, all in black. There the similarity ended. Far from being "in mourning for her life," Aunt Kitty giggled, which, much to her embarrassment, made her false teeth slip. A protective hand would go over her mouth, but the smile wrinkles would persist around her eyes. She played all the children's games, and since she was most generously proportioned as well as old, this always made us nervous when it come to "musical chairs"—would Aunty Kitty hit the chair or the floor?

She was my mother's oldest sister. Once, traveling by train with my mother in Europe, she was overcome by a need to relieve herself. The ladies' loo was long occupied. Finally, in desperation, she forced open the window of their compartment, downed her bloomers and let fly. My mother remonstrated, to which Aunt Kitty replied: "Oh Minnie dear, don't be silly, no one will recognize me."

The children's games were an essential part of our Christmas. They came after the dining room had been cleared, after coffee and liqueurs in the drawing room. The favorite games were Up Jenkins and "the smelling game." In the latter, you were blindfolded and led down a long table with a succession of plates or glasses that held lemon, cinnamon, bay leaves, whiskey, garlic, pepper, rose leaves, mint and so forth. Someone would keep score. After a strong whiff of either garlic or pepper, you were either insensible to smells or you were sneezing. My brewer grandfather Labatt was once handed a glass of his own ale to smell and announced with great authority and certitude that it was "prune juice"—a judgment he was not allowed to forget.

The responsibility for all these festivities, the scheduling,

menus, invitations, gift wrappings, shopping, flower arrangements, and the immense tact required to avoid hurting the
feelings of some family member or other, all fell on my mother.
How she managed it I'll never know. Without servants (there
were five of them) it wouldn't have been possible. She got support from my sisters, Katherine and Honor, but essentially it
was her show and took weeks of planning. Poor Mum; she
suffered chronically from "planitis" and we used to tease her
about it. It was no joke. She always woke early, and would lie
in bed stewing over the day to come. Christmas she could
manage, but it was the unknowns, the problems of her children and grandchildren, their marriages, health and for-
tunes—to say nothing of my father's—that were always with
her. No wonder she needed her early-morning tea and prayer
book.

Scattered through this house I write in are a dozen photographs of my mother, all but one tucked away in boxes, on
dusty shelves, in portfolios or scrapbooks. In one she appears
surrounded by my brothers and sisters, all dressed in white: a
sweet formal photograph of Edwardian family propriety.
There's a large Pre-Raphaelite portrait of her at seventeen,
beautiful with her hair up. Then, there she is with me as a
baby in arms before a Woodfield fireplace; sitting in the garden swing with me aged about four beside her; with my father
in a canoe, her hat surrounded by a halo of mosquito netting.
And there she is, alone, a slightly plump little elderly lady,
sitting in an old-fashioned deck chair, her hands holding needle
and thread above the mending on her lap. She smiles into the
camera. But who was she? Despite all our shared confidences
(she thought masturbation might lead to madness), I'm not
sure I know. She had an extraordinary generosity of spirit,
certainly, and a lively sense of humor—she literally laughed
until she cried, and then she would fumble for one of her
small lace-trimmed handkerchiefs, wipe her eyes and exclaim,
"Oh dear, how trying!" She had a love of the outdoors, an
immediate sympathy for the problems of her children and total devotion to my father. Whatever her problems, and they
were considerable during her last years, she relished life. She
was an acute observer of what went on around her, and good

at describing it. I can remember her talking about the butcher's frustration, or the rector's gaffe, or a play she'd seen as a girl, in a fashion that was halting but so vivid that it made the whole thing spring into immediate life. "Relish"—perhaps that is a key word in any assessment of my mother's character.

My mother's sister summed her up best. "Her entrance into a room is as though another candle had been lighted." Aunt Kitty owed the quotation to Robert Louis Stevenson, but the sentiment might well have been fashioned for Frances Amelia Labatt Cronyn, known to my father as "Jo." He came down the stairs to meet her once after one of her brief absences and said, "Oh Jo, this house is sad without you." And once I helped him roll up the front-hall carpet so that he might waltz with my mother to "The Blue Danube." A massive new gramophone had just been delivered to the house, but the sight of my parents dancing together was even more magical than that new possession. Open demonstrations of affection were rare where I came from; they were considered "soppy" and in poor taste. Yet the current of affection between my mother and father was as palpable at Woodfield as was the spring smell of paper-whites in the window boxes.

* * *

I had just one holiday with my father alone—well, we weren't alone exactly, there were other people about, but we were more intimately together than we'd ever been before or were ever to be again. We shared a tent: a tiny, dark green, waterproofed silk triangle that covered our blankets and kept out the rain—and it rained a lot.

Sir Herbert Ames, whoever he was, had organized a fishing expedition into the Nipigon region of northwestern Ontario, which was wilderness country then. There had been a rare family disagreement as to whether I should be allowed to go along; my mother and sister K (who was also my godmother) were on one side in the dispute, my father on the other.

"But Hume, dear, Sir Herbert and Lady Ames have no children. Won't it seem odd? And besides, Junior can't swim. Such a responsibility! Are you sure?"

The argument was unassailable—so my father took me. I was eight years old.

The train dropped us in the middle of the wilderness during the half-light of very early morning. There was no station, no road, no landmark of any kind, just a ragged ground mist, jack pines, caribou moss, blueberry bushes, and a delicious smell of damp earth.

With the train gone, there was an eerie silence, hardly broken when six Indians emerged from nowhere and, almost wordlessly, picked up the dunnage bags and rod cases and turned back into the bush—all except one of them. This one took a long length of rawhide from his pocket, attached one end to his belt and the other to my left wrist. We brought up the rear. I felt like Jim Hawkins attached to Long John Silver, only "my Indian" didn't limp. He had a long stride and the rawhide would snap tight whenever I tried to grab a handful of blueberries.

My Indian didn't speak a word of English. Not one word. We became great friends, despite his obvious anxieties about me. He couldn't swim either. And we were in country that was laced together with white water. This was a far cry from the placid ponds at the Farm. I found it terribly exciting and wanted to explore every pool, eddy, and pocket of foam. I was fishing mad. Any sign of a fish—a rise, a pink belly flashing in a rapid— could make me tremble. I'd grab a branch and lean out over the water with the rawhide taut and my Indian shaking his head in dismay.

There were six in our party: the Ameses, my father and I, and two "Americans." In those days, "Americans" was always said as though it carried quotation marks. It implied distance rather than disrespect—rather like saying "and two Martians." There was a guide for each one of us. Very posh. The Indian guides made and broke camp, cooked, carried the canoes, and guided us with great skill through dangerous rapids and across portages. (Something I was to learn to do in years to come— no easy job.)

The fishing was spectacular. Had I been allowed, I would have never stopped, but sometimes the weather intervened. One day there was a bad thunderstorm, with lashings of rain,

and there was nothing for it but to retire to our tents. My
father read aloud to me—probably one of Charles G. D. Rob-
erts's stories about wildlife.

I doubt that I paid close attention. I kept darting out of
the tent to examine the sky. "You can't go fishing," my father
said, "until there is enough blue in the sky to make a pair of
Dutchman's pants."

I did my best to put those pants together. "Look, there's
enough over there for one leg, and enough there for the seat,
and you'll soon have enough there for the other leg."

"All in one piece," was his stony reply.

Eventually, the sky cleared and we went to meet the Americans, who had been reconnoitering somewhere or other. Their
canoe was pulled up on the bank, their rods leant against a
tree; they were deep in conversation with my father. I was
allowed to borrow one of the rods. "Fish, way bottom," said
their guide.

He was right. There, only dimly seen in the bottom of a
pool, lay—not a trout surely, but a submarine. I cast upstream,
let the fly sink and drift slowly back toward the head of this
monster. As the fly got closer I twitched it. No interest. I tried
again and again. "No take," said the guide.

He was wrong. With the sunken fly no more than a couple
of inches from its head, the trout suddenly opened its mouth
and inhaled—probably out of irritation. I hooked him well and
he took off upstream like a rocket, came out of the water in a
beautiful rainbow of color, twisted, and came back down-
stream so fast that I was left with slack line, reeling frantically.
By this time I was in the water to my waist, with my father
hanging onto my belt. The Americans and the guide shouted
from the bank, "Keep the tip up! Keep that tip up! Reel, reel!
Don't horse him! Let him run! Reel!" I begged my father to
take the rod, but he wouldn't touch it.

The fish, a brook trout, weighed just under five pounds.
"My Indian" skinned it with enormous care and craft; sewed
the wet skin to a piece of birch bark and notched together a
frame of cedar. I carried it under my proud arm back to London, where my father had a taxidermist add a glass eye and
touch up the fading colors in oil: the wonderful pink belly,

the brilliant red speckles with their iris of bright blue. It was the biggest fish taken on the trip. When I last saw it—or its skin, just as it was originally mounted—it hung above the fireplace of the Potatuck Club, near Sandy Hook, Connecticut, not more than twenty miles from where I sit writing this, but a very long way and time from its catching.

There were other fishing trips with my father—and with my mother too. She was good at this sort of thing. In 1912 she had accompanied my father into the wilds of northern British Columbia. He was undertaking a land inspection on behalf of a group of Scottish investors. This was magnificent but rough country, and my mother was the first white woman to have seen parts of it. They lived under canvas and traveled by pack train. Supplies ran short. One day my father hoped to take a deer for the pot. The horses had been moving through long grass, which always made them nervous, and my father was on his hands and knees, maneuvering through the grass with his rifle, trying to position himself for the best possible shot. Suddenly one of the horses lashed out with a hind foot— and caught him full in the chest.

He was carried to his tent, and for two nights my mother sat up with him, holding his rifle across her knees. This watch made the guides even more nervous than the horses had been. Carrying hot tea for my father, the chief guide approached the tent with great caution. He handed the tea through the tent flap, looked down at my father, and tried to think of some words of comfort for my mother. "He'll be spittin' blood soon," he said.

Of our fishing trips together, the best were to La Roche, a private club deep in Quebec's Laurentides Park. We traveled by train to Baie St. Paul, then by horse and *planche* (something like a buckboard) to Lac à Gravelle, and from there we walked— a very long walk to the log cabin on the Rivière de l'Enfer, the River of Hell. Not well named, I thought, for something so beautiful, with its boiling rapids, deep pools and long placid reaches all teeming with trout. This was in the days before lumbering operations intruded and sawmills polluted the water. Wildlife abounded. Your canoe would round a bend in the river and surprise a beaver working on a dam, or a straddle-legged moose feeding on water lily roots nearby. The beaver's tail would hit the water with a crack like a pistol shot, sounding the alarm before he dove. The moose would raise its head, cascades of water pouring from its palmated antlers, stare, then crash wildly off through water and bush like a locomotive gone off the rails.

It was the camp's guardian, an *habitant* named Thomas Louis Fortin, who taught me how to bring the canoe close to a river-feeding moose without frightening it—too close sometimes. The moment you saw the great animal you froze. If the wind was from the moose to you, you might get close. It would stare long and hard at this unfamiliar object on the water, but sensing no alarming smell or movement, it would put its head back into the water again for another mouthful of the tubers. At that point you paddled hard but with the paddle blade never leaving the water and turned sideways to position for the next stroke.

The trick was to gauge the length of time the animal would keep its head under water—until you had to freeze again. Little by little you would draw closer, but woe betide you if your paddle hit the gunwale. The moose's hearing and sense of smell were as acute as its eyesight was indifferent. Eventually of course some errant eddy of wind, some man smell, would reach it and that would be goodbye.

One of my few duties at La Roche was preparing my mother's morning bath, which meant building a smudge against the ever-present black flies. The men soaped and swam from the canoe landing in water so glacial it took the wind out of you. My mother had found a bathing spot a couple of hundred yards from the cabin, where an eddy at the foot of a rapid had scooped out the bank and left a small, gravel-bottomed pool. There the beautiful, clear, brown water turned round on itself, creating an ice-cold but golden whirlpool bath in the early morning sunlight. I had to gauge the breeze and build the smudge—birch bark, twigs, balsam and caribou moss—so that the pungent smoke would drift across the spot where she stripped off, then dried herself after her bath. Once the smudge was built and burning, I would leave. My mother's modesty was total. Despite having produced five children (all born in her own bed), she would never suffer the indignity of a proper gynecological examination. How Dr. Moore, the family physician who delivered us all, had functioned prior to these births, I can't imagine. Such modesty was later to cost her dearly. She died of a cancer that was originally cervical and that might—so I was told—have been arrested had it been discovered in its early stages.

On the walk to and from my mother's bath I would frequently bump into a friendly skunk or porcupine. It would waddle out of my way, amiably, as though I was a nuisance rather than a hostile intruder.

There was an unspoken but carefully observed rule that on the trail, over the many long portages around rapids, no one spoke. You couldn't avoid the sound of footfalls, but these might be covered by the burble of rushing water. Chatter was another matter entirely and not to be tolerated. To this day, I grow uneasy when walking through the bush with people who insist on talking; it's no way to see anything.

And how much there was to see, to smell, to hear and savor: great blue herons fishing along the shore who would flap silently away as the canoe approached, their great wing span making them look like the pterodactyls I'd read about in Wells's *Outline of History;* loons who would pop up on one side of the canoe, then dive and appear far off on the other side, and laugh. Sometimes when the day was overcast, or in the evenings, you would hear the loon's "great cry": a long, sustained note, so different from the laugh and so mournfully haunting that you had a *frisson.* Then there were the wolves, rarely seen, yet heard at night with a howl that had exactly the same chilling effect. Near the trails, you might come on the sun-bleached racks of caribou, or, waist high in blueberry bushes, a foraging black bear, who would stand on hind legs, look at you in disbelief, then give a loud *woof* of disgust and disappear.

I think I spent three holidays at La Roche. Nothing again was quite to equal its special magic for me. As I grew older—and older—I was to go fishing in many other parts of the world; some of those expeditions were wonderful, particularly those in the Bahamas. But it's never the actual fishing that stays with you, only the quality of your surroundings: its smells and sounds—its feel—so that suddenly, years later, you can catch the odor of wet pine needles, or hear the happy giggle of fast water running over stones, and be transported back, immediately and totally.

In my early teens, I spent summers in Muskoka, Ontario. It was lovely country but pacified, a relatively conventional summer playground complete with speedboats, sailboats and regattas. The area around Beaumaris had attracted a colony of wealthy Pittsburghers. There seemed to be multiple families of Hillmans, Mellons, Blairs, Millers and Hilliards; warm and hospitable people whose children gravitated to the yacht club and lent a great liveliness to the months of July and August. The "cottages" were roomy, ours included, and guests seemed to come and go in overlapping shifts. I longed desperately for a motorboat, but my parents didn't believe in them— "stinkpots," they called them. Canoes and a sailboat were considered enough and of course they were. It was a good time for me, but my memories of those summers seem oddly trivial.

Our house there, Rockmont, was lit by gas jets. The gas was made by adding water to "carbide" in a smelly little shed down by the lake and fed into the system from there. Turning the gas on and off, lighting it and keeping the glass chimneys clean was a chore. I don't know what happened to the jet in the dining room, perhaps it had rusted, but when my father went to turn it off one evening, the jet broke away and a flame a foot high shot up toward the ceiling. I can remember my father appearing, oh so casually, in the sitting room where there was the usual collection of houseguests, and speaking very calmly to my mother: "Jo dear, I seem to be having a problem with the gas."

By this time we could all smell the problem. There was a concerted rush to the dining room, where a pall of dense black smoke hung under the wooden ceiling. Neither sand nor water would quench the flame. Finally, someone whipped the cloth from the dining table and managed to wrap it around the broken pipe, smothering the fire. Later, I asked my father what he would have done if he'd been alone in the house. There was a long pause before he replied: "I don't think I know—watch it burn down perhaps?" The answer was so startlingly atypical that I've never forgotten it.

In almost every Muskoka summer there were visits from my beautiful Aunt Lena Whitehead and her two sons, William and Robert. Like me, Bob had a taste for the theater. We used to play theater games (today, they would be called "improvisations") in which there were good guys and bad guys. Our main stage was the broad staircase at Rockmont that led from the sitting room up to the bedrooms. It provided a couple of useful landings where it turned, and in the action of the "play" and its many inevitable shoot-outs, we could get a fine theatrical effect by rolling down the stairs. Under the stairs was the fruit cellar, a dungeonlike storage area that smelled of apples. This was "the jail," and Bob still complains that he spent far too much time in it. What did he expect? I was nearly five years his senior.

Today, Robert is one of the most distinguished and respected theatrical producers in the English-speaking world. Over the years he has employed hundreds, perhaps thousands, of actors, but with a gross lack of familial feeling and a marvelous evasiveness, he has always managed to avoid employing me. I take it hard that the fruit cellar should be held against me. Still, professional distance has not impaired a friendship that has been one of the most important and rewarding in my life.

In 1927 my parents took my sister Katherine and me abroad. I'd been in England with them before but not on the Continent. My parents stayed in England, but K and I were to go on to Paris and then Spain. The trip was not to be entirely frivolous. I was to be exposed to Art and Culture, and there were endless tours through museums, galleries and cathedrals. K took these seriously and was determined to educate me, as befits the role of older sister and godmother. I grew bored.

The first incident occurred in Salisbury Cathedral. I'd had it with history and stained-glass windows, with tombs and memorial plaques. Besides, my feet hurt. I was tossing my hat in the air when suddenly it didn't come down again. It was perched at a rakish angle on the head of some medieval saint, his stone

hands worshipfully clasped, his stony eyes raised to heaven—
and now, to the brim of my hat. A verger had to be summoned. With the help of a long pole he recovered my hat and
unburdened himself further with an attack on all American
tourists, and particularly the sacrilegious behavior of their
mannerless offspring. I didn't like to disappoint him by pointing out that I was Canadian.

On we went through the cathedrals of Ely, Winchester,
Durham, and of course St. Paul's and Westminster Abbey. I
had my first Communion in the latter and wore a new pair of
soft shoes with crepe soles that were considered highly inappropriate to the occasion. Then there was a blessed hiatus in
the English educational tour. A Scotsman named Kenneth
Sanderson, an old friend of my father's, had asked me to go
trout fishing on Loch Leven and Loch Katrine. I traveled up
to Edinburgh overnight on *The Scotsman* and sat in the dining
car opposite an elderly Englishman who actually spoke to
strangers.

"How old are you, young man?"

"Fifteen, sir—nearly sixteen."

"A bit young to be traveling alone, aren't you?—but then
you Americans do get about."

"I'm Canadian, sir."

"Ah well, same thing."

I reached for my water glass, knocked it over, and a cascade went into my companion's lap—confirming his first sus-
picions.

Kenneth Sanderson's house at 5 Northumberland Terrace,
Edinburgh, was old, tall, and thin—as indeed was he. And the
house, like the man, was filled with treasures. The rooms and
walls of the successive staircases were crowded with steel engravings; the sideboards, mantels, shelves and tables were
crowded with beautiful silver. These collections were rare and
valuable, and at Kenneth's death were willed to the nation. He
was a distinguished lawyer, a bachelor with no family connection I ever heard about, and was looked after by a cook-house-
keeper and manservant. He might have been described as
lonely, but I doubt that he was; too much went on in his head.
He was passionate about both the arts and sciences, and had

the taste to talk about both simply but with an enthusiasm that was infectious. He gave me my first radio—a small box with an exposed crystal that had to be tickled by a wire arm to produce any sound at all through the clumsy earphones. I was encouraged to play it in the kitchen, I think because it required a very long aerial that could be conveniently looped around the housekeeper's washlines.

As promised, I was taken fishing, which proved rather unsuccessful. We rowed about the lochs, flogging the water, in a cutting wind and drizzling rain. I have never been so cold in my life. My fingers turned blue. After a couple of days of this, the weather worsened and there was nothing for it but to return to Northumberland Terrace. Eventually the miracle of the radio palled and Kenneth suggested that we go to a gallery. There was absolutely nothing I wanted to do less—except perhaps to be exposed to "Scotch mist" again. I temporized.

"I've seen a lot of pictures."

"Have you now?"

"Yes—a lot."

"And what did you enjoy?"

A terrible silence from me.

"Tell me about one picture."

"There were so many."

"And you can't think of even one?"

I couldn't, and felt ashamed. I went up to my room, put on my crepe-soled museum shoes, and braced myself for boredom.

When we arrived at the Royal Scottish Academy, Kenneth took me into the first large gallery and asked me to point out a picture I liked. I pointed at something.

"Ah yes," said Kenneth, "it tells a good story."

I don't remember just what I pointed at, but I suspect it was something like Winslow Homer's *The Gulf Stream*, which hangs in the Metropolitan Museum of Art: a large oil depicting a dismasted schooner, an exhausted man lying in the scupper, and a number of sharks waiting for him to roll overboard.

I pointed at something else, and Kenneth said, "Another good story—but did you notice the color?"

"It's red."

"Not entirely. The *focal* point is red, but there is green, yellow, blue, black, white, and *echoes* of the red which will bring you back to the focal point again. The painting is designed around those colors. Did you notice the composition?"

I didn't know what the hell he was talking about.

"Find another one you like."

I pointed at something else.

"Good, well composed. The artist not only feels for his subject but has arranged the elements in such a fashion as to speak to you, to enhance that feeling. You're interested in the theater. An actor may 'feel' his role, but if he doesn't speak loudly enough to be heard it doesn't mean very much, does it? Look at the rhythm of those vertical lines. . . ."

And he went on. *Composition. Focal points. Rhythm. Color. Design. Emotion.* I began to be intrigued. Kenneth said, "Well, now I think it's time to go home." I was shocked. We'd looked at only three paintings. We'd been in the building for only twenty minutes. I pointed to the next gallery.

"But we haven't been in there."

"No. But perhaps tomorrow. You've made three friends. That's enough for any day. You can always come back."

Dear Kenneth. I need not have worn my crepe-soled shoes. I don't really know how much he knew about painting and painters. Perhaps he was talking rubbish, but I doubt it. I do know that he gave me a priceless gift. He taught me to look, not just to see. He taught me to stop while I still cared. He taught me to go beyond "a good story" to the dim beginning of understanding an artist's craft.

And we did go back the next day.

SIX

It was at the Rodin Musée in Paris that I first saw a naked woman. There she stood, in all her three-dimensional bronze glory. Before that it had been paintings, photographs and discreet sculptures—most of them employing fig leaves or long, tactically arranged tresses. I was approaching my sixteenth birthday and I was fascinated. I suddenly developed a more immediate and basic appreciation of Auguste Rodin than of any other sculptor whose work I had seen previously.

In those days, the Parisian ticket brokers and travel agencies sometimes used large dolls to advertise the attractions of the Folies Bergère. These were sure sidewalk stoppers—or at least they stopped me. The prospect of those delicious, long-legged, bare-breasted girls, who wore G-strings rather than fig leaves, and whose hair provided anchorage for elaborate, plumed headdresses rather than a modesty cover, made me determined to see a performance of the Folies. But there were the difficulties, and these proved insurmountable. I didn't know my way around Paris; my French was of the fractured, school-boy variety; my sister held the purse strings and was very much in charge. The Folies were, quite definitely, not on our agenda.

M. Rodin and the Folies mannequins between them had excited a head of steam that was to be discharged in a curiously oblique fashion, via a pair of shoes. They were the same damn shoes that were found unsuitable for my first Communion in Westminster Abbey—the brown ones with crepe soles. We'd been invited somewhere or other for lunch and I'd been instructed to wear my blue serge suit. I wore it resentfully— but with the brown shoes. K protested. An increasingly bitter argument ensued, culminating in my shouting at her, "Go to hell!" I don't know which one of us was more shocked. She burst into tears and I felt terribly wicked. But I also felt relieved. It was some sort of declaration of independence. Nothing had happened to lessen the sexual tensions, curiosity and frustrations of my adolescence, but something had been achieved—at least I could choose my own shoes.

But when I went home, it was to a greater restlessness than ever. I'd discovered girls. Actually, I'd discovered them long before, but I was agonizingly unsure of myself. For one thing, I didn't like the way I looked. Perhaps no one does at that age. My self-image hadn't been helped by my friend Lucy Harris. She and her brother George were two of my close friends in London, Ontario—and remain so to this day. We were to go to the movies one afternoon, a whole gang of us, and I was sporting my very first pair of long trousers. I'd bought them that same morning at Graftons—charcoal gray—and there had been no time to have them shortened. I approached the theater very self-consciously, hitching up my new pants. I was late. The gang was already assembled under the Loew's marquee. Lucy spotted me half a block away and sang out, "Hey look! Here comes Fat now—in a long pair of black stockings." I could have killed her. I suppose I was about twelve at the time.

The most serious of my adolescent pursuits came five years later. Her name was Helen Beck and she was enchanting. Life bubbled in her like one of the Farm's most beautiful springs. Her eyes laughed even when she was serious. She wasn't conventionally pretty but she was irresistible, and as I think about her I smile.

One of the few positive elements in my chameleon's character may be that I look back on all the girls with such pleasure and affection. Even sixty years later, I look back and am smugly pleased. Some accepted me, some gave me the heave-ho; some were pretty, some plain; silly or wise, tart or Puritan, it doesn't matter. I owe them all my gratitude. My dalliance with Helen Beck lasted longer than most, and worried my mother. Beckie was three years older than I and I somehow managed to fit in with her friends, most of whom were older still. This disparity of ages was a problem for my mother, though not for me. Whatever else may have disturbed her, she may have felt that I was skipping some essential step—perhaps that I was rushing forward into some emotional catastrophe. She didn't disapprove of my taste. Indeed, she never seemed to disapprove of any of my girls—and I brought some distinctly odd ones to Woodfield. That I brought them at all pleased her, I think. But in the case of Beckie, the age difference bothered her enough to make her speak to my father about it—which meant that it bothered her a great deal.

I was summoned to the upstairs sitting room, where I found my father pacing. He began in peremptory fashion.

"Your mother is troubled by your relationship with the Beck girl."

"Yes sir."

"She's spoken to you about it?"

"Yes sir."

"Then why do you persist?"

"I like her."

There was a pause while he digested this. Obviously the problem wasn't going to be simple. Finally, he said, "That's reasonable enough—but we can't have you worrying your mother."

"No sir."

(Don't let those "sirs" fool you. In more casual moments I called him "Dad," but this was a formal occasion calling for "sir." If the ax was to fall, he'd have to wield it and there'd be no higher appeal.)

"What do you suggest be done about it?"

"I don't know, sir."

"She's three years your senior. Can't you find friends among your own age group?"

"Yes sir—but I can't find her."

I think my father was about to smile, but he resisted it and maintained a sternly judicial manner.

"Very well. Are you seeing her today?"

"We're playing tennis—sir."

"Well, from now on, you are not to see her"—I held my breath—"more than once a day. If you are playing tennis with her in the afternoon you are not taking her dancing in the evening. If you are spending the evening with her, you are not to play tennis with her in the afternoon. Is that clear?"

"Yes sir."

And the interview was over. As far as I remember, it was our one and only confrontation. I remember it with great affection and delight.

My father terrified my cousins. They spoke of "Uncle Hume" with awe as though he were some sort of ogre. It was the Presence that did it. Somehow, I had known from earliest childhood that he had a heart like butter. He may have frightened others, but never me.

* * *

Whatever my adolescent distractions—travel, rebellion, girls, or the itching foot—I was never again to stand in the first half of my class, let alone at the top. I continued all the old routines with resignation—serving time. The sentence was to be broken now and then by holidays, wonderful holidays, and of them all the best may have been in the Bahamas.

My parents wanted to escape some part of the Canadian winter. My father's health demanded it. They went by ship to Nassau, which was then a small, colorful, British colonial outpost bearing little resemblance to what it is today. It had no airport and no real tourist trade. A few Canadians had discovered it and even fewer Americans. It was essentially British, with all the strengths and weaknesses of colonial rule. The civil service was good, the courts absolute, and race relations amicable despite occasional prejudice and complete inequality between white and black Bahamians. In those days—sixty years ago—such things didn't trouble me. I doubt that I was even aware of them. All I saw were the magnificent untrodden beaches and water that was "gin clear," and to me more intoxicating. The colors changed and melded; dark blues and aqua-marine, jade, sapphire, emerald, varying like an opal.

On shore the flowering trees gave a different kind of color: hibiscus, oleander, shower of gold, and regally, above the rest, the royal poinciana, with its elongated seedpods that clattered in the wind and were known locally as "old women's tongues."

But none of the adjectives or names alone can capture the atmosphere. It was deeply sensual and deliciously languorous. You were drenched in sunlight, cosseted by warm and fragrant breezes. The body's metronome grew lazy. You slept. Time shuffled. Here the Spanish "*mañana*" became "by-'n'-by" or "an' God spare life." The latter expression was far from morbid, but a reasonable assumption that life in such idyllic surroundings was bound to be too short—that the doing of anything should not be pressed, and that today's pause might be of greater value than tomorrow's activity.

It was all new to me and totally enchanting. It still is—even though I don't much fancy Nassau now for all its progress. I speak of a time long gone. The beautiful island across the harbor that I knew as Hog Island is now Paradise Island, a gambling merry-go-round with all the attendant jostle of hotels and support services. But they have to rake the beaches now. The conch and lobster are gone. The gentle whispers of palm fronds in an evening breeze are drowned out by steel bands.

"Hog Island" transformed into "Paradise Island"? Perhaps progress got it the wrong way round.

Of course, this attitude is old-fashioned, creaky; the bleating of one of those you-should-have-seen-it-when septuagenarians who never stop muttering about "the good old days." And while Nassau has changed, hundreds of the out islands (or Family Islands as they're now politely called) have not. There, the pristine quality of the Bahamas remains nearly intact, and it was there, in years to come, that I was to rediscover all the old magic.

My parents first stayed at the antiquated Royal Victoria Hotel in Nassau, with its wide colonial verandas, rocking chairs, and beautiful gardens. After that, it was the then-new Hotel Montagu, and finally the move into a rented house on Cable Beach. This was well outside the town, and to begin with, we traveled back and forth by horse and carriage.

The house was called Westbourne, but more familiarly "The Three Sisters" or "The Holy Trinity." It was built in three sections, bound together with verandas on both floors—a lovely, ugly house. It sprawled along the beach on one side and looked across the golf course on the other. Years later it was to be bought by Sir Harry Oakes, whose very messy end in what had once been my mother's bedroom caused a famous murder trial. No foreshadow of such horror fell across Westbourne in the years we lived there—nothing but my father's illness. Of course, I saw it only on my holidays from school or university and not a great deal of the house even then. I was always off somewhere—generally on the water, or in it, or under it. Most probably the latter. Having discovered that other magical country beneath the surface, a rainbow world of silent but ever-moving life, I spent waterlogged hours just watching. I was an early skin diver, having brought mask, snorkel and flippers back with me from the Mediterranean. I took the steel stays from an old beach umbrella and had them barbed in the local ironmongery. Spearfishing was primitive then: no weight belts or spring guns, no admonitory literature, and certainly no scuba. You speared only what you would eat. Shark were commonplace and barracuda almost constant companions. You treated the first with respect and the second with a toleration bordering on contempt.

Much of my time was spent alone. My father would play a little golf and sunbathe. My mother attended to Westbourne and a constant stream of older guests, and wrote endless letters. I hung around the Prince George docks, the sponge and fish markets, Charlie Turtle's boatyard and Hall's Curio Shop.

Mr. Hall wore a seaman's cap, indoors as well as out, and always spoke in a very soft voice. Unfortunately, he was afflicted by a terrible stutter. When this threatened to defeat him, he would stamp one foot in furious frustration, rather as though he were trying to crack a particularly stubborn nutshell, then begin all over again, in the same gentle tone. I must have exhausted Mr. Hall because I never stopped asking questions. His small shop was little more than a waterfront shack, but crammed to its bare rafters with the sea's curiosities and flotsam: delicately tinted glass net floats that had drifted all the way from Portugal, dried gorgonias, sponges of every variety, turtle shells, brain coral, shark's tails, pink conch pearls, tritons, bloated porcupine fish, and much more. The smell was overpowering. You couldn't tolerate it for long without a strong stomach. Luckily, I had one.

It was through Hall that I met some of the local fishermen. For a pound a day (five dollars then), I was to be allowed to go out with them. The understanding was that, once out, I stayed out, regardless of weather; that the boat was to keep any fish I might catch and, tacitly, that I wouldn't get in the way. The last wasn't easy.

The boats were small—sixteen to eighteen feet—with no motor, only the mainsail, jib and sculling oar. The gear barely left room for three men, and I was the fourth. You had to maneuver around fish pots, nets, and water glass and striking grains (lobster spears), lines and anchors. I found room for my feet where the mast stepped in. Holding the mast with one arm as the boat pitched and rolled, I could cast with the other. My rod amused these no-nonsense professionals; in the time it took me to land one fish, they'd take three on their handlines. But at least I contributed something to the catch—and I was in heaven.

I can't have been too much of a nuisance, because after a bit the fishermen would take me out overnight. We'd sleep on a beach at Andros or Eleuthera—a long sail from Nassau in a small boat—and fish from the following dawn to sunset. The meals were always fish, cooked over an open fire on the beach. The proceeding was simple. The fish would be gutted and laid unscaled on the coals without benefit of pan or kettle. It simply cooked in its own juices. When pulled from the fire, it looked inedible, burned to a crisp. It was placed on a sea-grape leaf and the charred skin scraped off. With a little native lime juice, the meal was delicious.

The drink was always tea. There was no alcohol. The fishermen were a rugged lot—they always are—but most of them were descendants of United Empire Loyalists: Godfearing and puritanical. They held strong prejudices against almost anything unfamiliar—and in some matters closer to hand. In a community like Spanish Wells, for instance, home for many of the most expert fishermen, black people were not allowed in the settlement after six in the evening.

Conversation between us was difficult. They talked little and when they did, I often couldn't understand what was being said. I remember being completely thrown when one captain explained to me that the wooden keel of his boat was cut from "nigger-whitey." Considering the prejudice, it seemed an unlikely description. I asked him to repeat it. That's what he said— and with considerable pride, too. It was sometime after that I realized the wood was *lignum vitae.*

After the last trip with my fishermen friends, I produced my pound note and had it pushed roughly away. "Keep it in your pocket," said the captain, and turned his back on me. It was one of the nicest compliments I ever received.

In the evenings at Westbourne, my father would sometimes take a solitary walk around the garden. The air was heavy with the scent of jasmine and frangipani. There was a murmur of waves on the beach. As it happened, the arc of the revolving beam from the Nassau light came to earth against our garden wall—a "tabby" wall, plastered over and painted pink. At regular intervals the wall would be swept with light before the beam passed on and out to sea. One evening I walked with my father and told him how much I liked that flash of pink.

"I hate it," he said. "It reminds me of the passing of time."

SEVEN

IN THE AUTUMN OF 1930 I went off to McGill University in Montreal. My brother Dick drove me to the train station. Of the five of us, Dick was the senior sibling and took his responsibilities seriously—at least toward his kid brother. He was a grave, enormously warm-hearted man, whose interests ranged over a wide spectrum: theosophy, extrasensory perception, electronics, aerodynamics (he flew the most beautiful complex kites), the church and, of necessity, accounting. He was treasurer of a large financial corporation. I always felt this occupation was a waste of his real talents. Dick had been trained as an engineer and had a strong inventive bent. It was he who made our first car heater (for an Overland touring car with isinglass side curtains), and the first electric kettle I ever saw. It had been confiscated from him at Ridley, where I inherited it twenty years later. It still worked perfectly—until confiscated from me a second time.

Dick had a workshop in the basement of his house on Waterloo Street. I must have been about fourteen when he taught me how to make gunpowder. It's not difficult—though I've forgotten the formula. Learning to make it led me to a number of experiments on my own. I was mad about fireworks, and had been reading about submarines, so I decided to build an underwater bomb. Dick suggested that I try a couple of empty shotgun shells as a casing.

"Pick up some twelve- and sixteen-gauge shells on the skeet range. One will fit inside the other. Fill the small one with powder. Thread a high-resistance wire through the casings— there's some on the top shelf. Dip the whole thing in liquid paraffin, attach your wires to a dry cell with extra-long leads, and there you are. Don't forget to turn off the Bunsen burner after melting the paraffin, and *don't* even light it until you've put the powder away. Got it?" And he went upstairs.

I thought I'd got it. I found the shells. They fitted together perfectly. I mixed the powder, filled the case and fitted the shells together—a small red cylinder with a brass cap at each end. I melted the wax. Now, how was I going to get a hair-thick wire through the middle so as to explode the whole thing? I had an inspiration. Heat a darning needle, hold it with pliers and run it through the cardboard casings. I relit the Bunsen burner, put "the bomb" in a vise and heated the needle. Dick came back to check on my progress.

"What are you up to?"

"Heating a needle."

"Why?"

"I'm going to make a hole for the wire. Then I'll dip the whole thing in wax so it'll be waterproof."

"I see. Have you put in your powder?"

"Of course."

There was a long pause before he continued.

"You've loaded the bomb?"

"Right."

"And you're heating a needle—red hot?"

"Right."

"And you propose to shove it through the casing?"

"That's right. It should go in easily."

"I'm sure it will—and the casing is filled with gunpowder?"

"Ri—" Oh my God! I was about to blow my face off.

I was never allowed to be alone in his workshop again.

Dick's very real mechanical aptitudes had been interrupted by the war, the R.A.F., an early marriage, and children. The practical business of making an immediate living took over.

Like my father, Dick was a big man, but more heavily built. I used to admire and envy his bulging muscles on the tennis court. He took none of his ever-changing preoccupations lightly. When he studied a subject, it was studied, and as he drove me to the station he was studying me. Finally he blurted it out.

"I suppose you know something about women?"

What boy of nineteen is going to answer "Not a damn thing"? My reply was almost disdainful. "Oh, of course." Dick was relieved. "Well—that's all right then."

And that was the total substance of my formal sex education. (I don't count Cap Iggulden's fulminations about self-abuse.) If only Dick had cross-questioned me about my sexual experience as carefully as he'd done years earlier about my underwater bomb, I just might have avoided some future explosions.

In Montreal I was consigned to the temporary care of one of my mother's younger sisters, my Aunt Babs. I adored her. Babs (the "Aunt" was dropped quickly) was a merry widow and a wealthy one. She was also a lady of taste and discrimination. She collected beautiful paintings and spent hours at the piano. She went to the theater and to concerts—taking me with her. She played golf, rode, and traveled a lot. Whatever problems she had were submerged by a spontaneous gaiety of spirit. She called me "Treasure" and spoiled me rotten. Her apartment at the Glen Eagles, and later her house on St. Sulpice Drive, were always open to me and my friends—but to be used with discretion. She never criticized my behavior or self-indulgence, though she was obviously aware of both, and she expected no less from me.

In this regard I made one dreadful mistake. One morning I awoke with an appalling hangover. I don't remember where I had been the night before, only the headache and a determination never, ever, to drink red wine again. As I hadn't appeared at breakfast, Babs knocked on my door, stuck her head in and asked "Are you all right, Treasure?" I groaned, sat up in bed very carefully, and stuck out my tongue. It was a hideous shade of purple. Babs laughed and said, "I'll be back in a minute." She returned with a liqueur glass filled with a muddy brown liquid. "What's that?" "Fernet-Branca—the hair of the dog. Knock it back." Shuddering, I did so. "I'm going riding, Treasure. Back in a couple of hours. You better rest."

When she got back, looking very smart in her riding clothes, I was up, but pale and wan. She was bubbling. "I think I'll have a drink," she said. My stomach turned over and with solemn priggishness I said, "Before lunch?"

That did it. The air congealed into frost. Babs turned from the sideboard and gave me a long, cold stare. "Yes. Before lunch. Do you mind?" It was the only time I remember her being angry with me. I can still feel the draft.

Delightful though it was, I couldn't stay with Babs forever. I had to find a place of my own. There were university residences, of course, but I'd had it with institutional dormitories. As for the fraternities, I was a very fresh freshman and hadn't joined one. I hadn't been asked. This was a particular blow to my vanity, as I was a "legacy" of both Zeta Psi and Kappa Alpha. My father had been a Zete and my uncle a Kap. During the "rushing" weeks, I'd been interviewed by senior members of both fraternities—and found wanting. There were generally two interrogators at these meetings, one your apparent advocate and sponsor, the other suspicious, if not downright hostile. The scene was rather like one of those old cops-and-robbers movies in which the suspect is grilled by two detectives who've decided beforehand which roles they are to play—one is the good guy and one is the bad guy. I remember one such interview in which the "good" said, "They tell me at the gym that he's a very good boxer," to which the "bad" replied wearily, "So what? We've got enough athletes." It was supposed to be a pejorative comment, but I couldn't have been more pleased. No one had ever referred to me as an athlete before.

Eventually, I was accepted by the Kaps, but it was very touch and go. The day of formal invitation was almost over, the day in which final bids were to be made to prospective candidates. I was obviously at the bottom of the barrel and was seeking comfort in the bar of the Ritz Carlton Hotel. This was precisely the sort of freshman behavior that was frowned upon by other undergraduates—I should have been drinking at the Pig and Whistle, which I frequently did, but it was at the Ritz that an emissary from the Kap House found me. There must have been a frantic, last-minute tallying up of freshman acceptances and the discovery that they were short their quota. At any rate, I squeaked in—perhaps to their regret. I never did manage to complete my full initiation requirements, and I was as recalcitrant a fraternity member then as I've been an unsatisfactory club member since. (I've been a member of one New York club for fifty years that I've certainly not set foot inside fifty times, and I remained a member of another for ten years before resigning out of shame for my lack of contribution.) I've simply never learned the trick of it, or the habit. I tried, but it became a duty rather than a pleasure, and besides, I had other things to do.

Nevertheless, I wanted to join a fraternity. No one twisted my arm. I wanted to belong. That called for some unspecified conformity, and whatever the requirements, I didn't measure up. My friends were mavericks or at least rugged individualists, my habits questionable, my manner sometimes aloof and easily construed as arrogant. As for my tastes, they were both champagne and beer. It confused people.

Many years later, I was to sit in Phil Silvers's dressing room at the Shubert Theater, spinning him some sort of tale that left him puzzled. We laughed a lot but finally he said to me, "Hume, you're some sort of . . . Shakespearean hoodlum, aren't you?" It was an odd but intended contradiction—perhaps more descriptive of what I'd like to be rather than of what I was. I've always wanted my bread buttered on both sides.

Among the marks against me as fraternity material were my frequent visits to the Beaux Arts nightclub. I learned about this after the fact. Almost always, I used to go alone. I'd sit in the corner beneath the bandstand and would be joined by a couple of chorus girls and, between sets, by the orchestra's conductor, Izzy Aspler. We got along well. I found these new friends more stimulating—and the girls more attractive—than the few I'd met in lecture halls or at student gatherings. I liked to dance and I liked the surrounding feel of show business— no matter how tacky. I became an habitué. I had an in at the Beaux Arts, and when seniors came in and were unable to find a table, but saw this punk freshman in his corner, it did nothing to win me their approval.

How could I afford nights at the Beaux Arts, drinks at the Ritz, and similar extravagances? The answer is simple. I was rich. My family took care of all my university fees. I had no rent to pay as long as Babs would put up with me, and I received an allowance of two hundred dollars a month. In 1930, that was lavish. There was only one catch. I had to account for my expenditures. This required a certain amount of what is now known as "creative bookkeeping," and was a terrible bore; but without submission of the previous month's account, the following month's allowance would not appear.

The whole allowance proceeding had started while I was at the Ridley Lower School. I got three dollars a month pocket money then. One dollar per week for three weeks (mailed punctiliously by my father's secretary, Rose Merrit) and then a week with nothing. The theory was that this would teach me thrift. It was pointed out that if I saved a quarter from each of the first three weeks' remittances, I could still afford the tuck shop on the fourth. This theory collapsed in practice. When I got to the Upper School the monthly amount was increased to fifteen dollars—three lovely, crisp, five dollar bills—an increase of five hundred percent. Wow! But the same rules still applied, and I was generally broke by the month's end. There would be a frantic scribbling in my account book—periodically inspected by my brother Dick, or, more tolerantly, by Miss Merrit—to ensure the next remittance.

Now, at McGill, the amount had been increased again, this time by nearly fourteen hundred percent. My old Lower School friend and protector (in the days of McGoohey and Madox), James Carrington Harvey III, helped me to spend it.

Jim was a sophomore and knew his way round. He also knew just where he wanted to live: the Chateau Apartments on Sherbrooke Street. It was a preposterous address for an undergraduate; a great gray pile conforming to its name, complete with uniformed doormen and elevator operators. The rent for the most humble of its apartments—two rooms on the ground floor facing on both the street and driveway—was ninety dollars per month. How we ever got in I'll never know; I can only suppose that the collapse of the stock market the year before had something to do with it. We decided to take in a third student, bringing the ante down to thirty dollars a month each—only one seventh of my allowance. Even Dick would approve of that, however little he might have approved of some of my other expenditures.

Jim was a rather dashing figure. He had an entourage consisting of Hector Curdle, his batman or valet, and an off-white English bull terrier called Sikes, who drooled and had bloodshot eyes. Sikes wasn't housebroken and for some reason or other seemed to favor my bed as a resting place, with the result that it was frequently damp and smelly. I'd rail at Jim, who found it amusing but would take Sikes out for a walk—long after the event.

Hector was a twisted little man, of indeterminate age but certainly much older than we were. I felt sorry for him; Nature had done him dirt. He had almost dwarfish legs and a badly bent back. He barely came up to my shoulder and he wasn't too bright. I never quite understood his duties and suspect that Jim employed him more out of compassion than need. Hector spent a lot of time fussing over his employer's considerable wardrobe.

Jim wore a dark Chesterfield coat, a bowler cocked at a jaunty angle, and yellow suede gloves. He also had a cavalier attitude toward money. I once hesitated over buying something, because I couldn't afford it, and Jim looked at me pityingly.

"You don't *pay* for it—you *charge* it."

"But you have to pay for it someday."

" 'Someday' may never come."

The third member of our Chateau household was Colin Keith, recruited from the engineering school. Colin was of Welsh descent and known affectionately as "Taffy." He was wedge-shaped: tall and enormously broad shouldered, with the head and face of a Stone Age man. He had a heavy, square, underslung jaw and above it a surprisingly beatific smile. He enjoyed drinking, smoking his pipe, and working at the intricate drawings on his drafting table, which took up far too much space in our cramped quarters.

We were an odd triumvirate. If you'd lined us up on Saturday night, dressed in our tails, white ties and top hats, we'd have looked like graduated penguins—Taffy at the top end and I at the bottom. Saturday nights were special during "the Season." There were "coming out" parties then. If you were on a list, you would be invited. You were formally introduced at a reception line. You danced (wearing white gloves), drank punch, ate supper, and sometime after midnight, escorted some "nice" girl back to wherever she lived.

It was after all this that the fun began. We'd take off for far less formal surroundings below St. Lawrence Main—some of them real sleaze spots. Our appearance there couldn't have been more inappropriate if we actually had been penguins ("college kids—slumming"). Sometimes there were fights, but Taffy's size didn't invite them and Jim's good humor diffused a lot of resentment.

I have the feeling now that we were all faintly ludicrous—figures from a cartoon by John Held, Jr., that hilarious cartoonist who satirized the flapper age, the Charleston, necking, mini-miniskirts, hip flasks, and raccoon coats. But I had a ball.

If you're wondering where my studies (commerce and finance) came into all this, they hardly intruded. I attended some lectures on political economy given by Stephen Leacock, whose *Nonsense Novels* had delighted me; but I found the lectures dry and tedious—not at all what I'd hoped for. I went to my English lectures and spent desultory hours in the Redpath Library. It was only in the English department's work done on stage at Moyse Hall that I really became involved. This led to my participation in the university's Players' Club, the Red and White Revue, and finally in the performances of the Montreal Repertory Theatre. All the latter extracurricular of course, and not at all what I was supposed to be about, which was preparing to be a corporation lawyer.

So there I was, pissing away time and opportunity; spending hours in amateur theatricals; trying, quite unsuccessfully, to get some girl or other to go to bed with me—and boxing. I was "sowing my wild oats" like any other overprivileged young man with roots in the Edwardian era.

Boxing isn't a sport that tolerates being out of training. I was on the university boxing team but in laggard condition. There were a series of matches held in the suburb of Notre Dame de Grace. The opposing club was made up largely of blue-collar young men who could fight—none of your fancy Dan stuff. My featherweight opponent was a steelworker, heavily muscled and more of a street fighter than a boxer. He held his gloves at waist height, leaving his head unprotected, and stood flat-footed, legs astride, waiting to throw a punch that counted.

I outpointed him easily. First his nose bled, then one eye puffed up, but it didn't seem to bother him. He just stood there stolidly, blinking and looking confused, as though he had a too-persistent wasp buzzing around his ears—which, come to think of it, is a fairly accurate analogy.

I grew cocky. I dropped my guard and came in close, bobbing and weaving, trying to tempt him to throw a punch and open up even more. That was a serious mistake.

I didn't even see the blow coming. It was a right cross that jarred every tooth in my head. The force of it made me do a sort of back somersault into the ropes. It was the first and only time I got knocked down. The local crowd couldn't have been more pleased. Then I made another mistake. I was on my feet again before the referee even got his arm up, but so stunned that I saw six opponents across the ring. A more experienced boxer would have finished me off in short order. I was literally saved by the bell.

I won the next two rounds on points and was given the decision. The audience booed. They knew, and so did I, that I'd been beaten.

That was one lesson. A few weeks later, I was to get a second, but of an entirely different variety.

EIGHT

THE GIRLS LINED UP for our inspection: about eight of them,
dressed or undressed in whatever manner they felt would be
most seductive. Mine wore nothing but high heels and long
black silk stockings, held up by scarlet garters that boasted tri-
color rosettes, rather like those of the Legion d'Honneur—she
was after all a French-Canadian. Next to her was a girl wearing a sheer, full-length nightgown. Another patriot wore a
cache-sexe shaped like a maple leaf, with tiny pasties to match;
another, some sort of velvet saddle and harness, catering I
suppose to the kinky trade. They were all completely at ease,
watching us with amusement. We were the ones on show. They
smiled; we fidgeted and affected a worldly casualness that none
of us felt.

The whole thing had started in a booth at the Prince of
Wales Tavern, more familiarly called the Pig and Whistle. The
four of us were talking about sex and lying in our teeth; at
least I was, the others had had some experience. There was a
discussion about the merits or drawbacks of various local
whorehouses. Because I couldn't contribute to this, because I
found courage in the group, because I wanted to show off,
and not least because I was randy, I rather think it was I who
said, "Let's go." The aficionados chose a place just off St.

Catherine Street—nothing fancy, just a cathouse dependent on low prices and high turnover.

I pointed—oh, so casually—at the girl with the garter rosettes. She can't have been much older than I was. She had a pretty figure and straight blue-black hair cut in a pageboy bob. She stepped forward, took me by the hand and said, *"Je m'appelle Michelle."* Then she led me upstairs, her bottom undulating nicely at each step.

The room was little more than a cubicle, with a cot, washstand, a bedside table and chair. She took a clean towel from a pile on the stand, poured water from the pitcher into the basin, held out her hand and asked for three dollars, which she tucked into the top of her stocking. I undressed, putting my clothes on the chair. She kicked off her shoes and proceeded to wash me and at the same time carry out an examination for obvious signs of venereal infection. All very clinical. She lay back on the bed, held out her arms and the whole business was completed in perhaps sixty seconds. At least I knew how the pieces fitted together.

"Votre premier fois—n'est-ce pas?" I didn't trust my French to try to persuade her otherwise. What would have been the point, in view of the performance? I nodded dumbly and she patted my shoulder.

"Très bon, chéri."

I think she expected me to move. I didn't.

"Et maintenant? Encore?"

I nodded again and she giggled.

"Mais plus lentement, peut-être."

It may have taken a minute and a half the second time round, and it cost another three dollars. When Michelle was finally able to sit up, she reached for the towel, combed her hair, and opened the drawer of the bedside table. From it she took a long green card and a conductor's punch. The card was already heavily perforated. She punched it twice again, then put it away. (This may sound unreal but is strictly true.) I think I managed a *"merci beaucoup"* with the tip that I laid on the bed. I left her squatting on the po. She waved to me, saying, *"Bonne chance,"* and I found my own way down the stairs—no longer a virgin.

It was neither a glamorous experience nor a disgusting one. It wasn't the best way, nor was it the worst. I'm not prepared either to bless or to judge it. What has been accomplished in the broad field of sexual education over the past half century I'm not qualified to debate. My own education was to continue as it started.

Flo's was a call house on Milton Street and a distinct step up in both the social and economic order of brotheldom. No girls lived under Flo's roof. When they were summoned, they arrived discreetly dressed. There was no parade, and the tariff was ten dollars. You could pay it by check if you so chose.

The house itself was a single family residence on a quiet street in what was then a middle-income neighborhood. It was ordinary, comfortable and clean. The ground floor consisted of an entry hall, a parlor, a dining room which doubled as a second parlor or even a waiting room when business was brisk. Flo's johns were kept carefully segregated, as a matter of discretion. Upstairs there were three or four guest rooms and, quite apart from these, Flo's own quarters, which were frilly and cheerful but which I was only allowed to see once, when she was in bed with a severe cold. I sat on the end of her bed, drinking a cup of tea and marveling at her curlpapers. She was a very ample lady of about fifty, retired from active service and, as far as I knew, her own boss. She always wore something tent-shaped, a cross between a hostess gown and a muumuu.

Flo ran a very tight ship. She catered to a carriage trade, as she defined it. A new customer had to be introduced by an old established one. There was no walk-in trade and there were rules: no drunks, no rough stuff, and you had to be out of her house by two in the morning. If anything got out of hand she wouldn't hesitate to call the police, who chose to be sympathetic.

Her young ladies were all moonlighting and seemed to enjoy their work. Most of them had steady jobs but wanted a second income. If you ran into them outside, which I did on two different occasions—once behind a counter and once waiting on my restaurant table—they cut you dead. The rules said you were not to be acknowledged outside Flo's premises.

I don't remember who introduced me to Flo. I do remember her parlor—and her kitchen. You sat in the former waiting for your girl to arrive. It was a nervous wait. What would you draw? The radio was always playing. You could order a drink and there were magazines which you pretended to read while listening for the doorbell. The front door would be opened by Flo's maid. You'd hear a murmured exchange behind the sliding double doors while the girl hung up her coat, then the doors would slide open and Flo would carry out the introduction. The girl would sit beside you on the sofa, pull her skirt demurely down over her knees and perhaps accept a drink—generally a soft one. You did *not* rush off upstairs. You talked. You "became acquainted." She would admire your taste in neckties; you might comment on the little gold cross she wore around her throat (and which she kept on even when starkers). You might even hold hands, but no more—not in the parlor.

I suppose Flo's place was a kind of club—catering to the beastly habits and hypocrisies of depraved men? (Flo told me that most of her clientele were married.) Whatever it was, I enjoyed it. I was comfortable there and became a familiar of Flo's. We'd sit in her kitchen drinking tea and gossiping to one another about our quite diverse problems. I was able to make her laugh, but one afternoon when business was slow, and she was out of sorts, she suddenly burst out at me.

"You're a funny kid!" she said. "Funny—but a kid, a baby. What are you doing sitting here talking to a fat old whore? Why aren't you somewhere else—or upstairs?"

I started to protest, but she cut me short.

"Oh, it's all right. You're welcome—and there are damn few customers I let come into my kitchen. You want another cup of tea?"

When, inevitably, I came down with gonorrhea, I went straight to Flo and told her I'd caught it from one of her young ladies. I felt it was less a complaint than a public service, but she was outraged.

"You've been catting around—or having it off with one of those 'nice' girls who don't know a douche bag from duck soup. I can't make you wear a rubber, but if you won't, you deserve what you get. Don't come back to my house without a doctor's certificate."

She heaved herself up from behind the kitchen table, snatched for her purse and pulled out a bill, which she slapped down in front of me.

"Look at that—and that's only for last month."

It was a doctor's account in three figures.

"Every one of my girls has to have regular examinations. Don't tell me you caught it here."

But I had—and I paid for it.

A "dose of clap," as it is so poetically termed, was not to be taken lightly in 1931. There were no antibiotics. If the infection isn't checked, there's a painful side effect known as chordee, which I refuse to go into but which can make urination agonizing. There's also the danger that treatment, if not skillfully administered, can drive the infection "posterior," which results in further unpleasant complications. I managed to gather the whole sweet bouquet.

At least I had the sense to seek out a doctor immediately. He was a urologist with the good Presbyterian Scots name of MacDougall, and was frightfully jolly. As a recommendation, this proved not to be enough. Taffy was to come down with the same complaint a few months later (not caught from me, I hasten to add), and went to the same doctor. Taffy reported that "Dr. Mac" showed him to the door, slapped him on the back and said, "Just do as I told you. Go home, drink plenty of water, and don't worry. Some of the best men in this town have had it—not to mention any names, the mayor."

Dr. Mac treated me with potassium permanganate, the specific in those days. It was administered through what looked like a horse syringe—a forbidding-looking vial containing a purple solution. The end of the syringe was inserted into the penis and the liquid driven slowly up the urethra by a careful depression of the plunger. It was a messy business, and after the first few treatments I was required to learn to do it for myself. I spent a good deal of time mopping up purple stains from the bathroom floor.

The infection persisted for weeks but came to a head one evening while I was in rehearsal. I can't remember just what it was I was rehearsing, but it must have kept me thoroughly occupied. I needed to go to the bathroom. On the other hand, I didn't want to interrupt what was going on. When there was finally a break, I rushed to the men's room. I stood in front of the urinal and nothing happened. Absolutely nothing.

After rehearsal, in some distress, I tried to reach Dr. Mac, but it was a weekend and he was away skiing. Jim Harvey suggested that I call his friend Dr. Frank Scully, who lived at the Ritz Carlton just across the street from the Chateau. It was after midnight, but I was worried and in pain. I woke the doctor up and explained my problem. He groaned, sleepily, and told me that whatever else might ail me, my anxiety had probably contributed to a nervous stricture. He called an all-night drugstore and prescribed a sedative.

"Drink it down and then walk. Keep walking. If that doesn't relieve you, call me back—I may have to catheterize you."

And he hung up. I didn't know the word *catheterize* and I thought he'd said "castrize." I'd never heard that word either (I don't believe it exists), but it sounded ominously related to *castrate* and I *did* know what that meant. I'd once watched the gelding of a horse.

I put down the telephone and turned, ashen-faced, to Jim and Taffy. I explained my understanding of the conversation, and a terrible, apprehensive gloom settled on all three of us.

I got the sedative and drank it down right there in the drugstore. Then I started to walk—up and down Sherbrooke Street, in subzero weather. Even the cold didn't help. Nothing helped, nothing worked, and the pain was becoming unbearable. I woke Dr. Scully again about three A.M. "I'll pick you up," he said, and appeared in a taxi not ten minutes later, wearing pajamas under his overcoat. We drove to Sir Henry Grey's private hospital, blessedly nearby, where they seemed to be expecting us. "I'm going to put you to sleep," said Frank.

When I woke the next morning, it was with enormous relief, and the discovery that I was attached to several rubber tubes. My door opened and a large silver-haired man walked in. "I'm Dr. Grey," he said tersely. He lifted my limp wrist and took my pulse in silence. Satisfied, he went back to the door, put his hand on the knob and turned before opening it. "If you were my boy, I'd give you a sound thrashing," he said, and stalked out.

My next visitor was not long in arriving. It was Babs. Jim had called her and she'd obviously had a chat with Sir Henry.

"Hello, Treasure. You're in a pickle, aren't you? Well, these things happen. Bear up." She smiled reassuringly and galloped on. "I felt I had to call Dick. I can't pretend I don't know you're in hospital, can I? But I didn't find it necessary to go into any sort of detail. Said you'd be out in a day or two anyway. That all right?" I couldn't think of anything to say except, "Thank God Mum and Dad are in the Bahamas."

They did discharge me a few days later—without benefit of tubing. I walked with a limp for a bit and had to use a cane. It put an end to my boxing and my infrequent attendance at lectures. I couldn't bear the inevitable inquiries: "What happened to you?"

And that was that lesson—but fortunately, no more than a caution, no scars.

Frank Scully became a good friend. He found my passion for the theater amusing and would call me "Mansfield" after the great American actor Richard Mansfield, who was popular at the turn of the century. Frank's own interest in the theater was not entirely impersonal. He was fond of an actress who was the leading lady of a stock company in Washington, D.C.— a very good company, one of the last to survive that spoiler called "talking pictures."

Before long I faced my final first-year examinations at McGill. I simply ignored them. The university authorities knew that I had been absent (a freshman roll call was recorded at lectures) and that I had failing grades in most subjects, while doing surprisingly well in others. It was a pattern which confused my sympathetic freshman adviser. "I don't understand it," he said reproachfully. "Four F's and two A's. You can't be stupid—how are your eyes?"

I think I may have had an advocate and supporter in the dean's secretary. She was a distant cousin named Daisy Field, who was fond of my mother. Whether it was Miss Field, the confusion, my frequent appearances on university stages (where I'd drawn some attention), my boxing, or a bureaucratic bungle, I was accepted as a "partial" student for the following year. Quite undeservingly, I'd been spared the embarrassment of flunking out.

At the end of my freshman year, I took off with Frank Scully for Washington and my introduction to professional theater. Frank's friend, Nancy, turned out to be endearing, and introduced me to the company's director, an Englishman named Clifford Brooke, who might well have been cast as Mr. Pickwick. I was allowed to hang about backstage, a rare privilege, and to attend rehearsals, which was even rarer. I was in heaven. I learned a lot quite quickly, most of it from being put severely in my place. The company's comedian, Forrest Orr, was more amusing onstage than he was off. Trying to be helpful one evening, I pointed out that his false moustache was a bit lopsided. He glared at me and snapped, "A professional never criticizes another actor's makeup!" I don't believe I've ever done so since.

Eventually, to my delight, Clifford Brooke gave me a job. I was engaged at fifteen dollars a week to play a paperboy in *Up Pops the Devil*. I had one line which I rehearsed to death and, cliché though it may be, I stepped out onto the stage of the National Theater for my first professional appearance— and promptly forgot my line.

This is the essence of one of the most moss-grown jokes in theater history. A young actor, after appearing for years as no more than wordless "atmosphere," is given his first line. It reads "Hark! I heard a pistol shot." In a fever of anxiety he stands in the wings rehearsing his line and waiting for his brief but glorious moment. On cue, he steps onstage and shrills, "Hark! I heard a shistol pot—a postal shit—oh fuck!" and he stamps offstage in disarray.

Up Pops the Devil was the last play of the National's spring season. I went back to London, Ontario, after it closed, taking a new actor friend with me—the one who wore the suede shoes. It was later that same summer that the tea party took place on the Woodfield lawn. *Up Pops the Devil,* indeed.

When I look back at the number of amateur performances in which I appeared during the school year of 1931–32 (*The Road to Rome, Morn to Midnight, The Adding Machine, Dr. Faus-*

tus, Alice in Wonderland and others which I've forgotten), I wonder how I managed to learn the lines. Just half as much effort applied to political economy and all the rest of it might have earned me an eventual degree.

In the summer of that year, I went off to New York carrying a letter. It had been written by Martha Allen, artistic director of the Montreal Repertory Theatre where I'd appeared in a couple of plays, and it was addressed to Miss Margaret Linley, casting director of the Theatre Guild, probably the most prestigious producing organization of its time.

What did I expect of my letter of introduction—that it was a passport to fame and fortune? Possibly. I certainly expected something. I've learned better. No responsible individual, be he (or she) casting director, producer, director, star or stage manager, can justifiably recommend you for a job without personal knowledge of your capability. Your work has to be seen. An introductory letter may open a door, accomplish a tenuous connection, may even lead to an audition, but that's it.

"Martha speaks very highly of you, Mr. Cronyn," said Miss Linley.

"Yes, she was kind enough to give me a copy of her letter."

"Are you a member of Actors' Equity?"

"Not yet."

(An infamous catch-22: You cannot get a professional job unless you're an Equity member; you cannot become an Equity member without recognizable professional experience.)

"I see. Well, your best chance of employment—people will want to know what you have done—is to find a job, any sort of job, an apprenticeship possibly, with one of the summer stock companies. Do you know Arthur Sircom?"

"I'm afraid I don't know anybody—not in this country."

Miss Linley looked tired. She drew a yellow pad toward her. "Let me give you some names you might call." I didn't realize how kind she was being. Dozens, perhaps hundreds of actors, professional actors with impressive credits, trooped through her office every week seeking employment, and here was this Canadian kid with a strictly amateur background taking up her precious time.

She handed me a list of half a dozen names and telephone

numbers. There was a pause. She looked at me, puzzled, before saying something that is engraved on my memory.

"Mr. Cronyn, I think you may have a difficult time."

"Oh. Why?"

"Because you don't look like anything."

Because it sounded rude, she hurried to explain that my accent was odd, my appearance was odd, my clothes were odd. Well, not odd exactly, but unexpected. I didn't fit into any immediately recognizable category. She couldn't pigeonhole me as a type. Miss Linley was very nice about all this and at pains to explain that my most likely chance of employment was to walk into an interview and have the interviewer feel, "That's it—that's the type: typical young student or banker, stockbroker, bohemian, bum; arrogant, shy, educated, illiterate . . ."

For the beginner particularly and, sadly, later on even for the seasoned professional, one's capability as an actor is not the essential question, but rather "Is this the type?"

As a footnote to the above, Margaret Linley subsequently left the Theatre Guild and joined what was then a major talent agency, A. & S. Lyons, Inc. Among her clients was the young man who "didn't look like anything." This possible deficiency became Maggie's problem. After all, hers was the job of persuading managers that I was the ideal actor for whatever part they were trying to cast. Actually, I've always suspected that the deficiency was one of my few assets. I was difficult to type; and when I consider the range of parts I was allowed to play over the next twenty years, the suspicion seems reasonable.

I walked out of Miss Linley's office neither richer nor poorer. I don't know what I may have done with her list, except that I never pursued it. The next morning I took off for California to deliver another letter of introduction. This one had been provided by my uncle, Edward Cronyn. "I knew an actor once," he had said with the rather surprised air of one who might admit to having been on friendly terms with a Ubangi chieftain.

It was my first trip to California, and I chose to fly, which my family found mind-boggling. The elapsed time from New York to Los Angeles was 33 hours. The plane from New York to Salt Lake City was a Ford trimotor, which was a little like being encapsulated in a Mixmaster. The connecting plane from Salt Lake City to Los Angeles was small, holding the pilot and five passengers. I had arrived in Salt Lake City feeling exhausted, thirsty, partially deaf and queasy, and I itched abominably. The heat was oppressive. I asked the small plane's pilot if it would be a mistake to drink some water. He said he thought it might be. It was. I've had some rough trips in bush planes since that epic flight, but none that made me sick. This was a first and only, not helped by the fact that the passenger in front of me kept swigging from a pint of bourbon. The whiskey fumes wafted back, hastening my reach for the airsickness bag. Ironically, only the drinker and the pilot remained immune to the alternate sensations of driving madly over a curb as we hit an updraft, and of falling into a bottomless pit on a downer.

I stumbled into my Los Angeles hotel, collapsed onto the bed fully dressed and slept for ten hours. When I woke I was scratching, and discovered that I was host to a fine crop of body lice. My first mission in the City of the Angels was to find a drugstore and a supply of blue ointment. I drenched my underwear in lighter fluid and set fire to it in my hotel room wastebasket.

I can't blame the crabs on the aircraft but on the bright lights of Broadway. In my forty-eight hours in New York, I had drifted from theater to theater in the Times Square area, and on my last night there ended up in a taxi dance hall. Was that the source of my itch or was it my hotel bed? If it had been anything more intimate I would remember.

The actor to whom I was carrying Uncle Ed's letter was Lawrence Grant, an English character actor who at the time I met him was working with Ronald Colman and Fay Wray in a film called *The Unholy Garden*. I know that somehow or other Lawrence got me onto the set and introduced me to its stars. I watched the shooting goggle-eyed. At one memorable moment Ms. Wray (later to be immortalized as the girl held high above the head of King Kong atop the Empire State Building) got something in her eye and I rushed forward to lend her my handkerchief. I wasn't to see her again until eight years later when we were in the same stock company at Skowhegan, Maine.

My mother's bargain with me had been that if I spent a second year at McGill and still wanted to go into the theater at the end of it, I should have a choice of attending either the Royal Academy of Dramatic Arts in England or the American Academy of Dramatic Arts in New York. I chose the latter. Why? Perhaps because it was closer to home; perhaps because the border between the United States and Canada seems more tenuous than all but the most passionately nationalistic of Canadians is prepared to admit; perhaps it was the A.A.D.A. catalogue, which listed as graduates Spencer Tracy, Edward G. Robinson, William Powell, Rosalind Russell, and a host of other theater and film celebrities more familiar to me than their R.A.D.A.-graduate counterparts. Whatever my reasons, I was accepted into the fall class of 1932.

Fifty-six years later, on May 1st, 1988, the academy paid tribute to me and to Jessica Tandy in a gala ceremony on the roof of the St. Regis Hotel. It was attended by the Canadian prime minister, the premier of Ontario, the Canadian ambassador to the United States and a great many professional colleagues, whose presence was even more of a tribute than the occasion itself. I sat through the entire proceeding in a fog of disbelief and apprehension over my ability to express an adequate thank-you. The one thing I kept thinking about was the enormous satisfaction and pride it would have given my mother.

NINE

IN THE UNITED STATES in September, 1932, the Great Depression was in full swing. Three-point-two beer was just legal, or about to become legal. Prohibition was on the way out, but speakeasies of every description still flourished. There were apple sellers on the corner; something like thirty million people were unemployed. They slept by the hundreds in Central Park during the summer months—and went relatively unmolested, then, in a common bond of misery. Bank holidays came and went.

But I was rich. I had one hundred and seventy-three dollars a month, the U.S. equivalent of two hundred dollars Canadian, and felt vaguely ashamed of such affluence. I turned up at the American Academy of Dramatic Arts wearing a bowler hat and blue serge suit, and the first student I met was a tall, handsome midwesterner who had on a pearl gray Stetson. He smiled broadly down on me, shoved out his hand and said, "Howya." He was immensely affable and I thought we might share an apartment. However, "Howya" was committed to the Y.M.C.A. I ended up sharing a one-room studio apartment with a student called Peter Barry, who, when we first met, took one look at my bowler and blue serge and said, "You planning on a wedding or a funeral?"

91

Peter Barry was born Bert Bacherig, from Nashville, Tennessee. It's improbable that he coined his new name from James M. Barrie, but there was a connection. Peter was an original, another of my mavericks. A master of fantasy, he saw the world through some sort of cockeyed prism and turned everything and everybody delightfully upside down, including me.

James Thurber once described his near-blindness by saying, "Where you see a paper bag blowing down the street, I see an old lady turning somersaults." Peter shared such miraculous visions. If I'd hunted throughout Manhattan, it's unlikely that I could have found a roommate whose personality was so different from my own. Where I was compulsively tidy, Peter was outrageously sloppy. Where I took too much too seriously (including myself), he was marvelously giddy and satirical. Where I counted pennies and kept accounts, he was happily irresponsible. Peter found my solemnities hilarious and poked endless fun at me. One day after I'd walked into our studio and found it in even greater disarray than usual, I drew a line down the middle of the floor and said, "Okay, Peter, now that's your side of the room. Do what you damn well want with it, but keep your stuff the hell out of mine!" Peter looked at me in bemused bewilderment, but I heard him describe the confrontation later: "Hume got so cross—he had on his baby bonnet and flap shoes and stalked around the apartment shouting at me." The image of flap shoes and baby bonnet came from burlesque, but is very close to Disney's Donald Duck.

My account-keeping also amused Peter, perhaps because by the twentieth of any given month he'd be broke and have to borrow from me. This usually meant his suffering a lecture on the virtues of thrift. He'd listen to me owl-eyed and impervious, and having got the ten dollars needed (which he always repaid) he'd take the first opportunity to describe the transaction to our friends: "Have you ever seen Hume's accounts? Great stuff. They go like this:

Bus 15¢
Cleaner 75¢
Lunch 45¢

Paper 5¢
Orchids $17.50

Orchids for God's sake!"

What I spent on girls gave Peter a good deal of leverage, because he always succeeded in making me feel guilty, even if he'd not been able to come up with his share of the rent—or at least not on time.

Peter had a deep distrust of banks. He might have kept what money he was able to collect under the mattress if we hadn't slept in Murphy beds that swung up into a wall closet. All that tilting, to say nothing of the fact that his bed was never made, would have probably dislodged his treasure.

A couple of years after we parted company as roommates, I ran into Peter and his friend Hans Hasler on the street. It was a bitterly cold night, but Peter had his rather seedy camel hair coat open and thrown around his shoulders like a cape; a long, fringed silk scarf was wound around his neck, with the fringe falling to his knees. His hat brim was turned up all along one side in the rakish manner reminiscent of John Barrymore. Peter always wore Adler elevator shoes to compensate for his five-foot-five-inch height. These pitched him forward onto his toes so that he appeared to be leaning into a high wind. By comparison, Hans, or "Hansel" as Peter called him, seemed even taller than he actually was. Peter always referred to him as "my personal storm trooper." Hans wore no hat, his overcoat was too short for him and his enormous hands, purple with cold, clutched a crumpled brown paper bag.

They insisted on buying me a drink. We went into a bar filled with mirrors. Peter tossed his coat over the back of his chair, removed his hat and carefully checked his profile and hair in the nearest mirror. He was a terrible but endearing poseur: an "actor-laddie," on and off. Some of my friends, particularly the girls, found Peter's affectations irritating. Not I. His constant performance was sustained with such a sublime and amusing self-confidence.

"And now, my dear Hume, regale us with tales of your career!"

I don't know what I replied to that somewhat barbed inquiry. I only remember that when it came time to pay the check, Peter waved me aside, turned to Hans, snapped his fingers, and said: "Hansel—give." Hans scrabbled around in the brown paper bag in his lap, and handed Peter a huge wad of dollar bills. My look of incredulity must have been obvious.

"We too are employed, you know," said Peter. "How much have we left, Hansel?"

"Nine hundred and forty-one dollars." Hans turned to me. "We sold a story yesterday—Pete likes cash."

Peter paid the check, leaving an extravagant tip; pushed back his chair, flung his scarf over his shoulder, draped his coat, and went to the nearest mirror to adjust his hat at precisely the right rake, then teetered toward the street door.

Outside, we turned in different directions. I watched them cross the street, Hans still clutching their precious bag. Peter took his storm trooper's arm as they came to the curb, then waved back at me. I wasn't to see him again until some years later, when we met in California. Peter was writing for television.

Among Peter's minor talents—and he had many—was one for doggerel. He wrote a verse about me:

> If one could be what one might wish
> He'd choose to be a rake,
> A gentleman in button shoes,
> Who's always on the make;
> But since he is no roué
> And a conscientious soul,
> His pipe dreams are all hooey
> And he labors toward a goal"

I'm damned if I can remember the rest of it. I wish I could. It was quite true that I wished to be something I was not. I'd had an oddly formalized upbringing: near-Victorian standards, church school, discipline and rigidity. I was rebelling against them all, but I hadn't quite yet escaped that bloody blue serge suit and bowler hat, and all those confusing, inherited inhibitions: one must never do this, one is obliged to do that—or one is beyond the pale. It's hard to transcend one's inheritance. It would stun Peter Barry—long dead now—to hear that he helped me. His constant affectionate mockery of me was, somehow, clarifying.

Inhibition is a major stumbling block for the actor. If, for instance, you've been taught that any outward display of strong emotion is unseemly—tears, rage, uncontrollable laughter—then how do you lend those reactions to the character whose play-wright-creator demands them? You can always fake them, of course, but even a clever fake is mere competence, and not good enough. That was one lesson I had to learn at the academy—and over and over again for years to come.

A school's quality is determined by the strength of its teaching staff, not by its facade, the chandelier in its reception area, and least of all by the glitziness of its catalogue—which is most frequently the student's introduction to the institution. The academy had some wonderful teachers—particularly Philip Loeb, Eddie Goodman, Arthur Hughes, all professional actors of distinction, but at the top of the list was Charles Jehlinger.

Jehly, as he was referred to behind his back, never to his face (more appropriate nicknames would have been Steel, or Granite), has become a sort of mythic figure among academy graduates. There are none alive now who knew him as a young man, so all of us remember him as gray-haired, rather deaf and a trifle withered. Appearances were deceiving; he had an explosive energy and a total intolerance of fakery. He was a short man; he had to look up even to me. He would thrust his face up into mine and say, "You're a fool, boy. Oil and water won't mix. You can't criticize and create at the same time. You're a fool!" And then would come a mannerism that I've never heard anyone mention in any of the endless reminiscences about Jehly. He would laugh. His face would split open and out would come a breathy exhalation, "Heh, heh, heh," and then the face would snap shut again as suddenly as a sprung trap. I found the total effect terrifying. There was no humor behind that laugh—or if there was, I was too numb to recognize it. Perhaps the laugh was Jehly's way of modifying the awful severity of his censure. Perhaps it meant to convey "There's nothing personal about this. You may not be a total fool, but you've been caught out. You're lying—*demonstrating* (ultimate sin), not *being*. Shame on you!"

Trial by Jehly was traumatic. The first year, the "junior"

student was not exposed to the trauma until the examination plays in the spring. At that time, the staff made decisions on whether you were worthy of being invited back to the academy for a second and final year or whether you were to be cast into outer darkness.

I believe the first of my examination plays was a now-forgotten drama called *Milestones*. On my very first entrance, Jehly's voice boomed from the darkened orchestra: "Already bad—go back!" There were three of us entering together, but I was the last to appear. We retired in confusion, closed the door and started in again. As I appeared, a second time, the voice said, "Back!" and after a third try, "BACK!" We hadn't even opened our mouths, for God's sake! Mercifully, I've forgotten what my failing was, but once the entrance had been executed to Jehly's grudging satisfaction, it went downhill from there. This, our dress rehearsal, barely managed to get through the first act of a three-act play; and by the time we were dismissed, the cast was jelly and Jehly appeared to be Simon Legree.

Jehly rarely explained his objections. He expected the student to discover and rectify his or her lapse and get on with it. Occasionally he'd use metaphor (such as "oil and water don't mix") or a pet aphorism: "Continue thought, theme and mood until something comes to change." That one usually meant you'd been found guilty of anticipating what came next, or trying to remember the lines, fumbling with a prop, or fidgeting in an uncomfortable costume—anything that might break a total concentration on the playwright's moment. I think Jehyl saw our student productions in moments. He knew the plays so well—they were repeated over and over again by successive classes—that he could ignore the rhythm of the whole and deal with the particular. After all, he was a teacher, not the director. That unfortunate individual had to pick up the bits later and put them together again.

Occasionally one of Jehly's cries of outrage would backfire. A favorite bellow of his was, "What is this wait!?" He couldn't abide what he considered an actor's self-indulgent pause. "What is this wait!?"

Jehly paid a hurried visit to the men's room late one afternoon toward the end of a long and exhausting rehearsal.

"Continue!" he barked as he left. When he returned to his seat the play was galloping on until suddenly there was a long and appalling pause. It hung there, inviting retribution. Finally, he thundered: "WHAT IS THIS WAIT!?" A terrified stage manager stuck his head around the proscenium. "It's the end of the play, Mr. Jehlinger."

Upon completion of my junior year I thought seriously of leaving the academy. I'd had nearly nine months of instruction in body work (dancing and fencing), voice production, life study, scene work and much else, and been through the mill of the examination plays. I'd worked hard and happily—harder and more happily than at any schooling I'd faced before—but I was tired and somewhat disenchanted. I'd been asked to return for the senior year, but I was tired of classes, I wanted to get out and *do* it if I could, rather than talk for another year about *how* to do it. I was of six minds about my next step. I took my quandary to Emil Diestel, the academy's secretary and second in command.

Mr. Diestel, or more familiarly "Dee," was a tall man with prominent teeth in a cadaverous face. He was patient, avuncular and soft-spoken—he had to be, dealing as he did with problems ranging from the school's finances all the way to the repeated absences of some particular female student with difficult menstrual periods.

I knocked on the door and heard him say, "Come in, come in." He tilted back in his swivel chair, clasped his hands behind his head and added, "What can I do for you?" It was like being in the confessional, but with the benevolent priest face-to-face. When I had said my piece, Dee tilted forward again and his elbows came to rest on the chair arms, with his hands forming a little A-frame over his lap.

"Mr. Cronyn, if you are to get on in this profession, it will not be because of the American Academy of Dramatic Arts—but in spite of it." He then went on to suggest, quietly and patiently, that I might wish to reconsider; to remind me that I'd acknowledged taking much from the school and that while I had to adhere to the senior curriculum and continue those sometimes stultifying exercises, I had much still to learn.

It was Dee's understatement that did it. I not only decided

to return to the school for my final year, but asked if I might take the examination plays all over again with the succeeding junior class. As that class was short of men, I was allowed to do so without fee, and so exposed myself to a second trial by fire at the hands of the magnificent but dreaded Jehly.

Upon graduation from the academy a year later, I sweated out a letter of thanks to Jehly and received this handwritten reply, dated May 22nd, 1934, from the Santa Barbara Biltmore:

Dear Cronyn,

Your letter, forwarded to me here, gave me great pleasure. It is an appreciation—deserved or undeserved—that gives me renewed ambition to be more worthy of it. That is possible even at *my* age. In your last two performances I felt that you were an unusually good actor for your age and there is nothing to prevent your attaining genuine artistry if your [and here there is a word I can't read—could it be "new"?] attitude doesn't waver. The *base* of your work is genuinely sound; never let go of it. What you need now is experience in your medium, experience in life and never-ending increased knowledge of life and appreciation of beauty in all directions. . . .

The letter continued for another half page talking about his holiday in California and closed with "Sincerely always, Charles Jehlinger."

*   *   *

The summer of 1933 was a welter of colliding emotions. On June 19th my father died. I came back from New York by train. As I rode from the station I was aware that flags were at half mast. My mother, in black, stood in the driveway next to a magnificently flowering rosebush covered in scarlet blooms. Some images cannot be erased.

My father was laid out on a chaise lounge in the upstairs sitting room—the old day nursery. It was his particular place. They'd dressed him in his dark blue velvet smoking jacket. Sunlight streamed into the room from the open French doors, and I sat down on a straight chair beside him. We were alone. I felt numb, wondering what I should be feeling. At some point I put out my hand and gently stroked his hair as I'd seen my mother do at the end of a bad day. It felt like corn silk, and the scalp beneath it was cool. After a bit I left, closing the door carefully behind me so as not to disturb him. I went through the empty house, down the veranda steps and out into the back garden. I walked around the lily pool. There was that goddamn legend carved into its cement lip:

> The kiss of the sun for pardon,
> The song of the birds for mirth—

I don't think I read beyond that point. My father was dead and I could not cry. Not yet. For him, "the passing of time" had ended; and for me, the lighthouse beam which he so hated had gone dark.

There was an obituary on the editorial page of the *Ottawa Evening Journal*. It reads in part

> Hume Cronyn, dead in London, Ontario, was of those rare types who, gifted with fine attributes of heart and intellect, and singularly qualified for public service, lack the instinct for practical politics necessary to supreme achievement. No one who watched his short career in Parliament could doubt his attainments. On his mother's side a Blake, he had a background and a tradition which could not be mistaken. But he had also the Blake sensitiveness, a shyness which made him shrink from the harsher contacts of politics, and this, with a curious humility, robbed him of ambition.

There follow two paragraphs dealing with my father's political associations and activities, and then the final paragraph.

> Personally, Hume Cronyn was everything that enters into the definition of a gentleman. Courteous, kind, considerate, there was about him a stately dignity and a chivalry which made him stand apart. Cultured, widely-traveled,

educated, a lover of books and games and good comrade-
ship, he was an ideal companion, who made and held fast
to friends. Public life would have profited richly from his
civilizing influence.

*   *   *

My father's death left my mother desolate. I had already
committed to going abroad with a group from the New York
School of the Theater—now defunct. We were to take classes
in Bath, England, and, under the aegis of the Mozarteum, in
Salzburg, Austria. My mother decided to join me in Austria,
but instead of staying in Salzburg she went to the Schloss Fin-
stergrün in Remingstein, on the edge of the Austrian Tyrol.
The schloss, a beautiful medieval castle, belonged to the Gräfin
(Countess) Szapary and accommodated a few selected paying
guests.

I remember driving my mother into the cobbled and deserted courtyard and searching for a knocker or a bell to ring.
A small heavy door at the base of one of the towers finally
opened, revealing an elderly lady with short-cropped iron gray
hair. She wore mountaineer's boots, thick black woolen stockings, a practical, short pleated skirt, a white blouse, and a cha-
telaine at her waist. Ah, the housekeeper, I thought. "I have a
letter of introduction to the Gräfin Szapary," I said. The
housekeeper smiled. "I am the Gräfin," she replied. So much
for illusions based on fiction: in my mind's eye I think I had
pictured a countess as wearing purple satin and pearls.

I was equally unprepared for the theater of Max Reinhardt. Part of our privilege as summer students at the Mozarteum was to watch his rehearsals of *Faust* and attend the
performances of *Everyman*—not to mention the magnificent
concerts conducted by Bruno Walter. I had never seen such
epic, bravura productions. My recall of *Everyman* today is far
more vivid and moving to me than any of the New York plays
that I was to appear in subsequently for hundreds of performances each.

Our principal classes at the Mozarteum were given by Frieda
Richard, as an acting instructor, and by Harald Kreutzberg,
who at the time may have been Europe's foremost exponent

of modern dance. I can remember Kreutzberg's assistant, Ilse Meudtner, who moved like quicksilver, smiling pityingly on this ragtag group of American students, so lacking in physical control or even simple coordination—and I had thought I could get by with only one year's formal training!

When my session at the Mozarteum came to a close, my mother and I drove across the Alps into Italy. My photographs, all carefully labeled by my mother, range from those taken in Venice to those from Capri, and a great many from in between: Florence and Rome of course, the hill towns, Pompeii, and on and on. All in ten weeks? I suppose we were true tourists, but the pace must have been wearing on my mother. However, perhaps that's what she needed: to run away, to keep running, to smother the images of the recent past with an overlay of as many new ones as possible. She wore black, but she rarely spoke of my father, and I saw that control break down only once, and then very surprisingly. I was aware that she slept badly, and I tried rather unsuccessfully to get her to rest after lunch. We stopped at a small *taverna* on the outskirts of Montefiascone. The photograph shows the two of us sitting in the backseat of an open touring car holding wineglasses; it is duly labeled "Montefiascone, Thursday, 11:30 A.M., August 31st, 1933" and below that, "As we were leaving the town we stopped at a small inn and drank some of the wonderful Est-Est-Est."

We did indeed, and Frances Amelia Labatt Cronyn, aged sixty-four and recently widowed, got drunk. There were no two ways about it; only two glasses and she was smashed. My mother was not a drinker, but she was exhausted, and under great emotional stress. We were laughing about something or other, then suddenly the laughter turned to tears and, to the horror of our driver, great racking sobs of anguish. I sat by, helplessly, holding her hand. Mum slept well that afternoon.

The very last photograph in the series shows a pretty girl sitting on a beach and is labeled "Capri—one of Hume's bathing friends." I recognize the blond hair and smiling face but could not put a name to her to save my life. She was obviously a casual though attractive friend. My affections were fixed elsewhere—on a fellow student at the academy named Emily.

I adored Emily. I was hopelessly and totally in love for the first time in my life. Descriptions of someone with whom you are besotted are not merely subjective, but almost impossible. Em was beautiful, kind, generous, possessed of a lovely sense of humor (I can still hear her laugh), intensely loyal, sensitive and talented. Were there no negatives, then? Was the ultimate disaster of this relationship wholly my fault? Quite probably; but a large part of the pain involved—and my God, I found it painful—was that I never knew, still do not know, why we parted.

Searching for a possible negative, in an attempt to lend balance to this nonportrait, the only thing I come up with are some lines in Robert Browning's "My last Duchess": "She had/ a heart—how shall I say—too soon made glad,/too easily impressed."

Considering the fact that those lines in Browning's poem are spoken by an absolute bastard of a husband about his wife, I do myself no favors. Was I too demanding, too overbearing? Quite possibly. Em was torn by fierce loyalties: to me on the one hand and to her family on the other. The family, Em's father in particular, did not much care for the theater and all its works. How they happened to allow her to go to the academy in the first place I can't imagine, but they did, and we met. We became lovers.

TEN

IT WAS A LOVELY TIME. I had a wonderful girl and, in my final year at the academy, more work than I could handle. It was a prescription that then and now—fifty years later—is hard to beat. Unhappily, it was not to last.

Following my graduation in the spring of '34, Emily and I joined the Barter Theater Company in Abingdon, Virginia, along with two fellow students from the academy, Virginia Campbell and Dick Clark (the one with the Stetson hat). The Barter Theater had been launched the year before by a marvelously inventive actor turned manager named "Massah" Robert Porterfield. Bob, a large shambling man with a persuasive Southern accent and engaging smile, could have been an irresistible snake-oil salesman. The description is not meant to be pejorative. Bob was generous, kind, and totally dedicated to a dream: his own theater, a popular, affordable theater for these hard times; perhaps even a state theater. He realized all of it. A job that we—the collective dogsbody of the company—had to try to fulfill was to live up to Bob's easy promises. Massah Robert found it easier to say yes than no. Could we give an added performance? Could we play without scenery or props? Could we appear for some high school a hundred miles away at ten in the morning? Of course we could! Bob dis-

pensed the company patronage with the glad hand and winning smile of a born politician.

I bore the title of production director and was, on the letterhead at least, Bob's partner. What I had done to earn such
an exalted position was highly questionable. I think my principal qualification was $2,000. I came up with half that amount
myself, thanks to an inheritance from my father, and raised
another five hundred dollars apiece from Emily and Virginia.
Money, cash, in 1934 was very hard to come by. The Barter
Theater Company's policy was to charge an admission of 35¢
or the equivalent in barter: vegetables, eggs, chickens, fruit, or
the occasional multiple admission equivalent: a whole Virginia
ham. The actors ate the ticket price.

Finding the hard currency to supply necessities other than
those required by a company's appetite wasn't easy. Our first
purchase on behalf of Barter was a secondhand truck. We
loaded this up with discarded flats, curtains and a small broken-down manual switchboard, all of them scrounged from
theatrical warehouses or failed New York productions.

The four of us, Emily, Virginia, Dick and I, drove this load
from New York to Abingdon. Precisely what I did there as a
production director besides act—and I did a great deal of that—
escapes me. My only accomplishment of record was an inventory of the props room (I still have a typed copy) which, on
arrival, I found to be a jungle of theatrical rubbish. However,
one acting job, in the leading part of a new play, was to lead
to my first New York engagement. Burgess Meredith was engaged to play "my" role in New York, and I was his understudy, also playing a small part of a man in his mid fifties. I
was twenty-three at the time. The play, *He Knew Dillinger*, re-
titled for New York as *Hipper's Holiday*, opened at the Maxine
Elliot Theater and lasted one performance—or was it three?

In the spring of 1935 Emily and I joined the New Jitney
Players, a touring group, headed by Ethel Barrymore Colt
(daughter of Ethel, and niece of Lionel and John). We carried
a repertoire of three plays: Goldsmith's *She Stoops to Conquer*,
Boucicault's *The Poor of New York* and a children's play. We
appeared in a series of one night stands in a wild assortment
of halls, tents, churches, and at least one hospital for the in-
sane, where I remember a male nurse collecting all scissors

and knives from our improvised makeup tables so that no in-
mate be tempted to pinch them while we were onstage.

Again, the actors did everything: drove the truck, set up
the scenery, took it down again, performed, struck the set,
loaded up again and moved on to the next stand. Generally,
we slept in "tourist homes" or "guest houses," where a bed was
to be had for as little as 50¢ a night—a dollar, tops. It seems
incredible now, but during the thirties these "tourist homes"
were commonplace: private residences where the owner might
pick up a little extra money by renting out a spare room. There
was one of these where I spent the night—or at least part of
it—sharing a double bed with our electrician, Maynard Sam-
sen. "Sammy" was plump, fair haired, and had a delicate pink
complexion. I woke up at about two in the morning to find
the lights on and Sammy sitting up in bed scratching himself.
He was covered with huge red welts.

"I've been bitten," said Sammy.

"Let's get out of this bloody bed." I threw back the covers,
turned out the lights and waited. We waited a long time, with
my hand on the light switch.

"What the hell's going on?" asked Sammy plaintively. I hit
the switch and rushed to the bed. There they were: half a
dozen "B flats"—or less whimsically, bed bugs—all looking for
Sammy. We caught three of them in a bedside glass and
propped the evidence between two pillows, with a little note
explaining our precipitous departure. The hotel we eventually
wound up in charged us each a dollar. It was an outrageously
extravagant night.

In the summer of 1935, Emily and I were married. We
stood up one afternoon in New York's Collegiate Marble
Church, with Virginia Campbell and Dick Clark as our witnesses, and were pronounced man and wife. No representative of either family was present.

I'd made a special trip to London, Ontario, to tell my mother
what was happening, but Emily's family were entirely in the
dark. She had agreed to marry me only on condition that her
family not be told—not for the time being at least. That "time
being" was to stretch on and on, and was the foundation of
failure.

My proposal to Emily must have been one of the most damp

and dismal romantic happenings in history. We were sitting on a banquette in a near-empty dining room of the Beaux Arts Apartments on East 44th Street. She sat on my left, a small, dark-haired girl with the figure of Aphrodite and the most lustrous brown eyes, eyes that I'd heard described as sad. Certainly there was no sparkle in them at this moment. She looked extremely grave, though that was not uncharacteristic. She knew that I wanted to marry her and almost surely anticipated what was coming. Anyway, I proposed. Emily accepted—and promptly burst into tears. That should have told me something. The tears were not of joy or even relief but were, I believe, of some deep inner conflict that defied rational explanation. What was it? I don't know to this day. I was to relive that scene over and over again. I'm doing it now, as I write this; and I still don't know.

Of course I was totally mad to agree to a marriage based on the condition that it be kept secret from the girl's family. But I was very much in love, and I believed that Emily loved me. That she was torn by conflicting loyalties I knew, but I quite failed to recognize the extent or nature of her loyalty to her family. She had two brothers and a sister. I'd met all of them and we seemed to get on well. Emily's mother was a beautiful woman with prematurely snow white hair and a gentle patrician manner. In contrast her husband, Em's father, was definitely a man of the people, a "good ol' boy" whom everybody referred to as "Mr. Frank." He was small, leathery, seamed, and wiry—like a coiled spring. He was also deaf, which perhaps contributed to a manner suggesting an amiable but barely controlled frustration. The family were kind to me. I'd been invited to visit them in Georgia and less obviously to stand inspection. After all, I was Emily's "beau." Actually of course I was Emily's husband, but only she and I were aware of that. What the family were seeing was not a prospective son or brother-in-law but a confused and unwilling wolf in sheep's clothing. It was a weird situation.

Em's family was wealthy, not show-off rich, but more than merely comfortable. Mr. Frank seemed to have a finger—*all* his fingers—in any number of pies; one of them was a farm where he bred cattle. I remember him pulling his car onto the shoulder of the road so that we could admire one of his herds. There followed a dissertation on the importance of breeding and of bloodlines. Mr. Frank was obviously proud of his stock. The implications of this friendly little lecture were hard to escape. It wasn't until some twenty years later that I discovered that Mr. Frank had sent an emissary to London, Ontario, to investigate my own stock and background. Apparently I passed—it was the emissary himself who told me of his research—but that passing grade alone was not, I suspect, sufficient to reassure a possessive parent.

At the time of my visit to Emily's family I was, rather unsuccessfully, trying to write a play. I thought things might go better if I could hole up somewhere alone, in isolation, away from all the distractions of New York. Emily suggested that I might use her family's country place where, providing I could look after myself, I would certainly be isolated. The house saw little use.

We drove about fifteen miles out of town, turned off on a side road and eventually entered a long driveway, which wound its way around and between a series of ponds until we came to the house. This "country place" was at least twice the size of the house in town: two long wings, one on either side of the main living area, which was two-storied with a cupola on top. It perched on rising ground like some monstrous bird of prey. The architecture was rustic and on first impression distinctly Gothic in feeling. What had it been built for? Enormous house parties—that had never taken place? There were at least eight or ten bedrooms.

It was spring; rain was falling when we arrived, and there was a chill wind. The trees had not started to leaf and the ponds we'd passed were the color of tomato bisque from the runoff through red Georgia clay. First appearances were neither cozy nor encouraging. Emily walked me through the house. I deposited my meager food supplies in a large "cold box"— shaped like a coffin—in the kitchen, crossed through the pantry into a billiard room, its green baize-covered table dusty with disuse, and on into the enormous sitting room. The scale of this room allowed for massive stone fireplaces at each end. The mantels were half-hewn cedar logs, and one of them bore a small stuffed alligator looking very much the worse for the attention it had been given by rats. Behind a door in the corner of the room a circular staircase wound its way up through a tower to the cupola and led out onto a large flat roof space. From there one had a lovely view of the ponds and countryside, but in this raw weather it was not a place to linger.

When Emily had driven away, I chose a bedroom close to the sitting room, unpacked my few things, set up a card table near the fireplace, found a stepladder and swept the alligator remnants from the mantel, lit a fire and fixed myself something to eat. The house made noises, creaking like a ship's hull in the wind and rain. It was definitely spooky.

I can't say that I ever settled in, but after a day or two some sort of routine developed. I made myself sit at that card table scribbling unsatisfactorily or staring morosely into the fire. When I could bear it no longer, I would go for a walk, kicking at pinecones and carrying a fishing rod—although I couldn't even see my lures in that red gumbo water. I usually ate my meals in the kitchen standing up, and it was following one of these unproductive fishing expeditions that I opened the cold box and found some of my food supplies missing. At least I thought they were missing. I was pretty sure that I'd had six lamb chops; now there were only three, and what about the bread and eggs, hadn't they diminished? Perhaps I'd eaten them and forgotten; I never paid much attention to food, so that was possible. But you have to *cook* lamb chops and I hate cooking, so surely I'd remember that. Oh, well. I don't think I mentioned this puzzle to Emily when she next came out, or perhaps I did and she simply replenished my larder. Em appeared fairly regularly, if all too briefly, and I began to feel that I was being granted conjugal visitation rights. That's probably unfair. After all, I'd agreed to the condition of our marriage: that it be kept secret from her family. I was now paying the first installment on that condition, and the payments were going to increase until they became unsupportable.

(There is a mystery in all this that neither notes, scrapbooks, letters or diaries can unravel. I was a camera nut in those days. I took a photograph of Emily by moonlight—no auxiliary lighting or flash involved—that shows her seated, leaning against a porch support, with her arms folded. It was taken at the country place and prominent on the third finger of her left hand is a wedding ring. *A wedding ring?* Worn while she was staying with her family? Impossible! Did she put it on that evening just to please me? Have I got the time frame wrong? Is my memory so fallible? The answer could be yes to any one of those questions. I'll never know.)

The house was always cold, so I kept a fire burning all day long. When I went out on one of my despairing walks, I wore a heavy sweater. One day I couldn't find it. I decided on some hot soup instead, but the soup cans had disappeared. I opened the cold box. It was empty—not a damn thing left. I'd been cleaned out. There was no doubt about it this time. I went to the bedroom—more furious than frightened—to see what clothing I had left and slammed the bedroom door behind me. The impact dislodged the Yale lock on the inside of the door and it fell at my feet. On examination it was obvious that the lock had been pried off and replaced, so that while it appeared to be in place, any pressure put on the outside of the door would break it loose. That did it. I had an unseen but thieving visitor. I checked every door and window in the house, walked out to the highway, and thumbed a ride into town. There I bought another sweater, more food and a second-hand .32-caliber pistol.

At this point I suppose I could have called Mr. Frank and told him what was going on. But a sweater? Some food? A broken lock? It all sounded so trivial. Besides, I did not want to appeal to Emily's father. Anyway, nothing happened for a day or two except that the sun came out, making the rooftop an attractive alternative to one of my broody walks. I carried an old piece of carpet up the tower stairs, lay down, and read a book instead.

I heard my visitor before I saw him. He was on the opposite side of the nearest pond. Sound travels easily over water and I could hear the footfalls in the dead leaves. Although I couldn't see him in the brush, it seemed quite clear what he was doing. He would walk a dozen paces, then stop. Walk again, stop. He was checking the house from every angle for signs of occupancy. I crawled to the roof edge and looked over. He broke out of the bush almost directly beneath me: a tall, lanky, black man with a gold tooth, carrying a six-foot length of board. I noticed the tooth particularly because he was looking up and I was afraid he'd seen my head over the parapet. However, he was concentrating on the windows; he'd place the board against the top of the lower window frame then hit the butt end of the board with the heel of his free hand to see if the window would budge. I watched this operation along the side of one wing of the house until he disappeared from view.

As I crept down the staircase I heard a window go up somewhere in my wing. The visitor had gained entry to the house. I'd left the door ajar at the foot of the stair but there was room to hide behind it and look through the crack. The man went into the kitchen then came back into the sitting room. He noticed the tower door was ajar and moved toward me to investigate. As he approached I swung the door open, standing there with a gun in my hand. If I was nervous—and I was—he was terrified. He leapt backward, his hands reaching above his head and shouted, "Don't shoot! Don't shoot!"

I felt sorry for him. I told him to go out on the terrace and when we got there to sit down at one of the wrought-iron tables. I stood and, trying to control the quiver in my voice, made a little speech. I explained that I'd been watching him for some time, and how fortunate that was for him, otherwise he might have been shot. I told him that if he'd come to the house and asked for food I'd have given him some. I ended up by saying:

"Now go home and tell all your friends that there's a very nervous man living up here with a gun in his pocket. Tell them that if they have any business at this house to come in daylight, singing or shouting, making a lot of noise, so that I'm not surprised. I don't like surprises. You'd better go now."

I thought I'd done this rather well, but it had a curious effect. The visitor grinned at me, leaned forward in his chair and fished a cigarette butt out of the ashtray—one that I'd left there after my morning coffee—and said, "You got a light, boss?" This was, as the English say, distinctly cheeky. Perhaps I'd made a mistake in telling him to sit down. Perhaps it was the quiver in my voice and my northern accent; whatever, all I could think of to say was: "Put it back." He grinned at me again.

"It's only a little stub, boss," he said, and sat there as if prepared to continue an amiable discussion.

"This gun is loaded, you know," and I fired a couple of shots into the azalea bushes. My visitor got up very quickly, dropping the cigarette butt back into the ashtray.

"Yes suh, boss. I figgered it was loaded."

I watched him amble down the driveway, cross the rustic bridge, and disappear. That, I hoped, was the end of that— but it wasn't quite.

I told Emily about the incident; she told her father, and he must have told the police, because later that night I saw headlights on the driveway and County Car #13 pulled up under the portecochere. I opened the door to admit two large, smiling policemen.

"Heard you had a little trouble up here. I'm Sergeant Spradling, this is Officer Factor."

I told them the story. They asked for a description of my visitor: age, height, weight and so on. They were extremely polite and friendly, very respectful of Mr. Frank, and curious about his house.

They refused my offer of a drink, but followed me into the kitchen. My pistol was lying on the counter and I had no license for it. I had a bad moment when Sergeant Spradling picked it up and hefted it. "Ah see y' got y'self a pop gun," he drawled. He put it down again, drew his own heavy-duty .45 from its holster and said with obvious pride, "Now see this. Just hit a man in the arm with this and it'll knock him down."

The officers didn't stay long. They asked me—politely again—about what I did for a living, seemed interested when I told them I was an actor but less so when I had to admit I knew no movie stars, and were genuinely puzzled by the fact that I was in Mr. Frank's house writing, or trying to write. "Kinda lonely up here all by y'self, ain't it? We'll look in time t' time, see how y' gettin' on."

What I didn't expect was to have them back again within a couple of hours. I was in my pajamas. They had a terrified black man in tow. Without preamble, Sergeant Spradling demanded, "This y'r boy?"

There was a striking resemblance: same build, same angularity, facial features, even haircut—but no gold tooth. I explained the difference to the officers and the black man blurted out, "Yassah! Dat's m' brother."

The sergeant spoke softly. "And where do we find him, boy?"

The answer was immediate. "He done lit outa the county. He knew."

Knew what? Knew that he was in trouble and would probably be picked up for questioning? I was to learn over the next few days that these officers also knew. They knew the good guys, the bad guys, those with political influence like Mr. Frank, the rich, poor, the troublemakers. They knew their county, and presided over its order with great apparent affability and an absolute sense of righteous prejudice.

Mr. Frank showed up at his country place the next morning. He was not pleased. "We've lost a dozen pair of blankets out here. I've been trying to catch that rascal for six months—served him right if you'd shot him." I think I muttered something about shooting an unarmed man, or at least looked appalled, because Mr. Frank added, "Not seriously—just in the leg or something." I had a mental picture of myself trying to decide which leg it should be—left or right?—and what if I missed?

There were no further intrusions, except very early one morning when I was woken up by some noise outside my window. Through the mist I saw a dozen men in striped uniforms tidying up the grounds: raking leaves, carrying logs, and preparing a large barbecue pit. They were a prison gang, detailed to do a little favor for Mr. Frank. By noon the driveway was clustered with cars and the party was on. It was some sort of political rally: food, drink, and speeches, all alfresco. Nobody came into the house. I don't even remember Mr. Frank being present, and certainly I'd no advance notice of the event. It was a bizarre happening straight out of a Fellini movie—but then my entire stay at "the country place" had been that and continued so.

My friends the policemen would look in on me from time to time—always after dark—and ask me if I wanted to go out on patrol with them. I'm sure this was contrary to regulations, but I wasn't about to pass up such an opportunity.

I sat in the backseat of County Car #13, where there was a locked steel box bolted to the floor at my feet. On inquiry I was told it held a machine gun. A machine gun?

There had been a series of kidnappings in recent years, the most infamous of which was that of the Lindbergh baby in 1932. My uncle, my mother's brother John Labatt, had been kidnapped and held for ransom (with, thank God, a happier outcome) two years later—just a year before this midnight patrol of the Georgia countryside. The sergeant and his buddy had read the news reports. We talked about them. Whether there was a connection between the outbreak of kidnappings and the machine gun, I don't know—I find it hard to believe that it was standard equipment—but at any rate, there it was.

"You want to try it out?"

"When? Where?"

"We'll find a place."

And they did. The car was pulled over to the side of the road, the box unlocked, and the gun thrust into my hands.

"Just let fly at the hillside there. Press the trigger and hang on—a couple of bursts should give you the feel."

It nearly knocked me over, and the noise was horrendous. Unquestionably this little demonstration was outside regulations. Perhaps I'd acquired status or privilege because of my uncle's kidnapping, but more likely it was the long shadow of Mr. Frank—a courtesy to one of his guests.

The countryside was sparsely populated and seemed deserted. We traveled for miles over dark roads. Occasionally the car's searchlight would be switched on and its beam would probe through a huddle of shacks. Only once did I see a man walking—a young black man. The car pulled up beside him.

"You're out late, boy."

"Yassuh."

"Where you travelin'?"

"My gran'ma's place—just roun' that bend. She sick."

"Uhuh. Well, you get on then, and stay there."

"Yassuh."

He moved quickly away ahead of the car. The road was narrow, with steep embankments on each side. The car moved after him. He walked more quickly, the car's headlights not more than ten feet behind him. He had a red bandanna in his hip pocket. The car picked up speed. The man started to trot. The car went faster, until the man was going full out and the car's bumper not more than three feet behind the bandanna. Finally there was no other course: he flung himself down the embankment and somersaulted into the dark ditch. I could not see him through the rear window. Sergeant Spradling and Officer Factor found it all pretty funny.

I did, however, go out with them a second time. The car radio chattered and we were directed to a fire. It was a large building, perhaps a barn, but so engulfed with flame you couldn't be sure what it had been. No sign of fire engines, but a certain amount of rubbernecking traffic that had to be moved on. The officers took care of that while I sat in the car watching.

A black man carrying a bucket came running toward me, his figure clearly silhouetted against the flames behind him. He hesitated for an instant to look over his shoulder at the burning building, then charged on—and completely disappeared. It was as if the earth had suddenly opened to swallow him up. One moment he was there, a solid, three-dimensional figure, and at the next, gone—vaporized.

I heard the trunk of our car open and saw the sergeant extract a coil of rope. He ambled in the direction of the disappearance. What *was* going on? I got out of the car to follow the sergeant and became aware of faint cries for help. The bucket carrier had fallen down an open well.

"Save your breath, and grab this." The sergeant lowered the rope, but there was a struggle in getting the man out, and in the middle of it the rooftree of the burning building collapsed. It came down with a tremendous crash and a great shower of sparks. Involuntarily, we must have let the rope slip. The man in the well fell back again and we had to start over. Finally, we got him out; very wet, but miraculously unhurt. He wiped his face with both hands, grinned at us, and said, "Lost m' bucket."

As we returned to the car, the sergeant said, "They can take anything."

Later that night, or more accurately, early the next morning, County Car #13 was dispatched to the scene of a highway accident. Nobody had been hurt but the two cars involved in the collision were badly damaged. One was a big Buick sedan with wooden-spoke wheels, the other a battered Ford pickup—or what would be called a pickup today. The Buick's left front wheel had been broken on impact so that it rested on its spokes, and before the car had come to a full stop, the broken spokes had marked the tar surface of the road like a gigantic pastry wheel. Clearly, the Buick had been well over the center line. The Ford was as far to the right as it could get without being in the ditch, and its left side from radiator to rear bumper was a mess.

The Buick's owner was white; very big, very genial, very talkative, and very drunk. He wasn't falling-down drunk or even staggering, but you had only to get within three feet of him and you could smell the liquor. He drew the sergeant aside to give him his version of the accident; speaking confidentially, but gesturing extravagantly, pointing up and down the road, indicating the skid marks where he'd applied his brakes—which of themselves should have been a dead giveaway—and even leaning into the Buick to sound its horn.

While this was going on, Officer Factor was examining the black truck driver's registration and license. They exchanged only minimal words. The white man was still talking. I heard the sergeant say, "Well, whatever. We've got to get your car off the road." It took all five of us to do it because of the broken wheel. The black man helped, although he was old, fragile, almost wraithlike.

With the road clear, there remained the question of what to do with the cars, neither of which could move under its own power. The sergeant said he'd send out a tow truck.

"I ain't got no money for a tow," said the old man anxiously.

"Cost you a lot more if we have to do it for you—and there'd be a fine."

As we drove away the black man was still standing in the

middle of the road looking puzzled. The white man was behind the wheel of his Buick smoking a cigar.

When we got to the garage the sergeant ordered a tow
truck to pick up the Buick. Officer Factor went into the office
for a cup of coffee. I asked what would happen to the pickup.
The sergeant shrugged.

"But it was the other guy's fault."

"How would you know?"

"It was obvious—you saw the spoke marks."

"Uhuh."

"He was driving on the wrong side, and he was drunk."

Factor returned with a paper cup. The sergeant took me
firmly by the elbow and steered me back to the county car.

"Why don't you just let us handle it, huh?"

It was the equivalent of "Mind your own damn business."

"We'll take you home now."

We drove in silence. When we arrived, I thanked them,
politely.

"You tell Mr. Frank we took good care of you, y'hear?"

That was the last I saw of them. A few days later, I returned to New York—alone.

ELEVEN

UNEMPLOYMENT IS the hideous portion of almost every young actor at the start of a career. I was luckier than most, but in the middle and late thirties I had my share of it, and found it demoralizing.

Here I was at the age of twenty-four, with school, university, the academy, Barter, the Jitneys, even a New York production behind me, ready to go. Go where? Counting amateur and school productions, I'd appeared in at least twenty-five plays, about half of them as a professional—meaning I'd been paid something or other. And now? I was lost. No job. No comforting structure provided by a school schedule. I was fortunate not to be buried in some menial job just to eat. Or was I? I might have learned a thing or two washing dishes, or sweeping floors, that I needed to know. After all, Jehly had said, "What you need now is experience in your medium, experience in life, and an appreciation of beauty in all directions." I couldn't find the first, I sidestepped the second in the menial forms immediately available to me, and—quite unconsciously—settled on the third. *I had to do something.* I had to employ myself, and being of an altogether too orderly mind I decided to give myself some sort of work schedule. It would be a lifeline, something to hang on to.

I've always kept some sort of week-at-a-glance diary. Today it is oppressively full, then it was depressingly empty. So, quite arbitrarily, I decided to fill it up. I would give myself appointments.

Monday A.M.: Gym—P.M.: The Met.
Tuesday A.M.: Read Cymbeline—P.M.: Do the rounds.
Wednesday A.M.: Swim—P.M.: Concert matinee.
Thursday A.M.: Do the rounds, [etc].

And so it went.

It was in this fashion that I became addicted to regular exercise, saw my first operas, read T. S. Eliot and Strindberg, was introduced to the American Museum of Natural History and learned to haunt the Museum of Modern Art and the Metropolitan. I couldn't draw at all, but I'd take a sketch pad to the Met and (copying from portraits by the Flemish masters) draw noses, beards, eyebrows—anything I thought might be useful one day in creating a particular makeup. I also learned to look for body language—although the living models in waiting rooms, subways, and cafeterias were a richer resource than figures on canvas. Zoos were another haunt. The actor can learn a lot from watching animals, both alive and sculptured. There used to be a black marble panther, crouched to spring, at the head of the stairs from the Met's main rotunda. Wonderful. Such compressed energy, such grace, such menace.

This business of "doing rounds" was job hunting: knocking on doors, trying to circumvent receptionists, trying to crash auditions for which you hadn't been called; hoping to remind managers, directors, agents, casting directors that you were alive and of course extremely talented. It was an extraordinarily dismal activity to which the usual response was "Don't call us, we'll call you." I never got anywhere doing the rounds.

More productive was "networking," as I believe it is called today. Whom did you know who might know something you didn't know? You might learn that producer X had just bought a play, that director Y was casting from his apartment instead of his office, that unfortunate actor Z was about to be fired and they'd be looking for a replacement. You followed up and hoped for the best.

Garson Kanin had been a senior at the academy when I was a junior. I'd watch him act in the senior-class plays, and he was very, very good. He and a fellow senior, Martin Gabel, seemed to me to be the best, and I was determined to meet them and learn from them. I asked them both to dinner and to my delight they accepted. They looked around the not very distinguished dining room of the Beaux Arts and Gar said, "How can you afford this?" Considering the fact that my share of the rent came to only $37.50 per month, it could hardly be considered luxurious living, but these things are relative and I was immediately uncomfortable, on the defensive. I explained my remittance and hurried on to talk about their work as seniors and my admiration for it.

"You're both marvelous, and yet entirely different—the only thing you seem to have in common is that you're both Jewish."

Gar and Martin exchanged a look.

"Of course, that's not surprising is it—so many of the world's great artists are Jews."

I suppose I sounded condescending. At any rate, the remark was not well received. Gar put down his fork. "Now, for God's sake, Hume," he said "don't tell us that some of your best friends are Jews."

In 1935, Garson was an assistant stage manager and understudy in *Three Men on a Horse,* an immensely successful farce, playing at the Playhouse Theater on West 48th Street. It had been directed by the legendary (even then) George Abbott. The management was planning a road company, and Gar suggested that I might be able to do his job on tour. He gave me the date of the casting audition and told me what duties might be expected of me as an A.S.M. I had seen the play—I saw *every* play in those days as part of my week-at-a-glance program—and knew that my chances depended on how successfully I might persuade Mr. Abbott that I could "cover" one of the principals. I chose the character of Frankie and without shame dressed as closely as I could to his costume in the New York production.

It was midsummer. I showed up in the alley leading to the

stage door of the Playhouse Theater and found myself in a long line of actors and actresses waiting their turn to audition. Mr. Abbott and his staff ran these auditions with military precision. When my turn came, a script was thrust into my hands and my name was announced along with that of the part for which I was reading.

"Mr. Cronyn, as understudy to Frankie and assistant stage manager."

I don't remember who read with me, only that halfway through the scene, an abrupt voice from the darkness of the orchestra said. "Thank you. Very nice. We'll let you know."

Onstage, but just inside the proscenium, sat Edith Van Cleve, one of Mr. Abbott's assistants, with a clipboard and checklist. I gabbled in her ear. She gave me a doubtful look but then, bless her, rose and addressed The Voice. "Mr. Cronyn thinks he could also cover Erwin." (Erwin Trowbridge was the leading character in the play.) There was a short, barked laugh— little more than a snort—from out front, and The Voice said, "Well, he's twenty years too young but he's here, let him read it. You read with him, Edie."

The Frankie sides were exchanged for Erwin sides. We read and were allowed to play out the scene without interruption. There was a pause; a shuffle between seats from out front, and The Voice materialized at the footlights. It was Mr. Abbott.

"You read that very well. Go over to Mr. Yokel's office and tell them that you're engaged to understudy Frankie *and* Erwin in the Boston company, and as assistant stage manager.

Eureka! I had a job. As I hotfooted over to the Yokel office—he was the producer—I wondered if I dared ask for seventy-five dollars a week, and whether either of the actors engaged to play the parts I was to understudy would have the grace to be sick.

I sat in the producer's office, waiting in a lather of anxiety. Finally the general manager, Carl Fischer, appeared from some inner sanctum.

"Is your name Cronyn?"

"Yes sir."

"They want you back at the theater."

"But Mr. Abbott told me—"

"Right away."

"But I'm supposed to understudy and stage-manage . . . assistant stage-manage . . . in the Boston company. I'm supposed to—"

"They want to talk to you again—now."

I left the office most unwillingly. Oh God, they've had second thoughts. Mr. Abbott had said I was twenty years too young—and he hadn't even let me finish my first reading for Frankie. I crawled back to the Playhouse.

Gar met me in the alley. He'd been waiting for me.

"What took you so long?" He didn't even give me a chance to answer. "Boy, are you in luck! Mr. Abbott wants you to read Erwin *again*. Tomorrow."

I stumbled backstage and waited while other actors finished their auditions. What was going on? I knew they'd cast an Erwin for the Boston company—I'd seen the announcement in the paper—so that pipe-dream possibility was out. Was Mr. Abbott really so concerned about my age? When at last I was led into his presence, he said that I'd read well, but that he wanted me to audition once more, and this time with Margaret Mullen, who was one of the leading actresses in the New York company. He turned to Gar. "Will you call Maggie for me and explain the situation—three o'clock tomorrow at the National. And oh yes, you'd better give Mr. Cronyn a script."

He turned back to me. "Look it over." All of this was brief, almost curt. He put on his hat and headed for the stage door; a big, handsome man, very erect, almost military in bearing, who did not waste or mince words; one of the great directors of the American theater and an absolute master of farce.

"Look it over," he'd said. I spent most of that night "looking it over," and turned up at the National Theater the following afternoon, word perfect, palms sweating, to audition. We were allowed to run through whole scenes without interruption. I could feel Maggie willing me to do well with the generosity of any good and secure actress (she'd been playing the part with the New York company for months).

Mr. Abbott stalked down the aisle.

"I'm going to have you play Erwin in the Boston company. Do you know how much money to ask for?"

"No sir."

"You should ask for two hundred dollars—and get it."

"Yes sir."

"You can pick up a rehearsal schedule at the office."

It was one of the oldest and most improbable theatrical scenarios in history: "Young actor auditions for humble understudy role and winds up playing leading part." You might add the word "brilliantly" to this fantasy formula, but that's not quite how it went for me.

The Boston company of *Three Men on a Horse* gave its first public performance for an invited audience on the set of the New York company, at the Playhouse Theater on West 48th Street. The house was packed. I was in a froth of nerves. In this condition either one of two very unhappy things can happen to the inexperienced actor: he can overplay abominably, or in an effort to avoid that, underplay, directing his performance into his navel rather than to an audience.

At the end of the first act of this first public performance, a grim-faced Mr. Abbott appeared in my dressing room. As usual, he wasted no words.

"What do you think you're doing?"

"What?"

"You're not playing as we rehearsed."

"I think I am."

"Well, you're wrong. You've no energy. You're slow, your timing is off, you're not making your points. Now play it as we rehearsed it or you're fired!"

He left, and I was stunned. I had about five minutes in which to collect myself, and in those five minutes rage took over. *That son of a bitch—I'll show him! He wants more energy: bigger, louder, funnier—I'll show him!*

At the end of the second act, Mr. Abbott didn't even bother to come into the dressing room. He stuck his head around the door, said, "That's fine," and disappeared.

Years later, in reminiscing about *Three Men* with George, I said: "That was a terrible thing you did to me in mid performance."

"Not at all," he replied. "I knew that all you needed was a good kick in the ass."

While it worked in my case and at that time, I wouldn't recommend such an approach to other directors. It could prove disastrous. Directors have to have the fortitude to sit through numbers of inadequate or perhaps downright bad performances, when actors are first meeting an audience and discovering the pitch of their roles.

The character Erwin is described in the stage directions as "meek" and "shy"—rather negative characteristics. The trick with such characters is to make them positive and yet stay within the honest bounds of the personality the playwright has conceived. Conversely, an aggressive, dangerous character is often far more affecting when played quietly—almost shyly—than with overt forcefulness. These observations are general but boil down to an age-old actor's dictum: "When playing an angel, look for the devil in him; when playing a devil, look for the angel."

George Abbott was brilliant in the matter of character— and of comic timing, of pace. He was ruthless in eliminating the small laugh (often to the dismay of the clever actor who'd discovered it) that might impede the pace of a scene driving along to a major point and a much bigger laugh. Mr. Abbott also ran a very tight ship. No liberties were taken with either his script (he'd coauthored *Three Men on a Horse* with John Cecil Holm) or with his staging. An actor himself, he understood the process; he welcomed suggestion, appreciated inventiveness, but demanded punctuality at rehearsals and a strict attention to the business in hand. This discipline translated into performance, and discipline in farce is essential. Beware the funny man–actor whose specialty is a new and inspired bit of dialogue or business in every other performance.

If you are not lucky enough to cut your teeth on Shakespeare, you're fortunate to be exposed to farce for the discipline it imposes, the attention to timing, and its demand on the character you are playing. The nature of good farce is not in the number of slamming doors or near-naked ladies discovered in our hero's closet, but in that "willing suspension of disbelief" that allows an audience to go along with an outrageously improbable story and still persuade themselves that such things might actually happen. The key to that belief is character. If you believe in the truth of the character, and his/ her reaction to the patently absurd, you're a long way home— be you audience or actor.

TWELVE

Three Men on a Horse ran for seventeen weeks at the Plymouth Theater in Boston and another sixteen weeks at the Garrick in Philadelphia—a seeming lifetime now for a straight play. In Boston there was a seafood place I used to go to between performances, and I remember walking in one afternoon and realizing for the first time that I was recognized. Much more important, I was not only recognized, but people were smiling—smiling at *me*. I've never forgotten the wonder I felt. Years later, after I'd appeared in films and on television, recognition became commonplace, and so did that fairly standard phrase used by generous people on the street who say: "I want to thank you for the pleasure you've given me." The pleasure I've given? So often I've wanted most desperately to believe that, to be able to say to myself in times of stress or estrangement, "I've given pleasure"; but I've never really felt it in my bones, only that I've done a job. Such a confession probably implies a distinctly odd or perverse nature, but at least I don't confuse it with modesty. I have my fair share of arrogance. But on that particular afternoon in Boston, in that restaurant where no one spoke to me but just smiled, I felt wonderful, rewarded beyond measure.

There was one other unforgettable incident during that

Boston run, and it also took place following a matinee.

The Plymouth shared an alley with the Colonial Theater. Playing at the latter was Alla Nazimova in Ibsen's *Ghosts*. I'd seen this extraordinary European actress in London, England, in 1927 and been absolutely riveted. When she opened in New York—subsequent to her Boston engagement—Brooks Atkinson of the *New York Times* had this to say about her performance: "Nazimova has flooded the whole play with the light of exalted acting."

I was determined to see this great actress in one of her matinee performances (we had matinees on different days fortunately) but kept putting it off because I insisted on a good seat and these were hard to come by. I would have to wait.

One afternoon I was sitting in my dressing room, wiping greasepaint from my face, when there was a knock on the door. It was the stage doorman.

"There's a dame here to see you."

"Who is it?"

He shrugged. "A dame—from across the alley."

I asked him to show her in. A dame from across the alley? I was looking into the mirror, but the door was directly behind me. When the knock came and the door opened, I saw her reflection in the mirror. I stumbled to my feet.

"Madame Nazimova!"

She smiled. I was speechless.

"Yes. Good afternoon, Mr. Cronyn. My, you are very young." She had a marked accent.

I mumbled something: "This is a great honor," I think. She smiled again.

"Well, I had to come back. I have been playing this dreary play" (she was referring to *Ghosts*) "for so long and needed to laugh. Friends told me to come and see you—and I have laughed. Thank you."

And she was gone, as suddenly as she'd appeared. I suppose the whole exchange had taken less than thirty seconds. I sat down again, staring into the mirror, immobile. From strangers in a restaurant, a smile; from Nazimova: "I have laughed." Professionally, my cup ran over. But personally, it was bitter.

I could not get Emily to come and live with me. She'd appear for a weekend now and then, and there would be hours of ecstasy followed by hours of argument. Then, inevitably, she would announce that she had to leave, and I would take a long toboggan slide into depression. It was a situation that could not continue, and I was the one who precipitated the divorce. I gave her an ultimatum: either that she come and live with me as a normal married woman might be expected to do, or that we separate—permanently. I could not wait to outlive Mr. Frank. She would have to choose. She chose divorce.

My lawyer in New York was an aristocratic gentleman named W. Herbert Adams. He was tall, silver-haired, and dressed in impeccable Irish tweeds. He did not handle divorce cases, and anyway, immediate divorce in New York State was impossible.

The only alternative was the state of Illinois, where immediate divorce was possible on either of two grounds: physical cruelty or adultery. Emily and I chose the former, with no very clear notion of what might be involved. Herbert had put us in touch with a Chicago lawyer who had agreed to handle our case on the strict understanding that both parties were agreeable to the action. It was of course collusive, and I only hope that the black comedy of the proceeding is now covered by some statute of limitations that allows me to write about it without going to jail.

Emily and I traveled out to Chicago together and shared a room at the Stevens Hotel. When we weren't in bed together, we held hands like frightened parents in a hospital waiting room. The Chicago lawyer was very matter-of-fact. If we insisted on "physical cruelty," there had to be witnesses to at least three acts of violence on my part.

"You mean I have to shove her?"

"Shove, hell! You have to knock her down, slap her, rough her up. Not kid stuff either. And there have to be three separate witnessed incidents. I suppose you could do one here in the room, one in the bar downstairs—we'll pick a quiet time—and maybe one in the street. How does that sound?"

I said it sounded absolutely appalling.

"Mr. Adams told me you were an actor."

"Not a good enough actor. Knock her down?"

"Well, you'll never get by with a little shoving. You'll be remanded to family court, where they'll give you a lecture and try to patch things up."

"I can't do it."

"Good. So it's got to be adultery. Much cleaner."

The lawyer went on to explain what that would involve. He would find a suitable co-respondent and make the arrangements for an assignation at an appropriate hotel. I would have to make sure that the desk clerk got a good look at the co-respondent when we registered as man and wife, and that once we got up to the suite (he did say "suite") and she undressed, that I was to send for drinks or cigarettes, making sure that the bellhop got a good look at the girl when he delivered them.

And one more thing: most important, I must *not* let the girl know that she was providing grounds for a divorce.

"Otherwise, she'll have you by the short hairs—blackmail."

"How do I manage that?"

"Just pay her and say good night. Say you've changed your mind."

"And she won't know? After going through all those preliminaries?"

The lawyer glanced at Emily. "We'll talk about it."

He got up to leave, and with a little twitch of his head indicated that I was to follow him into the hall. As we stood by the elevator he said, "Give her a little bang—it's safer that way."

As the elevator door opened he gave me a reassuring pat on the shoulder and added, "Your wife seems like a nice girl. I'm sure glad you changed your mind about physical cruelty."

It had been arranged that the lawyer and the co-respondent—a call girl—were to meet in the bar of the Congress Hotel at ten o'clock the following evening. I was to show up at 10:30. Emily and I spent the day looking at the Impressionists at the Art Institute and wandering, disconsolate, along Lake Shore Drive, trying not to think about the immediate future. We had a miserable late dinner together, and I went off to my appointment with all the cheer of a man going to the gallows.

I found the lawyer and the girl in animated discussion sitting at the bar. There was a very brief break for introductions and their conversation continued. I sat on the other side of the lady but couldn't hear what was going on because her body was angled away from me as she gave her full attention to the lawyer and because she seemed to talk from between clenched teeth. It was a curious speech pattern, affected, reminiscent of certain Long Island debutantes of the period—infinitely world-weary, a kind of muffled pseudosophistication, and damn hard to hear. The fact that I was excluded from the conversation to start with was not without compensations. What was I going to say to this lady when we were alone? "How long will this take?—My wife's waiting up for me." Or "Will you be offended if I *don't* screw you?" Or "I'm kinky—I just like undressing girls but that's as far as it goes."

Another compensation was that I could look the girl over without being caught doing so. She was about my age, very blond, a good figure as far as I could see while she was sitting down; taller than I, and pretty, in a sort of knife-edge fashion. A model, I thought, moonlighting. She was dressed in black, with a great swirl of silver fox around her neck and shoulders despite the summer weather.

When the lawyer got up to leave, there was an awkward moment. The girl looked puzzled, and glanced at me.

"You mean I'm with *him*?" she said to the lawyer.

He patted her on the shoulder in much the same fashion he'd done to me outside the elevator. "Nice guy," he said, and winked at me. "You'll get on just fine." And he was gone. We were on our own.

The girl swiveled on her bar seat. "So you're the John."

"My name's Hume—it's Irish."

"Lots of Irish in Chicago."

"Yes. I'm sorry, but I didn't catch yours."

She replied through clenched teeth. I couldn't hear her.

"I beg your pardon?"

"Florence—like Italy."

"Oh yes. You've been there?"

"Some day. You registered here?"

"No. No. I have a reservation at the . . ." I fished in my pocket for the piece of paper I'd been given, apologizing for

My father, Hume Blake
Cronyn

My father and I,
Woodfield, about 1914

My mother, Frances Amelia
("Minnie") Labatt Cronyn

Above, a Woodfield Christmas dinner, about 1935. *Back row:* my sister Honor (with baby), my brother Dick (far right). *Seated at table:* my mother (center) with my sister Katherine on her left. *Front row:* my brother Verse (center, with glassses), H.C. (second from right). Portrait on wall is of Mrs. Pritchard, one of David Garrick's leading ladies and my only (very distant) family theatrical connection.

Below left, H.C. camping, the French River, northern Ontario, 1928. Right, "What shall we do about Junior?"

J.T. and H.C. wedding,
Los Angeles, 1942

Only ten years later . . .

Friedman-Abeles

"You don't look like anything."

Erwin in *Three Men on a Horse,*
1935

Leo Davis in *Room Service,* 1937

MGM

The Quisling in *The Cross of
Lorraine,* 1943

Papa Leckie in *The Green Years,*
1946

M

Professor Ivan Ivanovich in
Chekhov's *The Harmful Effects of
Tobacco*, from *Triple Play*, 1958

Tchebutykin in *The Three Sisters*, 1963

Sosigines in *Cleopatra,* 1961

Richard III, 1965

H.C. with Spencer Tracy in *The Seventh Cross*, 1944

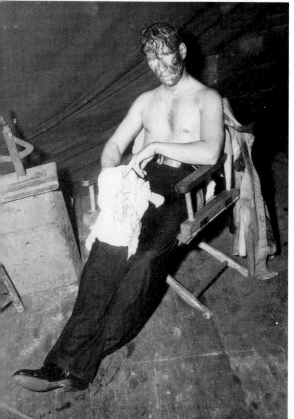

H.C., very wet, on the set of *Lifeboat*, 1944

H.C. with Tandy, 1947

Friedman-Abeles

Immediate family, 1952. *Clockwise from Jessica:* Christopher, H.C., Susan, and Tandy. Below, twenty years on: H.C., Tandy, Jessica, and Christopher (minus Susan, by then married)

not knowing my own address. When I produced it and read off the address, she looked pained.

"On the *south* side?"

"I hear it's very nice—I have a suite." I don't know why I clung to that word "suite." It must have been because I thought it might counter the disdain she felt for the south side.

"I never heard of it. Well, let's get going."

"What about another drink first?"

But I couldn't put it off forever. We got in a cab and when I gave the driver the address, he said—quite unnecessarily, I felt—"Oh yeah. Near the stockyards." When we arrived my heart didn't sink; there was no place lower for it to go. The hotel was on a corner, an old frame building not more than two or three stories high. It had a porch running around the sides at street level. On the porch was a line of rocking chairs, half a dozen of which were occupied by men in shirt sleeves and galluses, chairs tilted back, hats tilted back. It was like a scene from an old-time Western. I didn't dare look at Florence.

The desk clerk smirked, obviously expecting us. He shoved the registration form at me and slapped a key on top of it.

"No baggage?"

"Uh, no. Are they nice rooms?"

He smirked again. "Beautiful—I'll have the boy show you up. And you pay in advance."

The room was about ten feet square: it was largely taken up by a very big bed, but somehow they'd squeezed in a bureau, a chair, a telephone stand, and a clothes tree. I remonstrated with the bellhop, saying it wasn't what I'd asked for. Florence hissed something between her teeth, which of course I didn't hear. The bellhop said they had no suites but did I want two bedrooms?—and at that point I gave up. I overtipped the boy, closed the door and turned to Florence.

"I'm sorry. This place was recommended by a friend—it's not what I expected."

"It's got a bed hasn't it?"

And indeed her silver fox stole was already lying on it.

She undressed casually, pulling her dress over her head and smoothing down her hair, undid her bra, and stepped out of her half-slip. She wore no panties but a rather elaborate garter belt and long black stockings. These she kept on. The last things to come off were her shoes. I'd only got as far as my shirt and tie. At that point I pretended to rummage for cigarettes. Florence lay down on the bed.

I went through the prescribed drill: calling down to the desk for cigarettes and drinks, leaving the door open as I paid for them, and when it closed for the last time I stood with a trembling drink in my hand, facing the moment of truth.

Florence smiled at me. I smiled, knocked back my drink, and committed my adultery.

Afterward, we lay on the bed and talked—about what I don't know, but Florence actually unclenched her teeth and I remember thinking she had quite a nice voice: low and throaty, with a slight Southern drawl. It was the first relaxed moment in a long and painful day.

The court proceedings were almost immediate and mercifully brief. The desk clerk and bellboy appeared as witnesses. Emily had to take the stand as plaintiff and be identified as *other* than the woman who had registered at the hotel. The suit was uncontested and that was that—except for the emotional hangover.

THIRTEEN

IT WAS IN PHILADELPHIA again that the worst of the hangover caught up with me. I was touring in the next play I did for George Abbott: *Boy Meets Girl.* (Later there was another, *Room Service*; farces both, and both enormously successful.)

Divorce can carry a deadening sense of failure—when it's not an enormous relief—and no amount of bed-hopping relieves it. In Philadelphia my discontent came to a head. I could not stop thinking; so I fell into a pattern of busy oblivion. I'd play at night and then do a round of the late night spots, drinking. I've never been much of a drinker, but I could take enough to dull the senses and then fall into bed. I got up late, had brunch, and went to the movies. I must have seen every B movie in the Greater Philadelphia area. When I wasn't at the movies, I would wander, morosely, around Rittenhouse Park. I became an intimate of the pigeons there. Matinee days were a blessing, because I could lose myself in two performances.

Finally, when the depressions became unbearable, I telephoned home and asked my mother to come and stay with me. It was the only time she ever let me down. Of course she didn't really let me down at all: she had her hands full at home, she wasn't well, and her other children and grandchildren had

claims on her—a couple of them with their own marital difficulties. This dependence on my mother by the entire family
was typical. She was the rock—subservient to my father, but
the family foundation. She knew everything about me and was
a trusted, nonjudgmental friend. Even after our divorce, Emily went up to London, Ontario, to stay with her. Emily was
having her own problems. I remember a telephone call from
my mother after she had left. "Such a darling girl," my mother
said, "but I think—" and she groped for the right words "—I
think a little *mental*."

It's a hilarious old-world description: "a little mental." Poor
Em. She wasn't crazy, but savaged by conflicting emotions, as
was I.

I came slowly back to normal while appearing in Maxwell
Anderson's *High Tor,* which won a Pulitzer prize and ran for
about seven months at the Martin Beck. Once again I was
Burgess Meredith's understudy and—miserable opportunist that
I was—kept hoping he'd break an arm or leg so that I might
go on in his place. No such luck. He obliged me by breaking
an arm but went blithely on playing with his arm in a cast.
However, I had a respectable, if smaller, part of my own, and
the run of that play, unlike so many others, remains vivid because Peggy Ashcroft was the leading lady, and she, Burgess
and I were the first recruits in an acting class directed by Benno
Schneider.

Benno, an actor-director, had been a member of both the
Moscow Art Theater Company and the famous Jewish company the Habima. He was steeped in the Russian and European classics, and a wise interpreter of the Stanislavski method.
He was also an inspired teacher, and there are too few of those.

And here I quote a poem that I know as well as the Lord's
Prayer, and may have repeated more often. It was written by
the English poet Christopher Logue.

> Come to the edge.
> We might fall.
> Come to the edge.
> It's too high!
> **COME TO THE EDGE!**

So they came
and he pushed

and they flew . . .

Benno constantly led you to the edge and pushed—gently. Whether you flew or fell, you were richer for the attempt. It was under Benno's influence, and at Peggy's urging, that I attempted my first Shakespeare. "You'd be wonderful as one of the clowns," she said.

I was frightened of the Bard. My Shakespearean background was very shaky. At Ridley I'd been exposed to both *Julius Caesar* and *Macbeth,* in classes taught by Mel Brock, the basketball coach. As an interpreter of Shakespeare he was one hell of a basketball player. But Peggy suggested that I have a go at Launce in *The Two Gentlemen of Verona.* I choose the scene between Launce and his dog, being partially reassured by the pantomime involved and the absence of verse. At least it was a beginning.

It was during this period that I was summoned into the almighty presence of Mr. Harry Cohn, of Columbia Pictures. That studio was about to make a film of *Room Service,* in which I was playing at the time. Mr. Cohn's reputation has passed down through the decades as, to put it politely, an ogre. My one meeting with him does nothing to dispel that impression. Mr. Cohn sat at a massive desk at the far end of a big office. He was bullet-headed, and I was immediately reminded of the newsreel clips I'd seen of Mussolini—Il Duce. When I was ushered in, he didn't even bother to look up from his desk. I was just allowed to stand there, "cooling my heels" as they say. I had plenty of time to see that he was reading my resume. Finally, he pushed the paper aside.

"You wanted to see me?" he demanded.

"I understood *you* wanted to see *me.*"

"So, tell me about yourself."

I pointed to the paper in front of him. "I believe it's all there."

"This doesn't tell me anything—you're a Canadian—went to college—all that stuff—and you're working in that show we're

going to do—you'll have to make a test." The tone was so deliberately rude that I was immediately hostile.

"I don't think I want to do that."

"Why the hell not?"

"I'm playing the part eight times a week at the Cort Theater. Anyone who wants to see how I play it can see me there."

Mr. Cohn looked both incredulous and mad. "You don't
understand a damn thing about the film business." And that
was the end of the interview.

Mr. Cohn was right about one thing. I didn't understand
a damn thing about the film business. I'd never made a film;
it would not have been unreasonable to demand a test to see
how I photographed, even to see me with other members of
the film's cast. Besides, screen tests were common practice in
those days. All the major companies maintained a large roster
of contract players. Almost any young actor of promise was
tapped for a screen test, not necessarily for a specific role but
on the theory that he might prove useful.

It was on this theory that I was next approached by Paramount Pictures; only this time the approach was civil to the
point of being long-suffering on the part of the studio's New
York talent scout. We held several amiable meetings in which
I explained, solemnly and quite unrealistically, that I felt I was
primarily a stage actor and that I only wanted to make films
during the summer months—during the theater's off season,
from May through September; and that as I had a horror of
being typecast, I would not agree to a test unless I could play
at least four different characters from four different plays.
The Paramount representative looked at me, not so much incredulous as amused, and then asked gently, "Would it be all
right if we picked two of the plays?"

"Sure, that seems fair."

"I'll have to call the coast."

Paramount picked scenes from two broad comedies: *The
Milky Way* and *George Washington Slept Here*. They were about
what I expected, as whatever reputation I had was built on the
Abbott farces. I chose a scene from *The Last Mile*—very dramatic—and my other choice was about as unlikely a piece of
screen material as could be imagined: a scene from André

Obey's *Noah,* in which Noah, busy building the ark, has a long one-sided conversation with God about his difficulties. It's very fey material—the audience never hears God's side of the argument but must imagine it from Noah's responses.

Incredible though it now seems, Paramount built the four sets; I did my stuff, and the film was shipped off to California.

Eventually, word came back that I was to be offered a standard seven-year contract: exclusive services, forty weeks a year at a stipulated figure per week. The studio had an option to continue the arrangement or not at the end of each forty-week period, but the actor was bound for seven years if the studio so wished it.

"What about making it May to September?"

"Hume, be reasonable, no studio is going to give you that."

"But you promised. . . ."

"Hold it. We agreed to give you what you wanted for the test and I promised to pass on your conditions."

"What did they say?"

"They laughed and said 'get the test.' Look, Hume, there's a lot of money involved here. You can't expect a studio to make that sort of investment and then have to juggle its schedules just to convenience you—twenty weeks for God's sake—and only between May and September? Come on! With all due respect, you're a character actor, and even stars can't get that sort of deal."

There was a pause before he continued, tapping the legal form in front of him. "Actors have been known to change their minds, you know."

I turned down the contract, and my film test was filed away on some dusty shelf in California, where it stayed for about five years. When it was dusted off, it was so that it could be shown to Alfred Hitchcock.

Like many thousands of theatergoers everywhere, I worshiped at the shrine of Alfred Lunt and Lynn Fontanne. They were true theatrical royalty: consummate actors of the theater, and masters of high comedy—a rare commodity nowadays, requiring enormous skills. Because Jessica Tandy and I have not infrequently been compared to them, it might be assumed that we hoped to emulate them. Nothing could be farther from the truth. The comparison is a compliment, but the only thing Jessica and I have in common with the Lunts is that we are married and have been fortunate enough to have shared a long life in the theater.

However, nothing in that disclaimer is meant to detract from the great admiration, almost reverence, in which I held them as actors. How wonderful, I thought, to be a member of their company. In those days there were only two companies I yearned to join. One was Eva Le Gallienne's Civic Repertory Theatre on 14th Street, where there was a chance to play in the classics, and the other was with the Lunts. I wasn't to make either one of them, but in 1938 I got my chance.

The Lunts were about to do *The Sea Gull*, with Uta Hagen playing Nina. I was summoned to read for the part of Medvedenko, Masha's schoolmaster husband. Today, the character might be summed up as a wimp, but a rather touching and funny one.

The reading was held backstage, in whatever theater the Lunts were playing at the time, between a matinee and evening performance. An unusual arrangement, and one I think that was made to convenience me, as I had another job waiting for me that required an answer that very same day. I was not about to fall between two stools.

The stage manager read with me while Mr. Lunt watched. Ms. Fontanne did not emerge from her dressing room. At the end of the reading, Mr. Lunt said kindly, "Very nice, but do you think you could manage to make him a bit older?"

Here we go again, I thought, but replied: "I think so." We read the entire scene a second time, but being only a reading, it was static. There was no movement, and so much of the impression of age is a matter of how the actor uses his body. There was a long pause at the end of my second reading and finally Mr. Lunt said: "Pity . . . but you really haven't made him older, have you? You've just lowered the pitch of your voice."

I didn't get the job. Instead, I rushed over to Grand Central Station and caught a train to Boston where, with just eight hours' rehearsal the following day, I joined the company of a pre-Broadway tryout called *There's Always a Breeze*. The breeze wasn't strong enough, and when we came to New York, the play closed promptly.

Thirty years later, my friend Chuck Bowden brought Lynn Fontanne backstage in Milwaukee, where Jessica and I were on tour with *The Gin Game*. Ms. Fontanne, long retired, was living in Genesee Depot at the time, not far from Milwaukee. She came in on Chuck's arm: a small, fragile widow with white hair who, while retaining all her charm and vitality of spirit, seemed to have shrunk from her compelling stage presence. She sat and chatted with us about the play. It was a leisurely visit. At some point I recalled my *Sea Gull* audition and my disappointment over a missed opportunity. She smiled sympathetically and said something to the effect that between a matinee and evening performance Alfred should have been resting rather than auditioning. When the time came for her to leave, Chuck took her arm again and I followed. She paused in the dressing room doorway, put her hand on mine and said: "Mr. Cronyn, Alfred made a great mistake."

It was an infinitely graceful, if suspect, comment, and put me in mind of Nazimova's dressing-room visit of years past.

Between March 1938 and December 1940 I seem to have appeared in no less than seventeen plays. *Seventeen plays in twenty-two months?* True, eleven of those plays were done in stock, where I did a new play every week or, if I had a very major role, perhaps every two weeks, but that still leaves six done on Broadway. Flop, flop, flop—they followed one another like so many withered leaves blown across a small lawn of time. But I was learning. I look back on all of them now with wry affection.

Following the whisper of *There's Always a Breeze* was something called *Off to Buffalo*, memorable largely for the fact that it had five directors—one of the better of them being Milton Berle. Five! You can imagine what chaos that was. During a performance in Philadelphia (yet again) there was a riot, not solely because the play was so awful but because a large block of seats had been sold to opposing sides of a football crowd. They seemed intent on replaying the afternoon's victory and defeat and eating at the same time. First there were jeers and catcalls and then the food began to fly. It became bedlam. There were cries of "Shame!" "Sit down!" "Shut up!" I was hit on the ear with a hot dog bun. Instead of bringing down the curtain, a paralyzed stage manager—safely out of the line of fire—allowed the performance to continue, although the poor bloody actors couldn't possibly be heard.

It was then that I had a minor inspiration. I stopped trying to be heard. I moved round the stage through a very animated scene mouthing the dialogue, but making sure no sound escaped my lips. The other actors quietly followed suit. Gradually the audience became aware that something very odd was happening on stage. It must have been as if they were viewing a film in which the sound track had failed; here were all these gesticulating actors racing around, apparently screaming at one another, and yet not a sound. What was going on? For a few moments there was total and sublime silence, while the audience accommodated itself to the idea that the actors were fighting back. Then there was a smattering of laughter, which grew into a great wave of applause, and we were allowed to finish our terrible performance in relative peace.

It was one of my first lessons in crowd control. Unfortunately, it wasn't to be my last.

Toward the end of 1940 I joined the Group Theater for what turned out to be their swan-song production: Irwin Shaw's *Retreat to Pleasure*, directed by the great Harold Clurman. I can't fairly say I belonged to the Group but rather that I was co-opted into it when they felt they had no one within the established company to play the part offered to me—a very good part too. I wish I could lay claim to a greater participation in the Group's history, because during the decade of the thirties they were the most dynamic acting company in the English-speaking world. Disciples of Stanislavski, rebels against the Theatrical Establishment, they were fed by the passionate plays of Clifford Odets, and their ensemble playing was a revelation, as was their sense of truth in performance.

Clurman was certainly one of the most exciting directors for whom I have ever worked. When it came to character analysis and motivation, he simply had no equal. He loved to talk and he talked wonderfully, with great animation, infecting the actors with his own energy and insights. But he had one curious lack. He did not "stage" a play well. Traffic was not his strong suit. The actors kept bumping into one another, and furniture was a hazard. I felt that whenever there were more than three people on stage, Harold became nervous. If it was a party scene and movement had to be choreographed, his natural ebullience would vanish and he would retreat into glum silence.

I remember John Emory, playing a gentleman of distinction, making one entrance in top hat, tails, and white tie. (This was not the usual proletarian Group Theater production.) He was greeted by the daughter of the house and immediately removed his hat. The girl's mother was also present. John hung onto his hat. There was a brief dialogue exchange and then John, tired of holding his hat, said, "Harold, where do you suggest I get rid of this?"

Harold frowned. A pause of deep concentration followed and then he said, "Why don't you just wear it?"

Wear a hat in his host's sitting room with two ladies present? I have never forgotten the look of stunned disbelief on John's face. It was hilarious. I don't know how that particular dilemma was resolved, but just before the first public performances, a stage manager was brought into rehearsals to sort out some of the most awkward staging. I think Harold was relieved.

This stage manager was also an actor, and I'd seen him give some brilliant performances—an adjective I don't use lightly. Without ever contradicting the director's intention and always suiting "the action to the word, the word to the action," Elia Kazan proceeded to solve our problems with tact and encouragement. He and I have now been friends for fifty years.

Retreat to Pleasure had no out-of-town tryout. The Group had no money for that. Instead, we gave a number of paid previews. One of these was a benefit for a Jewish organization, perhaps the Hadassah or B'nai B'rith. They were a good audience—up to a point. And that point came during a satirical scene about anti-Semitism. Remember that this was 1940. Hitler had overrun Poland, the pogrom was in full force, the holocaust had been launched and Jewish sensibilities were very, very acute.

As the offending scene was immediately removed from the play, I doubt that there's any record of it, but my memory of it goes something like this: The mother and daughter referred to above (played respectively by Helen Ford and Edith Atwater) are seated on a balcony overlooking a Florida resort beach. They spot a man they've met the night before and obviously admired. This gentleman is just entering the water. The ladies exclaim over his perfect manners, his gallantry, physique, intelligence and general desirability. They watch him through binoculars.

"He's swimming out to the raft."

"Doesn't he swim well!"

"There's someone already on the raft."

"Who is it?"

"I think it's that terrible woman—you know, the tramp."

"You mean the one with the bleached hair and too-tight dress?"

"Yes. I saw them dancing together last night."

"I wondered about that—let me see." (Pause for binocular business.)

"What's going on?"

"He's climbing onto the raft. . . . He's sitting beside her. . . . He's got his arm around her."

"Disgusting!"

"Mother, I think he's Jewish!"

Now, while Irwin undoubtedly wrote the scene with far greater skill and wit than I've managed in this re-creation (the only words I can swear to are "I think he's Jewish") it's still very dangerous stuff. And at that particular time it was explosive.

A seismic shock ran through the audience and then all hell broke loose. The riot in *Off to Buffalo* pales beside this one. Mr. Lee Shubert, standing in the back of the house, got knocked down while trying to arrest the stampede of angry customers. The curtain had to be lowered. The bewildered actors slouched off to their dressing rooms wondering what had hit them. The scene had never been challenged in rehearsal; we'd all thought it was funny. But the audience was outraged.

I had been sitting in my room for about five minutes when

an agitated director and ashen-faced author appeared and said that I must go out and talk to the audience.

"*I* must? Why me?"

"Because they *know* you. They don't know us."

"But, for God's sake, you're the director and you're the playwright—and you're both Jewish. I'm a charter member WASP."

"Yes, yes, yes, but they *like* you, and at the moment they hate us."

It was true that the audience liked and sympathized with the character I was playing—but what was I going to say? Whatever it was, it had to be said immediately. While a relative if sullen peace had been restored, the more deeply offended were picking up their hats and coats and leaving. A good portion of them had already left.

The stage manager drew back the curtain for me and I stepped out onto the apron, to be met by a stony silence. It said louder than words, "This had better be good." I don't know what I said, but I'd made it a condition of my breaking the ice that Harold and Irwin follow me and offer their own explanations. I don't know what they said either—but we did resume the performance. It wasn't easy.

I think it was George Kaufman who, when asked to define satire, replied rather gloomily that satire was what closed on Saturday night. Well, we didn't close on Saturday, but I don't think we ran for more than three weeks. My list of flops was becoming extremely impressive. Something had to be done about that. I decided to become an actor-manager.

Of course, it didn't happen like that. I didn't just wake up one morning and say to myself: "Whoops, I'm an actor-manager!" There was some sort of evolution filled with anxieties; with "ifs," "ands," "buts" and "maybes." I went to my friend Audrey Wood, a prominent literary agent who specialized in plays. Audrey knew me as a struggling actor. She listened sympathetically while I explained that maybe, if, perhaps, I wanted to produce something—not necessarily a play with a great part for me, but something that *I* liked, something of quality.

Audrey left her office and came back with three slim

manuscripts bound in blue paper covers. "I don't quite know what you're looking for, but read these. It's not *a* play—it's three one-acts. New playwright, you won't have heard of him. Read them. Tell me what you think."

I glanced at the covers dubiously. Three one-acts? That was box-office poison. However, I took them home and read them. Then I read them again. And again. They were totally unlike anything I'd ever read before: lyrical, funny, touching—and original. Reminiscent perhaps of Chekhov but not really, the milieu being so entirely different. The culture seemed more foreign to me than that of the Russian countryside, but I was enchanted.

I went back to Audrey and asked if I might option these plays.

"For how long?"

I didn't know.

"I'll give you six months. Would fifty dollars a month be too much? He needs the money."

I took the option and sat down to draw up a budget. I'd had practice. I figured I could open the plays somewhere or other for about eleven thousand dollars. I "borrowed" five thousand from my mother and added two thousand of my own. That gave me seven of the needed eleven. But I was never able to raise another penny. I peddled the scripts around to various friends and established backers, but the reactions were always the same.

"Three one-acts! You've got to be kidding, and by Tennessee . . . who?"

"Williams," I said.

"What kind of a name is that?"

At the end of six months I went back to Audrey.

"I haven't been able to raise the money."

"But you'll renew the option? Another six months? You can afford it; you never stop working. Hume, he needs the money. He's bicycling around the South somewhere or other—and he's half blind. I keep waiting for the telegram that tells me he's been killed. There are six more one-acts. I'll include those too."

So, I had an option on nine one-act plays by Tennessee

Williams. (They were later published under the omnibus title of *27 Wagons Full of Cotton.*) I never got them off the ground. Well, not very far off, and then not until five years later when I directed one of them: *Portrait of a Madonna* with Jessica Tandy playing Miss Collins.

Perhaps I didn't try hard enough. Perhaps I was too busy acting—not only in my six Broadway flops but in eleven stock productions at the Lakewood Theater, in Skowhegan, Maine, during the summers of 1938 and '39.

"Summer theater" still continues, but it is not what it was. Certain summer theaters of my period carried a real cachet, among them Lakewood, the Bucks County Playhouse, Elitch's Gardens outside Denver, Ogunquit, the Falmouth Playhouse, and others. At the top of the list was Lakewood, the oldest and most prestigious summer theater in the country. I was lucky to join its company and even luckier in the parts I was handed, in plays by Shaw, Wilder, Coward, Odets and others.

Playing a new play every week—generally playing one at night while rehearsing the next for the following week—leaves little time for research, preparation in depth, or even learning the words. I don't remember ever actually sitting up with a wet towel around my head, but my lights burned late and I often stepped on the stage with little more than a fervent prayer. However, stock is a wonderful if dangerous experience for the young actor, wonderful in that you have to make every minute of rehearsal count; you have to get on with it, *do* it, rather than debate it. There is no time for self-indulgence.

Years later I was to work under the direction of Sir Tyrone Guthrie in rep, and play with Laurence Olivier on television, and while in both instances there was plenty of rehearsal time, I can still hear Tony say, "On, on, on!"

As for Larry, who always thought I talked too much anyway, I remember asking him for advice about a complex emotional scene I had to play, and getting the succinct answer: "Just give it a bash."

Well, in stock you have no choice but "On, on, on" and "Give it a bash." Of course you can't possibly be good—not really good—there's no time; and so the clichés of theater include the pejorative judgment, "Oh, it's a stock performance."

Lakewood attracted some impressive guests, not solely because of its company's reputation but also because of its beautiful location. The colony of small New England guest cottages bordered a lake, and the surrounding woods enveloped some attractive summer residences—but nothing crowded. It was peaceful, and its theater provided the only place of entertainment for miles around. Also, the company seemed part of the local community. Actors, once accepted, kept coming back—and it was a *company*. There was no jobbing-in of actors to play special parts, no stars as such, no "packages," and only one tryout that I remember: Lindsay and Crouse's *Life with Father*.

One of the guests who made a particular impression on me was Clifford Odets, though I think he was less attracted by Lakewood's theater and ambience than he was by the presence of Fay Wray in the company—the actress whom I had met on the set with Ronald Colman on my first visit to Hollywood and to whom I had oh-so-gallantly lent my handkerchief.

I had met Clifford before, but he didn't remember me. Now I was intent on being noticed. I not only admired him extravagantly, but I knew that he'd seen me in a number of plays at our theater, and I thought I was pretty damn good.

We were sitting in a booth somewhere or other, Clifford and Fay Wray, an actress called Claire (about whom more later) and I, talking as always about the theater: about plays, directors, and actors. Suddenly Clifford swiveled in his seat and gave me a long stare. Clifford was always very intense, even if the subject under discussion seemed trivial. (I doubt that there were any trivial subjects for Clifford.) He would fix you with a look like that of a basilisk, his eyes would open wide and seem to pop outward and there would be a significant pause before his pronouncement. The basilisk eye glared at me.

"You know every trick in the book, don't you?"

The tone was aggressive but then that was Clifford's style. I wondered what was coming next.

"What do you mean?"

"I've seen you in three plays now—all quite different—and they *loved* you. You can play anything, can't you?"

His eyes popped while he waited for my answer, but I didn't

have one. Clifford continued in what, for him, was an almost conversational tone: that of a doctor perhaps, talking to a colleague across a dissecting table—only in this case I was both colleague and cadaver. He went on:

"I think you must have a big closet somewhere with all your characters hung on hangers and when they hand you a new part you say: 'Ah yes, that will be number twenty-seven,' and you reach up, take it down, put on the character, and there you are. Only I don't believe a damn word of it—no matter how skillful you may be."

It was a devastating criticism; and it came from a man who was an integral part of the Group Theater, whose acting company I so admired. What Clifford was accusing me of was "facility"—a dirty word closely allied to "demonstrating," an even dirtier one in the actor's lexicon. In essence it means that the actor is giving a superficial performance, only skin deep, and that the guts of a character are never truly revealed, only demonstrated. It means that the actor has settled for *how* a given character behaves, reacts, but has scanted the *why*. *Why* must always come before *how*. If the actor understands why a character behaves as he does, how such behavior manifests itself will generally follow—and far more truthfully than otherwise.

On the other hand, facility, while dangerous, is not to be despised. To be able to do something quickly, to respond to direction immediately, to be able to make a radical change of course without hopeless internal confusion and time-wasting argument, are all immensely important. That kind of facility is invaluable in stock, in television and frequently in feature films—anywhere where the pressure of too little time prevents the actor from digging deep enough, from thorough preparation.

If the artist hasn't time to execute a complete portrait, a quick sketch is at least a beginning. But the sketch remains a sketch—and Clifford was complaining that my drawing wasn't up to it.

I didn't get up from the table and shoot myself. I was too depressed. I wandered out into the night holding Claire's hand and muttering to myself. I had been caught out. I hadn't covered my footprints; I'd been found guilty of "acting." The great Odets had condemned me for my lies.

"Truth" in the theater is just as chameleon-like as in real life. Actually, there is no truth in the theater or in any other medium of performance; there is only its *illusion*. You stab a man onstage and he falls dead in a welter of blood. "Truthfully" you haven't killed him. If you had, the acting profession would be far less crowded. If you are having an argument over a cup of hot tea, you're probably drinking cold water colored with a little vegetable dye and (if the director is a perfectionist) possibly with a small piece of dry ice popped into it to make it steam. And when you replace the cup in its saucer, you slip your little finger under the base of the cup so that your finger hits the saucer first avoiding a loud clink over some key word of dialogue. However, when the dyed glycerine blood, the "dead" actor's beautiful fall, the steaming tea and your little finger take over from the passion of murder or argument, you're in deep trouble. It is then that you're involved in a lie rather than the illusion of truth. Fifty years later, I'm still trying to achieve it—truth.

Clifford Odets did me a great favor. It wasn't the last time I had to be warned about facility, but it was the most memorable, and I believe I took it to heart.

FOURTEEN

IN AUGUST OF 1939, my mother visited me at Lakewood. She loved the place and enjoyed the performances, but she wasn't well and no one seemed to know the nature of the trouble. It was worrying. However, a greater worry obsessed her: the coming war. There were few Canadians who didn't see it coming, and as eighteen members of the family connection—admittedly a vast one—had lost their lives in the first world war, she was filled with foreboding. We sat on the veranda of an old hotel in Waterville, Maine, and discussed the implications. It was a beautiful summer evening, but the conversation was depressing.

The next month the war in Europe was a reality and I had dinner in New York with my cousin and fellow Canadian, Robert Whitehead. It was a foregone conclusion that we would "join up," but where and how? Bob asked me about my plans.

"I guess I'll go into the air force."

"That suicide squad? You're crazy! Why?"

"I don't know. My brothers were in it last time, and it seems cleaner than the trenches. What are you going to do?"

"I think I'll join the Canadian navy."

"The Canadian navy? Is there one?"

"Of course. They go up and down the coast hunting for

147

mines, and there's always the chance they won't find one."

Dear Robert: the eternal pragmatist. In the end, he did not join the navy but went into a service that seemed to take him into every hot spot in the world: Normandy, Anzio, Burma. Like his, my own course was totally unpredictable. I got myself up to Ottawa and volunteered for the Canadian air force. This involved a number of written and oral examinations, at which I did very badly. I remember the examining officer shaking his head rather sadly and turning to a fellow officer and saying, "Maybe Intelligence?" with the tone of one who has to dispose of some piece of embarrassing trash left on public property.

"What do I do now?" I inquired.

"You wait. We'll call you in turn. We have more volunteers than we can handle for the moment."

So I waited, and nothing happened. Eventually I contacted a cousin by marriage, General Harry Crerar, who was commander in chief of the Canadian Army, Since at twenty-eight I seemed to be unwanted as a combatant, I sent him a detailed plan for an army entertainment unit. Miraculously, I got a prompt and sympathetic reply, but Harry pointed out gently that the army had other priorities. He referred me to certain civilian organizations: the Red Cross, the Y.M.C.A., the Knights of Columbus, all of whom were supposed to be contemplating such an effort. But still nothing happened. Eventually, as a legal resident of the United States, I was drafted by the Americans in 1943 but failed to pass the medical examinations. By that time I'd acquired a beautiful five-inch scar down the center of my belly as a result of a laparotomy, and the U.S. Army took one look and relegated me to 4F.

As a consequence, I appeared in, produced, and directed a number of U.S.O. camp shows and organized two revues that played for troop establishments in Canada and at places like Governors Island and Fort Monmouth. These revues were probably most notable for their participants, among whom were Alfred Drake, José Ferrer, Tamara, Paula Lawrence, Keenan Wynn and Jack Gilford.

And that was the sum total of my "war record"— a fact for which I should probably be grateful.

＊　　＊　　＊

A group photograph of the Lakewood Company taken in 1939 shows an extremely pretty girl sitting in the front row. Her name is Claire. She is dressed entirely in white: white turban, blond hair falling to her shoulders, off-white sweater—it may be shell pink, but cashmere I'm sure—a twisted rope of seed pearls, white slacks with bell bottoms, white socks, and white moccasins. She holds a pair of sunglasses with white frames. Who was she? I'm not sure I know. I'm not sure I even knew in the Lakewood days, which seems a bit cavalier, as we'd decided to marry one another.

I gave Claire an extravagant engagement ring; the wedding invitations were ordered; we even had William Steig draw a cartoon for the cover of our invitation to the reception. It was to be ever so original, a skating party at the Rockefeller Center rink, and Steig drew a funny, charming picture of two kids waltzing together on the ice. Supper, champagne and wedding cake were to be furnished by the French Café, alongside the rink. No minimal observances this time, with only bride, groom and two witnesses huddled in the vastness of the Collegiate Marble Church. This was to be a celebration. And then the hand of fate took over.

My mother had to be rushed to the hospital for an emergency operation. The cancer was so far advanced that they simply sewed her up again, estimating that she had about eight more weeks to live. Claire was characteristically sympathetic and understanding, and we postponed the wedding. I spent a lot of time commuting between New York and Canada.

The situation dragged on. My mother was removed from the hospital in Toronto and taken home to her own bed in London, Ontario. She was happier there with her family surrounding her, but still required round-the-clock nursing. There was pain, constant discomfort and the miserable necessity of a periodic draining of her abdominal area because of the accumulation of liquid. She dreaded the appearance of that hollow needle.

It was a miserable autumn, spring and summer. Claire was living with her family in Pennsylvania. I seemed to see little of her—although I remember being booted out of the Algonquin

Hotel because I had Claire in my apartment after 11:00 P.M.

I spent much of my time rehearsing and playing in my various flops and making all-too-brief visits to my mother. Too much time went by. Eventually, my engagement ring came back to me and was followed shortly thereafter by a large package of wedding invitations—hundreds of them, all neatly packaged the way they'd come from the engravers. These had been sent to me by Claire's mother, who clearly felt that her daughter was being trifled with, and perhaps she was right. Besides all our other difficulties, I had also met "someone else," and *she* has a vivid and ironic memory of my taking her to supper and explaining in great fatuous detail my plans for what today might be called "an open marriage" to Claire. What total nonsense! All I remember about that supper was that my companion was strangely silent.

In October 1940, I had gone to the Biltmore Theater to see a performance of *Jupiter Laughs* by A. J. Cronin. In the cast was a fellow Canadian actor from London, Ontario, named Alexander Knox, and an English actress whom I had seen previously in *The White Steed,* Jessica Tandy. At intermission I went out onto 47th Street to smoke, and was mystified when I saw Miss Tandy come rushing down the theater alley and leap into a waiting taxicab. She was wearing a white dress—the same one she'd been wearing onstage. Where the hell was she going? The curtain would go up again in a few minutes, but what about the leading lady? She hadn't been killed off in the first act and yet I'd just seen her disappear into the hurly-burly of New York traffic.

I was to discover later that Jessica had a six-year-old daughter staying with her at a nearby hotel and had dashed back there to make sure that Susan Hawkins was quite safe, and hopefully sound asleep.

After the performance I went backstage to see Alex and was duly introduced to Miss Tandy. Did lights flash, bells ring? Were there internal fireworks? Nothing of the sort. It was all rather mundane, leaning in fact toward disaster. Alex took us both out to supper (he was obviously interested in Jessica), and I got launched on what I thought were some mildly amusing observations on the nature of English manners, and their quite contradictory idiosyncrasies. I suddenly heard Jessica say, "You *are* a fool," in a tone which implied that she'd been considering that possibility for the past hour or so. When supper was over, Alex drove Jessica back to her hotel and I went home alone.

When romantics ask me about how Jessica and I met, they are always disappointed by this account; and I can't say that the relationship rapidly improved. I did manage to persuade Jess to have supper with me again, alone this time. I can see her now: elbow on table, her head resting on one hand, turned toward me with a quizzical expression as I sounded off about Claire and just where the furniture was to be placed in our new apartment. She didn't call me a fool this time, but she must have felt it, or at least been bewildered.

> "Was ever woman in this humor woo'd?
> Was ever woman in this humor won?"

And was I wooing her, a married woman with a child, and I engaged elsewhere? Of course I was. But why? The odds were impossible. Jessica had no intention whatever of dissolving a ten-year marriage to Jack Hawkins, who, besides being the father of their child, was serving in the British army; and I, a divorced man about to launch into a second marriage to someone else, who was in a state of mental confusion that could only be illustrated by the *Laocoön*—that Greek statue of a man hopelessly struggling with entwining serpents.

Why then did I fall in love? Because that condition has damn-all to do with rational thinking. What attracted me? I can only come up with a laundry list of Jessica's attributes. First of all, her laughter. If I had to pick out one of so many, it would be her laugh—very frequently at my expense. I adored the way she made fun of me and the world in general. I was captivated by her sensitivity, talent, generosity to others, compassion, and of course her beauty and the fact that she seemed totally unaware of any of these qualities. She still is, and at past eighty now, more beautiful than ever. If, as has been said, you have the face God gave you until the age of forty and that, after that, you have the face you've made for yourself, then Jess's beauty is the sum total of her character.

Perhaps it was a growing awareness of my jealousy of anyone who attracted Jessica, or to whom she seemed attracted, which forced me to the realization that I was in deep waters—that I was hooked. Jess had an admirer, a very successful, very rich refugee French playwright who had a beautiful collection of Impressionist paintings. These hung on the walls of his elegant apartment in the Waldorf Towers. He asked Jessica to go and look at them—that old ploy—and she agreed. As this gentleman also had the reputation of a renowned lecher, I was not happy, though maliciously delighted by the outcome.

A friend of mine in the R.C.A.F. shared my passion for fly-fishing. He tied his own flies and had given me one as an affectionate souvenir. It was a very large salmon fly: beautifully made, very colorful, very decorative. I gave it to Jessica to wear on the lapel of a black suit she favored. She wore both to the Waldorf Towers. After a lavish supper served in the playwright's apartment, he showed her his paintings and then proceeded, quite predictably, to chase her around the coffee table. Somehow, in the ensuing struggle the playwright got hooked—literally. The point went in beyond the barb and he and Jessica could not disengage. So coupled, they repaired to a bathroom and the hook had to be cut out. He bled profusely. This cooled the gentleman's ardor, and Jessica bid him good night.

Jessica's public face is quite different from her private one. Casual friends might never suspect her capacity for rage. She's inclined to seem distant: very friendly but *very* private. She has many friends, few intimates. There's some mystery about her. I, who might be expected to know her better than anyone, have sometimes felt that I didn't know her at all. She's not a believer in "talking things out." I suspect she feels that a painful situation can all too often be aggravated by making a clean breast of everything.

To some extent she's undeniably right. Absolute revelation, confession, may be an enormous relief to one person while lumbering another with unnecessary pain. "Here! You take this problem. I'm sick of it." However, this reserve or forbearance—often generous forbearance—on Jessie's part should not be mistaken for a passive nature. Anything but. Outraged on one occasion by an insulting and airy condemnation of all women in general made by George Coulouris, Jess picked up her wineglass and threw its contents in his face. Unfortunately most of the wine ended up in Barry Fitzgerald's lap.

In a play I did with her years later, under the direction of an enormously celebrated but bullying English director, her temper finally snapped and she started throwing every movable prop within reach: ashtrays, cigarette boxes, cups and saucers. I was hovering behind a door waiting to make an entrance when something smashed against the other side of it and I heard her scream, "You sadistic son of a bitch!"

In the awful hush that followed, I tiptoed onto the stage and took her hand. I'd expected to find her in tears. Jess disengaged her hand rather abruptly and said, "I'm quite all right. I can handle this." The director was appalled, ashen-faced, which served him right. He was a prick.

It must have been about a year after my meeting Jess that we were sauntering down Fifth Avenue one Sunday evening, window-shopping. I was going through the worst of my jealousy phase, questioning her about this man and that one, asking for details, making innuendos, when she finally whirled on me.

"Now stop that! Just stop it! You say that you love me, then you love who I am, what I am. That's me! I am what I've lived through and that includes the lovers I've had, the men I've gone to bed with. Just stop it!"

And the miracle is that I did. My jealousy passed and I was never to feel it again, either personally or professionally. It was as though I'd been given an extraordinarily potent flu shot which quite killed the infection. I say "miracle" because it seems so rare that an argument, no matter how unassailable, can arrest a passionate emotion.

FIFTEEN

I WAS PLAYING Joe Bonaparte in *Golden Boy* at the Bucks County Playhouse when a script called *Mr. Big* was delivered to the New Hope Inn where I was staying. George S. Kaufman was to direct *and* produce this play on Broadway for the 1941–1942 season—the great Kaufman, whose last two directorial entries had been *You Can't Take It with You* and *Dinner at Eight*, both enormous hits. Mr. Kaufman was God and I was being offered the leading role in his new production. I was twenty-nine years old.

I handled the script with reverence as I carried it and a folding chair out onto the grass beside the inn. I read it carefully but with mounting anxiety. It was a wildly farcical satire inspired by the career of Tom Dewey, the *Mr. Big* of the title, who was then the New York State public prosecutor and who later became governor. And I didn't like it.

I didn't like it? Who the hell was I? I was obviously crazy, failing to see the comic potential, questioning the judgment of my betters. I accepted the job immediately and without demur. In the end that decision taught me something: never agree to appear in a play *you* don't believe in, regardless of auspices, unless you're broke. On the other hand, perversely, and in retrospect, I don't regret the decision. Working under the direction of George Kaufman was a joy. He was quiet, gentle but demanding, a perfectionist, and I trusted him completely and remember him with affection. In preparation for *Mr. Big,* I spent a couple of weekends with him and his wife Beatrice at their beautiful Bucks County "farm." The mail would arrive in the morning; George would open it and sit at the typewriter immediately to answer it—only a sentence or two perhaps, but immediate. He was meticulous. He had a trick of whipping out a pocket comb and running it through his thick, curly hair, as though that might preserve his compulsive sense of order. He also had a wonderfully dry sense of humor. He never punched a line nor allowed his actors to do so. I remember once asking him about a notorious musical comedienne with whom he'd worked. He thought before replying.

"Well, she can be difficult . . . she's not very bright . . . not much to look at either . . . she has a poor singing voice . . ." He seemed to search for a redeeming feature, then added triumphantly: "But she certainly can't act."

During the rehearsals for *Mr. Big,* my mother died. The prognosis of eight weeks had turned into eight months. Her death was a merciful release. I was given a couple of days of compassionate leave to go back to London, Ontario, and then I came back to work. In so desolate a situation, I was lucky to be steeped in the demands of rehearsing a very big part.

The entire action of *Mr. Big* centered around a murder investigation being carried out on the stage of a fictitious New York theater—a play within a play. The actual audience is witness to the murder and includes the presence of the state's prosecuting attorney, who immediately jumps onto the stage, takes over the investigation and makes a balls of it. That was me. In one scene I was to become hopelessly entangled in some fly ropes. I had the brilliantly stupid idea that it might be fun if the ropes were suddenly taken up and "Mr. Big" with them, disappearing into the flies—feet first. George went along with the idea in theory only. He wanted to see how it worked in rehearsal. The mechanics were left to me; after all, it was my neck. I had a strap made of harness leather to fit around my ankle, hidden by the cuff of my trousers. One of the loose ropes had a snap on its end, and with a little fumbling sleight-of-hand I was able to attach this to my ankle collar while seeming to disentangle myself from the coils I'd stepped into. On cue, up I went, feet first, disappearing behind the borders.

The effect wasn't quite as planned. For one thing, the moment I left the stage floor I started spinning like a top. Before they'd even had a chance to lower me, George came running down the aisle. "No! No! No! Hume, you can't do that! The audience won't laugh. They'll be terrified!" I persuaded him that if we could get rid of the spinning effect, I could arrange to go up head first, and that the business would seem less alarming but still get the desired laugh. George agreed, dubiously, to let me try it.

I stepped into a loop, the rope went up, I grabbed the line above me and was about to disappear when to my horror I found the first light pipe between my hands and my body. My feet in the loop kept going on up. There wasn't time to think. Instinctively, I let go of the rope and seized the light pipe—and there I was hanging upside down again; my feet in the rope above me, my arms hugging the light pipe below. At least a light pipe, weighted with all its lamps, and tied off at the pin rail, doesn't move easily.

A frightened stage manager appeared on the stage twenty feet below me.

"Are you all right?"

"Get me down."

"Just hang on. Frank! Release number seven—slowly!" Nothing happened. Number seven was the wrong line.

"No, no, not seven. Sorry. Try six. We've got to get his feet down. Don't worry, we'll have you out of there in a second."

"You'd better—my arms are getting tired." George appeared at the footlights. "Get him down, for God's sake!"

"We're trying. The line seems to be jammed in the block."

"Then lower the pipe."

I screamed. "NO! For Christ's sake don't do that! I'd have to let go of the pipe—I can't stretch! Feet first! Feet first!"

Eventually, they cut the jammed line; my feet and body swung loose, giving a terrible wrench to my arms, and there I was dangling from the pipe alone. Very, very slowly the pipe came down, and six feet from the stage floor I let go.

There was no discussion of trying the stunt again.

George never watched his own first nights. He prowled around backstage or paced up and down in the alley, combing his hair at nervous intervals. At the end of the first act he stuck his head in my dressing-room door.

"How's it going?"

"Pretty well, I think. They're laughing."

"Good." And he went back to the alley. At the end of the second act he appeared again.

"How was it?"

I shook my head. "Not so good—I'm afraid we're losing them."

George sighed. "Then we've probably got a flop."

There was no preamble, no fake encouragement. It was said quite simply as a statement of fact, and I remember it vividly. And of course he was right.

I did something that night that I had never done before, nor have since. I walked the streets—just kept walking, alone, for hours, waiting for the early-morning editions of the newspapers to appear. This was before the days of television reviews, and I wasn't sophisticated enough to know that if you had the right connections with copy editors or printers, you could probably get the gist of a review long before the paper appeared.

I expected to be hung, drawn, and quartered. I was "Mr. Big" and have rarely felt so tiny. I collected the various papers—there were numbers of them then—and sat in Child's Restaurant on Fifth Avenue in the upper forties to read the obituaries. We were indeed dead, but the reviewers spoke more in sorrow than in anger. They had great respect for George Kaufman. My memory is that the large company of excellent actors, Betty Furness and Fay Wray among them, were treated as gladiators in an unequal contest. As for me, where I expected to have my hide nailed to the barn door, it was barely tacked. But unmistakably I had another flop. I ordered some breakfast and went home to sleep.

I wasn't doing any better with Jessica either. I had asked her to marry me so many times that I had almost lost count. Her unequivocal nos lasted for about eighteen months, during which time she held my hand through the aftermath of my mother's death and the collapse of *Mr. Big*. She did two more plays in New York following *Jupiter Laughs*, having to wait a mandatory six months between engagements because of union rules affecting the employment of an alien actress. Both plays were failures and Jessie was flat broke. She'd been allowed to leave England with only ten pounds in her pocket as a result of wartime currency restrictions.

It was about this time that John Ford asked Jess to do a screen test. She went off to the studio with a bad cold sore on her upper lip and the last hundred dollars she had in the world tucked into the top of her girdle. She wasn't about to leave it in the dressing room when she changed into her costume for the test.

She didn't get the job and she lost the hundred dollars. When I asked her how it happened she said: "I don't know— perhaps I've been losing weight." She borrowed another hundred dollars from an old friend, the playwright Philip Barry, and I was furious that she wouldn't take it from me.

Although no play I did in those days seemed to run, I was comfortably off. This was not only because of the modest inheritance from my father's estate, but because I'd been lucky enough to invest in *Life with Father*. I'd seen the play tried out at Lakewood and I clung to the coattails of my old friends, Carly Wharton and Martin Gabel, who were two of the original producers. I was in pretty rich company, as Jock Whitney and his sister Joan Payson were the principal backers. There were only six or seven of us involved as backers, and the production had opened at the old Empire Theater to rapturous reviews. It had cost less than twenty-five thousand dollars to raise the curtain. By the end of its first-year run in New York, I had a profit of over one thousand percent. That sort of thing doesn't happen anymore.

A newspaper article of the period details the finances of *Life with Father* and lists the backers. My name appears as "actor and professional angel." Jessica asked me about the piece, and out of sheer, joking perversity, I explained that I was indeed a playboy backer—and added that I usually "bought" the parts I played in. It wasn't until she first saw me in *Retreat to*

Pleasure in 1940, which she'd attended in considerable anxiety, that she believed I might have some capability as an actor.

While Jessica was trying to make ends meet (a radio serial called *Mandrake the Magician*, in which she played the Princess Nada, was a great help), I was licking my various wounds, both professional and personal, and busying myself doing a number of shows for the armed forces. In the spring of 1942 I finally got Jessie to say yes. In the summer, she took off for Reno and a six-week residency at the Lazy A Bar Ranch, an establishment catering largely to divorce seekers.

I was only an occasional visitor to the Lazy A Bar, but it was while I was there that I got a message that Alfred Hitchcock wanted to see me in regard to a film he was going to make called *Shadow of a Doubt*. I learned later that he'd been running some film at Paramount when its casting director, Bill Meikeljohn, had suggested that he look at a test of "a New York actor" that might interest him. It was the four-character test I'd made for Paramount five years previously. **Blessed be Mr. Meikeljohn.**

SIXTEEN

I traveled from Reno to Los Angeles and stayed at the Beverly Wilshire Hotel. An old friend, Keenan Wynn, picked me up there and took me out to dinner. We went to Romanoff's and Keenan let me know that it was *the* place to go. The name meant nothing to me, but when we waltzed into the restaurant, I recognized the host and owner immediately. Keenan introduced me. I shook Mike's hand.

"We've met before."

I got a blank look. "We have?"

"Yes. At Harry's Bar, in Paris, several years ago. I bought a pipe from you—a Dunhill."

Light dawned and Mike took me by the arm. "Of course! And I didn't have a pot to pee in at the time." Then he added anxiously: "But you did get value received, didn't you? You did get value received?"

I assured him I had and he led us to a very good table right next to one where the unmistakable figure of Alfred Hitchcock was seated. I smiled but got nothing in return. I hadn't bought a pipe from *him*. We sat down and Keenan said, "What was *that* all about?"

I explained that I'd been standing in the bar in Harry's, drinking and smoking a pipe, when I became aware of the small man with the ugly face and big nose standing next to me. I thought I recognized him from newspaper photographs. The press had had a field day with the story. He was referred to alternately as Prince Michael Romanoff of all the Russias, Harry Gerguson from Brooklyn, or simply as a con man. I suppose Mike became aware of my scrutiny. He smiled and said, "You're an American, of course." "Close. I'm a Canadian." "Ah well. Little difference. Except for the education. The British tradition—much better."

He had a pleasant, deep, soft voice and spoke with a decided English accent. We made some small talk before I ventured: "You're Prince Michael Romanoff aren't you?"

"Ah, you know—very tiresome."

I never discovered precisely what he found tiresome, but after a bit he commented on my pipe-smoking and asked me if I'd care to buy another. He produced it from his pocket. "It's a good pipe—almost new. Dunhill of course. You see, I have no money, not a bean."

I was charmed by such candor and asked him what he wanted for it.

"Would five dollars seem excessive?"

I bought the pipe and paid the bar bill.

When Keenan and I finished dinner and he asked for the check, we were told that we had been Mr. Romanoff's guests. It was not the last meal Mike was to buy me.

The next day I got myself out to Universal Studios for my appointment with Mr. Hitchcock. I was waiting in a large reception room when a thin, gray-haired man with much-mended teeth walked through it, hesitated, and came over to me. "Are you Mr. Cronyn?"

"Yes. I'm here to see Mr. Hitchcock."

"Oh my. I'm afraid we've brought you a very long way for nothing. I'm Jack Skirball, the producer. You're far too young." Oh no, I thought, not *that* again. "However, you're here. You'd better meet him."

A few minutes later, I was ushered into the great man's presence. He was sitting with arms folded, tilted back in his chair. He wore a double-breasted blue suit; four fingers of each hand were buried in his armpits, but his thumbs stuck straight up. He weighed close to three hundred pounds and looked remarkably like a genial Buddha. He waved me to the chair opposite his desk and leaned forward, the chair creaking ominously.

"I believe I've seen you somewhere before."

I muttered something about the Paramount test and he said:

"No, not that—somewhere else—were you in Romanoff's last night?"

I told him the story of Mike and the pipe. He chuckled. "Lovely man, Mike—and good food. If he's a con man, we're all indebted to that profession."

I kept waiting for him to say, apologetically, that I was too young to play the part he had in mind. Instead he said. "Have you ever been in Santa Rosa? We're shooting the film there. Beautiful countryside. Miles and miles of vineyards. After the day's work we can romp among the vines, pluck bunches of grapes and squeeze the juice down our throats."

The mental picture of Mr. Hitchcock romping like a faun between the rows, with vine leaves in his hair, was too much for me.

"With all due respect, sir, it sounds more like a part for you than for me."

"What? Oh, you mean Bacchus—you're probably right, though I've never believed in typecasting."

He stared out of the window for a moment, considering, then back to me.

"We'll have to mess around with a little makeup—some gray in the hair perhaps—and glasses. We start shooting in about three weeks. Will you stay here or go back to New York?"

I couldn't believe it. Age had never been mentioned. There had been no talk larded with "ifs" or "maybes," no escape clauses ending with "We'll let you know." It all seemed to be an accomplished fact: I was to make my first film with Alfred Hitchcock directing. It was the beginning of a lifelong friendship and an enormously rewarding professional association.

The year 1942, *Shadow of a Doubt* and Alfred Hitchcock marked the beginning of a new career for me. I became a film actor, a husband and a father—not quite simultaneously, but in rapid succession. I started a new life.

My Webster's dictionary defines *kaleidoscope* as "an optical instrument which exhibits by reflection a variety of beautiful colors." It then goes on to describe how you put the tube to your eye, turn it, and with each turn the image changes; the colors blend or separate and finally come back to where you started. After a little while, the exercise, despite the color, becomes boring. The tube of my memory is rather like that. Making motion pictures is rather like that.

Between 1942 and 1948 I made about fifteen films, some of them eminently forgettable. Of those that are less so, the images remaining are strangely perverse, almost incidental.

In *Shadow of a Doubt* I remember one of my first lessons in film acting. I was seated at a dining table next to Teresa Wright. She had to say something to me which was shocking, and in reaction I stood up, pushing back my chair. I also stepped backward. Hitch spoke.

"That's all right, Hume, but rise and step *in*."

"*Toward* Teresa?"

"Yes, step in and lean forward."

"But she's just said something very offensive."

"I know."

"But . . . yes sir."

I made the move as directed, and it felt terrible, completely false.

"That's fine," said Hitch. "Let's shoot it."

The camera rolled; I stood and stepped back again, instinctively.

"Hume, you stepped back again."

"I know. I'm terribly sorry. It just feels so uncomfortable."

"There's no law says actors have to be comfortable. Step back if you like—but then we'll have a comfortable actor without a head."

I did as I was told. Afterwards Hitch took me aside. "Come and see the rushes. You'll never know which way you stepped. The camera lies, you know—not always, but sometimes. You have to learn to accommodate it when it does."

I went to see the rushes and of course he was right.

After work we did not go out and frolic in the vineyards, but the company frequently had dinner together. I would sit in the hotel bar with Hitch and watch him down three martinis before heading for the dining room. There, Hitch and Alma (Mrs. Hitchcock) would preside over a specially ordered dinner (the lamb *must* be pink) and a buzz of conversation. The martinis, the meal, his immense weight, to say nothing of the day's work, would take their toll until Hitch's chins would rest on his chest and he would start to snore gently. Alma would reach out her forefinger and, with the gesture of someone lifting the latch on a garden gate, chuck him under the nose. It always seemed to me like a frightful indignity, but Hitch never seemed to mind. He would smile, reach for a toothpick, and with his free hand coyly cover his mouth while picking his teeth. Eventually, he would catch the thread of the conversation and rejoin us.

We did a certain amount of location work on the streets of Santa Rosa. This always attracted a crowd. I was amazed at how considerate they were. From the moment the assistant director called, "Quiet please!" until they heard Hitch say, "Cut!" there wasn't a murmur; but when the camera had to be moved or the lights repositioned, a great babble would break out. People would seek more favorable viewing positions or pursue Joe Cotten or Teresa or Henry Travers for autographs. I was ignored—with one exception. A girl of about twelve, aware that I'd participated in the scene she'd been watching, rushed up to me, thrust her autograph book into my hands and said, "Sign it please." I did so—it was my first film autograph—and handed the book back to her. She frowned over the signature for a moment, then said: "Now, hurry up and get famous!"

On September 27th, 1942—after completing *Shadow of a Doubt*—Jessica and I were married at the Beverly Vista Community Church by a Dr. Stewart. Dim photographs show a great many candles and even more gardenias. Jessica wore a suit of pink and and gray doeskin. I'd brought the material back from the Bahamas a year previously. Our reception was held in the garden behind Romanoff's and Mike did us proud. Our wedding cake was one of those elaborate affairs with a miniature bride and groom molded from sugar on its top. June Havoc was seen to cut off this decoration and wrap it in a napkin, announcing that she was taking it home to her daughter. I hope the daughter enjoyed it.

Living in California was not simply different, it was revolutionary. We had a house, we had a garden, there were oranges, lemons and avocados growing right outside the door. We had constant sunshine and I had an immediate family. Jess's daughter Susan came out to join us from New York, where she had been staying with wonderfully kind and generous friends. She was only seven years old and now she had a stepfather; it must have been traumatic for her. I've never felt that I was a very successful parent, either with Susan or with my own children, Christopher and Tandy, who were born of my marriage to Jessica. Perhaps my inadequacy had something to do with my own upbringing, to the series of governesses and boarding schools. It was far from an unkind atmosphere, and I worshiped my parents, but it was a world where the child was to be seen (on special occasions) but not heard. I suspect that I tried to impose that kind of rigidity on my own kids. It didn't work. My standards belonged to another convention, place and time.

However, I can remember only one real confrontation with my stepdaughter, very early in our life together. Jess and I were in the study of our rented house when Susan suddenly appeared demanding attention. She was in a fractious mood and I'd been at the studio all day and was exhausted, a dangerous mix. Whatever it was that Susan was asking for, it was one of those rare occasions when Jessica felt she had to say no. A battle ensued, and Susan was very rude. I tried to make a point of keeping clear of these inevitable differences between mother and daughter by maintaining a discreet silence, but this time my temper snapped. I sprang from my chair, seized Susan with a hand under each arm, carried her upstairs and deposited her on the landing all in one move.

"If I ever hear you speak to your mother like that again, I'm going to spank you!"

Susan was much more startled by the headlong rush up the stairs than she was frightened by my threat. She glared at me a moment and then roared, "YOU QUIT THAT!" In retrospect it's both trivial and funny, but at the time it upset all of us a lot, especially Jessica. When I came downstairs again, I found her in tears.

I never did spank Susan, and when, at about the age of twelve, she came to me and said that she'd like to change her surname to Cronyn, I felt proud and rewarded. To all my children I have always been "Father," because for Susan "Daddy" belonged to Jack Hawkins—and of course the two younger ones followed the lead of their older sister.

After *Shadow of a Doubt* I made a film which I absolutely hated and in which I was very bad: *Phantom of the Opera.* I overacted abominably. I made two classic mistakes: trying to make more of a small part than there was there, and accepting the job in the first place. I remember the conversation that led me into this mess. My agent at the time was Sam Lyons. He sat behind his desk talking around his cigar.

"Whadaya mean y' don't wanna do it? You're new out here. Nobody knows you. Exposure! Y' gotta have exposure. I keep callin' and they say 'Who? Hugh who?' Y' can't afford to be choosy. Someday maybe—not now. I gotcha six hundred bucks a week—y' think that's chopped liver?"

And he went on like that. So, I accepted the part. Once again I made the same mistake I'd made with *Mr. Big,* agreeing to do something for which I had no appetite, and this time for far less compelling reasons. I was a slow learner.

I don't know how I happened to be cast in *The Seventh Cross.* Perhaps it was the release of *Shadow of a Doubt.* It was an M.G.M. picture starring Spencer Tracy and was to be directed by Fred Zinneman—his first "big" picture. The auspices were terrific and what's more, I had a wonderful part. I suggested that Jessica might play my wife and they agreed. It was the first of the many times we were to act together.

The company of *The Seventh Cross* was a motley collection of nationalities and accents. The Swedish actress Signe Hasso played opposite Tracy, I was Canadian, Jessie, English. There were Czechs, Hungarians, and many German Jews, most of them refugees of distinction. Early on in the shooting I spotted a woman who was hauntingly familiar but whom I couldn't place. I turned to an assistant director, pointed, and said, "Who is that?" He shrugged. "Another Kraut." I sought out Freddie and asked the same question. "That," he said, "is the great Helene Thimig, Mrs. Max Reinhardt . . . and she has one line." My God. Ten years earlier, as a student at the Mozarteum, I had watched her play the leading female role in *Everyman,* and now she was reduced to one line—and probably happy to get it.

A few weeks later I was to be in a scene where, outside my lodgings in Berlin, I am getting off my bicycle and am picked up by the Gestapo for questioning. In the fright and confusion of the scene, I try to put the bicycle into the Gestapo van. The incident is watched by my landlady.

This was an awkward piece of business, not in the script, and I had persuaded Zinneman to let me try it. It proved difficult and I thought I was going to lose a moment that was true, touching and funny. The actress playing the landlady said something to Freddie in German. I don't know what it was, but it was obviously helpful. We got the shot and afterward I turned to the "landlady," thanked her and asked her name. A diminutive lady of middle years, with a careworn face, she held out her hand and said, "I'm Helene Weigel." *Helene Weigel?* There she stood, the original Mother Courage, the wife of Bertolt Brecht, a pillar of the Berliner Ensemble, one of the truly great acting companies of the European twentieth century.

These names, Thimig and Weigel, will mean little or nothing to young readers, but meeting them on the set of *The Seventh Cross* made me sharply aware of the plight of the refugee. And we were surrounded by them: Thomas and Heinrich Mann, Bertolt Brecht, Schoenberg, Kurt Weill, Jean Renoir. I met them all, but really knew none of them. Not all of them were political refugees. Some had left home because the wartime climate had made their professional worlds impossible. Jessica, for instance, had left England when there was a job waiting for her in New York—or so she thought. (It turned out not to be true, and she went to work in the British embassy as a cipher clerk.) Whatever the reasons, the presence of these refugees in Hollywood added an unusual and healthy mix to a stagnant cultural milieu. I remember once flying into Los Angeles at night with my friend Joe Mankiewicz, and amid the vast panoply of lights below noticing one curiously dark and dead spot in all that glitter. I pointed it out to him, saying, "I wonder what that is?"

"The public library, of course," said Joe.

In preparation for *The Seventh Cross* and even during the early days of shooting, Jess and I would sometimes go to Zinneman's office at night, rearrange the furniture to simulate the set, and work out with Freddie the mechanics of the next day's work. We not only played our own scenes but often those of other characters as well. It was great fun, reminding us of the theater, and gave us invaluable rehearsal and an insight into the problems of a director. Freddie could share these in private, whereas he could not possibly reveal them before an entire company and crew.

Where Hitchcock had seemed imperturbable and totally secure, Zinneman seemed to be in a constant state of anxiety. Seen in my mind's eye, he always has a furrowed brow. He had reason to frown; this was a big-budget film and in Spencer Tracy he had a very major star not noted for treating fools gladly. Freddie also had a fellow German as a cameraman. Older than Freddie, surly, but very well established, he always seemed to feel that he knew better than the director. His lighting took hours. Walking onto the set, threading one's way through the light stands, was like entering a bamboo thicket, and some lamp or other would inevitably get nudged and have to be refocused. I could see Freddie's furrows deepen as he looked at his watch.

In my first year in Hollywood, to be able to observe Hitchcock, Zinneman and Tracy work was a revelation. I found the whole process fascinating and asked endless questions—too many, probably. I can remember Hitch ostentatiously hiding behind a newspaper as he saw me approach. Freddie talked freely off the set, but I rarely spoke to him when we were working; he always had other things to worry about. Spence was monosyllabically tolerant. I was sitting next to him one day as we endured another lighting wait, when a visiting journalist was introduced and proceeded to ask some questions. Spence proved to be a dry well, and finally the journalist in desperation turned to me.

"This is your first film, isn't it, Mr. Cronyn?"

"Not quite—my third."

"Oh, I didn't realize . . ." He turned back to Spence and said jocularly, "And how is this young fellow doing?"

Spence threw a sour look first at him, then to me and growled, "The son of a bitch would fix the lights if they'd let him!"

I tried never to miss watching a scene when Tracy was playing. His method seemed to be as simple as it is difficult to achieve. He appeared to do nothing. He listened, he felt, he said the words without forcing anything. There were no extraneous moves. Whatever was provoked in him emotionally was seen in his eyes. He was praised for his naturalness, for being "so real," but it wasn't real. Acting never is. His was a finely honed craft.

Spence was a lovely man, a lovely, troubled artist whose pains I could only guess at, but he had a rough tongue on occasion—particularly after a drink or two. I was sitting in his dressing room one evening after work, drink in hand, when Katie Hepburn walked in. It was the first time I'd met her, and I was on my feet immediately. Spence was feeling morose and made no effort to move or to introduce us. Perhaps he assumed we knew one another. I introduced myself. We shook hands and she said, "I hope I'm not interrupting anything—please sit down."

She was tall, slim, beautiful and very direct, and her look was as firm as her handshake. I was aware that she was appraising Tracy and conscious of his mood. She turned to him and said cheerfully, "How are you doing, old man?"

"On my ass."

"Problems?"

But he was drinking and didn't bother to answer. She continued, "I think I'll get myself a drink."

I got up once again. "Can I get it for you?"

"She told you to sit down." It was said as though I might be hard of hearing. I sat down. Miss Hepburn got her drink and joined us—well, me anyway. Spence seemed withdrawn into sullen reverie. I wondered what was wrong; he'd been talkative enough before Miss Hepburn arrived, despite the irritation he expressed over the time it was taking to light our scenes. Miss Hepburn talked to me, ignoring Spence's silence. She asked me about the film and what I was playing; she knew the script well. She was charming. At one point she produced a cigarette and I got up to light it for her. That did it. Spence exploded.

"Why don't you two find a bed somewhere and get it over with?"

I stood there, frozen, until the match burned my fingers. Miss Hepburn just smiled.

Spence waved at me. "Sit down, for Christ's sake! You keep bouncing around like corn in a popper!"

I finished my drink and left. But it wasn't the last time I was invited to Tracy's dressing room. I liked and admired him, and he could be just as funny as he was sometimes savage.

The Seventh Cross was released in the season of 1944 and I was nominated for an Academy Award in the "best performance in a supporting role" category. I didn't win; Barry Fitzgerald did, for a beautiful job in *Going My Way*. However, I had a rewarding nomination—which was unkindly followed by many months of unemployment. I didn't like this at all. I could take only so much sunshine. It wasn't a matter of my not being offered parts; I was under term contract to M.G.M. and that busy and prestigious studio had a very full schedule of productions. Messengers would bring scripts to my door periodically; I would read them, say a polite "No thank you," and would hear no more about it, except on those rare occasions when the irate producer or director involved would call to scold me about my lack of judgment, and ask why the hell I failed to appreciate the opportunity being offered. The reasons were almost always the same; either I didn't like the script, or the part was a pale copy of something I'd done before. I had to be careful about expressing such reservations and became a master of evasive argle-bargle on the telephone.

Legally, of course, Metro could have suspended me, but they never did. For this I believe I had one man in particular to thank: Benny Thau. Mr. Thau was the studio's supreme commander of all "talent"; some thought of him as Lord High Executioner and referred to him unlovingly as Old Stone Face. Not me. Somewhere under that granite impassivity was a warm heart and a sense of humor. He would listen to me with weary resignation while I explained why I didn't want to do something, and even more important, when I did. Could he arrange for me to be tested for such and such a part, regardless of the fact that I was the wrong age, height, color, perhaps even sex? He would sigh deeply and say, "We'll see about it."

My self-imposed exile from the studio was demoralizing, so I sat down to write my first screenplay. It was called *Angel of Miami,* the name of a schooner, and it was about castaways on a tropical island. *Robinson Crusoe* did it better. However, it kept me from getting waterlogged in the pool and miraculously it sold. R.K.O. bought it and it was never heard of again.

Eventually, a script arrived from Metro that I *did* want to do. It was *Ziegfeld Follies,* and I was to play opposite Fanny Brice in a sketch she'd made famous on Broadway with the great vaudeville comedian Willie Howard. The sketch was called "The Sweepstake Ticket" and was the purest farce, a burlesque standard. Well, I hadn't done that before; at least not on film. We were directed by an old hand at musicals, Roy Del Ruth. For a man surrounded by clowns, music, beautiful show girls and lavish sets, he seemed singularly depressed. We would start our day's work with Mr. Del Ruth riffling through the script pages, looking glum. He would slap the book shut, sigh heavily, and say, "Oh well. Let's shoot it." It was not a beginning calculated to inspire a great comic performance.

SEVENTEEN

CHRISTOPHER WAS BORN in 1943 and Tandy two years later. By that time we'd moved out of our rented house and bought one on North Rockingham Avenue in Brentwood. It was what the real estate agent called "Mediterranean"—a sort of bastard Spanish: red-tiled roof, arches, patios, balconies; an old house set well back from the road, with a generous garden that terraced down the hill on the west side overlooking Mandeville Canyon. The view across the canyon was to the Santa Monica mountains, and in a break between these hills there was a glimpse of the blue Pacific.

The house had had various owners, one of them being Johnny Weissmuller, of Olympic swimming fame, the star of a number of Tarzan films. Perhaps he had been responsible for the large swimming pool. It was placed between the house and the road in a grove of half a dozen beautiful lemon eucalyptus trees. These doubled the work of the man who came to clean the pool. He kept suggesting that they be cut down. No way. They're gone now, but we enjoyed their grace and fragrance throughout our tenure.

On the canyon side of the garden, smack up against the property-line fence, was a small, dilapidated, garden toolshed. I had this converted into a one-room studio, with my desk in a cantilevered window nook facing the mountains. There was a miniature fireplace, a built-in bunk bed and a bathroom about the size of a small closet. The interior was of unpainted tongue-and-groove cedar. It was a lovely, quiet, reclusive spot where I spent many hours. I took Robert Ardrey down there one day just after it had been finished. Bob had done a lot of his writing in a cramped and shabby hotel room on West 44th Street in New York. He looked around my ivory tower and said, "Nice—now all you need is the talent to go with it."

Life, for this actor in Hollywood, was full of unexpected joys. I do not look back on it as many of my contemporaries appear to do as a wasteland, an exile into corruption. First of all, I was very happily married. I had three healthy and sometimes fascinating children, and for the young ones at least, there was the illusion of permanence. We had a home, a house filled with light and frequent laughter. We had dogs: Tempo, a magnificent-looking but cowardly Alsatian, and a cocker spaniel named Paprika. I can remember once wheeling Tandy down Rockingham Avenue in her pram when we encountered another dog, an aggressive boxer. Paprika held his ground, fangs bared, but Tempo immediately tried to climb into the pram with Tandy.

The family was together on weekends and almost every evening, which was an improvement on having the parents playing in a theater somewhere or other. On occasion, Jessica has remarked that I "missed a great deal" when the children were very young. It's been a remark made in regret, never in accusation; but it has troubled me—not knowing quite what it was that I missed. Babies are inclined to alarm me. Even now, when I'm sometimes allowed to hold a great-grandchild in my arms for one of those generational photographs, I must admit to feeling that the baby views me with deep suspicion and to wondering just how soon I can tactfully hand it back to one of its parents. But as my own children grew older, I can remember with pleasure playing with them in the pool, teaching them to swim, and reading aloud to them in the evenings. I didn't miss everything.

Jessica and I had many friends who were writers and directors, but it was among the actors that we found spontaneous gaiety even when they were complaining. Actors can be wonderful companions, occasionally gloomy and sour like the

rest of humanity but essentially lovers of life. The best of them
are keen observers of behavior and can be hilarious commen-
tators on it.

A gang of us used to meet on weekends, most of them
members of "The M.G.M. family"—which is how the publicity
department, under the direct influence of L. B. Mayer, liked
to think of us. These gatherings would shift from house to
house, but those I remember best were at the house of Gene
and Betsy Kelly. There would be touch football in the afternoon, food, drink and almost inevitably a long evening given
over to "the game." This was an elaborate form of charades
peculiarly suited to actors. We usually played in violently com-
petitive teams. The trick was to pick a series of phrases or
quotations so outrageous that they would defy the abilities of
the most accomplished pantomimist on the opposing side. There
were very strict rules; strict time limits, strict prohibitions against
the use of a foreign language and so forth. The job of referee/
timekeeper was unenviable.

While Gene and Betsy, who seemed to share some sort of
radarlike communication (God help you if they were together
on the opposing team), were the acknowledged masters of the
game, it was Laird Cregar I remember best. Everything about
him was oversize, both physically and emotionally. He was an
accomplished character actor who, tragically, died too young
to be remembered by any but a few of today's film buffs.

Laird played the game with a relentless passion that would
have been boring if his spectacular furies at losing hadn't been
so hilarious. He would rail against his teammates for their
blindness and insist on acting out his clues all over again to
impress them with the clarity of his performance. Sometimes
indeed I suspected his team of being intentionally obtuse just
to provoke one of Laird's magnificent eruptions.

When the game palled, when the cheating became too fla-
grant or Laird's overdrive too exhausting, there were other
forms of entertainment. It was at Gene's house that I first heard
Judy Garland sing "Over the Rainbow" and Nancy Walker sing
"Pass That Peace Pipe." Hugh Martin and Ralph Blaine played
us the whole score of "Meet Me in St. Louis." All these were
months in advance of the release of the films involved. Hoagy
Carmichael would play the piano and sing his blues songs in

that persuasive rusty voice of his. There was a lot of talent in those rooms. One night Paul Draper, surely one of the great classical tap dancers of all time, hopped onto a glass-topped table—yes, it was very heavy glass—and danced for us. The effect was magical. He seemed, like Ariel, to dance in the air.

Such was the wild, woolly and scandalous party life of Hollywood as we knew it. Perhaps this was an age of relative innocence, before drugs played any significant part in it. Of course there were other parties in other houses, some ribald and less innocent, and there were the high-stakes poker games popular with studio executives, producers and high-powered agents, but we were not invited to those. Much has been made of the stratification of the film community's social life—of the "A" and "B" lists—but we were never conscious of it. For us it was a case of like seeking like.

I remember going to the house of Robert and Janet Nathan, where we were likely to meet refugees such as Thomas Mann or Arthur Rubinstein; to Dick and Tinx Whorf (Dickie was a Renaissance man, able to turn his hand with equal facility to acting, painting, scene design or directing); to Dore and Miriam Schary, where the talk was of liberal politics; to Bill and Greta Wright, who had a beautiful old house close to ours, filled with pre-Columbian sculptures; to Lenore and Joe Cotten, who gave elegant dinner parties; to Ira and Lee Gershwin, whose collection of French Impressionists was startling; and to Keenan and Evie Wynn, Robert and Helen Ardrey, friends from the theater. It's a diverse list and contradicts the insularity of Hollywood—at least in the forties.

Those were boom times in the film business. It was said that you could run a picture backwards and it would make money. The major studios had a vast number of people under exclusive contracts, not only actors, but writers, directors, producers, designers, scenic and makeup artists—the list goes on and on, without touching on the craft unions.

Jessica was placed under contract by Twentieth Century–Fox and given her first American film part by Joseph L. Mankiewicz. For her it was not a great role, but for me it was the beginning of one of the closest friendships of my life, one that happily endures to this day. I love Joe. We are godparents to one another's children; we have shared a great deal of laughter and a few tears, and supported each other in extremis. Ultimately, I was to make three films under Joe's direction, and if my performances were any good, I owe much of that to him. But the thing I prize most is his friendship.

Joe is as well-read as he is opinionated, a marvelous raconteur, and possessor of a biting wit. He has brought me sharply to heel more than once when I became lost in some extravagant nonsense. I remember once handing him something written in my eccentric longhand and hovering behind his chair saying anxiously that I hoped he could read it.

"Not only can I read it, I can correct your spelling at the same time."

When Joe was a producer at Metro he attended some sort of executive conference presided over by L. B. Mayer. The subject under discussion was a film in production difficulties and way over schedule, and there was a suspicion that someone was being self-indulgent. The director was Mervyn Le Roy. Joe murmured, "*Le roi s'amuse.*"

L. B. turned to Joe. "What? . . . What was that?"

"Nothing."

"You said something—in French, wasn't it?"

"I just said that I hoped Mervyn was enjoying himself," replied Joe blandly. "It's a difficult film."

When Joe won the New York Film Critics Award for his work as writer-director on *All About Eve,* I attended the ceremony with him. It was held in a roof restaurant on one of those towering midtown office buildings completely surrounded by glass. New York was at his feet. Joe was introduced to the assembled guests by Bette Davis, and her praise of his various capabilities was so extravagant as to be almost embarrassing. It was also longwinded. I glanced at Joe, wondering how he was going to handle such effusiveness when he had to acknowledge it. He was looking out of the window, frowning. When finally he rose and crossed to the microphone, there was a great round of applause. He let it die out completely and then said slowly, almost diffidently: "I must thank Ms. Davis for an overly generous introduction . . . and assure all of you that on the seventh day I rested."

EIGHTEEN

SOMEWHERE IN THIS PERIOD I was loaned out by M.G.M. to Fox to appear in a film called *Lifeboat*. It wasn't one of my more rewarding roles, but that didn't matter, I was back with Hitchcock again. The film was an uncomfortable one to make, physically uncomfortable, because of its nature. Nine of us huddled together in a lifeboat on frequently stormy seas for the best part of three months. To call it close quarters would be an understatement.

No part of the film was actually shot at sea. It was made entirely either in the studio or in a tank on the back lot at Fox. This tank had a chute at each of its four corners—the kind of chute you might see in miniature at a children's playground. At the top of each chute was a container holding four thousand gallons of water. When the contents of all four containers were released simultaneously, sixteen thousand gallons of water hit the tank below in a cataract that completely buried the boat below and overwhelmed its occupants. The boat was held in relatively stable position by a maze of underwater wires. The actors weren't.

On the soundstage the lifeboat was mounted on a mechanical rocker and sat about eight feet off the stage floor. You got in and out of the boat by ladder. Behind the boat was a process screen on which was projected the sky, scudding clouds, and the rolling sea in all its moods. The rocker had to move the boat in a manner appropriate to the wave conditions shown on the process screen—sometimes pitching wildly, sometimes rolling gently, occasionally in a flat calm. There was a large demand for antiseasickness pills among the actors.

The film posed technical difficulties that were meat and drink to Hitch. He rejoiced in solving them. Because the process screen placed sharp limitations on his camera angles (you could rarely lose the screen except in closeup), Hitch compensated by the variety of his compositions. At one time, he had been an art director. He could draw. Hanging on the camera dolly was a clipboard holding a pad of legal size plain paper, with each sheet divided into three sections by perforations. In the center of each section was printed a square, simulating a frame of film. Hitch would reach for the clipboard, rapidly sketch in the desired composition, tear off the section, hand it to the cameraman and say, "This is what I want." It was a skill I'd never seen before or since, and it saved an enormous amount of time in discussing camera positions, lenses, and the positioning of actors. Everything was there on that piece of paper.

The cast of *Lifeboat* was impressive, but its leading lady was *the* leading lady and no one was allowed to forget it. Tallulah Bankhead was not to be crossed. She has had so many admirers that this lone dissenting voice can hardly damage her heavenly state. She was famous as a young woman for her looks, her scandalous behavior and above all for that low-pitched, throaty voice. One of my reservations about the lady was that the voice was heard all too often. She was a compulsive talker with a reputation for wit. My own estimation was that this was based on the law of averages: anyone who talked as much as Tallulah did was bound eventually to say something witty. Unfortunately, I saw more of the termagant than the wit.

While the set was being lit one day I was rehearsing with Henry Hull, an actor with a long and enviable theater reputation. (I have never forgotten his marvelous performance as Jeeter Lester in *Tobacco Road*.) Henry was no longer young and had some difficulty with the lines. We were running the scene. I stood in the stern; Henry faced me and behind him was Tallulah—talking. Henry had a longish speech dealing with another character, named Mrs. Higgins. That name, for reasons unknown except perhaps to the legal department, had been changed several times from Higgins to Higley then back again to Higgins. Tallulah had only caught up with the first change. Henry was concentrating on his words. "Such and such and so on and Mrs. Higgins and so forth." Tallulah barked: "It's Higley, Henry!"

Hull made a face of exasperation and went back to where he'd started. "Such and such and so on and *Mrs. Higgins* and so forth."

"For Christ's sake, Henry, it's *Higley!*"

Hull didn't turn around, he simply snarled over his shoulder. "HIGGINS! Tallulah."

What happened next is hard to exaggerate. Over Henry's shoulder I watched Tallulah swell up like a cobra about to strike. She started slowly at a bass pitch that rose to a genuine scream. "Don't-you-speak-to me like that . . . YOU GOD-DAMNED OLD HAM!"

I swear the stage walls trembled and leaned outward. The company was paralyzed. Hitch quickly went to the water-cooler. He hated confrontations.

An occasional blowup on a set where all day long, day after day, actors are wet, uncomfortable, and too closely confined can be forgiven. For instance, we all had about six changes of identical wardrobe; the theory was that at least one of them would always be dry. It was a fine theory. In practice I found that by three in the afternoon I would be sitting in the rays of a "brute"—one of those enormous two-thousand-watt lamps used for simulating sunlight—trying to dry out and keep warm.

As I said, blowups are forgivable providing they're not habitual. Later in the film, word reached the set that the Italians had capitulated and that Mussolini had fled. Walter Slezak, an Austrian who gave a superb performance as the captured German U-boat captain (which was, I suspect, a contributing factor to the obvious hostility Tallulah felt toward him), said something like, "Well, thank God that part's over. Perhaps it will spare more unnecessary bloodshed."

Again, Tallulah went through her cobra phase. She wheeled on Walter.

"I-hope-they-spill-every-drop of German blood there is. I hate them all! And I HATE YOU!" And again the stage walls quivered. There was a deathly hush followed by Walter's reasonable voice. "I'm sorry about that, Tallulah."

Miss Bankhead was not a believer in underwear—not even panties. She was also a born exhibitionist. The ladder into the lifeboat was portable and steep, and Tallulah had to hike up her narrow skirt to climb it. She hiked it up to her waist. The first few times this happened the crew were startled; after that they yawned. They had seen it all before—and better.

Most of the actors would have taken their positions in the boat before Tallulah arrived. I was lying in the bottom of the boat one day, which meant that Tallulah had to step over me. She glanced down at me and said, "Getting a good look, Hume?" I muttered something noncommittal—and afterwards wished I'd had the courage to say, "Yes . . . give me a stick and I'll kill it," which was the punch line to one of Hitch's more bawdy jokes.

These exhibitions by Tallulah aroused no one on the set except a visiting lady journalist for one of the popular women's magazines. She had watched Tallulah climb into the boat and her sense of propriety was deeply shocked. She complained bitterly to the head of the publicity department, saying that Miss Bankhead's behavior was an offensive reflection on American womanhood. As a result, a terse memo was sent to our unit manager, Ben Silvey. Either Miss Bankhead must wear more clothing or the set would be "closed." Closing a set is a terrible nuisance. Policemen have to be posted at the doors to the soundstage; the press is barred, and anyone entering must produce an official pass. Since people from various studio departments are required to come and go all the time on short notice, a strict closing can slow things up considerably. Ben Silvey, a very big, genial man, somewhat overweight, always seemed to be perspiring. The memo put him into a lather; we already had enough problems.

Hitch and I had lunch together on the day of the memo. When we returned to the stage, Ben was waiting for us at the door, mopping his face. He explained the problem to Hitch and the difficulties that would ensue; he went into considerable detail, handed the memo to Hitch and ended up by saying, "So, Mr. Hitchcock, would you like to talk to her?" It was a desperate plea rather than a question. Hitch read the memo; he looked at Ben solemnly.

"Ben," he said, "I always try to avoid departmental disputes, and in this case it's difficult to know where the responsibility lies. You might say it was a matter for wardrobe . . . or makeup . . . or perhaps hairdressing."

He handed the memo back to Ben and proceeded onto the set.

No one ever did talk to Miss Bankhead. The set was closed.

I'm bound to acknowledge that professionally, Tallulah's behavior was impeccable. She was on time, she knew her lines, she took Hitch's direction beautifully, she always turned up to play a scene with the rest of us even though she herself might be off camera, and I never heard her complain about the working conditions. These were pretty rough; not only were we frequently wet, cold, and covered with diesel oil (I can still smell the stuff), but working in the tank was particularly hazardous—especially for me. I had to play a scene where the boat is caught in a roaring gale and my character gets washed overboard. I have read of cases where a man was washed overboard by one gigantic wave and washed back on board again by the next. Such was the scene I had to play, but there was no possible way to arrange this action without mechanical aid: that meant fitting the actor with a harness and attaching wires that hauled him out of the boat on cue, and then hauled him back in again. The mechanics were complicated and they were not about to let me attempt the scene. They planned on using a stunt double. The stuntman was about my height and coloring but bigger-boned, heavier. They rigged him up; released the water down all four chutes, and the boat practically disappeared in a maelstrom of white water. The double went overboard, was washed back in again, the camera (on a crane) moved in to show me lying in the bottom of the boat—and revealed a total stranger. It was as though the whale had spit up a Mr. Smith rather than Jonah. This wouldn't do at all.

There was nothing for it but to have me do the business myself. I put on the harness, feeling distinctly nervous, and they wired me up. The water came roaring down the chutes once more and over I went, only to be immediately buried in the turbulence which swept me under the boat and into the web of wiring that held it in place. I got tangled, and it was not a lot of fun. They told me afterward that when I failed to pop to the surface immediately, the stuntman dove in but couldn't find me. Stuntmen are like that. Theirs is a profession for which I have great respect. The best of them are very courageous, very cautious, and cool appraisers of the difficulties and dangers they may have to face. They also have a sense of responsibility for the safety of the actor they are covering.

When I finally did surface, lungs bursting, I was whipped back into the boat much too fast. The mechanics had been geared for the stuntman, who weighed thirty or forty pounds more than I did. I hit the gunwale so hard that I cracked two ribs and had to finish the film strapped up like a mummy. I remember the discomfort, but I don't remember missing a day's work.

There were two other films in which I chose to take damn-fool chances: *A Letter for Evie* and *Brute Force*. Both were directed by Jules Dassin (pronounced with a heavy French accent), an American who, like his colleague Joe Losey, has made many of his most memorable films abroad. They were both victims of the black list and the McCarthy era. I had known Julie since our earliest New York theater days, and I am forever grateful to him for casting me, in these two films, in parts which were a study in total opposites. One was a shy, diffident, decent man; the other, Captain Munsey, was a sadist of malignance and perverted power.

A Letter for Evie owes something to *Cyrano de Bergerac* in that both are the stories of plain men who undertake to write love letters for their more prepossessing friends, and end up revealed to the lady involved as the true lover. In *Evie*, the companions in arms were both G.I.'s, and in one scene, which took place at a carnival, a group of us played a game in which the prize was a kiss from a pretty, scantily clad show girl. There were six of these girls, each one standing at the end of a tight wire stretched across a sawdust pit. The game consisted of each participant trying to cross the wire and reach the girl to claim the kiss. It was of course the shy and inhibited one, played by me, who managed to negotiate the wire. The other contestants, all played by professional wire walkers, had to teeter violently and comically, and then fall off. Julie said he could never shoot the scene satisfactorily unless I walked the wire. They built the set in advance so I could rehearse. Under the guidance of one of the professionals, I practiced and practiced and fell and fell. To call it a bruising experience is an understatement. There was no danger in the fall itself; the pit was not more than six feet below me and there was a thick bed of sawdust. But as I fell, the wire would rip up my side like a paring knife on a carrot, so that from anklebone to armpit I became a mass of yellow, green and blue bruises. Jessica was horrified. Perhaps I should add that I did wear a metal jock strap.

In the second film for Dassin, *Brute Force*, there was a climactic scene in which Burt Lancaster, as a prisoner involved in a prison riot, confronts the sadistic prison guard Captain Munsey, played by me, on the top of a watchtower. They fight. Burt, who had at one time been a circus acrobat, was in magnificent physical condition and weighed about two hundred pounds. He could in reality have picked me up with one hand and wrung me out like a washrag. As a concession to the casting and the totally unbelievable match, it was agreed that before the struggle began, Burt's character should be shot and wounded. Even so, Julie staged one of the most murderously filthy fights ever photographed, so filled with kicks to the groin, eye gouging and karate chops that when the scene was cut together, it was considered altogether too violent for the public and portions of it were eliminated. Today, it would probably seem commonplace.

At the end of our fight Burt had to pick me up bodily—despite his having been "shot"—hold me above his head, and hurl me over the parapet of the tower to my deserved death, while a crowd of rioters in the prison courtyard below cheered. Very dramatic stuff but decidedly hazardous for me; and again Julie asked me to take the fall myself rather than use a stunt double. This meant a free-fall of about twenty feet, down from the tower to a specially built platform piled with mattresses and surrounded by padded railings to keep me from bouncing off. I've forgotten to mention an added hazard: the tower was on fire. While fires on sets are controllable, surrounding flames and smoke do not promote a sense of security, let alone confidence. I took the fall only once, with multiple cameras rolling, landed on my butt, climbed down from the scaffolding and went home fairly shook up. If I'd landed on my head, I could easily have broken my neck.

What impelled me to such idiot behavior? I didn't *have* to do any of these things. As Hitch had said to me on my first film, "the camera lies"—at least as frequently as it reveals an unsparing truth. The scenes described above could have been, *should* have been, done by a stunt double. I think the most compelling reason for my agreeing to do them myself is that it was *my* part and I wanted to play *all* of it, rather than hand part of it over to a stuntman. Added to that was sheer vanity. I was young, in good physical shape, athletic and cocky. Whatever the reasons, they were all terrible; and today I would advise any actor never, never to agree to do anything hazardous in a film if a stuntman is available. If he isn't, insist on getting one. He'll do the job better than you can and with far less risk to either one of you.

In the period 1942 to 1947, between my marriage to Jessica and her return to New York to appear again on the stage, I made about a dozen films. Some I've mentioned, some I haven't. Trying to pierce the veil of memory is a little like leafing through an old photograph album. The snapshots curl at the edges, fade, change color, or come loose from the adhesive and fall to the floor as you open the book. You pick them up and jam them back in any old place, and wonder where does this belong, when was it taken, where? I try to ignore those and concentrate on the pictures still firmly in place, where the image is so vivid you even remember the necktie you were wearing.

One of those memories is of *The Green Years,* a lovely story by A. J. Cronin, in which I played a penny-pinching sanitary inspector, Papa Leckie. Jessica, who in real life (forgive the ingallantry) is a couple of years my senior, played my daughter. Yes, daughter.

Jess had made a test and was immediately given the part. She was newly pregnant at the time, but as the film would be finished before the pregnancy showed, we didn't feel it was necessary to reveal her condition to the studio. Then there was a change of directors and the film got postponed for several months. That blew it. I can remember sitting in the M.G.M. commissary with Jessica explaining the situation to Victor Saville, the new director. Victor swore gently and looked reproachfully at me. "We'll have to recast." Of course. While we were delighted by the prospect of having another child, it was a pity to lose the opportunity of working together again, and besides, Jess was having a less satisfactory time at Fox than I was at Metro. They simply didn't seem to know what to do with her there.

I kept running into young actresses on the lot who were testing for the part of the Leckie daughter. All of them volunteered that before making their test they'd been shown the one Jess had made and been told, in effect, "This is what we want." Such a proceeding was highly unusual. As the date to commence shooting *The Green Years* got closer and closer and the part of Leckie's spinster daughter remained uncast, there was a great deal of speculation as to what the outcome would be. Victor resolved the mystery in a conversation with Jessica. "If you're willing to do it, I believe I can shoot it so that no one will ever know you're not a virgin." That was going to be quite an accomplishment, as by now Jess was in her seventh month and very big.

Never has an actress been shot behind so many pieces of waist-high furniture, carrying so many trays or bundled up in so many shawls. And never has an actress been treated with more loving care and consideration on the set. The director, assistant directors, and crew might have all been in training for service in a maternity ward. Jess was made to take regular rest periods, lunch was served to her in her dressing room, and her working day was short. With the timing that only an experienced and gifted actress can accomplish, she managed to give birth to our daughter, Tandy, one day after completion of principal photography: November 26th, 1945.

NINETEEN

Not all my energies were occupied in filmmaking. I maintained a passionate interest in the theater. A group of actors formed a "studio" in Hollywood, which they called the Actors' Laboratory Theater, more familiarly known as "the Lab." The hard core of the organization was made up of former members of New York's Group Theater, by this time disbanded: Morris Carnovsky, Roman "Bud" Bohnen, Art Smith, Phil Brown, and a host of new recruits with a theater background who found working in films unsatisfying, among them Anthony Quinn, Larry Parks and Vincent Price.

A loosely knit collection of people supported by the film industry, the Lab was held together by the practices of the Group, a hunger for the theater, and a political bias to the left that only became evident in policy discussions or its choice of plays.

As an example of the latter, I remember the controversy over a proposed production of Sartre's *No Exit*. John Huston was going to direct the play but was finding conditions in New York unsatisfactory. He suggested that he bring his cast out to the Lab to rehearse, and open the play there. The Lab had a lease on a small, shabby theater in Hollywood, just off Sunset Boulevard and immediately behind the landmark Schwab's

Drug Store. As with all small nonprofit theater companies, there
was a constant problem in finding attractions that would bring
in an audience and so pay the rent. Here was a heaven-
sent opportunity: Sartre was an exciting new playwright,
Huston a fine director, and the play itself filled with clash-
ing emotions and conflicting philosophies—or so I remember it.

In the windy discussions that followed Huston's proposal,
it became clear that a group of the Lab's founders was opposed to the presentation of any play by Sartre, on the grounds
of his shifting political attitudes. From having been a darling
of the Communist party-line, he had become anathema. The
argument was made that the Lab had a responsibility to its
audience, namely, to protect it from the dissemination of unacceptable ideas or the work of playwrights judged politically
unreliable. Unacceptable to whom? Judged by whom?

I got to my feet and said I thought the argument was spe-
cious rubbish. Were we about to undertake the role of censor,
prejudging what an audience should or should not see? Suppose an audience came to the play and were so deeply offended that they tore up the seats and threw them at the stage.
How wonderful! At least we would have moved them, made
them participants, something more than polite zombies ap-
plauding on cue.

It was of no avail. Huston had to take the play elsewhere.
However, with the exception of one or two skirmishes of this
nature, the political juggling at the Lab didn't affect me. I found
the dialectic argle-bargle boring and ignored it. Perhaps I was
what one of the the Lab members so bitterly called me, "politically naive." What interested me and ultimately Jessica was
the productions and the classes. There were a bright bunch of
students involved—one of whom, Joe Pappirofsky, was to make
theatrical history as Joseph Papp.

Little by little the Lab began to acquire a reputation for
the quality and originality of the work done there. Strictly
speaking, of course, most of us were moonlighting; we had
bread-and-butter jobs during the day. It was during weekends
and in the evenings that we turned to the Lab for a stimulating other-life.

The Lab proposed a bill of one-act plays by Tennessee Williams—three of the very same plays that I'd held under option seven years previously. The wheel of fortune had turned. It was suggested (or did I suggest it?) that Jessica play Miss Collins in *Portrait of a Madonna* and that I direct it. The play was a lovely, touching portrait of a lonely spinster suffering the bedevilment of violent sexual fantasies and the illusions of social ostracism. I had always loved it and welcomed the chance to direct it. It was to be the first of a number of times in which I was to direct Jessica.

I've been asked so often "What is it like to direct your wife?" that by this time it would be reasonable to expect that I might have developed some neat, nice, pat answer. But it isn't so. It's like that other frequent question, "How have you made it work?" referring to nearly half a century of marital collaboration. The only honest answer is "I don't know." What else am I to say? Certainly it is rewarding, loving, occasionally painful, filled with secret insights, disagreements and consequent compromises, but as for a formula, we haven't got one. We have a meld of differences.

But I do wish she wouldn't rehearse alone in the bathtub. It makes me feel laggard, as though all those hours spent on a rehearsal stage or in the film studio weren't enough, and that I must be shirking because I want to come home, just read the newspaper, and forget about tomorrow's hurdles.

To say that Jessica's performance in *Portrait of a Madonna* took the town by storm may be a cliché, but it is not, I think, an exaggeration. The reviews were lyrical, and I remember the visits backstage by David Selznick, Charlie Chaplin, Hitch and George Cukor and the extravagance of their compliments. There was only one dissenting voice and that came from Twentieth Century–Fox. What did Jessica think she was up to? Didn't she realize that she was under exclusive contract to them, and no one had given permission for this excursion into the theater? The fact that the work had been done entirely on her own time and that *their* actress's reputation was enhanced had no effect whatever. Joe Mankiewicz wrote the following letter to Darryl Zanuck, but it cut no ice either.

January 16, 1947

Dear Darryl:

I think you owe it to yourself to devote one half hour of an evening to attend the one-act play that Jessica Tandy does at the Las Palmas theatre in Hollywood. It is one of a group of one-acters presented by the Actors Lab.

I have rarely seen acting to equal hers, and even more rarely seen a very tough, invited professional audience brought cheering to its feet as spontaneously. By the way, she does not play an Englishwoman.

Tandy has it all over Bette Davis as an actress, and is certainly more attractive. It would be a great pity if we were to miss out on a possible dramatic star by the unfortunately too prevalent custom of doing nothing with a vibrant personality and great talent.

I am taking the liberty of sending substantially this same memo to many of the producers on the lot. I know you won't mind.

J.L.M.

Fox didn't penalize the erring Miss Tandy, but they pouted. M.G.M. couldn't have cared less about my own involvement.

Somewhere in this period, I was able to pay a visit to New York and called on my old friend Audrey Wood. She handed me a new play by Tennessee Williams, with a curious title: *A Streetcar Named Desire.*

No, I didn't realize that I was reading one of the theater masterpieces of the twentieth century, but when Audrey asked me, almost casually, if I had any idea who might be suitably cast as Blanche Dubois I didn't have to think twice. Audrey let me a carry a copy of the script back to California to show to Jessica. Subsequently, Tennessee, Elia Kazan (the director), and Irene Selznick (the producer) came out to California to see Jessica in *Portrait,* and the rest is, as they say, "on the record."

*   *   *

Los Angeles had a few good art galleries. We used to prowl through Hatfield's in the Old Ambassador Hotel, or visit Stendahl, who dealt out of his house. He had a mind-boggling collection of pre-Columbian sculptures and sold many beautiful pieces to Charles Laughton and our friends Bill and Greta Wright. But it was in the house-gallery of James and Annie Vigeveno that we spent some of our best times. James had been a dealer in Holland before the war, and could talk about European artists and their work endlessly. We would go there in the evenings, drink tea and listen to James, and he would produce yet another recently acquired treasure. I think his fellow refugees trusted him. So many paintings had come out to California secreted in someone's baggage or rolled up under the arm. James would either buy them outright or take them on consignment.

I suppose I owe my interest in paintings, and my first stirrings as a collector, to Kenneth Sanderson and those unwilling visits to the Royal Scottish Academy in Edinburgh, which I've written about previously. However, I didn't immediately go out and buy something; I was too unsure of myself for that and besides, in London, Ontario, there wasn't much to buy. One bookshop carried a small stock of etchings and steel engravings, and remembering Kenneth's enthusiasm for this genre, I acquired a few of those and hung them proudly in my room at Woodfield.

It wasn't until 1937 that I bought my first oil and thereby, as they say, hangs a tale.

I was playing in *High Tor* at the time (one of my few New York hits) and my route to the theater carried me through the R.C.A. Building. Among the various shops in the rotunda was one dealing in rare books and paintings. Prominently displayed in the window was a large seascape; massive rock formations on each side framed a small beach, and crashing in on it was a great wave just about to break. The artist had caught it at its crest, and sunlight, streaming through the curl, made the water seem translucent, a beautiful jade green. It was almost photographic in its reality—rather like one of those illustrations by N. C. Wyeth (only not so good) that were to be found in books I grew up on: *The White Company, Treasure Island* and *Kidnapped.*

For weeks I used to stand in front of that window waiting

for the wave to collapse into white foam and wash about my legs. Finally, I went into the shop and asked a very pretty salesgirl what the painting cost. Three hundred and fifty dollars. That was too much for me. The charming girl suggested that I might want to consider buying it on time—a sort of layaway plan. Would fifty dollars per week be acceptable? I said yes and so bought my first oil. I went into the shop weekly to put down my fifty bucks and became quite friendly with the girl. At the end of the seven weeks, I carried the painting back to my apartment and hung it in triumph. Not long after, the trouble started.

I grew tired of waiting for the wave to break and instead fixed on the rock formation to the right of the canvas. There, in profile, was the silhouette of one of the Trafalgar Square lions—or was it the one outside the New York Public Library? Never mind which, it was *there*. How had I missed it before? Now it became an obsession. I couldn't look at the damn painting without seeing my lion. I even said to one of my friends, "Do you like my lion?" when I meant to say, "Do you like my wave?" I was going crazy of course; the artist had seen no lion. He probably hated all cats.

Perhaps I could exchange the painting for something less troublesome. It was worth a try anyhow. I went back to the shop and waffled about an exchange—the canvas was too large for the space in which I'd hung it, or my wife (I didn't have one) hated it, or some lie. My old friend the pretty salesgirl listened in sympathy. "But I thought you loved the painting."

"Oh I do . . . I did . . . but you see there's this bloody lion . . ."

And then it all came out. I wasn't married. The space was fine; it was just that I was losing my mind. The girl smiled at me in compassionate understanding and said, "No problem. Where do you live?"

"On East 44th Street."

"Oh, that's not far. The young man who painted it is a friend of mine. I'll bring him over and he can touch up the rocks—and no more lion."

"You mean have him paint it out? I couldn't ask an artist to do that!"

"I'll ask him. He won't mind. Playwrights change lines in their plays, don't they?"

And I actually let it happen. That's the shameful part of the story; the rest of it is pure comedy.

On the appointed day, my friend the salesgirl showed up with her artist friend in tow. He was very tall, wore paint-spattered trousers and grubby white sneakers, and carried a small case like a toilet kit. He took one look at his painting and had the grace and generosity to say, "I see exactly what you mean. Well, we can fix that pronto."

He rummaged through his bag, producing brushes and several twisted tubes of paint.

"Oh my God, I didn't bring white lead."

"I'll get it! I'll get it—just tell me where."

"There's a place on 42nd Street—about eight blocks from here I'm afraid. I better go myself."

"No. No. You both have some coffee. It's fresh. There, in the kitchenette."

I was so eager to show my appreciation, to collaborate in this act of vandalism, that I'd accept no argument. I bolted out of the apartment and ran down 44th Street. I thought I remembered an artist's supply store near Grand Central Station—closer than the one he'd mentioned. I bought a tube of white lead and rushed back.

The door to my apartment opened into a sort of dogleg passage which led into the sitting room. If you were in there, you couldn't hear the front door open, and the passage was carpeted. Clasping the little paper bag holding the paint tube, I walked into my sitting room. There was no sign of the girl, but over the end of the sofa, which faced away from me, was a leg, presumably attached to a body. The heel of the grubby sneaker pointed to the ceiling, the toe to the floor; below it was a green sock, and an expanse of hairy calf. The rest was obscured by the sofa back.

I must have got out of there even more quietly than I'd come in, because when, after a decent interval, I telephoned from the lobby, the girl's answering voice was entirely unruffled. I read off the label on the paint tube and asked her if I'd got exactly what her friend wanted. There was a brief, muted inquiry at the other end before she came back and said, "Exactly." I apologized for being late, said I'd had trouble finding the art store and would be home in about ten minutes.

The actual touch-up can't have taken half so long. A daub here, a dab there, and the lion was exorcised. The painter and his girl departed, leaving me to the untouched coffee and my retouched painting. I don't believe it was a conspiracy on their part so much as a case of happy serendipity.

I felt more at ease with my painting after that, but never truly fell in love with it again. Some years later it was disposed of at a church bazaar.

I continued my collecting, such as it was, buying prints and reproductions and from the F.A.R. Gallery on Madison Avenue, a group of posters by Toulouse-Lautrec and Mucha. These were first-run lithographs, rare today, but they cost me about fifteen dollars apiece. I gave some away as Christmas presents. One of them, a picture of Jane Avril doing the cancan, still hangs in the apartment of my old friend Arlene Francis—a loving reminder of fifty years of friendship.

It was not until the mid forties, after my marriage to Jessica, that the collecting took a more serious turn, and then it may have been prompted as much by our owning a house and having wall space as by anything else. Up until that time, I'd stuffed things away in portfolios in my two-room apartment in New York. But there were other, equally important motivations in our collecting: we had great fun; we seemed to favor the atypical work of painters rather than the ones most immediately recognizable; we bought not only paintings but pre-Columbian sculpture and Chinese ceramics of the Tang period. We certainly didn't buy as investors. Consider: at one time I had, "on approval," two paintings from the Hatfield Gallery. One was a van Gogh portrait of the Bébé Roulin, the other a portrait of Renoir's favorite model and reputed mistress, Gabrielle. Hatfield had suggested a package deal—thirty thousand dollars for *both* of them. I felt that was more than we could afford. After a month on our walls the paintings went back to the gallery. A van Gogh and a Renoir for thirty thousand dollars . . .

By 1947, ten years after I'd bought my first oil, the one of the wave and my lion, we'd acquired works by Picasso, Rouault, Renoir, Modigliani, Derain, Forain, Grosz, Vlaminck, Cassatt, Utrillo, Boudin and of course the posters by Toulouse-Lautrec and Mucha. It's an eclectic list and sounds terribly rich. It would be now, representing a not-so-small fortune, but it wasn't then— and we had two salaries, which made it affordable.

We were adventurers rather than connoisseurs; we'd found a new passion outside our work and were indulging in it. Today, we don't own a single work by any of the artists mentioned above. They all disappeared to help finance a new adventure.

TWENTY

Following our work together on *Portrait of a Madonna,* Jess and I took off for the Bahamas. I'd chartered a boat and we sailed from Nassau to go bonefishing in the waters around Andros. The fifteen-knot wind blew constantly, our anchorages were uncomfortable, the head didn't work, and we had a stubborn, monosyllabic captain who hunched over his radio all day and insisted on running his generator at night. It was not a promising start to our second great adventure, one that was to continue over a period of eighteen years.

Like poor Miss Collins in *Portrait,* we are all possessed from time to time by mad fantasies. One of my more persistent ones had been to own an island in the Bahamas. It started back in my teen years, when local fishermen had taken me into the waters off the lonely but beautiful cays surrounding New Providence. I knew a lot of people in Nassau at that time, and a few of them were aware of my crazy dream. To most of them, the "out islands" were a place to go fishing or pigeon shooting. But live there? Never. You couldn't get anyone to work; you would be robbed deaf, dumb and blind; people were illiterate; a line of supply impossible; and so forth. None of this turned out to be true.

One of my Bahamian friends, whose name appears earlier

in these fragmented memoirs, was Charlie Turtle. Charlie didn't seem to think I was crazy.

"What are you looking for?"

"An island . . . somewhere."

"There's many an island. What sort?"

"Oh, not too big . . . somewhere I might build a house . . . maybe . . ." And I trailed off. I didn't really know what I was looking for, and Charlie's air of patient resignation recognized that.

"You look for five things: fresh water, a good anchorage, height of land, arable soil, and because you're a tourist, a beach."

"Where do I look, Charlie?"

His reply was unhesitating. "The Exumas. God made no other islands like them."

"Any particular island?"

"Have a look at Children's Bay Cay. Crown land—beautiful." He smiled, in reverie. "I always put in there on my way to George Town."

"What's there, Charlie?"

"Nothing. Absolutely nothing. . . . Beautiful . . ."

Another old friend, the real estate agent Harold Christie (he'd found Westbourne for my parents), also knew of my interest. He agreed with Charlie about the Exumas, but had never heard of Children's Bay. He wanted me to look at a place called Leaf Cay.

"I'll tell you what we'll do. I'll lay on a charter—seaplane— I'll pay half, you pay half. It will run you down there and back, won't take more than three or four hours. Carry a picnic, have lunch on the beach, look around. Swim. Your wife will love it."

I explained that we were just off to Andros and would have only three days left in Nassau on our return.

"The day after you get back then. Only three or four hours—maybe five. Great fun. I'll see to it. Chicken and papaya all right for the picnic? What do you want to drink?"

And it was settled.

When we got back from Andros, Jessica wanted nothing so much as a hot bath, a toilet that worked, and a meal that wasn't peas, rice and conch. She also wanted to put on a pretty dress and high heels and to window shop along Bay Street. But reluctantly she agreed to our little five-hour expedition—which in fact was to last five days.

We didn't go alone. Harold had made a few changes.

"The plane has seven seats, so I've asked old Charlie Turtle to go along with you. He knows those cays like the back of his hand. And Fred Wanklyn and his wife Susan would like to join you. Nice couple, and he's attorney general of the Bahamas—could be useful—and a fellow named Charlie Chaplin, *not* the actor. Decent sort, very quiet—English, interested in fish. But you're paying half the shot . . . any objections?"

It sounded great to me. The morning was beautiful, and we took off.

The beach at Leaf Cay was glorious, but the island itself seemed to me to be one large salt pond surrounded by a rim of rocky scrub. It didn't appeal. We explored, we swam, we worked up an appetite, but there was no lunch. The picnic had been overlooked. Not to worry, said the pilot; we could proceed to George Town, Exuma, and find something simple there.

Elizabeth Harbor, formed by Great Exuma on one side and Stocking Island on the other, must be one of the most inviting in the world, but the wind had come up again and we made a bumpy landing. The plane's floats yawed wildly as the pilot tried to keep a straight course through the whitecaps.

A boat put out from the government dock to fetch us; and going ashore, the pilot confided that he had a little problem. The plane had an oil leak and he'd found bits of mangled metal in the residue. He'd have to see to it.

It must have been a long look. I heard later that the plane never did leave Elizabeth Harbor—ever. It sat there, bobbing, for months, and despite the expertise of mechanics flown down from Nassau and the replacement of various parts, finally and ingloriously sank.

(Years later, when Children's Bay had become more reality than dream, I played with the idea of learning to fly, acquiring a plane of my own, and using it in the Bahamas. I sought advice from Jimmy Stewart, the only person I knew with considerable experience as a pilot. Jimmy is famous for his laconic speech.

"A seaplane?" he said.

"There's nowhere else to land."

"Salt water, huh?"

"That's all there is."

"Who'll service it?"

"I'll find someone in Nassau. They have planes going in and out of there all the time."

"How much flying you expect to do?"

"Oh, whatever's necessary to get my license, and after that maybe a few weeks every year."

There was a long pause before the verdict; then Jimmy drawled, "Well . . . sounds to me like a dandy way to drown." I dropped that fantasy on the spot.)

Once ashore at George Town, it became obvious that we were going to have to find another means of returning to Nassau, 150 miles away. Susan Wanklyn suggested that her husband might telegraph the governor and ask him to send down a plane to rescue us, but he brushed that aside. "Can't do that. We're not on official business, you know. This is just a lark."

I suppose it might have been a lark if the wind hadn't kept increasing, if we had had proper food, adequate clothing and a place to stay. Charlie solved the latter problem. His brother Morton, he said, had a house (the only house) across the harbor on Stocking Island. We could crash there.

We bought some canned goods from the small waterfront store and arranged for a boat to carry us over to Stocking. It was wet going and chilly. With Charlie's blessing we broke into the house, and somehow or other managed to put kerosene into the gasoline-powered generator and gasoline into the kerosene stove. We were damn lucky not to have blown ourselves up. We never did get the generator working, but there were candles. The house was musty with disuse and the wind moaned around it. We went to bed.

The next day was more of the same: wind and "hoody" skies (a graphic Bahamian description of an overcast). Again, the toilet wouldn't work because of dependence on the pump, which in turn depended on a resentful generator suffering from kerosene indigestion. Jess had to throw a blanket over her shoulders when she went out to use the bushes.

Despite the chill, Chaplin and I went spearfishing. The water was roiled up and we returned with only a few small but very welcome grunts. Fresh food! I'd noticed that Chaplin had eaten very little breakfast and even less lunch. I said something to him about it and he mumbled that bread and canned milk were fine. When taxed further, he admitted to having ulcers and finding them unreceptive to canned pork and beans.

So it went. It wasn't a very encouraging introduction to the Exumas. On the third day a U.S. Navy P.T. boat plucked us off Stocking Island and carried us back to its base on Great Exuma. The base was in the process of being decommissioned, and the skeleton crew remaining were bored and lonely. Their eyes brightened when they saw the two very attractive women in our party. Jessica and Susan were assigned to the moth-balled officers' quarters while we men were segregated else-where. The grub was fine, but yet again the toilets didn't work, even in the officers' quarters, and there was no hot water. There was always the sea and the men's showers, but the girls seemed to avoid those. Jessica began to complain that she smelled.

On the fifth day, the governor did send down a plane. I think they began to miss their attorney general. The day was as fair and beautiful as the previous ones had been uncom-fortable. We persuaded the pilot to fly over Children's Bay Cay and circled it twice before going on to Nassau. The island appeared to be about a mile and a half long by about a half a mile wide at its broadest point. There was one obvious hill and seven beaches, but it was impossible to judge the topography from the air. The whole island was covered by a dense scrub.

With only twenty-four hours left before the departure of our already postponed flight to California, I walked into the Crown Land's office and—without ever having set foot on it—made application to lease Children's Bay Cay.

The agreement provided that I might lease for a period of five years, but within that time I must "improve" the property ("improvement" not defined) by spending a specified amount of sterling. After that, upon payment of a further sum, I could apply for a grant in perpetuity. Our total commitment to the Crown Land's office—*including* the required improvement—was about fifteen thousand dollars. I had my island in the Ba-hamas, at least in theory. Now we had to get back to California where I was slated to play Dr. Robert Oppenheimer in *The Beginning of the End*; and Jess had to arrange to move to New York for the rehearsals of *Streetcar*.

We flew out of Nassau, leaving fantasies behind us, to join the real world, and to grapple with questions to which there were no certain answers.

Would *Streetcar* be a success? If it was, it meant Jess was committed to living in New York for a minimum of nine months. She had been "loaned out" by Fox to Irene Selznick for the duration of *Streetcar* but was expected to return to the fold once the engagement was over. Were we to sell the California house? Furnished or unfurnished? Start all over again? Where would we live with three children in Manhattan? What schools?

And in the middle of all this I bought an island? Crazy.

To start with, of course, Jessica would live in a New York hotel. Then there would be the pre-Broadway engagements in New Haven and Boston, and finally the opening at the Ethel Barrymore Theater on West 47th Street. There, the die of our family's immediate future would be cast. In the interim I was to become a commuter—that is, when my film assignments would allow it.

So much has been written about the original stage production of *A Streetcar Named Desire* that I am not tempted to add to it. Besides, I was on the periphery, the actress's husband. Among the authoritative versions of what transpired during rehearsals are Elia Kazan's overwhelming *A Life*, Audrey Wood and Max Wilk's *Represented by Audrey Wood*, and Donald Spoto's *The Kindness of Strangers*.

I don't remember the opening night of *Streetcar*. I was probably too nervous. Most certainly I was there, and according to at least one of the accounts mentioned above, the ovations lasted for a good thirty minutes. My only vivid memory is of the rehearsal and tryout period: a meeting on the sidewalk with Tennessee and Kazan during an intermission while the play was out of town. None of us of course knew that we were discussing a landmark production—one of the great plays of the twentieth century, a masterpiece. I thought the play was too long, and that about ten minutes needed to come out. It was not a new argument; with Tennessee's approval, Kazan had already cut five or six pages in rehearsal. Suddenly, Tennessee turned to me and said, "All right, *you* cut it." It was not a joke, not a put-on, not ironic. When I protested he said, "No. I mean it—I can't do it."

I couldn't either. I tried. I holed up in my hotel room with a script and a stopwatch. At the end of hours of consideration, I estimated that my cuts added up to approximately one minute and fifteen seconds' playing time. The fabric of the play was simply too tight. If you cut, you lost something contributive to the whole.

Maybe the play wasn't too long after all.

TWENTY-ONE

I LAY NO CLAIM to the gift of prescience. I'm a compulsive planner, but that's no more than a futile if optimistic defense against a threatening future. Fortunately, most of the terrible things I can see ahead of me have never come to pass. However, if I have a plan, if I can look in my diary and see that on such and such a day I will do this and that, I feel relatively safe—well, safer. If I have a diary entry, I can persuade myself that half the battle that lies ahead is already won. I'm sure my death is going to be a terrible personal inconvenience. I doubt that it will have been planned, and diary entries will be left undone. Perhaps I won't care. That would be nice.

Whether it was before, during, or after *Streetcar* that I did have a flash of prescience, I don't remember. But I thought I saw on the horizon a cloud in the shape of a black box. Television. I thought that with that cloud would come an end to the studio system with its vast list of contract players, and that one day M.G.M. would find itself, like the mythical emperor, wearing not much more than a jockstrap. Did I want to hang around for that? Did I want to hang around anyway? I would walk up Rockingham Avenue and down Bristol, around the circle at Sunset and home again, chewing the inside of my cheek in anxiety and trying to decide what my next move should be. I was quite sure that I was never going to become a star. I was a useful character actor, just lucky enough—and stubborn enough—to have had a long succession of very different roles. And how long would that continue? After *Brute Force*, for instance, I was under real pressure to play every other miserable sadistic character that came along; if Granny was to be pushed down the stairs in her wheelchair, or some child raped in the bushes, the script would come to me. My old acquaintance, the specter of repetition, would flap its horrid wings before my eyes, and I would threaten to gnaw a hole in my cheek.

When finally I took my problem to Benny Thau and asked to be released from my M.G.M. contract, he listened impassively, as always, and as always said, "We'll see about it."

I think Benny was surprised by my request. Actors of my status didn't usually ask for a release from their contract. They were far more likely to sweat out an option period, praying that the studio would pick up their contract and so guarantee financial security for another year. Option time is one of my few genuinely unpleasant memories of Hollywood in the days of the great studios. There was that look of anxious preoccupation on a friend's face; all the brave and generally self-deceiving talk of alternatives; the ground fog of fear that seeped up between the cracks of the pavement outside the elegant establishments of Beverly Hills. Will we be able to afford this tomorrow? What do "they" think I'm worth? Am I worth anything? And if . . . how do I pay the mortgage?

In playing Robert Oppenheimer, I faced that age-old problem of the actor required to portray a familiar public figure: how does one give a convincing illusion of the real man? There were newsreels, documentaries, endless press photographs, scientific papers which I didn't understand. I studied them all. I didn't want to attempt an imitation, but I needed a hook. In playing F.D.R. for instance, the actor can latch onto a particular voice, a speech pattern, the tilt of the head, the jaunty cigarette holder, a wheelchair, the blanket, and so forth. With Oppenheimer there seemed to be only that porkpie hat. So I wrote to him. I explained my limitations: that we had little in common except for our long faces and lean figures— though I was shorter than he was, and would have to wear lifts, those uncomfortable elevator shoes that made you feel you were standing on a ski run. I promised to try to capture his quality but begged him to be prepared to have family and friends say, "Oppie, he's *totally* unlike you."

I got a charming reply, and one day, Oppenheimer was ushered onto the set by our producer. We were playing a scene that required a long tracking shot across the desert at Los Alamos. The camera dolly, on tracks, pulled away directly in front of us for a considerable distance as we kept pace with it. General Groves, played by Brian Donlevy, was on my right, and Robert Walker, playing a young physicist colleague, on my left. We were discussing matters related to the bomb. We had just finished rehearsing when Oppenheimer appeared. He recognized me, took off his porkpie hat and skimmed it across the studio in my direction. I took off my own, which was a duplicate, and put on his, where it sat like a pea on a pumpkin. Returning his hat, I shook hands with him and got back into position for the first take. Then a terrible thing happened.

The director invited Oppenheimer to sit on the camera dolly directly below the lens. There he was, the man I was playing, not more than twelve feet in front of me, *smiling*. It was the most intimidating moment I ever spent before a camera. I wonder how Oppie would have felt if I had been leaning over his shoulder, grinning, during that first nerve-wracked countdown at Los Alamos.

"Action," said the director. The camera began its long pull back, the three of us started walking—and I promptly stumbled over the dolly track. "Cut. Back to your original marks, please, once more." We lined up for take two. "Action!" This time I must have traveled no more than six paces before I forgot my words. "Cut. Back again."

Bob Walker hissed at me: "Pretend he's someone else." Fat chance. My shirt was sticking to my torso with sweat. I don't remember what I did wrong on take three, but something. As we went back to the starting point, it was Donlevy, an old-timer, who said, "Hang in there, kid." Then the director's voice: "Hume, is something bothering you?"

"Yes. He is."

I didn't mean Oppie to hear me, but obviously he did. He

leapt from the dolly, saying, "How damn stupid of me!" and apologized profusely.

"My fault," said the director, "but I didn't think anything ever bothered Hume. . . . Stand behind the camera, Doctor. You'll see just as well." And we got the shot.

It wasn't a very good film. They tried to marry a docudrama to a romance between Bob Walker and Audrey Totter. It didn't work.

Whenever it was that I received my release from M.G.M., it left me free—but lonely. "Big brother," or Daddy, was not there anymore; neither were the weekly paychecks. It was clear that Jessica would be tied up for many months to come, playing *Streetcar* in New York. The children had already gone to New York to join her. What were we to do about our California house? What was I to do about me? I was seized by that age-old actor's panic that comes along with the end of every play, film, or manuscript: "I'll never work again." And then fate stepped in as it had once before, in the now familiar figure of Alfred Hitchcock.

He wanted me to help him prepare a screen treatment of the Patrick Hamilton play *Rope,* a story based on the infamous Loeb-Leopold murder of a young man in Chicago. But why me? I had no screenwriter credits. A couple of my short stories had been published; I'd written and sold a screenplay that was never made and that I doubt he ever saw. Perhaps he just wanted someone to talk to, to use as a sounding board for his ideas. Whatever his reasons, I wasn't about to question an offer that almost any screenwriter would have jumped at.

When Hitch found a story he liked, he enjoyed talking about it. He would spin the tale and dwell lovingly on its climaxes, its surprises, and how the camera would enhance these. I can see him now, seated, waving his thick, stubby-fingered hands about, simulating the camera movements, or making a frame to demonstrate precisely what the picture was to encompass or exclude. He thought in images. The story was to be pictorially revealed, not just told; and he brought together the gifts of art director and cutter in the telling. Sometimes his images were so bizarre, or became so fixed in his mind, that they proved a stumbling block to logic. When I questioned such moments,

Hitch would speak derisively of "the icebox trade."

For Hitch, the icebox trade was a group of people who had seen and thoroughly enjoyed a movie, then repaired to somebody's kitchen, raided the icebox (refrigerator), fixed themselves a snack, had a beer, and proceeded to discuss the film they'd just seen. "They'll always find flaws—no matter how much they've enjoyed themselves. I can't worry about that as long as they've been totally persuaded while watching the film." His contempt for such postmortems was absolute.

Hitch was in his element when there were horrendous technical problems involved in bringing a story to the screen, as in *Rear Window* (all shot from the point of view of one apartment and its window); *Lifeboat* (ninety percent of it shot before a process screen or in a tank on the back lot); or *The Birds* (handling all those birds, both indoors and out). I sometimes suspected that he chose such stories for the very technical problems which they posed. *Rope* was another example.

Rope was a story told in one location and in continuous time. Hitch had decided to make it in a series of very long takes, each the full capacity of a reel of film: a thousand feet, or about ten minutes of screen time. The only cuts were to be dictated by the camera running out of film. This concept, never attempted before (or since, as far as I know), was to serve this particular story. Whether it did or not I'm not sure, but it made for some very knotty problems in writing the treatment. Perhaps only a screenwriter will immediately recognize these: ten-minute takes that allowed for long shots, closeups, over the shoulders, inserts—but no cuts! The camera would have to dance, the lighting would be a nightmare, the actors would have to be meticulously rehearsed.

Hitch and I would sit in the garden of his Bel Air house, talk, discuss and argue; then I would go back to North Rockingham Avenue and put it all down on paper. We did not meet every day; I was too busy scribbling for that. When we did meet, there were certain hazards to be avoided; one of the most severe was that I should not get drunk. Hitch was a great believer in a relaxed approach to work, and before lunch the wine bottle would appear and he would descant on the vineyard, the vintage, and the nature of the grape as he poured

and poured again. It was a beguiling ritual but a very dangerous one for me.

Early on in our working relationship I discovered a curious
trick of his. We would be discussing some story point with great
intensity, trembling on the edge of a solution to the problem
at hand, when Hitch would suddenly lean back in his chair
and say, "Hume, have you heard the story of the traveling
salesman and the farmer's daughter?" I would look at him
blankly and he would proceed to tell it with great relish, frequently commenting on the story's characters, the nature of
the humor involved, and the philosophical demonstration implied. That makes it sound as though the stories might be profound or at least witty. They were neither. They were generally
seventh-grade jokes of the sniggery school, and frequently in-
fantile. I remember only one of them—which Hitch told in a
broad cockney accent that I can't reproduce on paper.

> Two teenagers run into a filthy alley, a boy pursuing a flir-
> tatious girl. The boy blocks her escape:
>
> BOY: Give us a kiss.
> GIRL: No.
> BOY: Why not?
> GIRL   *(simpering)*: I don't want to.
> BOY: Tell us your name then.
> GIRL: Noo.
> BOY: Why not?
> GIRL: I'll give you a hint.
> BOY: Wot's that then?
> GIRL   *(giggling)*: It's the stuff that sticks to the wall.
> BOY: Wot? . . . *Shit?*
> GIRL   *(outraged)*: Noooo! It's *Ivy*.

Hitch then went on to explain the story's contradictions:
how preposterous it was that the boy should think the girl's
name might be "Shit," and yet how logical considering their
location and his experience.

After several days' work together, punctuated by such stories, I challenged him—politely. "Why do you do that?"

"Do what?"

"Stop to tell jokes at a critical juncture."

"It's not so critical—it's only a film."

"But we were just about to find a solution to the problem. . . . I can't even remember what it was now."

"Good. We were pressing. . . . You never get it when you press."

And while I may have failed to appreciate Hitch's jokes, I've never forgotten that little piece of philosophy, either as an actor or as a sometime writer.

On another occasion, we were arguing about some story point or other, when he seized my pad and pencil and drew a large circle.

"This is the pie. We keep trying to cut into it here." And he drew a savage wedge into the circle's perimeter.

"What we must try to do is *this*—" and the pencil raced around the opposite side of his pie and dug a wedge in there.

I blinked. "What does that mean? . . . Turn day into night? Color into black and white? Change our antagonist into our hero? . . ."

"Maybe. What we're doing is all so . . . expected. I want to be surprised."

It was a very old lesson demonstrated in graphic form. Logic is so frequently boring. It's the contradictions that are fascinating.

In the year following *Rope,* Hitch asked me to do another treatment, this one based on Helen Simpson's novel *Under Capricorn.* It was to star Ingrid Bergman and Joe Cotten, a sprawling panoramic story of Australia in the days of penal transportation. Hitch wanted to shoot *Capricorn* in the same style he'd used so successfully in *Rope*—in a series of long takes. That was a mistake, and I knew it, but even I, as friend and collaborator, was not about to tell him so. You simply did not tell Alfred Hitchcock how to shoot—or how not to shoot—a film.

I went to London with Hitch to work on *Capricorn.* We would meet for our story conferences at Sidney Bernstein's offices in Golden Square. From the beginning, the work was fraught with problems. On one particular morning, with Hitch at the end of the table and Sidney and I on either side of him,

Hitch suddenly reared back in his chair, scowling like an angry baby, and announced, "This film is going to be a flop. I'm going to lunch." And he stalked out of the room, pouting.

I was appalled; Sidney was immediately solicitous. "Now, Hume, don't be upset. You know Hitch: he'll have a good lunch, come back, and everything will be serene."

It was true; I'd seen Hitch suffer these tantrums before. He never had them on the set; by the time we got there, the whole film was already shot in his head, down to every cut and camera angle. (He used to say that the actual shooting of a film bored him; he'd already made it.) But during a film's preparation he could become very mercurial; his emotional thermometer would soar to over a hundred degrees in enthusiasm, only to plunge below freezing in despair. We were alike in that, and I should have been more philosophical about the morning's upset. The trouble was that in this particular instance I had the awful, nagging suspicion that Hitch's premonition was accurate.

During the afternoon's work we found a way round the morning's gridlock, and while I found the detour less than satisfying, Hitch was restored to a benign humor. He asked me to have dinner with him at the Savoy. When I arrived he was positively purring. There were two long-necked bottles of wine sitting in the cooler. I remember that they had mauve caps.

"The last two bottles of this in the Savoy cellar . . . and we're going to drink them both."

The wine was "Schloss Johannisberger, Fürst von Metternich," of a rare vintage which I've forgotten. We had dinner, we drank the two bottles, and I staggered out of the hotel in need of fresh air and a long walk. I weaved down the Strand, across Trafalgar Square and along Piccadilly to my hotel and fell into bed. I remember that walk because of my anxiety over the treatment—but to Hitch, at least on that one evening, it was "only a film."

I should make it clear that on both *Rope* and *Capricorn* I wrote only the "treatments." The screenplays were written by Arthur Laurents and James Bridie, respectively. I never knew Arthur well, but Bridie—old enough to have been my father,

and the author of fifteen to twenty plays—became a great
friend. Among his best-known plays were *Storm in a Teacup, A
Sleeping Clergyman, The Black Eye* and *The Anatomist.* By profession, Bridie was a doctor, Dr. Osborne Mavor. I found his
accomplishments intimidating and the man himself endearing.
We corresponded for some years and in one letter he told me
that he'd written a play called *Daphne Laureola* and asked me
if I'd care to present it in New York. I read the play and simply didn't understand it. There was nothing for it but to write
back and tell him so. You can't fudge judgments with friends.
I quote exactly from his reply because it makes a very telling
point, offering a prescription for a good play that's hard
to beat.

> I honestly can't understand how any countryman of Wil-
> der, Saroyan, Faulkner and Tennessee Williams—let alone
> your bright, intelligent self—should find the play in the
> least bit obscure. But of course you aren't a fellow country-
> man of these persons. . . . The play is of course what *all
> plays ought to be*: *a story, a poem, and a philosophical demonstra-
> tion* [italics mine]. The story here is dead simple. . . .

There followed several typed pages outlining the story, his
employment of poetic symbolism, and its philosophical demonstration. I still didn't understand it.

Several months later the rights to *Daphne Laureola* were acquired by Laurence Olivier, and it was presented at Wynd-
ham's Theatre with Edith Evans to great acclaim. So much for
my opinion. Rather defensively, I add that when Leland Hay-
ward brought *Daphne Laureola* to New York—again with Dame
Edith and a first-rate cast—it lasted only a few weeks. As for
my adopted fellow countrymen, they (with one or two exceptions) didn't fare so much better in England either. The transatlantic traffic in plays is always hazardous.

Between the time of my morose walks around Brentwood,
wondering whether I would ever work again, and the time
that Jessica returned to California almost two years later, I
seem to have made two films; written the two screen treat-

ments for Hitchcock; appeared on Broadway in *The Survivors*—which didn't; and played Hamlet.

During this period, my son Christopher, aged about six, had his tonsils removed. Jess took him a game to play on his hospital bed. It was a board, rather like an enlarged chessboard but painted to represent a farm, with fields, woods, a stream, farm roads, etc. To be fitted onto the board were any number of miniature pieces: the farmhouse, barn, outbuildings, cows, horses, chickens, and so forth; all to be arranged to suit the child's fancy, then rearranged again. Chris was enchanted and announced firmly that when he grew up he was going to become a farmer. Reminded that he'd also said he wanted to become an actor, he had an immediate answer. "Well, I'll play Hamlet on Sundays."

I didn't quite do that, but it was damn close. I was allowed eight days of rehearsal. *Eight days* in which to learn and presume to play the greatest role in English literature? I must have been out of my tiny mind. What gall! What idiocy!

But I was certain that I would never get such an opportunity again and I grabbed at it. Today, knowing a little more, I would be about as likely to try to jump between the towers of the World Trade Center. This touring production of *Hamlet* had been directed by Robert Breen and was a joint presentation of the Barter Theater and the American National Theater and Academy (ANTA). Ultimately, the company was to travel to Denmark and perform at Elsinore. Breen, who had been playing "the gloomy one," didn't want to miss out on the Danish engagement but had to fulfill a conflicting commitment beforehand. A replacement had to be found to complete the American tour. I was that replacement.

Fortunately, I knew the play pretty well. Less fortunately, I had, over a period of twenty years, played the John Barrymore recordings of *Hamlet* until the disc was worn out, and when I got into rehearsal, I was haunted by that great voice and Barrymore's timing and interpretation. Those echoes were pure hell and made it doubly difficult to find my own interpretation and voice.

I played with the company for about eight weeks, touring, largely through the southern states. I believe the closest we got to a large metropolitan center was on the outskirts of Washington. There, one of the critics of that city's leading papers, headed his review "Hamlet on the Half Shell." While somewhat obscure, I don't think it can be interpreted as congratulatory. Nevertheless, I'm glad I did it, and when, fifteen years later, I appeared as Polonius in the Gielgud production of the play starring Richard Burton, it was comforting to have been at bat before. At least I felt I knew what the play was about—and there were no Barrymore readings to haunt me then.

When Jess got off her *Streetcar,* it was up stakes again and back across the continent. For the best part of the two years that she had been away we'd been able to make a near-ideal arrangement. We swapped houses. Great friends of ours, Virginia and John Becker, wanted to go to California. They took over our house on Rockingham Avenue, and we took theirs on Riverview Terrace. The latter, a small, private street running between 58th and 59th Streets, as far east on Manhattan as you can go without falling into the river, was enchanting and close to the children's school. Now the time had come to switch back again. Jess had to fulfill her contract with Twentieth Century–Fox. We hoped that on her return and as a result of her triumph in *Streetcar,* the studio might make better use of her.

The telephone rang about a week after we'd resettled into our own house:

"Miss Tandy? This is the casting department at Fox. Congratulations on your New York engagement. I'm sure you must be pleased. . . . Could you tell us how tall you are? . . . I see. Thank you very much . . . and welcome home!"

It was the only official studio recognition that she received, and it did not bode well.

Life has its chapters. You come to a dead halt and wonder: "What next?" When Jessie finished her run in *Streetcar* in June of '49 she'd given about six hundred performances as Blanche Dubois. She was tired, and the next job was immediate; too soon, in fact. She agreed to go to Stanford University and do a tryout production of *Now I Lay Me Down to Sleep.* I was directing—in fact I held an option on the play—and I suspect she agreed to do it largely to please me.

The novel *Now I Lay Me Down to Sleep* was written by Ludwig Bemelmans and dramatized by Elaine Ryan. It was a wonderfully bizarre, comic and touching story about a sweet but lecherous South American general in love with life, and of his pursuit of a shy, inhibited, Englishwoman in love with death. The characters were as bold and original as a Bemelmans cartoon, embodying both Bemmy's sophistication and childlike innocence. I was enchanted by them, by the fantastic story, by the lushness of the Ecuadorean settings and by the challenge. However, the play, to employ an overworked phrase, "needed work."

If my approach to *Hamlet* had been a leap between the World Trade Center's towers, the prospect of directing *Now I Lay Me Down to Sleep* was no less terrifying. The play had six sets and forty-seven characters! It was on the scale of a multimillion-dollar musical, and I'd only directed two plays previously: "intimate" productions of Molnár's *The Good Fairy,* with Walter Slezak, and *Portrait of a Madonna,* with Jessica.

But I took the risk all the same. I had an image of Orson Welles in my head. When Orson directed his Mercury Theatre's production of *Julius Caesar* in 1937, I'd seen it and been mightily impressed. There were those, including Jessica, who felt the play had been tarted up to serve contemporary relevance at the expense of William Shakespeare, but I didn't agree. I found the production spellbinding. Orson came into Sardi's one day when I was having lunch alone. He loomed over my table as I spoke with admiration of his work with the ensemble and particularly of the scene where the mob threatens Cinna, the poet (most beautifully played by Norman Lloyd), a scene often scanted in more conventional productions. I ended my hymn of praise by saying how much I admired his courage. Orson looked a bit puzzled. "Courage?" he said. He slapped a hand across his eyes, then took a giant goose step forward. It was a step into the unknown, and a demonstration of attitude that I've never forgotten.

So ten years later I took off for Stanford University in Palo Alto, California, and arrived in a tumult of actors and scenery. Akim Tamiroff was to play the general. He was wonderfully right for the part both in appearance and quality, but rehearsals soon made it evident that he was scared stiff. Jess, though tired, was solid as a rock. It was immediately obvious that ninety percent of my work would have to be with Akim—not to mention miles of scenery and the other forty-five actors, about half of whom were university students. (One of these was Jules Irving, who in later years was to become artistic director of the Vivian Beaumont Theater at Lincoln Center and the father of Amy Irving.) The students were all quite wonderful, and so was the technical staff in coping with a monstrous production that, among other details, required a full-scale earthquake— on stage.

Working with a frightened actor is always difficult. Complicating this particular situation was Akim's accent. As he became more nervous he became ever less intelligible, so that in the general's tantrums and epileptic fits he seemed to talk gibberish. Worst of all was his self-persuasion that he couldn't remember the words. Despite a solid theatrical background in his native land, his many years of filmmaking had allowed his actor's muscles to grow flabby. Memory, like every other skill, has to be exercised. During a stage performance, there are no retakes, no second or third chances. It was painful to watch Akim's fragile confidence turn into a creeping paralysis of anxiety. By the end of the second week of rehearsal, he wanted to quit. I did everything I could to support and encourage him, but patience takes time—time that I owed to the rest of the company and to solving the myriad technical problems. In the end there was nothing for me to do but to take him aside and make him a promise.

"Akim, you can be absolutely wonderful in this part. There's nothing in it you can't do brilliantly. That's already obvious and you've barely begun. Now, for God's sake trust yourself— and me. You're driving yourself mad over the words, but they will come . . . believe me, Akim, they will come, when you stop torturing yourself.

"You know what every scene is about, just concentrate on the other people and the moment. *Don't* look ahead, and the right words will come. . . .

"Look, I'll make a bargain with you. Stick with it as long as you can and stop worrying because . . . if at *any* time from this moment up until five days before the opening, you decide you really can't do it—which is rubbish—I'll take over and play the part myself. That's a promise . . . and there'll be no argument. I can't possibly do it as well as you can, but I'd rather try than have you continue to be so miserable. That affects the whole company. After all, this isn't life or death. It's only a play."

Thank God he didn't take me up on it. I could have probably handled the words, I knew the text so well; but what about the costumes? It would have taken a gross of safety pins to fit me into Akim's clothes. And what about the rest of the company, playing with a new actor and relying on a director who was on stage with them and couldn't possibly be objective?

Fortunately, none of these nightmares turned into reality. From the moment I put this safety net under Akim, he became infinitely more secure. His problems were largely psychological; he still stumbled over certain speeches, but far more important, he recovered his natural relish, a quality vital to the character of the general.

When I eventually directed the play in New York, in a production by George Nichols III and Nancy Stern, the part of the general was played by Fredric March and the part of Mrs. Graves by his wife, Florence Eldridge. Jess had commitments elsewhere and was, I suspect, relieved. Stanford had not been easy.

Working with the Marches was a joy. Freddy was not only a superb actor but had great panache: a charisma that overshadowed Florence and was absolutely right for the general. Florence, on the other hand, was, I think, an even better actor. Less flamboyant than Freddy, she was at least as talented and extremely intelligent. She was the balance wheel in their relationship. Generally, Florence looked on her husband's peccadilloes with the tolerant eye of a loving mother dealing with a naughty boy. Freddy, I must emphasize, was not a playboy. He was hard-working, generous to a fault, amusing, handsome, an occasional bottom pincher—and catnip to the girls. He couldn't help his wayward hands, and Florence, wise as she was, chose to look the other way.

Some years after Freddy's death, Florence told me the following story. When he was in the hospital and very ill, Florence spent most of her days with him. While Freddy slept, she would creep out of his room and sit in the sun-room at the end of the hospital corridor. She had been given a lot of books by friends who were aware of her painful vigil, and she'd take a couple of these with her and leaf through them as she waited. One of the books was about Carole Lombard, who had worked with Freddy in the film *Nothing Sacred*. Lombard, no puritan herself, recounted with glee that, being aware of Freddy's tendencies, she was fully prepared for him. When Freddy got his hand up her skirt, he discovered she was wearing a dildo.

"I read that and I was furious!" said Florence. "It seemed like such an indignity. I marched into his room and gave him absolute hell."

I asked her what Freddy had said.

"Oh darling, he couldn't say anything . . . he was dying."

Florence's anger had very little to do with Freddy's behavior. As she told me the story she was laughing. It was the "indignity" of the story—the light that it seemed to throw on her husband—that she resented.

When *Now I Lay Me Down to Sleep* opened in New York after the usual out-of-town preliminaries, critics found the play wanting: too episodic, too sprawling, unwieldy and lacking in substance. Worst of all was the opinion that Bemelmans's particular brand of humor was impossible to recapture on the stage. That upset me because I felt I understood Bemmy's humor very well. His was the sort of maverick personality that had attracted me ever since my school days: witty, mad, cocking a snook at the whole world; sophisticated, urbane, a true cosmopolitan. I kept getting letters from him—copiously illustrated in the margins—postmarked Paris, London, Rome, and so on. Most of these exhorted me to be of good cheer ("It's only a play") and to stop worrying. My favorite is all of twelve words long. Pasted onto the middle of his notepaper is a newspaper clipping surrounded by a black border. It reads:

> With extreme grief and reverence
> we mourn the loss of our beloved President
> ISRAEL MATZ

Out of respect to his memory, our domestic
and foreign offices and plants will be closed
Monday, February 13th.

EX–LAX, INC.

Bemmy's twelve words follow.

> Dear Hume
>> For heaven's sake
>> RELAX
>> Look what happened
>> to the President of
>> EX–LAX

And an excerpt from another one, dated April 11th, 1948,
written on the paper of Hotel Baur au Lac Zurich:

> Myself, have found that I am not much good close to
> production, my mind flies off, I invent new acts which never
> fit, my talent is that of a painter and I have enough trouble
> getting by writing; I think you are best left alone in all
> departments. I have the confidence in you that I usually
> reserve for the pilots on planes I fly, so that I can go to
> sleep quietly.
> My Rome address is the Hotel Excelsior.
>
> Yours, Ludwig

Bemmy was right about one thing, he wasn't able to be a
great deal of help where the play was concerned, except as a
one-man cheering section, and our dramatist, a very nice, very
nervous lady, was quite unable to pull the warp and the woof
together to make a tight coherent whole. This extravagant
production, despite Florence's and Freddy's excellent performances, closed rather quickly. Nonetheless, I wouldn't have
traded the experience for anything, and I got three letters of
appreciation from directorial experts (George Kaufman, Howard Lindsay, and Stanley Kramer) that meant much to me. It
was my first Broadway production as a director.

My second, done eight months later, was *Hilda Crane*, by Samson Raphaelson, where personally I fared rather better. Commercially, however, it was another failure.

This repetitious account of flops, as both actor and director may seem odd in a career which I hope is looked upon as fairly successful, but what the public at large refuses to recognize—and which, thank God, professionals forget—is that a long life in the theater is almost inevitably a history of commercial failure. The hits, the really substantial box-office successes, are few and far between. Failure is the norm; success the exception. It's like an old-fashioned bread pudding containing a few raisins, or one of those children's birthday cakes in which one or two dimes have been secreted. You have to swallow a lot before coming on a happy surprise. If an actor or director can *average* one genuine box-office success every five years, he or she hasn't done too badly. In over fifty years at bat I've just about managed it. And with that smug little pat of self-reassurance, I go back to 1950.

Jess and I did three plays together that year: the Bemelmans and *Hilda Crane* (in each of which I directed her) and Edmund Wilson's *The Little Blue Light*, in which we acted together at the Brattle Theater, in Cambridge, Massachusetts. My memories of the latter two productions are of the irrelevant snapshot variety. I see Wilson, bald-headed, flushed and perspiring, sitting on the floor, back propped against a wall at the first-night party. He is wearing a crumpled white suit with dark rings of nervous sweat around the armpits and is happily drunk, as well as being uncharacteristically benign.

I was thoroughly intimidated by Wilson; he was so appallingly erudite. There seemed to be no subject I could mention on which he wasn't a total authority. Even today, Edmund Wilson's writings on subjects as diverse as poetry, crime, social justice, American history, the Dead Sea Scrolls, economics, music and so on and so on, must make him one of the two or three outstanding critics-at-large of the twentieth century. Inevitably our conversations were all one-way streets—going his way.

Many years ago I was having dinner with Walter Lippmann in Washington. I asked him some ingenuous question about political problems in the Middle East. He sighed heavily, gave me a long, cold stare and then said: "Hume, I really can't discuss it with you unless you're better informed."

I kept waiting for Wilson to say the same sort of thing to me. He never did. He was tersely polite but adamant about his script. Nothing must be cut. This made for problems. It always does, particularly when you're dealing with an intellectual writer of reputation who is a stranger to the theater. It's been my fortune—and occasional misfortune—to work with a number of writers in this category. They seem to expect the stage to act as some sort of magic lantern that will project, magnify, and illuminate their words. They forget that they have collaborators: actors, directors, scene designers, sound engineers—and most important, an audience; an audience that is not reading but viewing; listening certainly, but absorbing the words in conjunction with images that, if anv good, may well tell half the story.

It was Somerset Maugham, I think, who, in an attempt to encapsulate his advice to young dramatists, said, "Stick to the point and cut." Wilson had difficulty with both of these injunctions. He'd written an awkward but fascinating play; challenging, dealing with matters of substance, but occasionally obscure, and much too long-winded. I took an option on the piece and, along with four partners, arranged a New York production. However, by the time that got under way, Jessica and I had both made other commitments. Burgess Meredith played "my" part and Arlene Francis took over from Jessica. With Melvyn Douglas, Martin Gabel and Peter Cookson rounding out the cast, it was a strong company.

After the New York opening, I got a long telegram from one of my partners. It was addressed to me at the Bel Air Hotel in Los Angeles, where I was doing God knows what, and read in part, "We cut another twenty minutes. Wilson attacked me immediately saying perfectly furious about those cuts. They all have to go back. Seeing my lawyer."

Incidentally, to his intimates Edmund Wilson was known as "Bunny," which must be the height of irony. I've never met a man less like a rabbit.

Following *The Little Blue Light* came *Hilda Crane.* I think of it and immediately see the ascetic face of Ms. Beulah Bondi—

familiar to filmgoers over decades. Beulah played Jess's mother and brought to the part not only her skill as an actress but a very suitable and characteristic austerity as well. In the heat of rehearsal I used the adjective *fucking,* and although I apologized immediately, Beulah found it hard to forgive, and I had to write a letter of further apology to her. I remember dwelling on my unsatisfactory upbringing and the corruptive influences of the theater, all of which was total nonsense, but she finally forgave me.

While hunting through an old scrapbook in search of a memory prod for *Hilda Crane,* I found two letters from our two youngest children. They were both written in the spring of 1950, when Tandy was five and Chris seven. Chris's letter is painstakingly printed; Tandy's was dictated to Wilma Schambera, the wonderful nanny who had them in charge at the time. She says: "I am writing this *just* as Tandy speaks." I quote the last paragraph of each letter.

> Dear Father, we've been waiting for you to come home. And put kisses and hugs.
> XXX OOOO   Love, TANDY

Chris's reads,

> I have always wanted to go to a ranch. We shall go together. How long will you be home?
> Love,
> Christopher

Even now, nearly forty years later, those two letters give me a sharp pang of guilt. What sort of parents were we? I've always thought we were pretty good—but that may be no more than comfortable rationalization. I certainly saw more of my young children than my parents ever saw of me. And I was all right. . . . Well, wasn't I? Don't answer that.

Except for a few weeks here and there, one of us was usually with the children. I can remember only one lengthy separation while they were young, and that came about in 1952 when we undertook a long national tour of *The Fourposter.*

TWENTY-
TWO

I WAS BABY-SITTING IN Malibu, California, while Jessica finished her brief run in *Hilda Crane*; there were just Tandy, Chris, the incomparable Ms. Schambera, and me in a rented beach house. We had sold the North Rockingham house, having made the wrenching decision to move back to New York—and the theater. When the house was put on the market, one of our first prospects as a buyer had been Piatigorsky, an immensely tall and amiable man who had a very public love affair with his cello. I can remember explaining to Chris that this imposing stranger strolling through our house was a world-famous musician and being surprised by the impression that it made on him. Later I heard him explaining to Tandy that the tall man was a famous *magician*—and of course he was not far off the mark.

Piatigorsky didn't buy, but Barron Hilton did. I remember the visitation by the Hilton delegation. It was headed by Conrad himself, founder of the empire, a bluff Texan who apparently lived by his own advice to "think big." I doubted somehow that Conrad would ever be cited for his bedside manner. He wandered through the house in company with his son, new daughter-in-law, and two other gentlemen I took to be a lawyer and an accountant. Conrad seemed to look at nothing and see everything. In my study, he spotted a framed diploma from the Mozarteum and asked what it was. It was written in German and I could only give him the gist of it. "You've got a German diploma and you can't speak German?" I had to admit I couldn't. Instead of being surprised he appeared pleased and said, "Good for you!" I decided I liked him.

Barron, the lawyer and the accountant asked predictable questions about acreage, taxes, insurance and so on. When the question of whether to buy furnished or unfurnished came up, Barron hedged, saying something to the effect that with all those hotels, furniture was no problem.

Conrad broke in. "Barron, if you want to buy, buy it furnished. These people have better taste than you do."

It was a horrendously tactless remark, followed by a long embarrassed pause before Conrad added, "I suppose that includes the pictures?" As the paintings, even at that time, had a market value approaching the cost of the entire furnished property, my negative answer was immediate and firm. Conrad grinned at me. Nice try. "Think big."

Anyway, there I was in Malibu, brushing the sand from a copy of the *Hollywood Reporter,* when I noticed a six-line squib announcing that Joseph Losey—an old friend from the Actors' Lab—was planning to direct a screenplay based on the recent two-character comedy London hit *The Fourposter.*

I found this item as intriguing as it was baffling. "A recent two-character comedy hit" produced in London and I'd never even heard of it? In those days, I knew what was going on in the English commercial theater. I picked up the phone and called Joe. It turned out that the play had *not* been a hit in London. In fact it had received some scathing notices. "Worst play ever written" . . . "piffle and balderdash." However, Joe believed in the screenplay and asked me if I'd like to read a copy.

I would, I did, and I agreed with Joe that this story of a marriage was heartwarming, touching, funny and affirmative. All those qualities appealed to me and still do. The original play had been written by a Dutch writer named Jan de Hartog. I contacted his American agent, Leah Salisbury, who agreed to send copies to me in California and to Jess in New York. I read the play and liked it even more than the screenplay, except for one scene at the end, which I felt didn't belong.

There is an old adage in the theater that requires a dramatist to "organize the emotions of the audience." This involves, among other things, a warning against abrupt changes in style: a comedy that suddenly becomes a tragedy or vice versa. Sometimes so drastic a change can work, but it must be carefully prepared for—as in O'Casey's *Juno and the Paycock,* where the play proceeds from hilarious character comedy to heartrending disaster. Beware the wrath of an audience who feel they've been led astray. Surprise in the theater may be an enormous virtue, but it must arrive in the context of probability or at least acceptable possibility.

All the same, I thought that Jess and I should give this play—and its last scene—a whirl through the summer theaters and discover how it played. There's nothing like an audience to confound a theory, or endorse it.

I telephoned Jessica and discovered she hadn't much liked *The Fourposter.* She found it ordinary, commonplace—a trifle. Now I had a problem. Certainly I didn't want to attempt the play with anyone else. Fortunately, I had some brownie points with Jess. She had thought she was dead wrong cast as Miss Collins in Williams's *Portrait of a Madonna,* but she had a triumph in the role. Now, I drew on this line of credit, and finally she agreed to a tryout at least. I made arrangements with Leah to tie up the American rights.

And then my troubles began. I couldn't get bookings. A two-character play? "Death at the box office." "Poison." The lady running the Casino Theater in Newport, Rhode Island, told me it was "a dirty play"—simply because the young married couple were shown climbing into bed on their wedding night. My old friend Theron Bamberger, who operated the Bucks County Playhouse, wouldn't have us at all (only to beg us to come to him late in the season after the initial reports of success elsewhere had reached him—he ended up as one of the investors in the New York production). We had to settle for some very odd bookings: London, Ontario; Sarnia, Ontario; Niagara Falls, Ontario (I was drawing heavily on my Canadian connection) and oddest of all perhaps, the Rabbit Run

Theater in Madison, Ohio. At Rabbit Run there were no bathroom facilities backstage. If you had to go, it meant racing around to the front of the theater to use the toilets provided for the audience. We gave an extra Sunday night performance at Rabbit Run as a benefit, with the proceeds going toward the building of a backstage bathroom. It was one of our proudest achievements.

In Sarnia, Ontario, we were presented by the Sarnia Drama League. At the top of their printed program was what I took to be a motto, or statement of purpose: "To celebrate with gaiety, with piety and truth, the divine pageant of the human soul." This high mindedness did not extend to the condition of the old—very old—theater in which we were to perform. The Imperial (rented for the occasion, I'm sure) was without doubt the filthiest theater I've ever set foot in, and I've played in more than my share of dirty ones. I'm sure that none of the ladies on the inevitable committee had even thought of inspecting the premises. Instead, they had concentrated on a gala cocktail party which we were expected to attend immediately prior to our opening-night performance. Even if the theater had been whistle clean, that wouldn't have been possible. It was our practice on arriving at a new stand to go directly to the theater, to hang out the costumes, inspect the set, turn around three times and try to collect our wits before facing the first-night audience. There was no time for bowing, shaking hands, polite murmurings, and—God forbid—alcohol, no matter how much you might need it.

The dressing rooms in the Imperial were beneath the stage. I remember Jess looking at the stairs and saying, "Oh my God—my dresses!" Her beautiful period costumes had been designed by Lucinda Ballard and paid for by us, and two of these costumes had trains. Lucinda, who had designed the clothes for *Streetcar*, was a rare artist, and no expense had been spared.

We dived into a shopping spree and cleanup, buying yards of shelf paper, Old Dutch Cleanser, Sani-Flush, sponges and mops. The "we" of that sentence were Bill Weaver, our stage manager, nicknamed Laughing Boy, as in even the most horrid crisis he was inclined to giggle; Jess and I, and Marjorie Winfield, familiarly known as Ol' Blue Jeans, because we never saw her out of them. Marjorie was my secretary, friend, confidante and confessor for fourteen years. She was a jewel. She's dead now, like so many of the people whose names appear in these pages, but I send her a kiss and deep posthumous bow in whatever place she blesses with her presence.

So, Marjorie and Jess were on their knees scrubbing, I was unpacking props and costumes and cleaning the toilets. Meanwhile, Laughing Boy checked out an extraordinary antique switchboard, wondering what might be done with too few lights. He had to do more than wonder when it came to the performance; the stage went totally dark during the first act, and there was nothing for it but to proceed by flashlight. The whole affair was a nightmare. Sarnia became our synonym for the pits. But after Sarnia, thank God, we played some thoroughly professional houses, including the Falmouth Playhouse, the Lakewood Theater in Skowhegan, Maine, the Olney Playhouse, and Bucks County.

We had opened in Westhampton, and it was clear from the start that we had a tiger by the tail. The play was immensely popular despite its dying fall at the end, when the gears screamed and the audience was plunged into gloom.

It was obvious that the play "needed work" and that we had to try to persuade the author to come across the Atlantic from wherever he was and do something about it. The first trick was to find him. His agents reported that de Hartog lived on a barge, and the barge moved. One week it was anchored in the Thames, the next in the Seine or somewhere in the Zuider Zee. I always seemed to miss him, and though I received an occasional charming letter, I got the uneasy feeling that he didn't much want to join us, even though it was his play. There were other problems, relating to his passport. As an alien who had been resident in occupied territory during the first years of the war, he was required by the U.S. government to have an endorsement from the mayor and chief of police in the city where he'd then lived, certifying that he had been neither a Nazi nor a collaborator. That requirement involved all sorts of bureaucratic tangles. The fact that de Hartog had written a book called *Holland's Glory* which was a rallying totem for the Dutch resistance, that he was an established anti-Nazi and something of a public hero, seemed to cut no ice at all. In one of our last transatlantic telephone conversations, he mentioned another difficulty: he'd broken a leg while diving, which made it difficult for him to travel. I was in despair. Our scheduled tour was drawing to an end, and we were in desperate need of the playwright.

We were playing at the Falmouth Playhouse on Cape Cod when Roger Stevens showed up. He was late for the curtain and missed the first scene. Nevertheless, he came backstage afterward and said he thought the Playwrights Company should present the play in New York. The Playwrights Company consisted of Maxwell Anderson, Robert Sherwood, Elmer Rice, Roger Stevens and John Wharton, a very prestigious consortium, and they had as their general manager Victor Samrock, one of the best in the business.

The conversation between Roger, Jess and me was very brief. Roger was due somewhere else that same evening and in six other places the following day. I was to learn that keeping track of Roger Stevens was at least as difficult as trying to find Jan de Hartog. However, in the few minutes we had together, we agreed on certain essentials. First, we had to get the playwright to see his play and, hopefully, to fix it. Second, we needed a new director, our first having defected three days before our opening in Westhampton. He was a sweet and talented man, but lacked experience and was consequently tentative. The timing of his withdrawal couldn't have been worse, but we parted friends and I took over for the balance of the tour—an arrangement that had domestic drawbacks.

The last engagement of our eight-week tour was at my old stamping ground, Lakewood. I persuaded José Ferrer to come to Maine and look at it. It was my prayer that Joe would agree to direct this play—or redirect it. I also hoped against hope that I could get the playwright there. Thanks to Roger's influence, de Hartog's passport difficulties had been resolved and now all he had to do was get on a plane. Day after day cables arrived from him explaining some further postponement. It became obvious that if he was to come at all, it was going to be a cliff-hanger. Finally, we got a cable saying that our wandering boy would arrive in New York on Saturday, and ending rather ominously with the inquiry, "How do I get to you?" New York is a long way from Skowhegan, Maine, and on Saturday we were to give the last two performances of the entire tour. If de Hartog was to see his play—and I was desperately anxious that he see at least two performances—it would have to be on that day.

There were no satisfactory connecting flights from New York to a commercial airport in our area. There was nothing for it but to charter. Would the weather be cooperative? How would de Hartog feel about an immediate bumpy trip in a small plane after flying all night across the Atlantic? And what about his broken leg?—and which leg was it? I reserved two seats on either side of the aisle so that whichever leg was immobilized could be held straight out in its cast.

Marjorie Winfield arranged the charter and undertook to meet our author and pay off the pilot. I couldn't do it; I had two performances to give and there were no understudies.

De Hartog didn't show up for the matinee. Marjorie had disappeared. There were no telephone messages. Between the afternoon and evening performances I wandered around the grounds keeping an eye on the driveway. If I'd been a nail biter, my fingers would have ended at my bleeding knuckles. Jessica was having dinner with Joe Ferrer. Finally, about forty-five minutes before the evening curtain, a car pulled up in a swirl of dust. I could see that Marjorie was driving. The door opposite her burst open and a big, blond, curly-haired man came bounding across the grass and embraced me. The son of a bitch didn't even have the grace to limp. The broken leg had been (to put it politely) a fabrication.

From the moment Jan arrived, and Joe agreed to direct *The Fourposter*, it was work, work, work, as well as perform, perform, perform. I had managed, thanks to the play's growing reputation among managers, to book an added two weeks on practically no notice. We played at night, rehearsed during the day, and learned the new words I don't quite know when or how. Jan came up with a new final scene within forty-eight hours, but it didn't stop there. He had other ideas for improvement, many of them sparked by Joe. They proved to be wonderful collaborators. We put new things in one day only to take them out the next. There was only one real blowup, when Joe, fed up I think with too many opinions from too many quarters, threatened to withdraw. I remember sitting with him in the back row of a theater somewhere or other while we discussed his sudden disenchantment. Sometimes, just some-times, in crisis, I'm overtaken by a sort of fatalistic calm. For-tunately, this was one of them. I pointed out that the play was going to go ahead either with or without him. Thank God he decided to stay with it, because without him I don't think we would have had the success to which he so richly contributed. Mr. Ferrer is a superb director.

So we plowed ahead. Jess caught a dreadful cold. I worried and paid the bills.

The Playwrights Company opened the Broadway produc-tion in Wilmington, and the Playwrights in person, excepting for Max Anderson, descended upon us. In the smoke-filled hotel room, following the opening-night performance, sat El-mer Rice, Robert E. Sherwood, John Wharton, Roger and I. Jess was still plagued by her cold and too exhausted to attend. (Or was she simply too wise?) Jan had returned to Holland, temporarily, to move his barge from some mudbank that threatened to leave it high and dry in the winter tides. Joe was boycotting the meeting. Again, he felt, with some justification, that there were too many cooks, and that this unannounced arrival of so many experts was unfair—be they producers or not.

I felt very lonely, but I sat dutifully with a yellow legal pad on my knee, noting the suggestions that came from left and right, and from the six-foot-six-inch recumbent figure slouched into an armchair directly across the room from me. Bob Sher-wood smoked and drank furiously while offering his criti-cisms. I suspected that he didn't entirely approve of the Playwrights Company involvement in this frivolous venture. Unhappily for me, most of Bob's criticism was aimed directly at my performance. I think he felt that my character, Michael, should have been more romantic, with greater charm. I sug-gested that "charming" and "romantic" were difficult qualities to apply as a sort of overall varnish, and that perhaps the au-thor had not thought of Michael in those terms. I did not add that even my mother, at her most extravagant, would have had difficulty in describing my personality as romantic and charming. But, after all, I was an actor. If those qualities were needed, I should at least be able to hint at them. I asked Bob to be more specific. I was already into my third page of notes.

With a glass in one hand and a cigarette in the other, Sherwood unhinged himself from his chair and came across the room. Towering above me, he launched into a description of Jessica's performance as Agnes. She was charming, romantic, witty, vulnerable, beautiful—in short, superb; and the clear implication was that I was no match for her. "This is after all a love story." I felt like Mr. Toad. The cigarette began to burn Bob's hand, and he peered myopically down at the table beside me in search of an ashtray. A dark object stood beside my cold coffee cup. It had been an opening-night present: a beautiful navy blue suede tobacco pouch given to me by Laughing Boy. With great deliberation Bob ground out his cigarette on it.

It was that kind of evening.

Throughout the latter part of our summer tour, from the moment that I became persuaded we might have a commercial success, I worried about the film of *The Fourposter,* and the competition it would offer to a stage version. An audience might well prefer to see Rex Harrison and Lilli Palmer playing Michael and Agnes. The film had gone into production while we were still touring, and the screenplay was the one Joe Losey had lent me. The original producer, at the time of Losey's involvement, was Irving Allen, who was having trouble getting it financed. When he discovered that I had acquired the rights to the play, Allen called and offered me the film rights for fifteen thousand dollars—a pittance. I passed, which was a serious mistake. However, I felt I'd bitten off all I could chew in acquiring the theater rights and financing the tour—besides, I suspected that the film might never get made. I was wrong. Almost immediately, Stanley Kramer picked up the rights, arranged financing and release with Columbia Pictures, and put the film into production. I knew that with Kramer, Rex and Lilli involved, the film would be one of quality. (And indeed it was.) But what about their screenplay? Did they really own it, that is, did they own *all* of it?

To understand what finally happened—and it strikes me as a rather unusual story—I have to go into the history of *The Fourposter* and am tempted to cluck rather pedantically, "Now, pay attention."

De Hartog wrote *The Fourposter* during the war while hiding as a "Mrs. Flyingheart" in an old ladies' home named Peaceful Haven in Amsterdam. When the underground finally managed to smuggle him into England, the manuscript was left behind, hidden in the linen closet of Peaceful Haven. You have to admit that that's not a bad start to Jan's account—and I have no reason to suspect another broken leg.

Eventually, Jan recovered his play but was unable to find a producer for it. He sold the film rights for two thousand pounds to Sydney Box, a British film producer. Mr. Box commissioned a screenplay but failed to make the film. However, the original play was published and subsequently produced on the stage, where it failed. Jan had done some rewriting for this English stage production, including an entirely new and very funny scene which Jess and I referred to as "the bottle scene."

At this point in the story, like you probably, I get lost. I don't know under what circumstances the film rights passed from an English film producer to an American one. I do know that I read all the various versions: the English film script, the American one, the published play, and the one as done in England. They all had significant differences, but the thing that struck me was that "the bottle scene," written by de Hartog *after* he sold his film rights, appeared in the American screenplay. Nobody seemed to be aware of this; not Columbia or its lawyers, not Kramer, not the author or his agents. A discreet inquiry on my part confirmed that the film of *The Fourposter*, now completed, had been made with an entire sequence to which they had no title. I took this little plum to Leah Salisbury, and Columbia was persuaded to delay the release of the film for about a year.

We opened the play at the Barrymore Theater in New York on Wednesday evening, October 24th, 1951. At the party afterward, Jan was sitting with his wife and his then father-in-law, J. B. Priestley. Jan came over to our table flushed with wine, opening-night success, relief, and his usual enormous exuberance, to present the following verbal bouquet: "Old J.B. had just made the most marvelous remark. He said to me, 'You see, dear boy, all we playwrights really need is a couple of actors stupid enough to actually believe what we write.'"

It's not the sort of comment this couple of actors is likely to forget, but it was passed on to us like a benediction and entirely without malice.

The Fourposter repaid its backers in six and a half weeks. Jessica and I played in it for about six hundred and fifty performances in New York and on tour. When we left the Barrymore, Burgess Meredith and Betty Field took over from us there, and they in turn, were replaced by Romney Brent and Sylvia Sidney.

I have a letter from Jan written on May 25th, 1989—thirty-eight years after that opening. I quote one paragraph: "How young we were, Hume. And how we loved each other. And what a joy it was to share that protracted feast of communal creation."

I try to avoid quoting reviews, but we got a letter in January of 1952 that I cannot resist including. It seems to sum up for me what *The Fourposter* was all about.

Dear Hume and Jessica Cronyn, José Ferrer,
and Jan de Hartog:
  We saw "Fourposter" last night through a film of tears, the most satisfying kind of tears because they were inspired not by sadness or solemnity, but by the recognition of the beauty that lies in all the married lives of all the stumbling, bumbling human beings who try to do their best with each other. Their combined intelligence is pitifully inadequate for the terrifying problems that beset them but having that incredibly hardy love that some couples share, they attain a kind of shaky and incomplete conquest over life. They may well call this happiness and be proud to own it. No wonder everyone cries. Everyone laughs, too, as far as we could see and hear, sitting in the audience last night, and everyone leaves the theater, as we did, with pride in the nobility of average people, and deep gratitude toward the four of you, who made such a beautiful evening possible.
  All our best wishes,
                    Sincerely,
                    Oscar and Dorothy Hammerstein

TWENTY-
THREE

I HAD TO JUMP overboard into water about waist deep. The
boat had a fixed prop and we couldn't go in any further. The
beach of lovely, firm, dazzling white sand stretched for a quarter
of a mile on either side of me. It was to become known as the
Home Beach. I waded ashore and set foot on Children's Bay
Cay for the first time since flying over it in 1946. Somebody
had lent me a machete—better known as a "cutlass" in these
parts—and I hacked my way through thick brush and a tangle
of love vines to the crest of the hill. At the very top was a small
joewood tree, bent and gnarled by the wind. I climbed up as
far as the tree branches would allow and there it all was—
much as God and nature created it. The shining sea; the wash-
board ridges of white sand shoals; the royal blue of deep
channels; the purple patches above turtle grass; the mottled
tan and blue—yet another blue—that warned of reefs or coral
heads; and closer inshore, jade, aquamarine, and, where the
ripples broke on the beach, the most delicate mauve that dis-
solved into foam and ran giggling along the beach.

> Then felt I like some watcher of the skies
> When a new planet swims into his ken;
> Or like stout Cortez when with eagle eyes

He stared at the Pacific—and all his men
Look'd at each other with a wild surmise—
Silent, upon a peak in Darien.

Of course, it wasn't the Pacific, there were no other men,
and I was certainly no Cortez. But there was silence and wild
surmise; and for this "harlotry player," as actors were once
known, it was a new planet.

I wished that Jess might have been with me—although she
wouldn't have fancied the climb up that hill. I was drenched
with sweat. I wasn't more than sixty feet above sea level, but
that's high in these islands, and the panorama seemed to stretch
to far horizons on every side of me. All those cays within boat
reach of Children's Bay—each one of them a beckoning adventure. All those cays with their romantic but idiosyncratic
names that were to become so familiar to me. Directly to the
south, the Brigantines; to the southeast, the tiny settlement of
Barraterre; to the east and west of us, Rat Cay, Lee Stocking
Island, Peace and Plenty, Bull and Cow, Norman's Pond, all
of them uninhabited and seeming likely to stay that way. To
the north were the wide indigo reaches of Exuma Sound, one
of the deepest rifts in all the Atlantic. From my perch in the
joewood, I could just make out the dull boom of the surf against
the rocky north shore of Children's Bay. I was to learn later
that when the sea was in a rage, the thundering waves on our
north shore could make our house-to-be shudder in response.

I climbed down from my tree thinking, "This is where we
will build our house," but before that even began there were
preliminary steps that must be taken. My agreement with the
Crown Land's office required that within the period of my
five-year lease, I had to "improve" to the extent of five thousand pounds—and my five years was nearly up and nothing
done. I felt like that madame of a South American brothel
who wailed in anguish: "Six o'clock, and not a girl dressed,
not a po emptied, and my house full of Spaniards!" I *had* to
"improve," and do it immediately, or I would blow the agreement under which I might establish a title in perpetuity. With
only a few months left to go, I committed to building the following: a deep-water dock (eight feet at low tide); a caretaker's

cottage, a warehouse (somewhere to store building supplies and equipment out of the weather) and a series of rough-hewn paths through the bush to join these various points and lead up to our eventual building site on the hill.

Everything, absolutely everything, had to be done by hand. Throughout the long building program that was to ensue, we had only one piece of mechanical equipment at our disposal: a gasoline-driven cement mixer. There were no power tools. There was no power, no generator. The building of the rain-water catchments under the caretaker's house and the warehouse were two of the most difficult and time-consuming tasks, all pick-and-shovel work and the judicious—very judicious—use of dynamite. One tank was to hold ten thousand gallons, the other eleven. There were wells of course, but these were shallow and, unlike the catchments, had no cement casing. They were little more than twelve- to fifteen-foot holes in the ground that tapped the fresh water lying under the surface limestone. Fresh water floats on top of salt water, so the wells rose and fell with the tide. Woe betide you if you overpumped one, or used dynamite at anything more than a surface level. In the first instance your well would turn brackish; in the second you risked opening up new fissures in the rock and your water would simply run away, disappearing into another limestone pocket. All the fresh water came from rains.

> Rain, rain gone away,
> Won't be back for many a day;
> Please help us save
> What little we have.

So goes the Bahamian jingle, as much a prayer as an observation on the weather.

With only days to spare, we completed our "improvement" commitment, and eventually received an illuminated scroll proclaiming to the world at large that by the grace of His Majesty King George VI, King of the United Kingdom of Great Britain and Northern Ireland, we and "our heirs and assigns, forever" were the proud possessors of Children's Bay Cay. There was one quid pro quo: a single peppercorn per year—

if it was demanded. The British Crown likes to maintain at
least a thread of demonstrable allegiance where its subjects are
concerned.

Now our problems multiplied. We'd made but a bare beginning. I had to find an architect, a builder, a labor force,
transport, and someone to oversee the whole business during
the many and prolonged absences involved in pursuing my
profession.

Up to a point, Jessica had kept her peace about my wild
schemes. Now she started asking irritating questions, like
"Where do we get our food?" or "What happens if one of the
children breaks a leg?" and of course, "Can we afford it?" To
all of these questions, I had lofty but very uncertain answers.
Once again, I seemed to be propelled by the philosophy of
Guthrie's "On, on, on!"; or Olivier's "Just give it a bash" and
Orson Welles' blind step into thin air. Mind you, at the time
of the Children's Bay Cay development, I hadn't even met
Guthrie and Olivier; so perhaps it was only my personal dream
or plain bullheadedness that drove me on.

Finding an architect was the first hurdle. After some false
starts, I was lucky enough to meet Kenneth Russel Miller, and
to him more than any other single individual I owe thanks for
the building of not only one beautiful house but two. However, the second wasn't to be built until the 1970's and is not
part of this story.

Ken Miller must then have been in his late twenties. He
had a job at this time as a draftsman with a big architectural
firm in New York. He clearly found this unsatisfactory and
wished to do something more creative. Because he had a nine-
to-five job, we used to meet in the theater between my matinee
and evening performances. I liked him immensely. Within forty-
eight hours of our first meeting, he came back to the theater
not only with solutions but with drawings—his drawings. How
on earth had he found the time? He must have spent a couple
of sleepless nights. From that point on I felt I had my house,
at least on paper.

I gave up my search for a conventional contractor almost
immediately. No one wanted any part of trying to build even
a modest house so far from a source of supply. Nassau was

approximately 150 miles from Children's Bay, across water.
There was no transport except for the weekly mail-boat, and
its schedule was subject to the weather and the whims of its
captain. And how about a labor force? Where would they come
from? Where would they live? What about basic communica-
tions (the nearest government telegraph office was a day's trip
away in George Town)—to say nothing of the skills required
of carpenters, masons and plumbers? We didn't even discuss
electricians.

I had planned on a bottled-gas stove, a kerosene refrigerator, and as for lighting, well, hurricane lamps and candles in
a pinch. It wasn't until we were well along with the building
that Jessica's anxiety about the children and her plain common sense dictated the installation of a marine radio telephone and a deep freeze. That meant generators, as the
maintenance of batteries seemed impractical. With the generators (there must be two—suppose one "give up"?) and telephone, we embraced our first mechanical monsters.

Because we couldn't find a contractor, we had to become
our own, but clearly, someone on the spot had to be in charge.
My old friend Paul Potter, manager of the Royal Bank of Canada, whom I had known since I was about sixteen, suggested
the name of Linton Rigg. It seemed that Mr. Rigg had fled
Nassau "civilization," and society in general, for the settlement
of George Town, Exuma. He was an American who appeared
to be more British than the British, the author of two books
on sailing and a onetime ship's architect. "At least he can read
a blueprint," said Paul," and I think he could use the money."
I telegraphed Mr. Rigg and he responded with an invitation
to come and stay with him for a few days in George Town. I
flew down immediately.

A telling description of Linton Rigg was provided in 1976,
when he died and was buried on the island of Carriacou in
the Grenadines. Just as he had fled Nassau, he left the Exumas in turn, and for the same reason—too much civilization.
An account of his death and burial—a black comedy if there
ever was one—was written by Francis Grant, Jr., and came to
me through our mutual friend Rodney Page. I crib from Mr.
Grant because I cannot swear to my own objectivity about Lin-

ton, although obviously we both liked the man despite his personality warts and aggressively contentious nature.

J. Linton Rigg, O.B.E. . . . born in Jamaica in 1895, where his family had lived for generations, grandson of an Anglican bishop, son of a clergyman . . . educated as a naval architect . . . lived near Baltimore, and for a while had shifted from yachts to fox hunting. He married briefly, once, had a daughter whom he never saw. . . .

Linton was a big man, quite deaf, very much self-centered. . . . He was an out-spoken racist, but had devoted black friends, a practicing snob who simply excluded from his view people he thought below notice . . . and a pronounced male chauvinist. Because of his deafness, he spoke in a very loud voice. He was quarrelsome, a monologuist, and an interrupter of other people's conversations, who bore no interruptions of his own. . . .

It's hardly an endearing description—and yet the second thing I noticed about Linton when we met was how popular he seemed to be with everyone with whom we came in contact. My first impression was of the actor Sydney Greenstreet: the same shape, corporation, thinning hair, and cryptic smile—even the same white suit worn in *The Maltese Falcon*. Linton paraded around George Town like some sort of patron saint. "Good mornin' Mr. Rigg, suh"; "Nice day, Mr. Rigg"; "God bless you, Mr. Rigg." It was true that there was a certain subservience in these greetings, but there were broad smiles, too, and a sense of genuine affection. Perhaps this was because Linton was "jolly." He loved to joke. It was only slowly that I became aware of his feuds. There was a small group of people with whom Linton would have no truck and for whom he had nothing but contempt. These individuals were cast into outer darkness.

Linton was living in a small four-room rented house with a kitchen and bathroom that appeared to have been tacked on as an afterthought. The toilet was flushed with a bucket of water, the flush mechanism having long since corroded into uselessness.

On my first couple of evenings in the house, Linton and I talked about Children's Bay and what might or might not be accomplished there. He was genuinely enthusiastic, but not overly concerned with the drawings I'd brought with me and inclined to wave them aside with a "Don't worry, we'll fix it" attitude. While this made me slightly uneasy, Linton's profound self-confidence was impressive, and his reassurance as to the quality of local workmanship available—under *his* direction—was comforting.

It must have been about my third evening in the house, when Linton produced the photographs. Our conversations had become more personal. Linton was a randy old man—and lonely. We were discussing sex. Linton suddenly rose from his chair and strode into his bedroom. He had an old rolltop desk in there, which, when opened, threatened a cascade of papers onto the floor. He scrabbled around inside the desk, slamming its small drawers and finally found what he was after. He dropped a small pile of snapshots into my lap. "Have a look at those." Most of them were of a black girl sitting on a beach. She was leaning backward, her arms stretched out behind her, her hands buried in the sand. She had a delicious figure, lovely breasts and a towel draped demurely across her thighs. Not knowing quite how to react except in admiration, I said, "Anyone I know?"

Linton looked dumbfounded. I thought he was going to call me "a cad"; say that a gentleman wouldn't make such an inquiry, or perhaps tell me to mind my own damn business. Not at all. In a whisper that echoed through the house, he said, "That's Alice." I said blankly: "Alice?" Linton looked even more perplexed. "Why man, she served you your dinner!" Now I was aware that someone had put the meal on the table and that the lady was wearing broken-down sneakers; the backs had collapsed, so that they were like scuffs and went slippety-slop across the floor between kitchen and sitting room. She had been wearing a man's hat and something quite shapeless, a sort of muumuu, that allowed no hint of the glories hidden beneath. I apologized for having been so unobservant; said Alice was beautiful and that Linton was a fortunate man. But the matter didn't end there.

"Hume, I don't know what your taste is in these matters, but . . . these women are very responsive and *discreet*. . . . I'm sure that if you care to pursue . . ." Linton left the rest hanging in the air, but some acknowledgment of the invitation seemed called for and I heard myself say: "Thanks very much Linton, but I think I can hang on until Jessica gets here."

Two days later Jess arrived and Linton took us both out for a sail in his boat, the *Barefoot Gal*. He was very proud of this boat; it had been built for him in Abaco to his very particular specifications. We sailed around Elizabeth Harbor, surely one of the most beautiful in all the Caribbean, under very "hoody" skies. I felt a storm was brewing. The water was alternately flat calm and then ruffled by cat's-paws and sudden erratic shifts in the wind. It was tricky sailing; however, Linton was a master sailor of vast experience in these waters and seemed totally unconcerned.

Jess was in the cockpit, Linton at the helm, and I was standing where I shouldn't have been, just forward of the mast, watching an ominous line squall bear down on us. The rain came, slowly at first in large drops and then more furiously, stinging the face as the squall hit us. We heeled over and I grabbed the jib to keep from going overboard. Why Linton hadn't lowered it, I don't know. The next thing I knew, I heard Linton bellow "Stand by to jibe!" I couldn't believe it. In this wind? If he'd shouted "Stand by to fly," it would have been more appropriate. I hunkered down, Linton threw over the helm and the *Barefoot Gal* didn't just go over, she somersaulted.

I came to the surface gasping, looking for Jess, and there she was only a few yards away resting on the rudder, which had broken away from its pins. She was laughing. Linton was looking absolutely furious and shouting something about his trousers. Fortunately, we were only about two hundred yards off the Stocking Island beach and in not more than fifteen feet of water. I was able to dive down and retrieve Linton's trousers, which had ten pounds in the pocket. That was his immediate concern—but it soon grew worse. A boat had put out from shore to help us; it was a powerboat piloted by the Turtle brothers—and the Turtles were on Linton's shit list,

though why, I never discovered. Linton took the rescue effort
with very poor grace. To have had his boat go over was bad
enough, but to be ignominiously towed ashore by a *power*boat
belonging to Morton Turtle was almost more than Linton
could bear.

Somehow or other the six of us managed to get the *Barefoot Gal* righted and resting on the beach. It was pelting rain
and in that wind very cold. Morton and Charlie urged us to
come to the house, but Linton would have no such hospitality.
"I'm going to bail," he said crossly. "You go." And we did. A
more considerate guest would have insisted on staying to help
Linton out, even though bailing in that downpour was idiotic
and the storm would soon pass. I gave up trying to remonstrate with him, left him to his grumpy chore and went up to
the house for hot tea heavily laced with rum—and there we
were once again, back in the same house we'd been stranded
in some years earlier when the plane had broken down on our
first trip to Exuma.

We did manage to sail back across the harbor to Linton's
anchorage, under a reefed sail this time and the cockpit still
awash. Alice gave us a hot meal and we fell into bed.

The next day I went down to the boat with Linton and
helped him complete the bailout and put the gear to rights.
The matter of Alice was on my mind. It was a fascinating puzzle and I approached the subject very tentatively. I've never
forgotten the conversation that ensued; it sticks in my memory
as the ultimate in racial prejudice.

"Linton, about Alice. It's quite obvious that you are a figure of great respect in this community. They treat you like
. . . like some sort of raj. How do you manage it? . . . I mean
that . . . that mixture of authority and moral rectitude . . .
I'm saying this so badly . . . and at the same time you have a
familiarity—even intimacy. . . . Alice for instance."

It was a stuffy inquiry, awkwardly put, but Linton took no
offense. I think he rather enjoyed the role of big brother explaining the mysteries of sex and interracial relationships (as
he saw them) to this novice.

"My dear Hume, you don't understand. If I find any one
of these women attractive and wish to take her to bed, I

shouldn't hesitate to ask and . . ." Then Linton became most profound: "And she would be perfectly free to refuse—*but,* I shouldn't dream of asking her to sit at the table."

That was Linton. Born in Jamaica, 1895; an unreconstructed Southerner by taste and inclination; the son of a clergyman; grandson of an Anglican bishop.

Not that Linton's clerical antecedents made him an automatic admirer of the church or its clergy. One of his feuds was with the rector of St. Andrew's parish, a certain Father Knifeton, whose church was almost next door. I don't know what the good father may have done to draw down Linton's wrath but I suspect that he may have felt that Linton was a corrupter of his flock. At any rate, Linton referred to him as "the miserable Knifeton."

On a Sunday morning, while Linton was shaving, there was a knock on the front door which I answered. There stood James Barr. James takes a little explaining. If Linton had been a military man, James might have been his batman. Whatever his position, he was a very big, omnipresent black shadow with a gentle voice and beatific smile that seemed almost an apology for his muscularity. I changed my mind about that voice and smile when, weeks later, on Children's Bay, I saw a dog snap at James's ankle. In a flash I saw James's long arm shoot out, catch the dog by its hind leg, swing it round his head and bash its brains out against the bole of a palm tree. Anyway, there was James smiling at me and when I said I'd fetch Mr. Rigg, he said, "No suh, this for you," and handed me a letter. Who, I thought, could find me with a letter in this place?

The letter was typewritten on the paper of St. Andrew's Anglican Church, George Town, Exuma. It went something like this:

Dear Mr. Cronyn:

Welcome to George Town. It has come to my attention that you are visiting the estimable Mr. Rigg. We have few visitors of your distinction and it would be a fine example to the community if we could engage you in this morning's divine service. I understand that you are an Anglican. I would not presume to ask you to address the congregation

on such short notice, but if you would undertake to swing
the censer and to join me and the choir in the chancel—
where you would be highly visible—we would be honored.

May I suggest you arrive at the vestry door not later
than 10:45 (the service commences at 11:00 sharp) so that
we may find you a suitable surplice and cassock.

Yrs. in Christ,

I. Knifeton

Rector

I was appalled. Me? Swing a censer? My great-grandfather,
also a bishop but militantly Low Church, would spin in his
grave, and Linton would have a fit at any suggestion of collaboration with "the miserable Knifeton." But how was I to frame
a polite refusal? I called to Linton, who emerged from the
bathroom, half-lathered, and handed him the Rector's letter.
He read it slowly and with great concentration, then handed
it gravely back to me, and said, "Damn decent of the fellow!"
Then he turned on his heel and went back to finish his shaving. As he disappeared through the bathroom door, I thought
I saw his shoulders heaving. I followed him and faced his image in the mirror. His lips were tightly compressed and his
face bright red from repressed laughter.

Of course, the whole thing was a hoax. Linton had pinched
the church stationery, typed the letter, forged the signature
and had James deliver it to me. It was the sort of practical
joke he relished. Months later, when the building at Children's
Bay was well under way, I got another letter in New York, this
one written under the letterhead of Her Britannic Majesty's
Geodetic Survey. It informed me that Children's Bay Cay was
sinking; that in the foreseeable future it would be entirely covered by the sea and that I, as owner, was responsible for any
loss of life as a result. Despite this preposterous premise, the
letter was written in such a persuasive bureaucratic fashion
and contained so much technical jargon relating to winds, tides,
rainfall and geological formations that it seemed possibly official. It wasn't until I got to the last paragraph and the signature that I became suspicious. Up until that point, I'd read
with horror. The ultimate paragraph said that Her Most Gra-

cious Majesty, mindful of the hardship that abandoning my property would work on me, was graciously pleased to award me similar acreage in the highlands of North Africa—and just when would it suit me to establish possession? The signature, written with a flourish, was that of Augustus Dinwiddie, director in charge of the Bahamian office.

The only legitimate item was the writing paper. Linton couldn't have faked that. He must have been a sort of shoplifter of official stationery—but the letters he composed were masterworks of parody.

A few weeks after concluding arrangements with Linton to supervise and coordinate the building effort on Children's Bay, I had a letter from Ken Miller, the architect. Ken said he wanted to chuck his job in New York and go down to Exuma to supervise the building of "his" house. He pointed out that he'd had some practical experience as a builder and understood the rudiments of carpentry, of masonry, even of the electrician's trade. I thought he must be crazy—and where would he live? Linton had already appropriated the caretaker's house. I don't remember what provision we made for poor Alpheus, the caretaker at the time, who was to be shoved out into the cold. Temporarily, at least, the workmen were to sleep on army-surplus cots under an immense army-surplus tent—a sort of canvas dormitory. Where might we put Ken? In the warehouse perhaps; but how was I to pay him? I certainly couldn't match what he was getting as a highly skilled draftsman in New York. And what would Linton's reaction be to another boss? I felt Linton wanted a free and creative hand. I remembered his rather airy dismissal of Ken's drawings and his "Don't worry, we'll fix it" attitude. Linton would take some handling.

On the other hand it would be a blessing, a huge advantage to have the architect on the site, and I might actually end up with the house Ken had designed. I called Ken and explained the difficulties, discomfort and limitations which I foresaw in his spending months in exile on Children's Bay. He'd obviously considered all of them before writing to me, and he seemed absolutely determined in his decision, providing I would have him. As for money, he required round-trip transportation *by boat*—he was adamant about that—the run of his teeth, and a very modest salary. I suggested a figure and he accepted it immediately. Ken's involvement proved to be the single most fortunate step in the whole campaign. Now, I had to deal with Linton. I composed a long and I hoped tactful cable to George Town pointing out the advantages of having Ken on the job and waited anxiously for a reply. It took a long time in coming and consisted of only two words: "Send Miller." Such terseness might be thrift but was more likely to be a grudging acceptance. Regardless, I told Ken to book his passage.

Our labor was recruited and supervised by Max Bowe. Max was shaped like a barrel. All that was missing were the iron hoops, but I felt they were there somewhere; there was a lot of iron in Max. His short legs bowed under his weight and he walked—rolled—like a seaman. I don't think I ever saw him without his cap, which was kept pulled down over his eyes— but the eyes missed nothing. Max was the single biggest landowner on Exuma. He controlled over six thousand acres, which were eventually sold off to developers and which remain largely undeveloped even to this day. Sadly for Max, the sale came at a time when he'd become too ill to enjoy the proceeds. When we met, Max was land-poor and glad to accept the job I offered. His own particular fiefdom was The Forest, the site of an old plantation house, long gone, where Max was emperor and dispenser of patronage, held in both awe and nervous respect. He was an educated man whom it was best not to cross. I wasn't privy to his dealings with the thirty-odd people he recruited to work on the cay, but sometimes suspected that they viewed him as a sort of Simon Legree. Max was the paymaster and paydays were ceremonial. He would sit at a small table which held a big pile of silver and pound notes, and with a tally sheet in front of him, he would bark out a name and the amount due. The man or woman would step forward and either initial the sheet or, more probably, make a mark. Max's accounts were always meticulous, but the procedure made me uncomfortable. Finally, I drew Max aside and suggested that if I supplied pay envelopes, he wouldn't have to announce the amount and count it off each time. I felt that the public announcement of a man or woman's worth was bound to cause

resentful comparisons and eventual trouble. Max held an entirely opposite view. "Mr. Cronyn, they *like* to know what
everyone gets—puts a fire under 'em." But I felt Max himself
supplied enough fire, and since it was my money he was dis-
pensing, I prevailed.

Despite my occasional differences with Max, I grew increasingly fond of him. I intervened a couple of times when
people turned up drunk and Max, who couldn't abide drinking, wanted to fire them out of hand. One hard case was Rit-
chie. I warned him and warned him and finally had to fire
him myself—such a nice man, always laughing, willing to do
anything, but frequently loaded. I watched him sail away with
real regret. I think he was the only worker we lost.

I suppose I didn't make things easy for Max, but he paid
me the honor of asking me to spend a night at The Forest
and of showing me his horses. I didn't know there was a horse
on the entire island, but there they were, two of them, beautifully groomed and Max's pride and joy. I think those horses
may have received more loving care and attention than anything or anyone else at The Forest.

We had dinner at a long table in the kitchen/sitting room,
but the only women at the table were Jess and my sister, Honor.
The other ladies present cooked, served, and hovered behind
our chairs with fans to keep the flies off. Max had the most
beautiful wife, Junoesque, handsome, dignified and imposing.
I spoke admiringly of her to Max and he said: "Oh yes, Mr.
Cronyn. . . . But she's *so* black!" Max himself was sepia-col-
ored.

One of Max's sons-in-law, Will Nixon from Steventon, a
carpenter, was to become a true friend and a man on whose
humor and wisdom I came to depend throughout our entire
eighteen-year stay on Children's Bay Cay. He looked like a
young, black Abraham Lincoln, and he seemed capable of
turning a hand to anything. Carpentry was pie for him, but
beyond that, he had a way with pumps, motors, anything that
had to do with a boat—indeed, anything at all. It was true that
I sometimes had to chide him about repairs accomplished with
string and chewing gum—not quite literally, but close. However, there seemed to be nothing he couldn't fix, even if string

and chewing gum were the only materials immediately available. The number of times I had to hail Will to the rescue are uncountable.

Will and I used to go fishing together. He is a marvelous fisherman and as knowledgeable about the sea as any man I ever met. But one thing he wouldn't do: he wouldn't get into the water with me. I was an enthusiastic diver and spear-fisherman, but Will chose to stay in the boat: "I don't go down there and trouble them, they don't come up here and trouble me."

One of my rare confrontations with Will came about over the security of our gasoline and diesel supplies. I'd been warned that as we were so seldom "in residence" and that as the caretaker's house was a good third of a mile away from our fuel depot, I must keep the drums under lock and key. Little by little the keys would disappear or the locks rust out. One day I told Will to buy new locks and to take personal charge of the keys. He gave me a long pitying look. "Mr. Cronyn," he said, "nobody goin' t' steal from you."

And no one ever did. A little something might be "borrowed" now and then, but my neighbors, many of them poor and unemployed, were as honorable as they were hardworking. So much for the advice I'd received in Nassau: "You'll be robbed deaf, dumb and blind." We threw our locks away and I was never to regret it.

With Linton, Ken and Max in charge and work begun, I left the Bahamas and went back to work. I'd get an occasional letter from Ken or Linton, and things seemed to be going reasonably well despite a constant need to improvise and the difficulty of arranging the transportation of materials to meet any kind of building schedule. I missed the day-by-day dramas, such as the one recounted in the following letter from Linton, dated September 30th, 1955, but it will give you a sense of the sort of thing that went on:

A couple of days after you had left, several of the men requested permission to go over to Barra Terra to buy groceries. I let them go over in the work boat in the evening after work. The next morning when I awoke at six, there was Richard Rolle standing at the door weeping co-piously. When I asked him what the trouble was he said, "Boss, they took my money and bought a sheep." When I asked him who "they" was, he could not tell. His story was that Cleveland had borrowed three pounds ten shillings from him to lend to James. I then sent for James, who denied that he had bought a sheep, and had no recollec-tion of having borrowed any money from anybody. None of them remembered if anyone had bought a sheep, but they all had seen the money on the table. As the money had obviously disappeared I then sent the boat over to Barra Terra to find out if a sheep actually had been bought, and if so to bring it here. Several hours later the boat came back with a sheep, and a receipt, signed by James Barr (who had not gone with the boat to get the sheep). As James cannot read or write, I at once knew that it was a forgery. Everyone accused everyone else of having a part in trying to sell the sheep to James, who said that he did not want it. Somehow, it was worked into the testimony that Edroy had on the previous week borrowed James' razor without his permission, and when James asked for it said that he did not have it, and then to me stating that he had the razor but did not like James' tone of voice in asking for it. Also it appears that the razor blade had been used to kill a chicken, and was no longer any good for shaving. James then accused Edroy of having been the instigator of the riot which took place at Georgetown at the time of the Queen's Coronation. As the issue became more and more involved, I finally had to call a halt to it. I told them all to shut up, to talk about it no more, and to remember that their only reason for being here was to build your house. I then said that I would buy the sheep, and so refund Richard Rolle for the money, which I did.

The next morning, Max came to me with a request that I call the men together and admonish them against swear-ing, as he said he had heard some very bad swear words used last night. So again I had to "hold court" and warn them all under pain of being "charged." But that was not all. That day Alpheus came and complained that I could

not keep a sheep here, as wherever I tied it up it was liable
to eat something that he was growing.

The object of all this is a poor wretched old ram, with
a face like Eleanor Roosevelt, with a tail that looks like a
dirty pipe cleaner, and a pair of balls that reach almost to
the ground. Some day we will eat him, but not until we are
half starving.

I had gone back to the United States to plunge immediately into rehearsals for N. C. Hunter's *A Day by the Sea*. I was
proud to be in it, a lovely, gentle, perhaps too talkative play
that had had a *succès d'estime* in England with a cast boasting
Sir John Gielgud, Sir Ralph Richardson, Dame Sybil Thorn-
dike, Sir Lewis Casson and plain old (though neither plain nor
old) Irene Worth, among others. Jessica referred to our cast
as "the lesser, or untitled company." Even so, throwing modesty aside, it was a distinguished one: Jessica, Dennis King,
Aline McMahon, that wonderful old actor Halliwell Hobbes,
yours truly (playing Sir John's role), and so on. It was directed
by Sir Cedric Hardwicke—the only title of which we could
boast—and it "didn't work."

In a reversal of form we opened the play in Los Angeles,
went on to San Francisco and from there to Broadway. During
the San Francisco run I received an urgent cable from Ken
Miller. All was not right on Children's Bay. Reading between
the lines, I gathered that we faced some sort of insurrection.
The trouble was not spelled out, but the cable spelled trouble.
Fortunately there was a hiatus between the San Francisco closing and our opening in New York. There was nothing I could
do but fly down to try to resolve the conflict. This involved
flights from San Francisco to New Orleans, from New Orleans
to Miami, Miami to Nassau and a charter from Nassau by seaplane out to Children's Bay. It was all very expensive and time-
consuming, but in those days, it was the only way to go. Not
for the first time did I question my sanity in building on a
remote Bahamian island.

In Nassau I made one of the very rare diplomatic moves
of which I'm capable. I loaded up the seaplane with four cases
of rum and three sides of lamb—I didn't feel I could count on

Linton's old ram. I guessed that part of the trouble was the result of weeks of grinding work, a little like building the Pyramids; everyone suffering the intense heat, boredom, the absence of even the simplest amenities, and the end of a honeymoon that had started with excitement and a prospect of months of employment.

On arriving at the cay I announced that we were all to have a two-day holiday at full pay, and that at the end of it there would be a dance on the seaplane ramp. The work crew was free to stay on the cay or sail home, as they chose. Before even getting into the nature of the trouble that lay ahead of me, I asked Max if he could round up an "orchestra" and persuade the men to collect their wives and girls to join us. This made for some transportation problems, and Max didn't approve of the rum, but he agreed to the barbecue pit (fresh meat in these parts was a rare luxury) and to the orchestra. The latter consisted of two guitars, a steel drum—cut from a diesel barrel—a mouth organ, an accordion, and a musical (?) saw. They were to give a performance of unrehearsed magnificence.

I'd arrived on the cay late in the afternoon and was exhausted. I made the foregoing arrangements; somebody gave me a dinner of conch, rice and black-eyed peas; and I fell onto a cot in the caretaker's house, putting off all serious conversation until the following day.

In the morning I took three long walks: one with Linton, one with Ken, and the last with Max. I encouraged them all to sound off and did little more than listen—which is not easy for me. Everyone had grievances. Ken was worried that the house was not being built to his specs, Max resented Linton, and Linton resented everybody.

After lunch I got them all together and tackled the difficult part. I remember the four of us sitting in the small sitting room of the caretaker's house, sweating, nervous, embarrassed. I started by saying how well I thought the work had gone since I left. And indeed it had gone well: the three ten-thousand-gallon catchments had been completed, all work below ground level, no breeze, pick and shovel, hours in a broiling sun; the stone walls had started up, some of the face stones covered with a beautiful pink coral encrustation that wouldn't fade.

I went on to say that I'd heard all the laments (though I was particularly careful not to repeat them, nor to quote anyone). I pointed out that no one present was indentured and that if any one of them wanted to chuck it and leave, there would be no hard feelings on my part. Then came the hardest part. I had to lay down the law. Two of these men were older than I and all of them more experienced. But if I didn't clarify the different spheres of responsibility, my island really might start to sink. I tried to be diplomatic.

It was pretty clear that the trouble was at the top. I'd formed a picture of Linton sitting under a beach umbrella outside the caretaker's house, where there was a nice breeze, and dispatching James Barr up the hill with some pronunciamento— carried in a forked stick perhaps.

The conference broke up without resolution but also, thank God, without confrontation, and the party that night was a huge success. Only one man got falling-down drunk, and that was the constable from Barraterre. I stumbled over him in the bushes beside the ramp, out cold. We picked him up and laid him reverently in the warehouse. He greeted me warmly the next morning and sailed blithely away to resume his official duties in the settlement. Work began again on Children's Bay Cay; and later that same afternoon, the seaplane came back to pick me up and carry me on the first leg of my trip to New York and the opening of *A Day by the Sea*.

The play failed, though with very creditable reviews for the cast. The biggest reward for me was a friendship with Cedric Hardwicke. Cedric had been a close friend of George Bernard Shaw; he'd appeared in many of Shaw's plays, directed *Pygmalion* when it was done in New York, and shared Shaw's cerebral wit. He was a marvelous raconteur, as well as being a skillful actor and director. There is a particular joy in working with actor-directors; they are sympathetic to the stumbling process by which an actor tries to achieve an impossible perfection. The best directors I've worked for have all, at one time or another, been performers. I can think of only two exceptions: Harold Clurman and George Kaufman.

Toward the end of his life, Cedric developed emphysema. He was broke, and the Actors' Fund came to his rescue. I'd heard that he was in New York Hospital and sent him some champagne and a basket of fruit before going to visit him. I walked into his room and there was the champagne, unopened, and the fruit basket still wrapped in its cellophane. Cedric lay propped up in bed with a huge canister of oxygen next to him. Attached to the canister were a series of rubber tubes terminating in a sort of mitt containing a mouthpiece. I sat in a chair with my back to the window. Cedric tried to talk. From time to time he would reach for the mitt and gulp a few breaths of oxygen. It was almost impossible to understand him. I moved from the chair onto the side of his bed.

"I'm sorry, Cedric, I didn't catch that—would you mind saying it again?"

Cedric looked vexed. He reached for the mitt, took a couple of long, difficult breaths and then laboriously uttered the understatement of the century.

"I said . . . I'm afraid . . . this puts an end . . . to my acting." He then leant back against the pillows, exhausted.

A few days later Richard Burton and I were two of his pallbearers.

TWENTY-
FOUR

THE PHOENIX THEATRE was the inspired and idealistic brain child of T. Edward Hambleton and Norris Houghton. It was their dream to create a popular nonprofit theater of distinction off-Broadway and to play for limited runs in what is sometimes called "sequential rep." It was a very brave effort, one that has been attempted so often in New York, and generally died of exhaustion. Yet the Phoenix was to have a long and distinguished career before succumbing. Today, maybe the dream can come true at the Vivian Beaumont of Lincoln Center under the artistic direction of Gregory Mosher.

The Phoenix's first offering was to be *Madam, Will You Walk?* by Sidney Howard, and Jess and I were asked to lead the company. I was also asked to direct it. Unwisely I accepted.

The play had a curious history. The respected playwright Sidney Howard was killed in a horrifying accident before he could finish it. (He was cranking his own tractor, which he'd left in gear. The tractor ran over him.) Howard's great friend Bob Sherwood undertook to finish the play, and it was produced by the Playwrights Company in 1939 with the great George M. Cohan playing the leading role of Doctor Brightlee. The play closed out of town when Cohan withdrew.

Some fifteen years later I undertook to play Brightlee, to

direct the Phoenix production, *and* to try to reconcile the
Howard and Sherwood manuscripts. As John Wharton says in
his *Life Among the Playwrights,* "Cronyn chopped out a lot of
superfluous verbiage and rearranged scenes as he saw fit. The
play then opened the Phoenix Theatre and launched that organization on its illustrious career."

I remember very little of all this except that I wasn't up to
it. I sweated over the rewrites—if they can be called that—
horribly conscious of the ghosts over my shoulder. I could also
hear in my head old Jehly at the American Academy screaming, "You're a fool, boy—a fool! You can't create and criticize
at the same time! Oil and water won't mix!" Obviously it was
a lesson I hadn't learned.

I got halfway through the rehearsal period and realized
that I'd bitten off more than I could chew. Howard had written a charming fantasy, but the character of Brightlee, a be-
nignly demonic figure, was a complicated mix of fantasy and
reality, and I was scanting my performance to concentrate on
matters of script and direction. Mercifully, Norman Lloyd, who
was also in the cast, offered to bail me out as a codirector, so
that while I was onstage, struggling with the realities and un-
realities of Brightlee, there was a talented and watchful eye
out front.

The play opened and received generally if not unani-
mously favorable reviews and ran for its appointed time. The
Phoenix was born. For me, it was on to the next thing.

In 1953 and 1954, Jessica and I were involved in a series
called *The Marriage,* first for radio and then television. While
it was my brainchild, its success was largely due to the quality
of the writing. NBC was the network, and I was the producer
as well as being one of the leading characters. I don't believe
the description *sitcom* had been invented in the early fifties,
but that's what *The Marriage* was, a situation comedy based on
the domestic trials and tribulations of a quite ordinary middle-
class couple with two children. It was *not* a spin-off of *The
Fourposter,* as has frequently been reported, but dealt with current problems of family life that we thought were relevant and
had a comic potential.

We must have done twenty-five to thirty radio broadcasts

when we were persuaded to switch to television. The shows
were to be done live and that meant a killing schedule—back
to the days of one-a-week stock. Jess and I talked about it a
lot. Finally we hit on a proposal which, to my considerable
surprise, NBC accepted. We would do eight weeks as a summer replacement, but with the promise that if, at the end of
that time, we didn't wish to pursue it, we could walk away
without further obligation. It was the kind of deal that could
never be made today; the network's initial investment in a series would be far too great even to allow contemplation of such
an arrangement. So, with an escape hatch at the end of the
tunnel and considerable advantage of having a backlog of thirty
radio scripts to draw on, we signed a contract.

Then Jessica discovered that she was pregnant.

Shades of the *Green Years*! This time, I don't believe we
told anyone. After all, by the time Jess's condition became obvious, we would have one of two choices: either to walk away,
or to incorporate the pregnancy into our ongoing stories—up
to a point. "Sufficient unto the day . . ." We already had a
hatful of problems. Our agents and many old friends thought
we were crazy to undertake a summer replacement when we
had other options. Summer replacements were considered dé-
classé; there would be insufficient time to build an audience;
sponsors, if any, would be hard to find for the summer months.
Added to this chorus of disapproval were the normal problems of putting together a production team: selecting directors, designers, writers, casting the company and combing
through our accumulation of radio scripts to find those most
suitable for translation into a totally different medium.

When it comes to preparation, I'm rather like the man who
insists on both a belt *and* suspenders to hold his pants up. I
knew that once we got into production, I would be too busy
trying to act to be a producer. So we went into rehearsal with
seven out of the required eight television scripts already completed, and for this I had to thank two people in particular:
Millard Lampell, who was the marvelous script editor and su-
pervisor, and Ernie Kinoy, who wrote at least half the scripts.

However, there are some events for which you can't prepare. Three days before we were to open the series, Jessica

had a miscarriage. It was a horrid blow for us and a nasty shock for NBC, which, at the last minute, had to substitute a film for the first episode of *The Marriage*.

When, ten days later, we did open, it was to unusually warm and enthusiastic reviews, not just New York reviews but also those from across the country. The show was referred to as "adult, funny, relevant and touching" and produced an avalanche of mail with a difference. Much of it came from professional people, and there were few of the grubby postcard variety that read, "You are one of my greatest fans *[sic]*. Send autograph and picture." Coping with these letters became a terrible burden and we finally had to resort to printed-form postcards, a procedure which I hate but which is inevitable if you aren't to spend twenty-four hours a day answering mail.

About half the way through *The Marriage* series, we had an episode directed by Marc Daniels, an old friend and a wonderful director. (Paul Bogart was another.) During rehearsals one day, Marc took me aside and said, "You know, Hume, you're never going to find a sponsor for this program."

"Why not?"

"You're blacklisted."

"I'm what?"

"Blacklisted. I've tried to get you for a couple of things in the past year, and been told that in some quarters you're considered 'politically unreliable.' "

"What the fuck does that mean?" Profanity may be the refuge of small minds, but I was outraged—and stunned. "What about Jessie?"

Marc shrugged. "Nothing, I guess—except that she's married to you."

I went back into rehearsal with my mind everywhere but on my job. What were my political sins? As a Canadian, I didn't even have a vote, for God's sake, and as an alien, I'd always been scrupulous about avoiding direct political activity. Certainly I'd insisted on employing actors and writers whom I'd been advised were blacklisted, but I had no patience with that, and there had never been even a peep of objection from the network—perhaps because there was no sponsor involved.

As soon as we broke from rehearsal, I took the express

elevator up to the offices of the president of NBC, Pat Weaver.
Pat was an old friend, but I don't think that was why I got an
immediate audience. I rather suspect that his secretary recognized the urgency of my fury.

I got to the point immediately and asked Pat if he was aware
that he was employing a producer-actor who was likely to sub-
vert the American Constitution, to say nothing of his own organization. Pat looked bewildered and said no, but that if my
political reliability was indeed in question, someone at NBC
would be aware of it. He spoke to his secretary and almost
immediately a gentleman appeared from the legal department. He was both cautious and tactful. He extracted the one
sheet of paper held in the file he'd brought with him and admitted that, yes, there had been certain allegations, but upon
investigation they seemed insubstantial and that Tandy and
Cronyn seemed to offer no threat to NBC or the American
way of life.

Pat was clearly untroubled by the matter; a couple of weeks
later he urged Jess and me to continue *The Marriage* into the
fall season and practically guaranteed that there would be no
lack of sponsors. I hedged, saying that we'd made plans to do
a tour of *Face to Face*—about which more later—but Pat had
done his homework and knew that our tour agreement with
the National Concerts and Artists Corporation provided a thirty-
day escape clause. We listened to his cogent arguments. "You've
done all the work, you've done a season on radio, seven television shows, you've had a great success—why walk away from
the rewards?"

I never found a persuasive reply. Instead, we went fishing.
Elia—"Gadge"—Kazan, his wife, Molly, Jessica and I chartered a boat and took off for a long, leisurely cruise through
my beloved Exumas. We were anchored in the harbor of
Compass Cay when the radio crackled and a message came
through to the effect that we were to have a visitor. This turned
out to be Ira Steiner of Ashley-Steiner, our agents at the time.
I could guess what he was after and who'd prodded him into
coming—Pat Weaver. I could also guess where Pat had got his
information about the cancellation clause in our *Face to Face*
contract.

The Fourposter,
Act 1, 1952

Alfredo Valente

The Fourposter,
Act 2, 1952

Children's Bay Cay, as I first saw it from the air, 1946

Five years later

Elia Kazan

Children's Bay Cay, the "Home Beach,"
about 1954

H.C., Children's Bay Cay, 1954

Elia Kazan

Children's Bay Cay, guest room, about 1954

Where it all started: shark fishing off Rose Island, Bahamas, with the fearsome Uncle Edward, 1928

Intrepid spear fisherman with grouper and yellowfin rockfish, Exumas, 1963

Jessica as Blanche Dubois in *A Streetcar Named Desire*, 1947

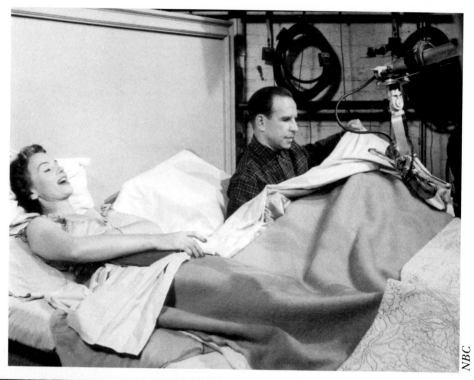

Above, *The Marriage,* for NBC-TV, 1953–1954

J.T. and H.C. in *The Honeys,* 1955

J.T. and H.C. in *The Man in the Dog Suit*, 1957

H.C. with Biff McGuire in Sean O'Casey's *A Pound on Demand*, from *Triple Play*, 1958

J.T. and H.C. in Sean O'Casey's *Bedtime Story*, from *Triple Play*, 1958

Kazan was totally disgusted. "For Christ's sake, Hume, when you say no can't you make it sound like no? All the way down here and we're going to have to talk about television? I'm going fishing!" And he did. As the little seaplane appeared, circling over our heads, Gadge and Molly took off up Compass Cay Creek, carrying their spinning rods. Ira came aboard and it began all over again. We were mad not to proceed with *The Marriage.* Did we realize how much money we might make? Then Ira produced his crowning argument.

"I'll ask you just one more question. If, a year from now, you could be where Lucille Ball is today, would you still say no?"

I looked past Ira to where Jessica was sitting. Her head was nodding up and down like that of a mechanical doll, slowly but very surely.

Ira gave up and went swimming. He was a strong swimmer and proud of it, but plump, heavily fleshed and consequently very buoyant. He found it difficult to dive. From the boat, we watched him thrash around in the water until finally Jess said, "What are you after, Ira?" He gasped, "Down there . . . a shell." Then Jess added insult to injury. She slid over the side, glided down the twenty feet, picked up the shell, surfaced, and put the shell in his hand. Ira was amazed. "How come you can do that?" Jessica smiled sweetly. "Ira, I can pick up a shell for you, but I cannot play in *The Marriage* week after week, after week. . . ."

Like Jessica, I dreaded the possibility of so much repetition. But unlike her, I was tempted—all that money! And I was spending it like a drunken sailor on Children's Bay Cay. However, my most serious anxieties had to do with being unprepared. If we were to proceed, we had to do it immediately and we no longer had a cache of ready scripts to draw on. I could see that these would have to be written as we played. I had visions of long, sleepless nights worrying about what we were to do, not only tomorrow, but in the endless weeks to come. I was frightened. I think I have more than my fair share of those actor's nightmares in which you suddenly find yourself onstage wondering what play you're in, or not knowing a line, or in the wrong costume, or stark naked.

At any rate, we "passed." We had our holiday and went back to New York to gear up for *Face to Face*.

Face to Face was one of those entertainments that is sometimes called a platform piece, for the very good reason that a platform is all that should be required by the players. Well done, it comes about as close as actors can get to fulfilling the oldest and most primitive of the theater's demands: "two boards and a passion."

Putting together an anthology program isn't easy. It just *sounds* easy. "Oh, you know, they're going to do a reading tour— just read, don't even have to learn the lines." First of all, we never actually *read* anything, even though the appearance of reading was sometimes required; everything was carefully rehearsed and committed to memory. Second, precisely what do you seem to read, or recite, or perform? With the whole canon of English literature, verse and drama to draw upon, there's an embarrassment of riches. One approach is to stick to a single author, as Emlyn Williams did with Dickens, Hal Holbrook with Mark Twain and Alec McCowen with the Gospel according to St. Mark. Each of these actors provided a brilliant performance of cohesive materials, and a wonderful evening of theater. Charles Laughton, on the other hand, "read" from a variety of authors and made his first appearance carrying a large pile of books. He practically staggered onstage under their weight before depositing them on the lectern, stage center. I always found this opening a bit intimidating, as though I might be committed to a long sentence in some musty library. If Charles didn't actually blow dust from the book covers, I felt he was about to. Of course, as soon as he began to read, all apprehensions were immediately dispelled; he was magical.

We chose the eclectic Laughton approach, but made far greater use of the platform than he chose to do. We "staged" many pieces, using a few straight-backed chairs as props, and with two of us involved we had the advantage of being able to use dialogue material. Our program ranged from Shakespeare to Ogden Nash, from Dorothy Parker to Tennessee Williams.

Even so, there were severe restrictions. We soon discovered that we could not do a piece simply because we loved it. I remember struggling with two beautiful narrative pieces: Alan Paton's short story "A Drink in the Passage" and a chapter from Sir Arthur Grimble's book *We Chose the Islands,* called "The Calling of the Porpoise." They were both wonderful stories, but we couldn't make them fit. There has to be a balance in the whole; sometimes the most effective of pieces make for terrible problems in what is to follow. You can't create one mood in an audience, then suddenly drop it and switch to a totally different one without a suitable and subtle transition. You can't weight the program in favor of one actor or another. You can do only so many individual pieces, so many dialogues; only so much drama or so much comedy. Putting a program together is rather like attempting to solve a particularly fiendish acrostic puzzle, and in the end only an audience can tell you if you've got it right.

If assembling a program is difficult, the touring requirements are even more punishing. We committed to about thirty engagements over a six-week period—an average of five a week, often in five different states. We lived in airplanes, buses and hired cars. Sometimes we played at ten o'clock in the morning, for schools and ladies' culture clubs, sometimes it was a matinee; more usually we played in the evening. We performed in front of movie screens, in gymnasiums, churches, synagogues, assembly halls, ballrooms, at least once on a basketball court, and sometimes, blessedly, in a theater.

The toughest engagements were those where our contract demanded our presence at a lunch before or reception after the performance. These social events were like a second performance, and required a calloused hand, a frozen smile and a strong stomach. Worst of all were the one or two occasions when an overeager booking agent and misguided sponsor failed to match the taste of their audience to the nature of the program being offered.

On December 7, 1954, we appeared in the grand ballroom of New York's Hotel Pierre before a black-tie audience largely drawn from the United States Department of the Navy. They were the guests of a naval engineering firm whose contracts must have been very lucrative. Ostensibly, the dinner was being given in celebration of the engineering company's fiftieth anniversary. December 7th also happens to be the anniversary of the bombing of Pearl Harbor. I can hardly believe that the dates were coincidental, even though there would be precious little to celebrate about "the day of infamy." Little did I know that we were about to drop some catastrophic bombs of our own making.

I have the elaborate and very expensive-looking program for that evening in front of me as I write. I'll spare you the dinner menu but list the wines being served during dinner and *before the entertainment*—of which we were only a part.

Harvey's Amontillado Sherry.

Meursault 1947 Goute D'Or.

Pommard 1945 Chanlains in magnums.

Veuve Cliquot 1947 in jeroboams.

Goldwasser 1598 Cognac (—*1598? Can that be possible?* Well, that's what it says).

Following the dinner menu is a page headed "Playbill." It reads as follows, with the exception of certain surnames I've omitted out of consideration for the possible painful memories of the artists involved:

Christmas March

*

The Cake Eaters Band

*

The Gypsies

*

Stan _____, pianist

*

Jessica Tandy and Hume Cronyn;
Excerpts from their National Tour of "Face to Face"

*

Virginia _____; Metropolitan Opera Star

*

Morley _____; Concert Star accompanied
by Marcel _____

*

Music by Stanley _____

I hope you've taken particular note of the *magnums* of red
wine, the *jeroboams* of champagne (to say nothing of the six-
teenth-century cognac), as well as the Cake Eaters Band. The
latter accompanied the triumphal entry of an enormous birthday cake in the shape of a battleship, with smoke belching from
its funnels. At that moment, the predominantly male audience
wanted nothing so much as to have the cake open to reveal
half a dozen dancing girls—topless, bottomless, and worthy of
a rude centerfold. What did they get from us instead? Chekhov, and Elizabeth Barrett Browning's *Sonnets from the Portu-
guese.* By the time we discovered our appalling mismatch—about
sixty seconds after we started—it was too late to do anything
about it.

For us it was an evening of total disaster. As for the reception of the unfortunate Metropolitan star who followed us, I
can only shudder. When we slunk down the stairs from the
ballroom we heard her bravely caroling "Chiribiri-bim . . ."

Despite the awfulness of that one evening at the Pierre, I
think that *Face to Face* has to appear on the credit side of our
theatrical ledger. At any rate, we got good reviews in Los Angeles and San Francisco, where we were presented in legitimate theaters.

Sadly, I can't say as much about our next joint effort. I am
still sad about *The Honeys* because I've always felt that we came
so close to a smashing success. What stood in the way I think
was the intransigence of the author, Roald Dahl. It certainly
wasn't his lack of ability. To quote one reviewer, "Mr. Dahl is
a brilliant writer of macabre humor," and indeed he was; he
made two of his short stories the basis of *The Honeys,* a farcical
black comedy. Unhappily, the wit and invention of the end
product were not enough, and Roald would not accept help
from any quarter, certainly not from the actors or directors

involved—and there were three of the latter before we opened in New York. Theatrical collaboration does not come easy to most writers who have become established in a different form. They are inclined to resent the intrusion of other opinions and look on it as destructive meddling, which is of course a possibility. But in the theater, collaboration is as inevitable as it is essential.

The play opened in New Haven and almost immediately the director, Reginald Denham, left us. Whether he chose to withdraw or was pushed I don't know, but things were downhill all the way thereafter. I had got on very well with Reggie—but then, I had what one critic called "a double-fudge sundae of a part." It was two parts, actually. I played dissimilar twin brothers, both of them equally obnoxious but physically totally different. Bennet Honey was neat, lean, arthritic, and wore an outrageous toupee. His twin, Curtis Honey, was bald as an egg, potbellied, and looked like an unmade bed. Photographs of Henry Ford, senior, gave me the image of Bennet, and an amalgam of Alfred Hitchcock and Truman Capote provided a physical key to Curtis. I used Hitch's pouty expression and Truman's high-pitched voice of complaint to try to draw an image of an overgrown, spoiled baby. Both characters had their individual tics and mannerisms. Elaborate make-up changes and wardrobe helped, but the trick was to make them both real, something more than cartoons. I had a wonderfully happy time working it all out. It was as close as I ever got to being the protean actor.

And then the roof fell in. Cheryl Crawford, our producer, came to me in New Haven and asked me to take over the direction. I was aghast. Reminding Cheryl that I was already playing two parts, I said, "No!" in a manner that would have pleased even Elia Kazan.

"Then what are we to do?" said Cheryl. I've learned since that you can say, "That's *your* problem" (indeed I've said it), but the conversation ended with my temporizing, saying that I would talk it over with Jessica and Dorothy Stickney, who played the two Mrs. Honeys.

So I did that, and I had what I thought was a searching talk with Roald that seemed to promise flexibility. As a result,

I agreed to take on the direction provided that the out-of-town tryout period be extended, that I was not to be credited as director, and most important, that Cheryl should somehow, anyhow, find a new director.

Throughout rehearsals, Roald and I had got on well enough, but once I had taken over as director and started to chivy him about his play, the relationship began to show signs of frost. Roald resisted change. I would sit beside him at a table with the script between us, and suggest this cut or that transposition, but to little avail. Roald had a curious habit that appeared only when he faced an uncomfortable decision. He would make a sound, a sort of prolonged "Hmmmm" that implied he was considering the suggestion—but it was almost invariably followed by "no." I began to dread these "Hmmmm—no!" responses, and in frustration took an actor's revenge: I incorporated the mannerism into my performance as Bennet Honey. Walter Kerr picked it up in his review: "Bennet is a palsied monster whose most emphatic utterances are preceded by a long low buzz from the depths of his being." I don't think Roald ever noticed, or if he did didn't recognize it.

We soldiered on through Boston, Philadelphia and finally Washington. I give Cheryl great credit for managing to extend our time out of town on such short notice. On the other hand, she had the most disconcerting habit of disappearing in moments of crisis—and there were a number of those. The most severe was in Philadelphia. I had been worried about Dorothy Stickney's health. We were giving eight performances a week as well as rehearsing every day, and Dorothy was not happy. None of us was. She called me at my hotel between a matinee and evening performance to announce that she would not be playing that evening; she was taking off for New York *immediately*, to keep an appointment with her therapist. My God! That meant we must either cancel the evening performance or put on a totally unprepared understudy. I couldn't reach Cheryl of course, so it was my decision. I opted for the understudy and rushed back to the theater to see what support I could lend. The understudy had not had one single rehearsal, and she covered both Dorothy and Jess. She said, quavering, that she knew the first two acts but would have to carry the book in the third. I helped her bring her stuff down from her third-floor dressing room to Dorothy's more convenient room on the stage level, turned her over to the wardrobe mistress, who had to try to get her into Dorothy's costumes, and went out onto the empty stage to pray for divine assistance for us all.

During the performance, a sneak thief managed to get into the understudy's deserted dressing room from a fire escape, and stole her purse. In it was not only her money, but her hotel-room key as well. The thief must have hotfooted it from the theater to the hotel, because when she got back there after a terrifying evening, she called me to say her room had been ransacked. Then she burst into tears. All I could do was to get over there and buy her a drink. Typical of the actress, what worried her most was not the loss of the money and half her personal wardrobe, but her performance. At least I was able to reassure on that point. She was a noble lady and a true professional. I salute her and apologize for not remembering her name.

After a couple of days Dorothy came back to us and Cheryl called me to say that she had persuaded Frank Corsaro to take over the direction in Washington. It was an enormous relief. The three previous weeks in which I'd tried to do triple duty had been absolute hell. Without Jessica's unfailing support—"It's only a play, dear"—I'd never have got through it but would probably have joined Dorothy on the therapeutic couch.

We opened in New York to what are called "mixed notices," which means that they are not good enough; and we closed after a short run. Sometimes I run into a fan who will say, "I saw you in *The Honeys*—it was hilarious." If they only knew.

TWENTY-FIVE

BILL WRIGHT AND Al Beich originally wrote *The Man in the Dog Suit* as a screenplay. I commissioned them to turn it into a play—and found myself back in the business of producing. We did two separate productions: the first in the summer of 1957, the second the following year; both in summer theaters throughout the northeast, both on tour. *The Man in the Dog Suit* was near ideal summer fare; light, amusing, affirmative, it was just the sort of thing for an audience of people who are on holiday and have little desire to engage their critical faculties. We frequently played to sold-out houses. Therein lies the cruel trap for managers trying out a new play on the summer-theater circuit and hoping to bring it to Broadway when it is "right." Summer-theater audiences are notoriously unreliable as a gauge of Broadway acceptance.

Halfway through the first tour I knew *Dog Suit* wasn't right, and yet I have a vivid memory of David Merrick sitting in my dressing room at the Westport Playhouse and offering to bring the play into New York the following season. Merrick was and is a highly successful producer, and the offer was horribly tempting. However, I'd made up my mind that we needed to do more work and felt sure we could improve the play. I was wrong.

The authors worked. A year went by, and the following summer we went back to it again with only marginal improvement. There was the same encouraging audience reaction and Bob Whitehead and Roger Stevens took over as producers, with that dear man Lewis Allen acting as their surrogate and associate producer on the firing line. The play opened at the Coronet Theater on October 30th, 1958, failed, and was buried. After so much work it was a particularly bloody blow.

The *New York Times*, in the august person of Brooks Atkinson, drove a couple of deep nails into the casket—right through the wood and into Jess and me as well. The most painful part of his review was its last sentence: "Why do Mr. and Mrs. Cronyn waste their talent on such tired nonsense?"

For the first and only time that I can remember in over fifty years of exposure to critics, I wrote Atkinson a letter of . . . what shall I call it? Protest? Refutation? Excuse? Exculpation? I quote just one sentence from it: "I simply want to explain that, right or wrong, *what* we undertook was not done frivolously, and that error in judgment can't fairly be ascribed to a lack of professional pride or to shabby intentions."

Atkinson sent a reply which was both charming and reasonable. He wrote:

> Opinions about plays are notoriously subjective. . . . No one can pretend to omniscience or infallibility in the sphere of opinion. But my only feeling about "The Man in the Dog Suit" is that it is a consistently hack job of characterization and writing. . . .
>
> Let me say that I am sorry to have given you a bad time. But since I know the quality of the work that you and Jessica do, I could not help brooding in the theater over the problem presented by a play I think is below your standards of artistic taste.

I suppose you could call this a standoff. I've never written to a critic since.

Between the two summer productions of *Dog Suit,* I directed a play by Molly Kazan (Molly Day Thacher) called *The Egghead.* It starred Karl Malden, and an important role was

played by Lloyd Richards, who later of course exchanged acting for directing and his triumphant work at Yale. Lloyd's understudy was a young man in his first Broadway engagement:
his name was James Earl Jones. Some ten years later Jessica
and I went to see this remarkable actor in *The Great White Hope*
and were so stunned by his performance that we sat in the
orchestra long after the audience left. I'd been so impressed
that when the final curtain came down and people stood in a
wild ovation, I had not even been able to applaud. When we
finally staggered to our feet, Jess said "Shall we go back to
congratulate him?" "Better not," I said. "He must be exhausted—and besides, I don't know him."

I didn't know him? As someone later reminded me, during
the rehearsal and run of *The Egghead*, I must have seen him
daily over a period of weeks. This is one of the most sad and
embarrassing facts of theater life—and in motion pictures and
television it's even worse. For weeks on end you work closely,
even intimately, with people in a highly concentrated effort to
achieve a common goal, a good production; and then you move
on to the next thing and the next and the next. Friendships,
intimacies, personal revelations become buried under layer after
layer of successive effort. Paths diverge—until one day they
cross again and there you are faced with a stranger whom once
you embraced. Today, when one of these too-frequent meetings occur, I take refuge in my poor eyesight, which is allow-
able as I have only one eye and less than perfect vision in that;
but it never happens without giving me a pang and a miserable sense of loss. So much shared; so much evaporated.

Of course, in the case of *The Egghead* I might be forgiven
for my lack of recall. Once again I was involved with an ob-
durate author of very little theatrical experience who was inclined to value the words on the page at the expense of what
was happening on the stage and in the audience. Going in, I
knew that Molly's play was flawed—but then most plays are.
You do the best you can. In this case I admired and respected
the playwright—a very bright lady indeed—and was surrounded by people of whom I was very fond. Those may not
be the best of reasons for directing a play, but at least they're
affirmative.

I'd known Karl Malden since he appeared with Jessica in *Streetcar*, and he is now one of my oldest and most trusted friends; a talented actor of great diversity and absolute dedication, and a wonderfully warm human being as well. It's a rare mix. Karl had a huge responsibility in the play. He *was* "The Egghead," the play's central character and pivot. He took my direction with unfailing grace even when he disagreed with it. He would try anything and so would the others: Lloyd Richards, Phyllis Love, and a strong supporting cast. I had no problems with the company, but I had big ones with the playwright. Molly had a message to give and she was damn well going to *state* it. She did not trust it to become implicit in the play's action. Atkinson in his review called it "a thesis play" and was accurate.

My experience with *The Egghead* is summed up in one epic meeting held in Molly's hotel bedroom after an out-of-town performance. Molly's husband, Elia Kazan, had come to see the play and brought Robert Anderson with him. Walking up the aisle after the performance, Gadge took me by the arm.

"Hume," he said, "she's got to cut it."

I said warily, "See what you can do."

We waited for Karl to get into his street clothes, then the four of us trooped over to Molly's hotel. The scene is etched in my memory. Molly lay on the bed propped up by pillows, one arm thrown over her head, one knee slightly raised. I was immediately reminded of Renoir's *Odalisque;* the positions were identical, only the clothes were different. Bob sat in the straight-backed chair beside her, Gadge straddled another at the foot of the bed, I was tilted against the wall behind him, with an exhausted Karl next to me in the only armchair. Karl and I were relatively silent. After all, with two of the most knowledgeable and influential men in American theater offering their opinions, what did we have to add that we hadn't already said?

Naturally, Bob, who had great influence with Molly as a playwright she respected, spoke more about the writing than its execution in performance. Kazan spoke about everything. The discussion went along smoothly, tactfully, for perhaps the first five or ten minutes, with Gadge paying tribute to Karl's performance and my direction, but dwelling particularly on the play's virtues: its wit, its humor, the theatrical effectiveness of certain scenes. Phrases like "beautifully written," "wonderfully observed," "brilliantly executed," and "you must keep that" cooed from Gadge's lips, and Bob Anderson would nod in agreement. I looked sidelong at Karl. He was following the interplay like a man watching a tennis match, his eyes darting from Gadge to Molly to Bob as he followed the ball. But for Karl it kept landing in the wrong court. He was drowning in the play's surfeit of words.

Then abruptly, Gadge said, "But you've got to cut it." The temperature at the bed immediately dropped by about ten degrees.

It is at a point like this in making a film that a director sometimes employs a "dissolve" to denote the passage of time. In this particular scene the image fades out and then comes back into focus, with no change of position among the principals but an enormous change in the tone of the dialogue. Gone are Gadge's honeyed phrases, and in their stead we hear the playwright's impassioned husband shouting, "God damn it, Molly, you've got no choice! . . . No one wants to hear that shit! . . . Boring, Molly, boring! . . . Ask Bob, ask Hume, listen to your audience for Christ's sake! . . ."—and so it went. In this tennis game the ball was no longer being lobbed but smashed across the net of the bed. It was a classic example of a rough passage in a marriage within the same profession. Here was a couple devoted to one another, each hoping to achieve precisely the same result, but approaching the problem from opposing artistic viewpoints. I'd been down this same road before with Jessica. It's not always conducive to a blissful domestic state.

Throughout the argument Molly remained imperturbable. The more vehement her husband became, the more maddeningly quiet and reasonable Molly appeared to be. She defended each specific point with a calm intellectual fervor of her own. An irresistible force met an immovable object and the immovable object won—or perhaps, in the long run (which we didn't have), lost.

We left the immovable Molly on her bed and staggered down the hotel hallway to the nearest elevator and bar. Karl,

Gadge, and Bob were depressed. Internally, I was giggling, indulging a shameful sense of "I told you so." After all, it was Molly's play and no one, *no* one, not Karl, not her husband, not an eminent colleague, not her director, was to be allowed to fiddle with it. It was something I'd recognized for weeks past, and while I thought Molly dead wrong, I had a sneaking admiration for her obduracy.

But of course the play failed—and I feel bound to add that even if Molly had decided to act on all our well-meaning suggestions, I could not swear that the outcome would have been different. Rewriting is a very, very difficult business. Cutting alone may spill the playwright's blood, but cutting *and* rewriting, during a tryout, calls on reserves of objectivity, invention and perseverance that at times, I suspect, defeated even William Shakespeare.

TWENTY-SIX

In the decade of the fifties, I was actively involved as actor or director in thirteen stage productions (ten of them with Jessica), three films, ten television productions, *plus* seven episodes of *The Marriage* (a TV series which I produced as well as played in) and seven appearances in *Omnibus*—each of the last a production in itself with a major responsibility. Jessica appeared in more than half of these TV productions with me; she also did three films on her own. It adds up to forty productions of one sort or another in ten years for me alone— and I haven't counted them all. At least I couldn't complain of stagnation. Looking back, I think we did too much and that we paid a price for it. But that comes later.

The 1950's are sometimes referred to as the Golden Age of Television. It was a comforting change to move from a series of theater failures into a field where we could seem to do no wrong. If that sounds arrogant—and it does—we have the writers and directors involved to thank for my cockiness.

We did some rubbish too—but consider the following list:

The Five Dollar Bill (Tad Mosel)
A Member of the Family (Horton Foote)
The Bridge of San Luis Rey (Thorton Wilder–Ludi Clair)

The Moon and Sixpence (Somerset Maugham–S. Lee Pogostine)
A Doll's House (Henrik Ibsen–James Costigan)
The Big Wave (Pearl Buck)
"Glory in the Flower"—for *Omnibus* (William Inge)
"The Adams Family"—for *Omnibus* (Henry and John Quincy Adams et al.)
Juno and the Paycock (Sean O'Casey)

At least four of the above were directed by Robert Mulligan, a superb television director, and in every case the writing was vastly superior to standard television fare. Also, most of the shows were done "live" from New York. You worked largely with familiar and accomplished theater people and went home to your own bed at night. There was another lovely bonus: the diversity of roles. I was allowed to play everything from an antique Chinese gentleman in *The Big Wave* to John Quincy Adams in *The Adams Family,* and from Krogstad in *A Doll's House* with Julie Harris to Captain Boyle in *Juno and the Paycock* with Walter Matthau. For me, all this was cake and champagne, but of course I didn't always get away with it. Jack Gould, the television critic for the *New York Times* in those years, faulted my performance as Captain Boyle, and he was probably right. I may have been miscast. Perhaps Matthau should have played the captain and I played Joxer, instead of the other way around. Anyway, Walter was outraged and wrote to the *Times* in my defense. It was a generous letter.

> Too many actors reaching a level of prominence are "playing it safe," meticulously guarding their professional appearances, encasing themselves in a protective shell of what has succeeded for them in the past. This kind of thinking is for banks and insurance companies. . . . If an actor hasn't the "guts" to try something different, be he good or bad, he's in the wrong field.

And some twenty-five years later in California, Walter did play Captain Boyle, with Jack Lemmon playing Joxer.

Omnibus was a prestigious show, a sort of classy catchall of infinite variety, as implied by its title. It was produced by Robert Saudek, and its host was the suave and ingratiating Alistair Cooke, whose opinions on almost any subject are provocative. In *The Adams Family,* the American historian Allan Nevins was the commentator who held the program together. All the dialogue was taken from the letters or speeches of Henry or John Quincy Adams or from historical documents of their period. It had to be exact. There was only one problem: the powers-that-be were of six minds as to precisely what excerpts were to be used on the show, and their opinions kept changing. Halfway through the rehearsal period it became obvious that the cast could learn nothing without the probability that it would be changed, and changed again, so TelePrompTer machines became a necessity. These monsters were strategically placed, but when we got to dress rehearsal, and the dialogue, under the tyranny of the clock, had to be either cut or amended right then to give it flow, the bedeviled TelePrompTer operator no longer had time to get a new printout. He had to make changes with a Magic Marker on the face of the existing paper roll. I can remember the poor man dashing out to his machine, crossing out six lines, replacing them with a connective link in unreadable longhand, and dashing back to make himself a note that at this point he would have to speed up his machine so that the actors were not left stranded. It was a hairy business and disaster was inevitable.

It came during a speech of John Quincy Adams to Congress. I was well into it when the TelePrompTer suddenly speeded up, eliminating four lines that had been cut and then, at the very last moment, reinserted. The operator had not caught up with this last-minute change. I was left with two fragments of a critical speech that did not make sense. (Remember, this was live—going out to millions of people as we played it.) I took one of the longest on-air pauses in television history and felt the sweat break out under my bald-headed cap. The operator, realizing that something had gone terribly wrong, reversed the TelePrompTer and it whirled back past the place where the cut had started. Then it whirled forward again as the frantic operator tried to find where he'd gone wrong. I was aware that one assistant director was desperately trying to manipulate the TelePrompTer roll by hand. He kept swatting at it like a man threatened by killer bees. This further complicated the operator's problem. Another assistant hurled himself onto the floor under the camera lens and held up a beseeching copy of the script. I could only just see the page and the agonized face of the man holding it. Reading the print was totally impossible. I *had* to adlib—I couldn't just stand there. "Gentlemen," I croaked from a very dry mouth—(and then another *very* long pause)—"Gentlemen, I am at a loss for words. . . ."

How we worked ourselves out of that mess I don't remember. I only know that I finished the performance with very weak knees and in terror that my rivers of nervous perspiration would break loose my bald-headed cap, and give John Quincy Adams a sudden miraculous growth of hair.

Saint Jessica, who was playing Mrs. Adams, met me in the dressing room with a stiff drink.

The Moon and Sixpence was, I believe, Laurence Olivier's first foray into television. He played Paul Gauguin and of course played it brilliantly. My own role was almost as good as his, and again Jessica played my wife. I knew Larry, but not nearly as well as Jess did; she had played with him on the London stage a number of times before. I was nervous, though I needn't have been. Olivier was just like any other gifted actor only more so, and by that I mean subject to the same anxieties, the same process of trial and error, the same generosity—and at the same time an impatience with what he considered unnecessary delay. I remember him turning once on me and Bob Mulligan, the director, when we were deep in a conversation about "motivations." "For God's sake," Larry snarled, "let's get on with it!" This was also the production in which I asked Larry for help in a particularly difficult emotional scene only to have him say, "Just give it a bash." Hardly profound, but very sound advice. In the clutches, an actor may sometimes intellectualize a performance into gridlock, when, if he had trusted gut instinct, he might have soared.

Olivier being Olivier, I remember certain things he said to me. At the height of his difficulties with Vivien Leigh, he sat in our New York apartment one evening and said quite abruptly, "You and Jessica are happy together, aren't you?" I could have answered immediately, "Yes, devoted," but Larry's question had carried a tone almost of accusation, and it would have sounded smug. I fumbled and equivocated, and while admitting to our happiness, added something fatuous about the inevitable pains attached to the marriage contract. Larry took a long pause, then put his head on the back of the chair, stared at the ceiling, and sighed. He said wearily, "I suppose all that matters is a bit of peace." It was a haunting comment, and there was no possible response but silence.

On another visit Larry asked to be shown through the apartment. He examined paintings and family photographs— those symbols of domesticity—like a city dog sniffing a country tree, but made no comment until we came to our daughter's bedroom. It wasn't an unusual room, but it was bright, with two window exposures, cheerful posters hanging on the walls, and gay curtains and a bedspread that matched. Tandy had her own desk for homework, and a bookcase. I would have thought it a fairly typical room for a ten- or twelve-year-old girl. Larry gave it a long searching look, then turned to us. "But what has she got to look forward to?" he said.

In 1962, staying with Larry in Brighton, Sussex, I told him I was about to play *The Miser* and he said, "Molière? Funny as a baby's open grave." You may imagine how that made me feel. Fortunately, he was dead wrong. The play can be both touching and hilarious.

Also in Brighton, I told him that I'd been offered the job of artistic director at both the Festival Theatre in Stratford, Ontario, and the Tyrone Guthrie Theater in Minneapolis. I'd turned them down, feeling either one would drive me to an early grave. But I felt insecure and a bit guilty about not accepting the challenge, and I think I was hoping to hear Larry say, "You were right!" He didn't. "Well," he said, "if you won't do it, you don't deserve to have it!" And that was that. It did nothing to reinforce my sense of judgment, but it didn't change my mind.

Playing Paul Gauguin in *The Moon and Sixpence*, Larry drew a masterful portrait of a tortured, complex man. The show was not done "live," but it might as well have been. We rehearsed it like a play, and the hours on the set were brutally long. The producer, David Susskind, was using a new type of film or tape where the color was almost impossible to match between takes. Consequently, it was like shooting *Rope* all over again. If there was a glitch, you had to start again from the beginning; there could be no such thing as "pick-up" shots. We were shooting in a studio somewhere in Brooklyn—a long ride from the city. Sometimes Larry would spend the night on the set, sleeping in one of the prop beds. When he didn't do that, he would take off for a gymnasium at the end of his day. He had always been careful about his physical instrument, realizing, as too few actors do, that it was an essential part of his professional equipment. But at the time, he was also preparing for *Spartacus,* a film that demanded he be in top physical shape. I marveled at his stamina.

Actors today, used to film and tape, or inexperienced actors, may not appreciate that in live television, you work always under the tyranny of the clock. Stretch one scene and in the following a desperate assistant director will be standing beside the camera making frantic gestures to indicate that the scene must be speeded up. Go too fast, or inadvertently cut something, and the same individual will be using hand signals that implore you to go slower. As you do it, so is it immediately broadcast. There is no rescue to be had in an editing room, and sponsors do not take kindly to having their commercials imposed upon. As a consequence, a live show is rehearsed very much as a theater piece might be, with one horridly important difference: the timing of the live television show has to be very nearly exact. (I exempt shows like *Saturday Night Live* and others of that ilk, in which buffers are built in.) Every scene is rehearsed to a stopwatch. There is room for experimentation and improvisation during rehearsals, but once the action, interpretations and camera moves are set, woe betide you if some member of the company takes off and does his own thing. The brilliant last-minute inspiration of an actor who decides to change the blocking, to take a series of long, indulgent pauses or, conversely, to race through a passage or try an arbitrary cut can throw his fellow actors into panic and drive directors and camera crews to madness. Bear this in mind while I describe an *Omnibus* show called *Glory in the Flower* by William Inge.

Jessica played the central role, and for once escaped being my wife. My own role was that of the owner of a shabby bar and diner, boasting a jukebox and tiny dance floor. It catered for the most part to truck drivers and teenagers. It was a hangout. As a proprietor anxious not to jeopardize his liquor license, I had to police the joint and make sure there was no underage drinking on the premises. In one scene, having become aware that four rowdy teenagers were passing a pint bottle among them, I had to confront these kids and demand surrender of the bottle. The bottle was not forthcoming. I had to search for it. All this had been rehearsed and I was supposed to find the bottle in the hip pocket of the young man nearest to me. At the final technical rehearsal, it wasn't there. I fumbled about, looking under the table, behind the seat cushions of the booth, under napkins, among the plastic flowers on the table, and then gave up. The camera stopped rolling.

"Where is it, Jimmy?"

The young man said, "Why don't you just find it?"

His tone was a challenge; it implied: "You're supposed to hunt, so hunt—let's make it *real*."

I tried to be agreeable. "Is it worth it? I think I can *act* hunting for it."

The director appeared from the control booth and asked for the bottle. It was produced from the actor's jeans, stuffed down behind his fly. The director stuck it back in the actor's hip pocket and told us to proceed. Time was running out and we still had to do a dress.

The actor involved was one I'd noticed on our very first reading of the script. He was blond, thin, handsome and had a very definite presence. He was also infinitely "laid back": not rude, not quite arrogant but with a manner that said "I'm here—pay attention—and I don't give a damn what you think." I'd never seen him before and couldn't remember his last name any more than I could those of the other dozen kids. I was lucky if I remembered their first names.

We finished the technical rehearsal and it was obvious that we had to plunge into the dress rehearsal with barely time to get into our costumes. I hate these last-minute rushes. They leave no time to check the props and none in which to compose oneself. That clock keeps ticking. You pray that nothing will go wrong and that you may get a breather before air time. I remember Jess saying, "Calm down, calm down!"

We got three quarters of the way through the dress without anything going drastically wrong, and reached a climactic scene on the small, packed dance floor. A fight broke out and I was supposed to wade into the melee and separate the two principal combatants. One of these was my cool friend of the bottle incident. The scene had been very carefully choreographed by the director so that the camera could follow the main action and not be blocked by writhing, closely packed bodies. There was also the danger that, if the fight was not executed precisely, someone might end up with a bloody nose.

My cue came and I waded into the heaving sea of humanity and was immediately lost. I couldn't find the bottle boy with whom I was to have the next exchange of dialogue; he simply wasn't where he was supposed to be. Where the hell had he gone? I looked wildly around, pushed people aside, crouched down, stood on tiptoe, but not a sign of him. Suddenly, a laconic voice from somewhere behind me said, "I'm here." He may bloody well have been there, but if I crossed to him we would both be out of camera range as well as the light. I heard a voice from the booth say, "Cut! Hold it! I'm coming down." And I lost my temper.

Actors rarely know their reputations with crews and casts. I've known some who considered themselves angels of light, but who are spoken of less than kindly by their fellows. God forgive me, I may be one of those, but I hope not. At any rate, I seized the young actor by the arm, whirled him around and pointed to the studio wall clock.

"See that? It says twenty-two minutes to air time, and we haven't yet finished the dress. I don't know about you, but I'd at least like to have time to take a pee before we do this for real. *For Christ's sake be where you're supposed to be!*"

Everyone went into shock. The young actor tore his arm loose and started to remonstrate. "I was trying something new. I wanted to confuse you. . . . You *should* be confused."

"I was! I am! But I can *act* confused. Keep that experimental shit for rehearsal or your dressing room! You're not alone out here!"

At which point the director arrived and said, "Cool it, cool it both of you! Jimmy, get your ass over here where you belong, and let's get on with it, *NOW!*"

In the few minutes' break between dress and showtime, coming out of the men's room, I ran into Jimmy in the hall. He said quietly, "Mr. Cronyn, I respect your work and you should respect mine. You shouldn't talk to me like that."

"You're right Jimmy, I shouldn't, and I apologize. But it isn't *your* work or mine. It's *ours*. We're all dependent on one another."

The show went on without incident, and some weeks later I ran into Jimmy on the street. In a very uncharacteristic manner he embraced me, and before I'd had a chance to say much of anything, he said, "I forgive you—you were nervous." To say that I was dumbfounded puts it mildly. However, we parted, smiling and the best of friends. I don't believe I ever saw him again—in person.

Later that year, Kazan and I were again on a boat together, and Gadge gave me a copy of his next film to read. It was a good script with a wonderful part for a young man.

"Who's going to play that?" I asked.

"A new kid, very talented," and he gave me the name. I suppose my expression or my silence must have betrayed me.

"What's wrong?"

"You're going to need all your patience"—and I told him the story of my experience in *Glory in the Flower*. It would have been kinder of me to keep my mouth shut, but that's not the way it works between friends. "He's still very talented," said Gadge, "and we've hired him." For those of you who haven't already guessed as much, the actor's name was James Dean and the film in question was *East of Eden*. It was later, I think, that Jimmy appeared in *Rebel Without a Cause*, and it was that very quality of "I'm here—pay attention—and I don't give a damn what you think" that served him and both films so well. Indeed, "rebel without a cause" says it all.

TWENTY-
SEVEN

SOMETHING FELL on my chest. There was a gentle plop. I opened my eyes, raised my head from the pillow and found myself face to face with a scorpion about four inches long. It was stunned by its fall from the rafters, and I was only half-awake. This does it, I thought. I've gone completely, raving, off my rocker. A house on a remote island in the middle of nowhere? I don't belong here. Jessica was right, I was certifiable.

The scorpion and I eyed one another warily. Who would move first? The scorpion's tail was curled over its back, threatening. I hurled back the covers, and heard the scorpion hit the opposite wall and scuttle away to some damp dark corner where it might hide. I sat on the edge of the bed, doubled over, with my head in my hands, staring at the rope matting on the floor, contemplating my folly and wondering where *I* might hide. I sat there for a long time.

It was my first night in my own house on Children's Bay Cay. I'd made my bed with very damp sheets and now I had to lie in it. Help!

It must have been about 5 A.M. It had been a miserable night. The storm had passed, but the torn sail still rustled against the side of the house. I stumbled outside and secured it yet again over the gaping hole—almost all of one wall—where

280

the plate-glass window was supposed to be. (The glass had arrived, shipped from the factory by way of Miami to Nassau, to
George Town to Rolleville, where it was picked up by our work
boat and carried triumphantly to Children's Bay. It had been
carefully crated, but when we opened the box we found it in
pieces; so we had to start all over again. The replacement glass
had not yet arrived.) Will Nixon, aware that a storm was coming, had lashed an old, worn sail across the opening to keep
me from being drowned in my bed; but the wind had got under the sail and torn the lashings loose, and I'd had to refasten
it again several times during the night. I gave up on my pajamas, which still lay in a sodden heap on the floor, and slept,
very fitfully, in the raw.

The rain had stopped. There was a wonderful smell of wet,
fresh greenery. The sea was flat calm. Nothing moved, and
there was total silence until somewhere in the bush a pearly-
eyed thrasher began rehearsing a few notes.

I went back into the house and peeled a grapefruit, then
carried the segments, dripping over my bare legs, out onto the
patio. Perched on the patio wall, stark naked, I ate my grapefruit and watched the sun come up: an enormous scarlet ball
sitting on the purple ocean of the horizon. Far to the west,
veils of rain, like gauze curtains, still hung from a mass of
dark billowing cloud that was turning pink along its upper
edges. No one was awake yet. I wondered where Jessie was.
What city? What in-between? I drummed my heels against the
patio wall to break the silence, and the thrasher found its voice
again. The sun was warm on my bare back. What a joy not to
have to wear clothes. I snatched up a towel and marched down
the hill to the beautiful horseshoe beach and fell into the comforting water. As I came back up the hill I noticed the hibiscus
were opening. Perhaps I hadn't made such a calamitous mistake after all.

The perilous voyage of the window glass was accomplished
safely the second time. It was manhandled up the hill by six
men and duly put into place.

Several weeks later we decided to try for a well at the bottom of the hill, to provide water for the oleander and hibiscus
that we'd planted along the main path up to the house. Water

was always a problem; once you'd decided to plant an area, a
well was demanded. We couldn't rely on our precious supply
of rainwater in the catchments to take care of the gardens as
well as the household and laundry requirements. That there
was water somewhere not far below the surface was clear
enough from the dense growth of scrub that it supported, but
just where would we find it, and how deep could we go before
hitting salt?

In the case of this particular well, we ran into a great slab
of limestone when we were not more than two feet down. There
was nothing for it but to move the site of the well or use dynamite. I hate dynamite, with its caps and fuses and unpredictable results, but that's what we chose to do. Everyone took
cover; we lit the fuse and waited—and waited. When the ex-
plosion came, there was a dull boom, a great shower of earth
and rock—and, just as we stood up, the sudden, unexpected,
almost musical sound of breaking glass from the hilltop. What
the hell was that? The house was at least three hundred yards
away. I raced up the hill.

There was a neat round hole in the middle of our new
glass window, surrounded by a beautiful spider web of cracks.
I found the stone on the opposite side of the room. It was no
bigger than a duck's egg. So we ordered our third window,
and of course had to wait months for delivery. In the meantime I had to go back to New York, but when I returned I
found the well, about twelve feet deep, with two feet of fresh
water at its bottom, a neat cement collar around its top, and
the gasoline-driven pump mounted beside it. The new window was in place and the view breathtaking—but my adventures with that window were not at an end.

I am not a dedicated bird-watcher, but I get great pleasure
from being surrounded by birds, seeing them, hearing them
call or sing. We've never lived anywhere, even in a city, without a feeder somewhere at hand. On the island there were
countless seabirds: many species of tern, "sea pies" (oyster
catchers), gulls, egrets, ospreys and many wading birds. On
land there were the ever-present banana quits, a lovely fly-
catcher known locally as a pickamadick, and the vocal and im-
pertinent thrashers. The last seemed almost tame in their

boldness, and to start with we did all we could to encourage them. That is, until they discovered the plate-glass window. As they became ever bolder they would perch on windowsills looking for a handout and see their reflections in the glass. At breeding time this spelled trouble. The male thrasher would view his image in the window, decide it was an interloper and, being madly territorial, would attack it. There would be a flurry of beating wings against the window followed by a screech of claws against glass as the bird slid back down onto the sill. This could go on for hours and apparently loosened the bird's bowels. I got tired of waving wildly through the window or dashing outside to say "shoo-shoo," to say nothing of sponging up the mounting supply of bird shit. Finally exasperation wore me down and I sent for the caretaker's shotgun. I wasn't a bit happy about the next step taken, but as a deterrent, it seemed to work.

> "God save thee, ancient Mariner!
> From the fiends, that plague thee thus!—
> Why look'st thou so?"—"With my crossbow
> I shot the Albatross."

Sometime in the summer of 1955 we had our first house guests at Children's Bay: Jerome and Joanne Hellman. Jerry had been an intimate friend for years, one of my closest and most valued, and remains so to this day. Like me, he is a small man, but unlike me, he has the physique of a miniature Atlas with a drive and dedication to match. We met in an agent-client relationship, but Jerry soon gave up agenting and became a film producer. As such, he has a long list of distinguished films to his credit, among them *Midnight Cowboy, Coming Home* and *The Mosquito Coast*. I've never known Jerry to do anything shabby, which is a considerable claim to make for anyone in our business. However, to balance this glowing portrait, he has one dreadful failing: he *will* make a mock of me. He has this disconcerting habit of reacting to my most profound statements with a giggle and, "Oh Hume, Hume, you *are* so funny!" When he has attained my years of wisdom, he may recognize that I am nothing to laugh about.

Joanne and Jerry arrived at the same time as our furniture. Thirty-five years ago, you could buy a lot of furniture for fifteen hundred dollars, which is what I spent one whirlwind day in Nassau, acquiring tables, chairs, chests, wrought-iron bedsteads and carpets of plaited rope or raffia. Admittedly, most of the chairs were wicker, and the bedsteads, covered with bright mattresses and plenty of pillows, doubled as sofas, but they all served. Jessica despaired of this kind of shopping expedition. She is a collector; she believes in buying piece by piece, after judicious consideration. I, on the other hand, want it all done now, or preferably yesterday. As Jess wasn't with me in Nassau I had a free hand. At her rate of acquisition, I felt we might take as long to furnish the house as it took to build—and that had begun to seem endless.

The cartons and crates were piled high on the patio, and Joanne and Jerry were instantly pressed into service to open them and distribute the contents around our naked house. They had no other choice if they wanted a place to sleep that night. I recommend friends whom you can put to work.

At our first island dinner together, Joanne was faced with a dish of greens, red peppers, and raw conch sprinkled with lime juice—all products of the island or its waters. She lifted her fork politely, then asked with some suspicion, "What is *that*?" I explained conch, and showed her the beautiful shell, but I don't think she was entirely reassured. It was the "raw" that put her off. The second course was fish with boiled green pawpaw (papaya), hardly ever eaten as a vegetable even locally because native Bahamians believe it corrupts the stomach. (If you look at the label of the content of a commercial meat tenderizer you will discover that a principal ingredient is papaya juice.) That parenthesis might give anyone pause, but don't you believe it. Cooked green pawpaw is tender as a mother's heart, absolutely delicious, and digests as easily as Pablum; however, I noticed that Joanne avoided hers.

Then during the night she was wakened by a harsh scrabbling sound from behind the chest of drawers. She woke Jerry. "What is *that*?" "A mouse," said Jerry unfeelingly, and went immediately back to sleep. That's no mouse, thought Joanne, and she lay awake nervously listening. As a matter of fact she was right. Summoned next morning, I went in and found a huge trespassing land crab stuck between the wall and the back of the chest. I picked it up, open claws lifted in terrified threat, and put it back outdoors. Joanne looked at Jerry. "A mouse, huh?" she said.

I suppose that this is as good a place as any to admit to certain island hazards. Plowing through the bush, one has to be aware of thorns and the needlelike spines of sisal and century plant. Then there are poison wood and manchineel, which are far more toxic than poison ivy. A scorpion sting won't really harm you, but you can take weeks to recover fully from the discomfort of the bite of a tropical centipede.

Beneath the surface of an endlessly inviting sea, there are spiny sea urchins, fire coral and occasional stinging jellyfish. The inquisitive and menacing-looking barracuda are never far away but are *not* a threat, despite their disconcerting habit of swimming along beside you and making a chomping gesture with their jaws which seems to suggest consideration of your testicles as an appetizer. There are—or at least were—sharks of almost every variety (excluding, thank God, the great white) around Children's Bay. It was commonplace to see them when snorkeling, and Jessica became positively blasé about their presence. However, they were treated with great respect. Anything over five feet long and we got out of the water.

My list of cautions sounds fearsome but is not intended as such. There are far more dangerous hazards to be found on the island of Manhattan—and there, common sense will do less to protect you than it did on Children's Bay. What I had to learn, I learned the hard way. I had to get seared a couple of times by fire coral before I learned to be careful when poking around reefs. I had to try to extract sea urchin spines from both my hands and feet to be taught to *look* before I placed either. I've been stung by scorpions, jellyfish and coral, but only because I was careless. I've never been attacked by anything—with one exception.

It was ritual for Jess and me to take an early-morning swim from the horseshoe beach. It was a lovely spot; a curving beach of powder-fine white sand about a quarter of a mile long, with palm trees and tall tropical grasses behind it. A protecting reef made it a gigantic natural swimming pool or aquarium, teeming with life: conch, spiny lobster and dozens of varieties of brilliant fish.

At certain times of the year this sea garden would be visited by schools of gaff-topsail pompano. This is a small, silver-scaled fish shaped like an oval saucer, with long, jet-black fins. They haunted the shallows, and they were incredibly curious, seeming almost tame. As soon as we got in the water they would appear, circling around us. I'll bet we could feed them, I thought. It was to be the story of the thrashers all over again.

The next morning I chopped up a conch into pieces about the size of the tip of one's little finger and put a supply into two small plastic sandwich bags. So armed, we went down for our morning swim and plunged in naked—we never wore suits—to meet our friends. The conch was a great success. After several days of feeding, the fish would actually come in to snatch a piece of conch from between our fingers. However, they were not stupid; they soon learned that the mother lode of conch was held in the bags and would attack those, tearing the plastic with their sharp little teeth and providing an immediate bonanza of food. So it went. Great fun. And then we got bored with the exercise and the sandwich bags were abandoned.

One morning after the abandonment, we went down to the beach as usual. I stood there enjoying the sun while Jess waded in. She was no more than knee deep when she laughed and said, "Here they are—the welcoming committee." She dove in, took a few strokes, then waded again. Suddenly she gave an offended yelp and grabbed her left breast. "One of the little bastards bit me!" she shouted. I doubled over with laughter. "It's not that funny!" she yelled at me. "Oh yes it is," I replied, "it's hilarious," and waded in after her. I hadn't got more than waist deep before I clutched at my crotch. I'd been bitten on the end of my penis. We both got out of the water in a hurry.

On following mornings we would go down to the beach, wade in, wait for the fish to surround us, then dash out and race a hundred yards down the beach and go in there. But the school soon caught on to this maneuver and would find us in no time. It was more than a week before we were allowed to swim again in peace.

Islanders require boats. Slowly, over a period of years, we

accumulated six of them. It was a strange fleet. Our first boat, without which nothing could have been accomplished, was the *Fourposter*. She was well named, having a beam about the size of a double bed; Abaco built, about eighteen feet long and immensely heavy. She was powered by a long-shaft British Sea Gull motor—and if that company ever wants an endorsement, it has a reverent one from me. It was the only motor of ours that never seemed to break down. If we ran out of gas, the boat had to be sculled, an art that I barely attempted and never mastered. The *Fourposter,* or "the work boat," as she was more familiarly known, never stopped wallowing between Great Exuma and Children's Bay. She carried every foot of lumber, every bag of cement, every everything that went into our building. Our smallest boat, the *Alleycat,* was a twelve-foot aluminum runabout powered by a 10-horsepower outboard and could be pulled up on the beach. Our largest—our flagship— was a beautiful twenty-three-foot Bertram named *Jessica,* with powerful twin inboard/outboard motors. In between were three others: a sailboat and two runabouts, one of whose motors was usually being fixed by Will Nixon.

As a kid, I'd spent a lot of time in boats—in canoes, rowboats, sailboats, that is—but motors were a forbidding mystery to me. As a mechanic, I have all the instinctive skills of an elephant learning to tap dance. How I ever managed to cope, even in a superficial way, with outboards, generators and pumps was a minor miracle. I had to learn.

I got a very sharp lesson along the way. Stopping in Nassau on my way down to the cay, I went fishing one Sunday afternoon with my old friends Paul Potter and Gurth Duncombe. The latter was Bahamian, the former might as well have been, as he'd been on the island for years. These were old hands who knew their way around. Their boat was a Nova Scotia–built eighteen-footer with an immensely heavy 100-horsepower Mercury outboard. We were trolling. About an hour out, the motor suddenly stopped. We immediately dropped anchor (rule number one) but couldn't find the bottom. The anchor line wasn't long enough. It wasn't my boat and I wasn't worried; the old hands would locate the trouble and fix it.

They didn't. They couldn't. It was my turn. I dried out the

plugs, adjusted the gaps, disconnected the lead to the carburetor—spilling a good deal of gas into the bilge in the process—blew the line clear, tested the battery; in short, did all the obvious things, to no avail. The offshore breeze was freshening, and lights began to come on at the increasingly distant shoreline. We were going to be *very* late for dinner. Well, that was some comfort; Nan Potter would begin to worry and eventually notify the air/sea rescue authorities. Of course, the ocean is a big place and it was getting dark. I wondered aloud if we had any flares should we hear a plane. No. Did we have a flashlight? No. Did we have running lights? Yes, but the battery was dead as a result of so many fruitless attempts to start the motor.

We drifted, with both wind and tide pushing us further and further away from New Providence.

By ten o'clock I knew we were in serious trouble. The shoreline lights had long disappeared, and the sea had become positively ugly. We were shipping water over the transom. We had to try to devise a sea anchor that would keep our bow into the wind. We had a big plastic garbage pail on board, meant to hold whatever fish we might have caught. I attached this to a line on the bow and heaved it overboard. It worked surprisingly well. Half full of water, it dragged our high bow round into the wind, so that our stern was downwind, and our drift rate cut in half. I prayed that the line wouldn't tear through the plastic.

By midnight the blow was at its worst and the boat pitching abominably. We lay on the bottom. I knew we had life preservers aboard (I had one under my head), but there was no fresh water and we were already thirsty. It was not a happy night. I made a number of silent vows. If I got back to Children's Bay, I'd see to it that every boat had a sealed bottle of fresh water, a waterproof flashlight and an extra length of anchor line.

Shortly after dawn we began to hear planes come over, but it was obvious they didn't see us. No waggling of wings, no dip down to signify that we'd been spotted. The sea was one vast, rolling, blue and white froth and our boat was blue and white. I added another vow; I was going to have the Bertram's cabin top or foredeck painted a bright orange.

Planes came and went at intervals. Finally, about noon, we were picked up by a tug just short of the Berry Islands. We'd drifted thirty miles from Nassau. We came into its harbor late that afternoon.

Early the next morning Jessica's phone rang in New York, waking her up. It was my secretary Marjorie Winfield.

"Don't worry, Jess! He's been found!"

"Who's been found?"

"Hume! I just heard it on the radio."

"I didn't know he was lost."

TWENTY-EIGHT

BOATS MEAN PARTS. Lots and lots of small spare parts. And on an isolated island, there is no friendly neighborhood mechanic to come to your rescue when you need a new cotter pin, a spark plug, a filter, a solenoid, etc., etc. The heavier or more bulky spares, anchors, lines, life preservers, fishpots, and all that sort of gear, were kept in the warehouse, but the smaller and frequently more critical parts were neatly arranged and labeled on the shelves of the storeroom. These reached from floor to ceiling, and I shared the space with a deep freeze that looked like a grotesquely oversized white-enamel coffin. That meant that sometimes Jessica and our cook, Carmen, had to have access to this sacrosanct domain. Their occasional presence was deeply resented. The storeroom was *mine;* and I lorded over it like a miserly emperor.

In the mid thirties, when Jessica had been at the Old Vic and Lilian Baylis was the impoverished empress there, the legend was that Lilian Baylis, Hon. D. Litt. Oxon.—always in mortarboard and gown for any ceremonial occasion—had a favorite and fervent prayer: "Dear Lord, send me good actors—and please send them cheap." This frugality infected her whole staff. Her wardrobe master, Orlando, was one who'd learned his lesson well. When Jessica came to him asking for a new pair of tights, he would smile wolfishly at her and say, "So you want new tights, do you? Let's see the old ones." Jess would present the distressed garment and Orlando would finger the runs and tears and say, "Very nice dear—new tights would be very nice—but you can't have 'em!" and send Jess back to her dressing room with a darning needle. Of course there is a simpler method of repair. If you're wearing black tights you paint your skin black beneath the hole—or red or green, as the case may be. It will never be noticed from out front. Unfortunately, most tights first give way in the crotch, which makes a problem for the painter.

When Orlando retired, an inventory of the vast wardrobe was required, and dozens of pairs of new tights, still in their packaging, were discovered. Orlando and I held something in common in our philosophies. You can't have too many spares.

In the year that Jessica was coping with Orlando and torn tights at the Old Vic, I was trying to reorganize the prop room at the Barter Theater in Virginia. Both experiences served me well on Children's Bay; I never stopped organizing, and Jess imported an old-fashioned treadle sewing machine.

Bob Whitehead, a frequent visitor to the cay, was and still is a compulsive fisherman. Our fishing rods on the cay were held in racks above head height out on the patio, and had to be lifted down from their perch with a forked stick. If you placed the stick properly against the reel, the rod couldn't fall out of the fork. I was in the sitting room making yet another list when I heard the crash. I walked out onto the patio and found Bob holding a shattered reel in his hands and looking dismayed.

"I'm terribly sorry, Hume, but . . ."

"It's all right, Robert. We have a spare," and I trotted off to the storeroom to unpack it.

Our son, Christopher, often joined Bob on his fishing excursions. Jess and I would see very little of them except at breakfast and dinner. The day after the broken reel incident, they both showed up for dinner looking happy, sunburned, but a bit sheepish. Robert owned up.

"I'm terribly sorry, Hume, but I lost the gaff. A fish swam away with it."

"A fish swam away with your gaff?"

"Yes. You see it was a big fish. I gaffed it, got the hook out, and was about to lift it into the boat when it gave a hell of a flap and tore the handle right out of my hand. . . . It was a *very* big fish," he added defensively.

"The handle cut through the water just like a periscope," said Chris, not too helpfully.

"It's all right, Robert, we have another one," and I went back to the storeroom to dig it out.

On the third day, Bob and Chris decided to fish from the point where Jerry Hellman and I had seen a big hammerhead. They took their lunch with them.

> Behold the fisherman!
> He riseth early in the morning
> and disturbeth the whole household.
> He returneth when the day is far spent
> smelling of strong drink
> and the truth is not in him

Well, the day was far spent when they came back, and we all had a drink before dinner. I got up to get another bottle of Canadian Club from the storeroom, and on my way out said, "So, how did it go today?" There was a long, curiously pregnant pause while Bob struggled with the truth within him. I turned in the doorway, glass in hand, propping the spring screen open with my shoulder. Bob gulped and shamed the devil. "I broke the thermos."

"Which one?"

"The green one . . . with the wide mouth . . . for ice, you know. . . ."

"Pity; that's the only one like that we've got," and I continued on my way. Unfortunately, the screen door slammed hard behind me. I swear it was not temper, but Bob and Chris found it unnerving.

Bob told me about the fourth day with considerable glee. He and Chris went back to the same spot carrying their lunch. When the time came to pack up and go back to the house, he said to Chris, Now, we haven't broken anything—let's not leave anything behind." He was holding an elastic band in his hand as he started to count. "Two rods, landing net, gaff—dear God, hang onto that gaff—lunch basket, tackle box, and I guess that's it. What do I do with this?" And he held up the elastic band. "Oh well, I guess it doesn't matter," and he chucked it over his shoulder.

Chris darted behind him and retrieved the rubber band. "No, no, no, Robert—elastic bands are very important to Father!"

I've never been allowed to forget that. Even now, some thirty-odd years later, the family will find me fussing about something and I will hear someone whisper, "Elastic bands are very important to Father." As a character reference, it belongs right up there with Spencer Tracy's "The son of a bitch would fix the lights if they let him."

Once the main house was built and livable, it became obvious that if we were to continue to have guests, to say nothing of our children's friends, we would need more room. It became equally obvious that if we were going to clear and plant, someone besides Rev Rolle, our beloved caretaker—his name came from the fact that he was a lay preacher on Exuma—and his wife, Lucy, plus their two young children, Sam and Magnola, would need to help from time to time. This involved bringing in crews from the nearby settlements about four times a year to clear, stump, plant, and hold back the bush that constantly threatened to take over anything already cleared. Sometimes I felt that I was surrounded by a jungle of gigantic Venus flytraps—just waiting for the unwary passerby to come along and be swallowed up.

"Coconuts!" said one of my knowledgeable Bahamian friends. "A bearing tree will bring you in about a pound a year in income." "Pineapples!" said another: "You have the right soil—you just need a well or two—and presto, you'll have a nice little pineapple plantation. There's a big demand for pineapples down here."

So we were to have coconuts, pineapples, a guesthouse, and a place for the periodic crews to live. What would we need to accomplish all this besides patience, determination and money, money, money? What we would need was Ken Miller, that's what—and with him the whole team back again: Max Bowe, Will Nixon, Jacob Smith and all. I contacted Ken and asked him to draw plans for a guesthouse and dormitory—always referred to by the crews as "the dormy." It turned out that Ken was just about to be married. He readily agreed to draw the plans providing he could bring his bride, Bobbie, with him for an extended working honeymoon. It was extended all right—to about six months. There was something providential about Ken's provisos. His first, upon starting work at the cay, had been that he travel down to the islands by ship. It was while on board that he'd met Bobbie, and now, here he was returning with her as his wife. All rather neat.

While Ken drew plans, I pursued coconuts and pineapples. My knowledgeable friend had said, "There's nothing to it. You stick 'em in the ground just as they are—shove 'em in anywhere and they'll sprout. But get 'em from Andros—beautiful—the golden coconut."

It sounded lovely. In my mind's eye I saw those magnificent groves of golden coconuts bowing gracefully in the gentle trade winds. And in ten years—maybe less—I'd have bearing trees that would pay me a pound per year, per tree. Great! I ordered three thousand coconuts and with considerable difficulty managed to arrange their shipment from Andros to the Exumas.

Of course, I didn't dwell much on harvesting, husking, and the shipment of the copra to the nearest processing plant. As a matter of fact, I don't believe there's a single commercial processing plant in all the Bahamas, or at least there wasn't then. I'd have had to ship the copra to the States. Golden coconuts indeed! And you can't just "shove 'em in anywhere" either. They do indeed sprout, they'll sprout lying on the dock, but your golden coconut can be a fairly fastidious feeder. It wants water, at least brackish water and the right mix of earth and sand. Of the three thousand we planted, about two thousand survived. They did look wonderful—but we never sold a single nut.

My pineapple venture was even less successful. I asked my friend and accountant in Nassau, Paul Gignac, to try to find someone who would sell me five hundred pineapple slips—the slip being a small plant found at the base of the parent fruit. Five hundred seemed like a nice round number. We might get through a couple of dozen while we were "in residence," and as for the rest, we could give them away or perhaps even sell some. I went about the business of preparing the ground. There was a spot I'd noticed about midway down the cay where the soil turned red, and I'd been told that this was perfect pineapple ground. Of course it would have to be cleared of brush, trees, and stone, and somewhere nearby we'd have to try for a well. After a few weeks we had a clearing about a hundred yards square, neatly surrounded by a dry wall made from the surface stone. All very tidy. The well looked less promising. It was temperamental; sometimes there was water, sometimes there wasn't. However, we proceeded under the happy assumption that rains would provide.

The pineapples didn't arrive. I kept bugging Paul on the telephone. "Where are my pineapples?" He'd found someone on Eleuthera who could ship the slips to Nassau, but from there they'd have to be transshipped to Exuma on the mailboat. "It all takes time and coordination," said Paul. I knew about that. After all, between us, we'd managed shipments of lumber, cement, roofing, drums of gas and diesel; what could be so difficult about a few tiny plants? I went back to New York dreaming of my coconut groves and the delicious Bahamian pineapple—smaller than its Hawaiian cousin but incredibly sweet and dripping with juice. My mouth watered. Someday I would sit down to a meal of genuine, sun-ripened, fresh pineapple and wash it down with genuine, fresh coconut milk spiked with rum.

When I next got back to the cay, there were still no pineapples, and my little plantation clearing boasted a healthy crop of weeds. Back onto the blower again, and a long-suffering Paul Gignac.

"Hume, try to understand something. We missed the first crop. If you want healthy slips, they have to be picked just right. They mustn't dry out in transit. Now, they've promised them for next week—or the week after—well, sometime this month. Try to be patient."

"Yes, Paul. I know, an' God spare life."

"You're learning—anything else?"

Paul had had years of running this sort of interference for me. How he'd managed to stick to it so long I don't know. A hotelkeeper was once heard to say of me, "Hume Cronyn knows exactly what he wants and he wants it yesterday." Paul would second that.

Eventually, I got word that my slips would arrive on Exuma on such and such a date and that I'd better send a boat to pick them up. I sent Rev to Rolleville in the work boat. He was gone all day. I was sitting on the terrace having an evening drink when I saw the *Fourposter* come wallowing back to our jetty. It seemed to be low in the water. I heard Rev before I properly saw him. Whatever his other qualifications as a lay preacher, vocal projection must have been top of the list. He talked to himself at high volume while he climbed the hill to our terrace, then appeared waving his arms, and launched into a booming tirade. He'd had a trying day, and I suspect a couple of liquid reinforcement shots to help him survive it.

"Boss, they ain't sent us no slips! They sent us five hundred pineapples—all ripe! What we gonna do with five hundred pineapples?"

Good question. I went down the hill with Rev, who was still fulminating, to inspect our cargo. There they were; a huge mound of fruit piled to the gunwales and ripe enough to draw the flies that buzzed around them. Well, it was too late to do anything about it that night. I'd have to try to get on to Paul over the ship-to-shore the following morning. I loathed the thought. The radiotelephone was the serpent in the garden— the bane of my existence on the cay.

In this instance fate was with me; I managed to get through early the next morning.

"Paul, I hate to trouble you, but about the pineapple slips . . . "

I heard him groan, "Oh God!" at his end.

"We seem to have five hundred pineapples, but no slips. There's been a screw-up somewhere. Are you sure they understood *slips*—not the fruit?"

"I'll try to get through to Eleuthera and see what happened—call you back."

It was a very abrupt conversation and I hung up, prepared to wait all day for a return call. That's usually the way it went, depending on the backlog of traffic on the radio frequency. In the meantime I had to sit by the telephone while the pineapples—still in the boat—grew ever riper in the sun. Miraculously, Paul was back to me within a couple of hours.

"Hume, you *have* the slips. They're attached to the base of the pineapples. You can't ship them unless they're attached to the mother fruit—they wither and die. Look again—those little green things attached. If I don't hear from you I'll know it's all okay."

I could hear the prayer in Paul's voice, but despite that I was stupid enough to say, "Oh . . . oh I see . . . but what am I to do with the pineapples?"

Paul's reply was unprintable.

But he was right. There they were, the little dears, a few small green shoots at the base of the fruit with separate root systems. We cut them away for our planting, but that still left us with the fruit to dispose of. We took a dozen for our own household use and distributed about forty others to people on the cay. How many ripe pineapples can one person eat in a week? What were we to do with the remaining four hundred and fifty? Rev said he'd take care of that, but he'd need Jacob to help him. I watched the still overladen boat put out from the jetty with Jacob enthroned on pineapples.

They came back that evening carrying a very heavy flour sack and looking triumphant. They tipped the sack upside down on the patio table and a great cascade of pennies, sixpences, and shillings poured out. It took me well over an hour to count it. There was about twelve pounds sterling, or roughly sixty dollars, in coins. Rev and Jacob had gone up and down the shore of Great Exuma hawking pineapples at about ten cents apiece. Very enterprising, but how was I to make use of all that change? I wasn't about to try to carry it back to the United States and dump it in front of some horrified teller at the bank, and I couldn't spend it on the cay. I gave ten dollars' worth each to Jacob and Rev as a commission, and divided the rest into six lots ranging in amounts from ten dollars to five, and we held a lottery. As it was free and no one got skunked (there

were only eight people on the cay at the time), it was considered a great success and cause for celebration. When we've
got our own crop, I thought, we'll make this an annual event.
"The Children's Bay Cay Great Pineapple Lottery." Alas, it
was not to be.

We planted our slips. The well went dry. In our first har-
vest I think we got eight bonsai-sized pineapples. I seem to
remember that they were absolutely delicious. I hope they were.
Counting labor and shipment, they cost about three hundred
dollars apiece.

Even allowing for the exaggeration of pride of ownership,
it seemed to me that Ken Miller did a wonderful job with both
the guesthouse and the dormy. While the latter was far less
elegant than the guesthouse, I had a particular fondness for it
because it offered so much more to the crews than they were
used to. The building consisted of a large common room with
a wing on either side. Each wing had four bedrooms with a
window and double bunk beds and each wing had a bathroom
and shower. All openings were screened. The kitchen facilities, such as they were, were provided by six outdoor hearths
(all built at waist height, in stone) that were supposed to cut
down the hazard of fire and allow simultaneous cooking options for accommodating differing tastes. This carefully considered brainchild of mine was never adopted. The dormy had
hardly been put into use before there were portable kerosene
stoves sitting on the hearth grills.

The guesthouse ran along a ridge of hill at right angles to
the main house but at a respectable distance from it. One end
jutted out over the end of the hill and had a cantilevered patio
outside the guest bed/sitting room and its dressing room/bath.
In a row behind this minisuite were four very small bedrooms
sharing one bath, intended for Chris, Tandy, their friends, or
any other spillover from the main house. All these rooms had
windows to the west and doors out onto a southeastern veranda that ran the length of the building. It was simple and
comfortable and surrounded by hibiscus, oleander and frangipani.

The work involved took months to accomplish, and I was
on hand only rarely. I would be in New York doing this tele-

vision show or that play or perhaps on location with a film. In any hiatus, even for a weekend, I would dash down to the Exumas and wander around through the chaos of building materials and workmen, only to recognize that my presence was entirely superfluous. They all knew what they were doing, I didn't even know what I was looking at. Everyone on the crew called me "Boss," but it was a purely honorary title. The real bosses were Ken, Max, Will and Rev—with Paul Gignac riding shotgun over the checkbook in Nassau. Ken and Max were responsible for the building program, Will handled mechanics (generators, pumps, boats, etc.) and Rev "the land" (clearing, planting, watering, etc.). All of these people were good and close friends who wanted to please me but looked on my periodic inspection trips and letters with a resigned, but I hope affectionate, tolerance. One day in the middle of a discussion with Will, he smiled wearily at me and said, "Boss, you goin' t' write me another of your lawyer letters?"

Sometime—in 1957 I think it was—I got a polite letter from the Royal Bank of Canada, in Nassau, drawing my attention to the size of my overdraft. Would I care to do anything about it? Paul Gignac had been nudging me on the same subject for months past.

On January 15th, 1958, at exactly 8 P.M., we auctioned off our collection of paintings at the Parke-Bernet Galleries in New York City. Among them were works by Boudin, Cassatt, Degas, Grosz, Modigliani, Picasso, Renoir, Rouault, Toulouse-Lautrec, Utrillo and Vlaminck, as well as a number of rather exceptional pieces of pre-Columbian sculpture and pottery. The sale netted us well under six figures and today—taking a wild, swinging guess—might have brought twenty million dollars. So much for my business acumen, my eye to the future, my crystal ball. At any rate I got rid of my overdraft. To give Jess her due, she thought I went too far and should have been more selective in our sale. Perhaps she was right, but I was— and still am—hagridden by an old tendency: "Off with the old and on with the new," which may help explain why we've had so many houses, and in my case, so many different, if related, occupations. I've been deviled all my life by this passion to change. Thank God it hasn't applied to wives or friends or

children. It's been largely related to "things": to houses, apartments, collections, even to professional endeavors—a compul-
sion which has made it unbearable for me to repeat myself if
I can avoid it. One of my friends once said to me, "You're like
that guy who found perfection—and was looking for something better." He was wrong; I haven't found better, only different—but that in itself has been exciting, an adventure. There
hasn't been a change that I seriously regret—sometimes a pang
perhaps, but nothing that has cost me loss of sleep. Not yet.
Change and adventure are synonymous in my book.

Occasionally people will say to me, "Don't you miss such
and such?" or "How could you bear to give it up?" and my
answer is "Easily," because I've always believed the grass will
be greener around the next bend in the road. It's a characteristic that can be very irritating—especially if Jess and I sally
forth on a picnic. She can barely restrain herself from saying,
"For God's sake—settle!" To date, and together, we've now
built or rebuilt seven different places in which to live, which
works out as an average of a new one every seven years. I've
enjoyed all of them without exception, if not all equally. But
once the books are on the shelves, the pictures hung, the garden acceptable, and the unpacking from the last move finally
and totally accomplished, I begin to develop a terrible case of
the itching foot. Only a saint, or Jessica, could tolerate living
with such an affliction. She recognized the symptoms long ago
and learned to say, wearily, "When do we start packing?"

In my own defense, I might suggest that nothing and no
one can take away from you what you've already had and really
enjoyed. In my mind's eye I can still see the geese come wedg-
ing into Mystery Lake in the evening; still hear the redwings
in the willow; enjoy the clamshell privacy of my little studio
on Rockingham Avenue; smell the nicotiana in the Woodfield
garden; hear the wind clatter the palm fronds or whisper
through the casuarinas in the Exumas. If you have truly loved
a place in which you've lived, in some fashion you will never
leave.

I was never to become a serious collector again. Indeed, I
never was a *serious* collector. I bought for fun, as the result of
an immediate emotional response, and my taste was as eclectic

as it was ill informed. In the early seventies I was to discover
the sculpture of the Inuit, more popularly known as Eskimo
art, related in feeling if not sophistication to the pre-Columbian works that had attracted me thirty years earlier. Large
pieces in calcite, serpentine, walrus ivory and whalebone are
often overwhelming in their magnificence. I doubt that I'll ever
build another house, but if I should be idiot enough to do so,
I doubly doubt that I'd sell my Inuit art to help pay for it.

*   *   *

It was a beautiful day: clear and fresh, the sky a brilliant
blue with only a few white powder-puff clouds to give it accent. The sun was hot but there was enough breeze to rattle
the palm fronds and ruffle the water on the lee side of the
island. Banana quits darted about the terrace, and a brilliant
green lizard sunned himself on the patio steps. The thrashers
were singing whatever song they fancied and a flight of black-
capped tern were fishing off shore, their white wings brilliant
in the sunlight as they hovered and swooped above the bait
fish just under the surface.

"God's in his heaven and all's right with the world." Except
it wasn't. A distinct air of melancholy hung over Children's
Bay Cay. I'd been aware of it from the moment I'd got out of
bed that morning. I'd swum alone, had breakfast alone and
walked down to the orchard alone—carefully skirting the
dormy, where people were packing up. The work was all done;
the crew was going back to Exuma. I dreaded the good-byes.
My plane wouldn't arrive until after lunch, so I had time to
kill.

Many years before, when I'd owned my first piece of land
in Redding Ridge, Connecticut, my neighbor, a grizzled old
New England widower named Charlie Stauffer, would watch
me from his porch rocking chair as I wandered aimlessly around
my ten acres and comment later that he knew I was back from
the city because he'd seen me out "takin' inventory." My per-
ambulations amused Charlie. In his view, if a man went outside, he went out to do something and obviously I did nothing.
But it wasn't nothing: I was indeed taking inventory, of the
black snakes in the old stone wall, the robin's nest, the trillium,

the resident groundhog and the lacework patterns of new leaves against a spring sky.

In just such a fashion, on Children's Bay, I wandered now down to the orchard. It bore no resemblance whatever to what Charlie would have termed an orchard; no neat rows of carefully pruned trees wearing white socks of insect repellent, but scruffy bushes planted at random wherever a pothole had gathered the rich detritus of the surrounding bush. On the other hand, the crop just might have surprised Charlie. We grew the best grapefruit I've ever eaten, limes in plenty, sugar bananas in the deeper holes where it was always damp. The Hayden mango trees looked promising, the papayas were heavy with fruit, and threading between the erratic plantings were the vines of yams and melons. I was proud of the orchard and its reliable well, even though it offered only a small measure of comfort on this particular day.

The work was ended—insofar as work ever ends on a project of this kind. The crew had been paid off and were leaving. Some of the boats had already set off for home, their sails receding in the distance, diminishing white flags on a turquoise sea. I delayed going back to the house for as long as I could. The little seaplane buzzed the cay and came in for its landing somewhere out of sight. When I got back to the house I saw Ken's gear piled on the patio and Will Nixon leaning against the wall of the house. It was an image I'll never forget. Will faced the wall, one forearm thrown up against the pink coral-encrusted stone (so carefully chosen for this particular spot). His head rested against his arm and his body angled out from it like a buttress. It was a pose of either prayer or mourning and did not invite trivial conversation. I tiptoed round him to get my sandwich only to find I had no appetite. I took a stiff drink instead.

I was not allowed to carry my bags down to the seaplane ramp. I tried to argue with Carmen, but she simply wrenched a bag out of my hand, looking sullen, saying nothing. As the stuff was being loaded, I felt a whack on my shoulder and there was Max, the tough, hard-bitten, indestructible Max, with a leathery hand held out. I shook it and winced. I tried to say something, but he pivoted away and stalked off down the beach.

I was suddenly furious. What the hell kind of parting was that? I was damn well going to say my piece. I took after him down the beach, spun around in front of him and started to talk. He pushed me roughly aside and went on—but he'd been crying. Simon Legree was crying! The world was coming to an end.

I retraced my steps, embraced Will, kissed Carmen, shook hands with Jacob and Rev, and climbed onto the plane after Ken. As we rolled down the ramp I saw Carmen cover her head with her apron.

The plane taxied out into the middle of the bay, took off, skimmed over Cay Head, gained height and circled, waggling its wings as we recrossed the ramp and the tiny cluster of figures standing there, looking up but not waving. Ken sat opposite me, his head pressed against the window. We passed over Lee Stocking, Norman's Pond, Peace and Plenty, and headed for Nassau where Ken would catch a connecting flight for home and his Bobbie. Neither of us had anything to say. I lit my pipe—it was allowed in those days. Ken kept his head pressed to the window. He made no sound, but little rivulets of tears coursed down his cheeks. All in all it was a very wet farewell.

I spent only enough time in Nassau to shop for some essential furnishings for the guesthouse and then returned to the cay. It was strangely quiet. I missed all the bustle of the building.

Sweating, I took my stuff up from the ramp and dumped it on the patio. Not a sound. No movement in or about the main house or from the guesthouse or the dormy. There was an eerie quiet where for weeks past there had been ceaseless activity, laughter, the sound of outboard motors and the growling of the cement mixer. Even the birds and the almost ever-present breeze seemed to have business elsewhere. It was very hot; one of those rare days when the sea is like glass, the bush droops and everything waits for some unknown, usually a radical change of weather. I looked at the barometer: it was falling.

I changed my clothes and went off to take inventory: down the hill, through the overgrown pineapple ground and into the coconut grove at Paddy's Cap. I stuck my head into the dormy on my return. It was deserted, but spit-and-polish clean, mute testimony to the tyrannical housekeeping of the departed "Big Rosie"—all three hundred pounds of her—whose particular care it had been. Sweat was trickling down my chest and back and gathering in a wet compress around the waistband of my trousers. To hell with this inventory, I thought. I was going to fall into the water. As I headed for the horseshoe beach, stripping off my clothes as I went, I realized that the sky had turned dark and the stillness had become even more oppressive. I dropped my things on the beach and waded in, not bothering to swim, but sitting neck deep on the fine white sand and watching the line storm approach from the northwest.

First there was a faint rumble of thunder, then the air moved. You couldn't call it a breeze, the mirror surface of the bay was hardly breathed upon. A long, slow dagger thrust of lightning split the gray mantle and was lost over the horizon. It was exciting. Another rumble of thunder—closer this time. And then a miracle took place. Suddenly the air above me was filled with yellow butterflies. They came over my head from the shoreline on my left, thousands of them, flittering across the water, freed by some command from their cocoons and bound for I know not where. Seen against that ominous leaden sky they were as brilliant as candle flames in the dark, and even more wonderfully cheering. Long after the rain came down I continued to sit there in a state of euphoria and grace, no longer lonely. Children's Bay Cay had had its blessing.

TWENTY-NINE

WRITING ABOUT *Triple Play* is a little like trying to recall a recipe for fruit salad thirty years after you first made it. It depended upon the season of the year and what fruit was available at the time. I suspect that in concept *Triple Play* was exciting and great fun (as any conception should be), but the child turned out to be something of a lovable bastard—a dear product of questionable parentage and shifting affections.

Jess and I must have begun by telling one another what fun it would be to play a wide variety of roles in short plays by master playwrights. It was just to be for the summer, of course, while we waited for the rewrites on *The Man in the Dog Suit*, which we'd tried out the summer before. The initial playwrights chosen were Chekhov, Sean O'Casey and Benn Levy. Somewhere along our circuitous route we dropped the Levy and substituted a short play by John Mortimer; and eventually we dropped that in turn and substituted Tennessee Williams. Consequently, we played the works of five playwrights before the New York opening and our passage into another oblivion.

The original company consisted of Biff McGuire, Frances Sternhagen, Brian Herbert, Jess and me, but as we changed plays, there were different cast requirements, so that before we'd finished, we'd been joined for indeterminate periods by

Helen Seamon, John Randolph, Margot Stevenson, George Mathews, Geoffrey Lumb and Francis Compton—wonderful actors all. To playgoers of the present generation, some of those names will be unfamiliar, but there wasn't one of them with whom we didn't enjoy playing. So, five playwrights and eleven actors were involved during the period (1958 and 1959) in which we struggled to find the right mix. We never did. We opened on Broadway with the work of three playwrights, six actors, and to "mixed reviews"—and you already know what that means.

A bill of one-act plays is notoriously difficult to pull off. If the plays are all by one playwright, at least there is the cohesive factor of one writer's work. Even then, however, there are difficulties: abrupt changes in style and mood, the shape of the whole—what comes first, what last—the probability of multiple sets, and recruiting a company of actors who can double or triple persuasively.

Once again, I was wearing three hats: producer, director and actor. I never learn; but this time, my fickle memory—given to wiping out the unpleasant and clinging tenaciously to what was affirmative—suggests that I had a good time. I had lovely parts to play, and was surrounded by skilled actors and the sort of support and guidance that only comes from a loving family. David Hays designed the sets; Anna Hill Johnstone did the clothes; Paul Foley was the production stage manager; and Marjorie "Ol' Blue Jeans" Winfield was his assistant. If I hadn't had to act, I could probably have stayed at home.

Paul Foley's name appears for the first time here. How can that be? Before he retired, Paul had stage-managed seventeen productions with me. Seventeen! I wonder how many other actor-director–stage manager collaborations have survived so much hassle and pain. Paul was the ultimate stage manager: knowing from long experience what was going to be needed by a director or actor before those individuals knew for themselves.

He also had the trust and sympathy of the stagehands, the master carpenter, electrician and property man. They would do things for Paul that no one else seemed able to accomplish. Paul was an intimate friend, a man of integrity, patience, hu-

mor and vast sympathy for even those, such as I, who, on occasion, must have driven him crazy.

Only once in all those seventeen productions did I see Paul
lose his temper, and that was when he put his hand on a pipe
stand that carried power to the border lights. There was a
short in one of the cables and consequently the pipe stand was
electrified. He gave a sort of strangled cry, and tried to tear
his hand away. I grabbed him around the waist (fortunately I
was wearing rubber-soled shoes), and yanked him loose. We
both tumbled onto our backs in the wings. I was badly frightened. I scrambled to my feet and gave Paul hell for something
he could not possibly have foreseen. Paul screamed back at
me, holding his burned hand, and cursing; it was all my fault,
if I would only stay out front or onstage where I belonged—
and if only I'd stop asking for the impossible—it would never
have happened. I don't know which one of us started to laugh
first.

Whenever Jess and I had the clout and the director's
agreement, we would write into our contracts that Paul should
be stage manager. He's gone now, and I miss him sorely.

Jessica had a wonderful range of parts: the mischievous
tart in O'Casey's *Bedtime Story,* which gave her a chance to display her beautiful legs; the moustached and padded old har-
ridan in *Pound on Demand,* and a tour de force as Miss Lucretia
Collins in Williams's *Portrait of a Madonna,* which she'd played
in Los Angeles twelve years earlier.

Through all the cast changes and switching of parts and
plays, there was one other constant besides Jess and me, and
that was Biff McGuire. Biff is about eight inches taller than I
am, with very broad shoulders, copper-colored hair, an infectious grin and a wit to match it. He would say something to
me in the heat and turmoil of rehearsal—generally when I was
being terribly intense or overly solemn—and I would turn away
to the next thing, having only half-heard him, and suddenly
realize that what he'd said was very funny. He spoke softly
and slowly, absolutely deadpan, and he always caught me un-
awares. I did more double takes with Biff than with any other
actor I've ever directed. Biff seemed to bear my direction with
a sort of resigned regret—as though I were telling him about

the expected death of a great mutual friend, when all I was saying was, "For God's sake, stand still," and all he was doing was laughing at me. As rehearsals progressed, Biff learned to block me with stock replies. I would open my mouth to offer some invaluable piece of constructive criticism, and before I'd got a word out, he would say, "Hume, I was *not* jiggling" or "I'll do it if you stop hitting me." This last was a real canard. I never, ever, hit him. He was too big. Oh, sometimes in performance I may have given him a slight nudge, my elbow might find its way into his ribs, or I may even have been guilty of the occasional pinch, just to let him know that he was out of position. But hit him? Never.

I have a letter dated June 29th, 1988—thirty years after *Triple Play*—written by Biff from the Seattle Repertory Theater where he was playing. In it he says:

> I am proud to say I no longer "jiggle" but stand perfectly still while addressing an audience. I know this revelation will make you very happy, for as I recall, most of my acting notes from you read "Stand still. Don't jiggle." Although in all honesty and fairness, a lot of that "jiggling" was the result of a young actor trying to escape the blows of an actor-director for not speaking his lines as quickly as possible.
>
> But all that pain aside, I do miss you two. Drop a line if you have time.
>
> Much love,
> Biff.

One of the terrible hazards of directing your fellow actors is that you may try to give their performances for them. This fatal temptation is hard to understand unless you've been through the experience of hours, days, weeks, spent out front directing the actors, willing them to perfection, body-English-ing their every move, and then have to climb up onto the stage with them and play your own part. Your whole focus must change immediately. You must concentrate not on them but on your own character's intention, and listen as *that* character, not as a director. The transition from one function to an entirely opposite one is not easy. Jessica has sometimes walked off the stage after playing a scene with me that I have directed and said, "If you don't stop moving your lips I may kill you." She doesn't mean that I was grimacing, but that I was saying *her* words under my breath.

In a 1961 copy of *Theatre Arts Magazine* I've found an article I wrote about *Big Fish, Little Fish*. The editor had asked me to keep a journal. There it all is: the whole rehearsal experience, though the dateline of the first entry was at first a mystery. Cincinnati? What was I doing in Cincinnati? And then it dawned. Jessica was on tour with *Five Finger Exercise*. She'd played a full season in New York and was now off on a national tour. The play by Peter Shaffer had been a great success but was to keep us apart for many months.

Big Fish, Little Fish had a wonderful cast: Jason Robards, George Grizzard, Martin Gabel, Ruth White, Elizabeth Wilson and George Voskovec. As for the director, Sir John Gielgud, I can only say that I found him as brilliant as it was difficult to keep up with him. He expected everyone to act as well as he did, which is an impossible order to fill. He was also given to lightning changes of mind, and a sort of machine-gun delivery of instruction that always made me feel that I was going to bump into myself going or coming. "Hume, cross left on that line. . . . No, that's wrong, go to the sofa . . . try it there. . . . That's terrible, cross right. . . . No! You just came from there. Try standing still."

I make it sound as though John's sole preoccupation as a director was mechanics, which is quite false. While he has an unerring eye for a stage picture and moved us around like so many pawns on a chessboard being photographed with a high-speed camera, he also has impeccable taste and can illuminate a character with a few well-chosen and very precise words. The depressing element in John's direction was that, as an actor, he could have made any of the changes he asked of us far more rapidly than could any of the clods he was directing—and we clods knew it.

Sir John hardly needs my admiration for him as a director; he won the Tony award for best direction both for *Big Fish* and for *Five Finger Exercise* with Jessica the year before. However, I often wondered just what would have happened if, while John was molding a performance and saying, "Move right, cross left, come down center, or stand on your head," the harassed actor had stopped dead and said, "Why?"—surely one of the most overworked words in any rehearsal process. It never happened, so I don't know the answer; but I suspect John's reaction might have been utter stupefaction followed by a stutter. I don't think John always knew the "why" until he'd got it right. He knew then, and that's fair enough. Personally, I like to be allowed to find my own whys once a director I trust feels satisfied, and John's ultimate choices always proved inspired. That last statement may confuse some of my actor colleagues. "You mean to say you're prepared to accept a direction you don't understand—and then rationalize it after the fact?" Yes, that's what I mean. Sometimes. When I know the director has taste. The actor cannot be in two places at once—cannot be both onstage and out front. What an actor "feels" is not always what an audience sees. Not infrequently, it is our job to "cover" a direction, to lend truth to a move, a reading, or a piece of business that feels awkward or even dead wrong for the character one is playing, in the interest of serving the whole. That judgment can only be made by the director.

Despite my extravagant admiration for John as an actor and director, I did not always find it easy to please him. For one thing, I was trying to cope with one of the most property-infested roles I've ever had to play. The character of Jimmie Luton was that of a gabby, frustrated little art instructor, a homosexual with all the instincts of Mother Hubbard. Jimmie never stopped talking, making beds, cooking, setting the table, tidying up, and so on. He gloried in being put upon and was hopelessly in love with "Dear William"—the Jason Robards character. Now, as an actor, I like props. I'm rarely happier than when speaking lines and having to deal with multiple physical activities at the same time. *But,* and it's a large but in my acting vocabulary, I have to know exactly *what* I am doing and *when.* This means that in the eyes of many of my fellow actors and the director, I become ridiculously obsessed with "business." ("I can't throw the sheet back on this line, it must be on the next!") The other actors sigh heavily as I go back to try it again, and the director looks at his watch. This impatient audience believes me to be "prop bound"—rather like an aggravated case of constipation—or worse. In my frequent moments of self-defensiveness, I prefer to call it "meticulous."

When I have one of these attacks, Jessica simply sits down, smiles in resignation and says, "Hume is packing a trunk." This refers to a piece of business in *The Fourposter* where I had a prolonged trunk-packing scene which, in braggart fashion, I claim the audience found hilarious, but which the rest of the cast (Jessica) found very trying during rehearsals.

My rehearsal journal begins, then, with the dateline "Cincinnati, Ohio, Saturday February 4th 1961."

Supposed to fly to New York for rehearsals starting 11 A.M. Monday. All flights canceled. New York snowbound. Decided on train to Washington. About to leave hotel when college girl appeared, asking to see Miss Tandy. The unannounced visitor had attended the matinee of "Five Finger Exercise." Long woolen socks, loafers, polo coat, and stars in her eyes. Intense fifteen minutes about THEATRE. Made me feel a hundred and eight. Anyway, let's go.

Sunday, February 5th
Arrived New York twenty hours later. "Where are the snows of yesteryear?" Right here, all of them! Walked fifteen blocks carrying three bags. Caught bus. Lew Allen (producer) called. Rehearsal postponed. Gielgud stuck in Montreal, Robards in Nassau, Grizzard lost. Cronyn pooped. Slept ten hours.

Tuesday, February 7th
Arrived Ziegfeld roof ten-fifteen. Met Jason going up in elevator. Most of the company already on hand. Lots of nervous jokes and overplayed camaraderie. Started to read on the tick of ten-thirty. No formal statements from anyone—no welcomes, introductions, explanations, or psycho-

logical investigation. Just, "Shall we read it?" Rather a relief.
We're off!

My voice sounds very loud, and the words meaningless.
Must make myself *listen*. Ruth White reads beautifully. John
Gielgud asks Hugh [Wheeler]'s permission to make a cut.

"Of course."

That's good. Hope it continues. Someone out front
laughs. Who the hell is out there, anyway? The voices continue, some loud, some whispered, some quiet, some delib-
erate. All nervous. Halfway through the first act someone
lets go with an unabashed and full-bodied fart. Everyone
feels relieved. We begin, tentatively, to talk and to listen.
Finish the first reading before the lunch break—start
blocking afterward.

Wednesday, February 8th

Blocked, cut, rewrote and transposed all yesterday
afternoon and today with only one official ten-minute break
outside of lunch. Whew! Must wear other shoes and bring
lunch with me. Finished long and complicated first scene
of first act. Five more scenes to go, and only seventeen
days before we face an audience. Well, don't think about
that! Must remember to go slow and concentrate on relationships rather than business. Johnny G. seems to have
sixteen new ideas a minute. Write in and erase, write in
and erase. Script covered with lunatic markings.

Lost an actor today. Part written out. Homework little
more than a mechanical review, and uninspired.

Thursday, February 9th

Long discussion today on the homosexual implications
in the play and the exact nature of the relationships between various characters. Opinions differ widely. We begin
to eliminate certain lines, and Hugh changes the color of
one of the key situations to avoid a seeming stereotype.
"The Best Man," "Advise and Consent," "The Devil's Advocate" and "A Taste of Honey" all involve homosexual
incidents in one fashion or another.

These attempts to prejudge audience or critical reaction are always tricky. You may end up safe but regretful.

Friday, February 10th

Still blocking first act. Very complicated. Set table, serve meal, dress, undress, dress again. Set up cot, make bed, etc., etc., etc. This one is going to be a prop man's nightmare—and mine—at least until I get the book out of my hands. I have Marjorie (Winfield, secretary-assistant) cuing me at night now, but it doesn't exactly rush along.

Saturday, February 11th

Stumbled through first two scenes of first act. Hugh doing some revisions of later material, so we're repeating rather than forging ahead. Good thing as far as I'm concerned.

Hugh read new material to company at end of day. Very good, we think, and are all encouraged.

Got home and felt lousy. Skipped dinner and went to bed. What have I caught and how long will it last? Hell, hell, hell! Why do these bloody ailments always smack you in rehearsal?

Sunday, February 12th

No rehearsal today. Lucky thing, too. Felt as though I'd been worked over with a baseball bat. The doctor says it's food poisoning. Whatever, it gave me an acrobatic night and I'm limp this morning—oatmeal, dry toast, and back to bed. I must be able to work tonight!

Monday, February 13th

Props, props, props. This must be the proppiest play since the creation of time.

Tuesday, February 14th

Thank God—a moment of euphoria. Unreal, and probably quite unjustified, but at least a scene seemed to go! Books and all—*it seemed to go!* There was contact and a brief moment of happening. A genuine "illusion of the first time."

Wednesday, February 15th

Every new play in rehearsal is a new discovery of an old lesson. The audience only cares about what it *feels*, rarely about what it thinks, even less about what it sees, except as such elements contribute to the emotion of the moment. The actor may be loaded with "understanding," on time for rehearsal, word-perfect, responsive to direction, a paragon of actor's virtues and discipline, and terribly dull!

Thursday, February 16th

Lines, cues and business. Lines, cues and business! Here I am, having done more plays, or at least as many, as any member of the company, caught in the oldest of traps. Mechanical repetition! Why, why, why do I never learn?

Friday, February 17th

One week from today we dress-rehearse in Philadelphia. Brr! Nine days of rehearsal behind us and eight ahead before facing an audience. I'm still carrying a script in the last act. Marjorie cues me until midnight, when I stop making sense. For Valentine's Day she gave me a gold paper heart plastered with dexamyl capsules!

Saturday, February 18th

John ticked me off today. It was done gently and with considerable forbearance. I know I'm driving him up the wall.

"Perhaps you could concentrate a little less on the business."

Dear God! I see those technical rehearsals coming; no time, a thousand props, and a never-ending weave of movement. If I don't pantomime it now, what will happen then? Chaos. Still, he's right, and I know it and must do it.

Sunday, February 19th

Jessica called from Los Angeles.

"I hope you're enjoying rehearsals."

I managed only a civil grunt. And yet six weeks from now I'll say, "Oh yes, very much," and mean it—I think.

It's a marvelous company. Perhaps the best I've ever been with. One of the depressing aspects of the crapgame that is the theater is the tendency to mutual disenchantment as rehearsals proceed and tensions mount. Here, of course, the director and principal players have an enormous responsibility. They set a tone, and you cannot do better than Gielgud, Robards, Gabel, Grizzard. They are not just talented, but thoroughly professional and generous as well, so the going is relaxed (my own tensions and anxieties being hopefully, if improbably, hidden). There is not an uncreative, let alone an incompetent player in the cast. And we are blessed in our author as well.

Hugh Wheeler, a successful novelist turned playwright, has extraordinary gifts. He is flexible, he is modest and very, very quick. Provided he approves a cut or transposition, it's done immediately. When a rewrite of consequence is required, he will look, listen, leave rehearsal, and return in a matter of hours—at the most, it's been a day and a half—with a really new and improved scene. Some of the best things in his play were written under great pressure.

Why then, with such a playwright, director and company, does the tenor of this diary seem so gloomy? Perhaps because of the accepted conditions under which we work. Even the actor in demand, provided he exercises any discretion—he better or he won't remain in demand for long—must wait months between engagements, and there is never room for him to fail. No wonder our courage is in question. Success, a hit, is all, and yet, after waiting, praying, and working for it, he must repeat himself, without seeming to do so, for hundreds of performances, a process almost guaranteed to stunt his development as an actor.

Are there no existing alternatives?

Yes: California, television, or off-Broadway theater, provided he can afford the latter. None of these are satisfactory either in themselves or in combination, for the simple reason that the best the theater has to offer in every department is neither required nor available in any one of them.

What then?

We must develop a new theater, and we will, but only after considerable agonies of death and rebirth. As a matter of principle, I dislike having to agree with Mr. Tynan about anything, but when he suggests that, in a very short time, Broadway will find itself with not more than a dozen theaters and all of them given over to musicals, I have no other choice. The bed we've made on Broadway is bloody uncomfortable, and I for one would like to climb the hell out of it. (Note: this was written in 1961!)

Monday, February 20th
At last I'm free of the script. Now all I have to do is act it.

Tuesday, February 21st
We're obviously overlength. But we must get through this hiccough stage before an accurate timing can be assessed, or even before we know precisely where the cuts are indicated.

We have a new cast member: the cat. Martin barely tolerates "Pussikins." His affection for her in the play will be a triumph of illusion.

Thursday, February 23rd
To Philadelphia. We were told we were to have our own parlor car, complete with two drawing rooms for conferences and those on-the-train rehearsals that rarely take place. I was lucky to get a seat in the diner. The Pennsylvania Railroad goofed, and "our" car was attached to another train. The company, mountains of baggage, a cat and a dog are spread through half a dozen cars. Pandemonium. It was almost worth it, as it's the first time I've ever seen the manager, Oscar Olesen, on the defensive—at least with actors.

Friday, February 24th
Stumbled through a technical of the first act last night. More of the same today. Dress parade and dress rehearsal tomorrow. Poor Mary Grant (the costume designer)—the

wardrobe has gone astray. John Maxtone-Graham, our stage
manager, looks more and more austere, and more and more
like Prince Philip on parade. The cat scratched Martin, and
she must be given a manicure.

Saturday, February 25th
Still no wardrobe. Dress-rehearsed in street clothes. John
G. continues to restage the first scene of the play. Please
God, let me remember what version we're to do on open-
ing night. The prop men are in labor, and the squawk box
over the switchboard competes with the dialogue as Ben
Edwards sets his lights. Isn't this jolly!

Sunday, February 26th
Project! Project! The Locust Theater in Philadelphia
could house a musical, and is magnificently unsuitable for
such an intimate play. We have an invitational preview tonight. Our first performance and our last to such an audience. It will *not* be a typical theater audience, and the
reactions can prove as misleading as helpful.
This is being scribbled while waiting for room service
at the hotel. I must be back at the theater in fifty minutes.
In the interim, I shall try to drown a flock of enormous
pale green butterflies with a comforting slug of bourbon.
"Do you mean to say you drink before a performance?"
"Yes, ma'am, I sure do!"

The Opening, February 27th
This is written the day after. I spent fifteen hours in
the theater yesterday. Not that there's anything very unusual about that, but it's trying! I had no lunch and a sandwich dinner in the dressing room. There were exactly
seventeen changes to absorb, and I became increasingly
peevish as the day wore on. At one point in midafternoon
I stepped down to the footlights and said, "Now, John—
John are you changing it because it will be better—or because you're bored?" John's reply to my question was gentle
and maddeningly benign. "But Hume, you'll manage it
beautifully." I did as I was told with very poor grace and

eventually retired to my dressing room to sulk.

(I don't think it's unfair to John to say that sometimes he *is* bored. He does everything so beautifully himself—and so quickly—and there he is stuck out in the third row watching us muddle along and repeat, repeat and muddle. Suddenly, after only half a day's work, you might hear John's singular and optimistic voice say, "I think we might break here, don't you—have a cup of tea—come back to it tomorrow after you've had another look. . . . "—and he's gone. Company dismissed.)

Later on yesterday afternoon Lew Allen tapped on my door with a friendly, "How's it going?" and got a definitely surly, "Don't talk to me," in reply.

I remember something Rex Harrison was quoted as saying in a magazine profile. He was seated in the house during rehearsals, and, pointing to the stage, he said to his interviewer, "You know, it's very exposed up there."

Most of the changes today were superficial, but they were changes and not calculated to increase one's sense of security. Half a dozen of them were serious, involving new or rearranged dialogue. John Long (dresser) was still cuing me at the half hour.

The reviews were one good and two indifferent, which is probably healthy. After all, this is another beginning rather than an end. To this point an essential element, the audience, has been missing. The next two weeks will be lived in a trancelike atmosphere of hotel bedrooms, rehearsals, performances, and round and round we go. Dear old Aunt Marcia, who lives in Philadelphia, will complain again that her favorite nephew failed to see her, and the room service, good or bad, will become intolerable.

About nine and a half working days left before we open in New York. That excludes matinee days and one day of technical rehearsal at the ANTA—say, roughly fifty hours. With John, of course, it will be less than that. Much less. He has a positive aversion to rehearsals, which leaves me torn between anxiety and admiration.

What will happen to us? How will we be received? I haven't the faintest idea.

I do know that Hugh's characters are rich and honestly drawn, and that the actors are likely to fare well. Much that the playwright has done may be overlooked, yet reflect favorably on us. Perhaps there's a rough justice in this. The playwright *can* go back to his typewriter—he may not want to, but at least he has that choice. The actor? A year or two years if he's in a hit, and if he's not, another wait. Another season, another Philadelphia and another bout with time and the pale green butterflies.

* * *

Big Fish, Little Fish ran for 102 performances at the ANTA Theater, New York. The play had good notices, on the whole. Some of us won awards, but nothing gave me more pleasure than Walter Kerr's notice in the *New York Times*. I indulge myself by quoting, because I was so proud of it: "Mr. Cronyn is so good it hurts." I treasure that review for a number of reasons. First, because I'd had such a struggle with the part of Jimmie Luton. Second, because in my own nature there is something that attracts me to what is both funny and touching. And third, because in the best of comedies—Chekhov for instance—there is much pain behind the character's bizarre and often ludicrous behavior. There was a lot of pain in Jimmie Luton. He was funny but he was touching.

Several weeks into the run of *Big Fish*, Jason had an off night, which means he'd behaved as I always behaved and had a drink before the performance. But I don't think he'd stopped at one, and I don't think he'd had anything to eat either, with the result that he was suddenly incapacitated. (I should add that Jason, who has never made a secret of his long-past drinking days, gives me cheerful and generous permission to tell this story.)

I was met just inside the stage door by Albert, Jason's dresser, a meticulous and caring little man who had once dressed me and whom I knew to be devoted to Jason. With him was John Maxtone-Graham, our stage manager.

"Mr. Robards is not well," said Albert.

"He's pissed as a newt," said John more bluntly.

There were raised voices from Jason's dressing room. I

knocked on the door and could hear the giggle in Jason's voice as he sang out, "Come in, come in whoever you are!" Betty Bacall (Mrs. Robards at the time) was with him and obviously not pleased.

Ms. Lauren Bacall is a lady with whom it is best not to trifle. Beneath that beautiful exterior, as a component of all her charm, talent, and character, is a repository of tempered steel, and on this occasion the steel was showing. She was both worried and angry, and it soon appeared why. It was not a question of that evening's performance alone but, far more seriously, of a court appearance that Jason had to make on the following day. Apparently he'd been cited for some sort of traffic offense, received a summons, and either forgotten about it or chosen to ignore it—not once, but a number of times. Ultimately, the case came before a judge who said that either Mr. Robards would deign to appear or that he would go to jail. Betty's wholly legitimate concern was that if the evening progressed as it started, and slopped over into the following day, that Jason might not make it—again. The other hazard was that if the evening's performance of *Big Fish* was canceled, the press might get hold of the summons story, and that the judge would not find this soothing. As Betty explained the situation, Jason listened with a maddeningly amiable expression. He beamed at me, nodded at Betty and said, "The eagle has landed," which did little to diffuse the tension. Albert kept pouring fresh cups of coffee.

John Maxtone-Graham, George Grizzard and I had a conference. We decided that we'd attempt the first act, and if that proved a disaster, John would make a tactful announcement in the interval, explaining that Mr. Robards was indisposed and would be replaced by an understudy for the second and third acts.

When Jason made his first entrance he looked infuriatingly gleeful, and when the audience gave him the receptive round of applause, he bowed to them. In mid-performance, he actually bowed! As he leaned forward from the waist I held my breath. What would hit the floor first, his knees or his head? Neither. He straightened up looking smug, and we were off into the dialogue. Jason was word perfect until George Grizzard came on. George played a character named Ronnie, but Jason now insisted on calling him "Grizzy," which must have confused the audience a little. I thought I heard the rustle of programs out front.

George and I had made a plan. We would flank Jason, one on either side of him, and move with him wherever he moved, shoulder to shoulder—rather like two elephants supporting a wounded third in between. Jason seemed delighted with this arrangement, and once he was aware of what was going on, would make new and quite unexpected moves to throw us off. He was enjoying himself. There was murder in my heart.

We got through the first act without any horrifying incident, and decided to plunge on into the second and third. Albert kept plying Jason with hot coffee. Betty had disappeared. At the end of the performance I got Jason out onto the sidewalk, determined to get him home. I'd promised Betty I'd do as much, but Jason thought it was a terrible idea. The argument got more intense, and I remember Jason saying, "Don't hit me, don't hit me!" Why friends like Jason or Biff McGuire—either of whom could pick me up and wring me out with one hand—should think I might even consider hitting them, I don't know. I haven't hit anybody since stepping out of a boxing ring for the last time in 1931. Be that as it may, I got hold of Jason's left arm and my friend Louis Cooper got hold of his right, and we walked and talked Jason into Louis' cab. (Louis Cooper was a taxi driver who had driven me to and from whatever theater I'd been playing in for years.) Once in the cab, there followed a long and acrimonious debate about where we should go. Jason would *not* go home and would *not* come to my place. Louis drove first in one direction, then in the other. Finally, we reached a negotiated settlement. We would all go to McSorley's Bar on the Lower East Side, where Jason would limit himself to *one* beer in exchange for the promise to be driven home afterward. I don't remember much about McSorley's except for the sawdust floor and Jason sitting on a barstool playing a ukelele and singing Irish ballads. This exercise quite restored Jason's good humor and depressed me. I just wanted to go home to bed.

Ultimately we got Jason back to the Dakota where Betty

and he lived. I asked Louis to wait for me. I intended no more than to escort Jason up in the elevator and propel him through the door of his apartment. It was about two o'clock in the morning, but Jason was as irrepressibly cheerful as when I'd entered his dressing room six hours earlier. Betty's mood hadn't changed either. She was still icy. She'd left our theater to go and see Richard Burton in *Camelot,* had supper with him afterward, and he'd brought her home. He was still there, sprawled in a big chair with a glass in his hand, when Jason and I came through the door. This two-person reception committee was not entirely welcoming. Despite our all being old friends, the initial conversation was strained. I began to feel that I was caught up in some sort of weird family drama with Betty and Richard cast as the disapproving parents, I as a temporary and aging nanny (I was more than ten years older than any of them), and Master Jason caught with his hand in the cookie jar and totally unrepentant.

I'd never taken my coat off, and was about to leave when Richard got to his feet, stood over Jason and launched into a scolding lecture on professional behavior and the actor's obligations to an audience and his fellow players. Jason's good humor suddenly vanished. He stood up with surprising alacrity and pushed Richard away from him. He shoved, he didn't actually hit him, but as Richard stepped back, his heel caught on a stool and he sprawled flat on his back. It was humiliating and dangerous. When a drinking Welshman and a drinking Irishman face one another with even a mild difference of opinion, almost anything can happen. I remember dashing in between them and having one hand on Jason's chest and the other on Richard's and saying something really profound like "knock it off." But it was Betty who defused the situation. She has a marvelous sardonic wit which can be either searing or restorative. In this instance she must have been inspired, because it made both men laugh. I wish I could recall her exact words. I know it had something to do with which one of them was prepared to show up onstage the following night with a black eye, but it was succinct and funny. I was too weary to take proper note. I made my escape, tottered to Louis' cab and was driven home.

THIRTY

JOSEPH L. MANKIEWICZ (despite what is now nearly half a century of intimate friendship, I have never discovered what the *L* stands for) was staying with me on Children's Bay Cay. He was holed up in the guesthouse, beavering away on a screenplay of Lawrence Durrell's *Justine,* and complaining in equal part about the no-see-ums which sneaked in through the screens to bite him, and the fact that I and Jean Vanderbilt, another houseguest, were having all the fun while he sweated and scratched.

I was monitoring the island telephone one morning when the call came through.

"Z.F.X. Come in please." I pressed the switch to reply. "This is Z.F.X."

"We have a call from Hollywood, California, for a Mr. M—
. . . " The name totally defeated the operator.

I said mercifully, "Mr. Mankiewicz? Who's calling please?"

The connection was broken by a great wave of static, and when finally we made contact again I heard the barking voice of Charlie Feldman, Joe's agent.

"Hume? Where the hell is Joe?"

"Next door, Charlie. Is it important? He's working."

"I don't care if he's on the can. Get him!"

And that was the first I knew of Joe's involvement with the film *Cleopatra,* a film that Joe is reported as saying "was conceived in a state of emergency, shot in confusion, and wound up in blind panic." I knew a little about its history to date. The whole world knew that. Elizabeth Taylor, its star, had come down with pneumonia, had had to have a tracheotomy and nearly died. The director, Rouben Mamoulian, had quit. At the end of six weeks, the English production, constantly plagued by bad weather, had only ten and a half minutes of usable film, and that at a cost of five million dollars (the figure would approximate twenty million today—or about two million a minute). The producing studio, Twentieth Century–Fox, had had a string of box-office failures, and its presiding emperor, Spyros P. Skouras, sat on a very wobbly throne. Now it was Joseph L. Mankiewicz to the rescue—and his introduction into a snake pit.

Weeks passed, then one day in New York, Joe called and asked me how I'd like to play "an Egyptian Polonius." The role was that of Cleopatra's prime minister, Sosigines, later described by Joe as "Cleopatra's Arthur Schlesinger," and known eventually to the company as Old Sausage Knees. There was no script for me to see, Joe having decided on an entirely new attack for the screenplay he would write, so I had to accept on faith. It wasn't difficult. With Mankiewicz, Taylor, Burton and Harrison, the scope of the story, a winter in Rome, and ten-week contract for me, what could I lose?

Well for one thing, almost a year of my life.

* * *

Cats.

They were everywhere. Cats stretching, cats yawning, prowling, playing, sleeping and screwing among the ruins. I stood behind some sort of guardrail looking down into the Roman Forum and watched them. It was one of those rare days of sunshine in that very wet autumn of 1961. But I was not working. I don't know why. I was being paid. I'd been paid for weeks past, having arrived in Rome in mid-September. Richard Burton had arrived the same day. He'd left *Camelot* and wanted to come to Italy by sea, to have a break before diving into *Cleopatra*. But they wouldn't let him; he'd had to fly. As it turned out, neither Richard nor I was to step before a camera until after Christmas, and by this time my threshold to Roman monuments had grown intolerably high. I knew every teat on the wolf that suckled Romulus and Remus. So I watched the cats instead. I identified with them. They weren't working either, and I shared all their activities, but unlike them, I was a stranger to contentment.

Part of it of course was Jessica's absence. While I was making *Cleopatra*, she was to make two films: *Adventures of a Young Man* and *The Birds* for Hitchcock. She came to Rome only twice and then for brief periods. Part of it perhaps was my fiftieth birthday the previous July. It was a milestone; a watershed of some kind or other. I used to ski. Most Canadians ski and skate. You'd get to the top of a new run and the track would stretch downward and disappear almost immediately over a bump in the hill. What lay beyond that? A jump? Ice? A threatening tree? All that you saw was a distant and noncommittal horizon of pale sky meeting blurry saw-toothed mountains. So, you'd push off, crouch down and hope for the best. At worst you might go ass-over-teakettle and break something, or merely suffer the shame of "sitzplatz" and a ride down the mountain on your rear end.

At fifty I felt I was on an unknown downward slope full of such bumps. Juggling these gloomy thoughts I shuffled along the Via Imperiali toward my hotel. What the hell was I doing here?

I had not become the actor I wished to become—someone in the mold of a Gielgud, Olivier, Richardson, Guinness or Alfred Lunt. I had wanted to play the classics, but in twenty-seven years had managed to appear in only two of them (*Hamlet* and *The Three Sisters*); whereas Jessica, with her English-theater background, had appeared in two dozen. In the theater I was established, but not a star—an asteroid, perhaps. The fact that my name frequently appeared above the title was irrelevant. In films I was just another useful character actor. Maybe I had a wider range than most, but I was never likely to become anything more than that.

It's odd how certain walks stick in the memory. Some are

treasure hunts—to a view from a mountaintop; to discover the sea; to come home again, to a lover, to firelight, a drink or a good book. And then there are the others, the worry walks, when you see nothing round you and get lost, first in a maze of internal argument—of perhapses and maybes—and then an abandonment of all sense of direction or place, when you stop and ask, "What the hell am I doing here?" So it was on this particular walk between the Forum and the Grand Hotel. Somewhere around the Quirinale I suddenly realized I didn't know where I was or where I was going.

"*Scusi. Dove Le Grand Hotel, per favore?*" I was answered in such rapid and voluble Italian that I didn't understand a word. Fortunately the accompanying gestures were direction enough.

I walked up the hotel staircase instead of taking the lift. I suppose I was still worrying that bone of professional discontent—and God forbid that I should let anything interfere with my habitual anxieties. Once in my room, I collapsed on the bed and switched gears. That is, I stopped worrying about my career and worried about my marriage instead. There was nothing wrong with it and so much that was right. Jess and I loved one another. The children were safe: Susan raising a family in California and married to a wonderful guy; Tandy at school in Germany and loving it; Chris at St. Marks and tolerating it. We'd offered Chris the same opportunity as Tandy: would he like to go abroad to school for a couple of years? I remember the brooding silence that followed our inquiry, and then his gloomy reply. "How will I communicate?" So, he stayed at St. Marks. Tandy had never even hesitated. "Oh that would be fun." Of course, Tandy had had a German governess, a wonderful woman, a refugee named Miss Bauer, who, where I was concerned, had only blotted her copy book once when she'd said, "Mr. Cronyn, you are the spoiltest husband I ever knew." Perhaps I was, and that was why I resented it. Perhaps it was my being spoiled that invited such broodiness.

At some point Chris and Tandy were both to visit me in Rome, and Jess too would come as soon as she wrapped her present film. So, why worry? Not a new worry, but a continuing one that had seemed to appear during Jessie's long tour of *Five Finger Exercise,* when I was doing six other things. And

that pattern had continued for a number of years now: we
would rejoice in coming together, and then there would be
another parting. We both worked so damn hard and we were
paying a price.

When you work together months on end there is also a
price. Month after month of the same bed, the same rehearsal
hall, the shared stage or film, the same supper and back to the
same bed again. Common problems, but differing and sometimes mutually abrasive solutions. I wonder how many plumbers
or architects or lawyers could tolerate the inevitable frictions.

"Hand me the wrench."

"What you need is a screwdriver."

"*I see the main exposure to the south.*"

"*But they ask for a north light.*"

"Her case rests on his infidelity."

"No, on their children's welfare."

The predictability of shared differences can be very wearing. Occasional separations can be very healthful.

"I'm moving into a hotel for a few days. Do you mind?"

"Of course not, but is there anything wrong?"

"Not a thing. Just me. Just a surfeit of togetherness—and
that bloody telephone."

"Have fun!"

"You too. You know where to reach me—but don't give
out the number. Oh, by the way, I love you."

"You must try not to state the obvious."

"Sure of yourself, aren't you?"

"No. But . . . " (and she quoted Millay) " 'I was not one
for keeping rubbed in a cage a wing that would be free.' "

It was not that our marriage, Jessica's and mine, was "in
trouble," but it was becalmed, in a doldrum—or so I felt. After
nearly twenty years we were drifting along, in and out of one
another's orbit: loving, respectful, sharing our problems and
those of our children; delighted to come together whenever
that was allowed and (never to be admitted) sometimes relieved when circumstance demanded a parting.

I got off the bed and looked in the mirror, brushed my
thinning hair and combed my new beard. Sometimes I felt
that the beard, grown for Old Sausage Knees, was the only

thing I'd achieved over the past few months.

"Oh come on Cronyn, cheer up. Your mother thought you were beautiful. Why are you always complaining? If this is mid-life crisis, it's a terrible bore and so are you. Lighten up, boy!"

I stopped talking to myself, put down the comb and went next door to bum a drink from Joe Mank.

This involved walking the few steps from my single room at the Grand to the door of Joe's much more comfortable suite. I knocked. Rosemary Matthews (now Mrs. Mankiewicz), his assistant, devoted friend, and worker of miracles, opened the door. Behind her I could see Joe sprawled in his large leather chair, a writing board on his knees, a dead pipe clenched between his teeth, wearing white cotton gloves. He looked like a dissolute butler recovering from a particularly vicious dinner party, pouch-eyed and sullen. Why a butler? I suppose it was those white cotton gloves. Our William used to wear them at Woodfield on gala occasions: I remember only because on one hilarious night in setting down the plates his glove came off and settled in someone's creamed spinach. Joe's gloves were a cover for some ointment or other. He'd developed a rash between his fingers—a reaction to nervous stress. I walked past Rosemary and Joe growled, "Hello m'boy. Pour yourself a drink."

"That's the only reason I've come. And what is today's latest disaster?"

"More of the same—why do I never see you at the studio?"

"Oh I'm there—on occasion—but you're always so damn busy. Besides, you don't need me."

And I *was* there—on occasion. I would get up at six. A car would pick me up and drive me to Cinecitta. I'd spend an hour in makeup, eating my breakfast while the makeup man curled my beautiful wig; then I'd climb into my elaborate costume—all skirts and rather drafty underneath—coil my gold chains of office around my neck, and wait . . . and wait . . . and wait. About lunchtime I'd be dismissed and driven home again, not having done a lick of work, and the next day would be the same. Demoralizing and boring.

I valued those periodic visits to the Mankiewicz suite. There was generally a fire burning. I came in out of the cold and the filthy Roman winter weather in more than a literal sense. I felt at home. Sometimes Rosemary would be there, sometimes not. Her presence was another warming factor. Joe would recount the day's travail, and whatever contempt or bitterness he might feel for the proceedings would be presented with the most marvelous humor. Shooting all day and writing at night and on weekends, he drove himself to a point that frightened me. There came a time when I thought he might die; that sitting there in that great chair scribbling, or in the confusion and chaos of the set, with dozens of technicians or actors pulling at his sleeve and demanding his attention, he would have a massive heart attack and fall dead. Of all his worries toward the end of 1961, I think the worst were the Roman weather that year (which constantly delayed exterior shooting) and the fact that he didn't have a finished script. He barely managed to keep ahead of the shooting schedule. At some point, one of *Time* magazine's senior people came to Rome, met Joe, and Joe asked if the visitor would like to come to the set. The *Time* man explained that he was leaving the following day and would have to choose between *Cleopatra* and keeping an appointment with the Holy Father. "Well," said Joe, "at least the Pope's got a finished script."

The writing weighed on him, but then so did another dozen factors: the political situation at the studio, where one faction believed that *Cleopatra* was terminal madness and another felt it would be the studio's salvation; the jockeying for position to inherit Skouras's crown; and the added complication of the Wall Street contingent interested in preserving their investment in Twentieth Century–Fox stock.

When the *scandale grande* broke out, involving Elizabeth, Richard, Eddie Fisher and Sybil Burton, matters grew much worse. All these people had a direct pipeline to Joe and all of them discussed their problems with him. He had to play Sir Oracle. That he was able to keep his cool throughout was a marvel.

The Taylor-Burton love affair was front-page news around the world for months on end—enough already. I knew all the principals involved and liked them all. Perhaps I had a particular sympathy for Sybil, for whom—though I haven't seen her in over twenty years—I retain an especially affectionate memory.

One day we finished work early and I had a drink with Richard and Elizabeth. In fact we had not one drink but several. I don't know what turn the conversation may have taken, but Richard suddenly said, "Hume, you don't approve of me do you?" Whatever it was, his Welsh intuition, my tactlessness, or the drinks, I got to my feet deeply hurt. I said, "Well, fuck you!" (hardly a witty rejoinder) and stalked to the door in offended dignity. I was furious at being exposed as judgmental. I liked Richard. He was a marvelously entertaining companion, a man of good will, but . . . how do I describe such a complex and driven personality? I think he knew that he was corruptible, and that it bothered him. Perhaps I was just jealous of his professional gifts—he had so many. Richard Burton was one of the very few actors I've known who was truly touched by the finger of God: his appearance, despite the pockmarked face; his quick intelligence, beautiful voice, and above all a Welsh lyricism of spirit that only money, notoriety and an overweening ambition to be a film star could waste.

I enjoyed all the people on *Cleopatra,* even Walter Wanger, who once referred to me—face-to-face, I must admit—as "the bearded hypocrite," not the most flattering of descriptions. He was aware of my friendship with Taylor and Burton but even more keenly aware of my closeness to Mankiewicz. I knew of certain crosscurrents in the developing backstage drama, of which Walter was ignorant or merely suspicious. He'd corner me and ask if such and such was true, or what Joe *really* thought about a particular problem. I knew far less than Walter suspected I did, but the questioning made me uncomfortable, and I would resort to double talk. Walter recognized it for what it was—an evasion tactic.

Actually, I felt sorry for Walter; he had a very sticky job as the producer of *Cleopatra.* He describes it without exaggeration in the book he wrote with Joe Hyams. *My Life with Cleopatra:*

"The logistical and transportation problems of maintaining our group—hundreds of actors, technicians, et al.,

—were immense and difficult. But it was the personal equation, the problem of keeping up morale, that concerned me as a producer.

"Some of our crew people came to Rome with only a few days' notice from the studio in Hollywood. They told family and friends they would return in weeks, which proceeded to stretch into months. Babies were being born at home; marriages threatened to go on the rocks; people were homesick and ill. Mail delivery became as important to us in Rome as to troops in the trenches. . . .

"And there were the personal problems brought about by the tension of too close association. Our job, plus the language barrier, kept us in our own little ghetto. . . . The forced intimacy took its toll in shattered friendships, arguments, and gossip."

This then was the atmosphere in which we were working. I couldn't wait for Jessica to arrive and restore some sense of normalcy to our lives.

Sosigines was a good part (in the Mankiewicz script), but as the character was not involved in any of the scenes of fighting or fornication, and as the first cut of the film was about six hours long—and eventually butchered in the editing effort to bring it down to half that length—most of Old Sausage Knees ended up on the cutting-room floor. A job that required my involvement for ten months resulted in a total film appearance of about five minutes. Measured in dollars per minute, I may have been as well paid as Elizabeth Taylor, but that was very small consolation at the time. I had some brief moral qualms about it but shrugged them off as a caprice of the wheel of fortune. Time and time again I'd sweated over failures that took months of work and their toll in anxiety and received damn-all in financial return. Now my dollar number had come up. Bingo! I bought myself a very snappy red Fiat sports car and on every occasion possible I fled from Rome. I drove along the coast, north to Porto Ercole, or south to Sperlonga and the house of my dear friends Virginia and John Becker. Virginia had been the roommate of my first wife, Emily, when thirty years earlier we were all students together at the American Academy. She'd held my hand through that painful divorce and during one of the worst periods, when I was on the verge of tears, I remember her saying, "Well Hume, you certainly are making character." In Rome Ginny came to my rescue again.

With Jess about to arrive I had to find another place to live. I didn't fancy our staying at the heart of things in the hotel. The real estate agent whom I was advised to consult was a *principessa*. Very elegant. I soon discovered that almost all the landlords with whom I came in touch were members of Rome's aristocracy. Perhaps the *principessa* believed in a closed shop. Finding a furnished two-room apartment with a kitchen and fireplace—the Rome winter was cold, and damp, the central heating sporadic—was not easy. I had almost given up hope when my noble lady told me of a *furnished* apartment under lease to an American couple who had been suddenly called home. Decisions had to be reached immediately and I could see the place only at night as the occupants worked during the day.

I went to the address that evening. It was raining and miserable outside. The apartment was on the ground floor of a palazzo in the Piazza Margana. Everything shown me in Rome seemed to be in a "palazzo"—where the grandeur of the title was belied by the shabbiness of the interiors. When the door opened I saw a very high ceilinged room, two great windows with curtains drawn closed, lots of cheerful lamplight, and a fire burning merrily in the vast fireplace.

"Hello," I said. "I'll take it."

"Don't you want to look around?"

"It seems fine."

"Well, some of the furniture is ours and we're taking it with us back to Mobile: that lamp, this rug—" She was small, blond, blue-eyed, snub-nosed and pretty. She had a lovely smile and a delightful Southern accent. I was paying attention to her rather than what she was saying. "The piano is ours and this table—"

I interrupted. "Is there a bed?"

"Oh yes indeed, a big one, but we seem to have blown a fuse in there. . . ."

"Never mind. What about the kitchen?"

"Through that door. Would y'all like a drink?"

The man, presumably her husband, had a napkin in his hand and I could see dishes on the coffee table in front of the fire. I refused the drink with thanks and started to back out. The man said genially,

"Ah unerstan' yoh wife is joinin' yew?"

"Yes, in a couple of weeks."

"Well naow, that's jus' fine. She may want to add a few things." He waved his napkin around the room in an all encompassing gesture.

"You mean for the kitchen?"

"Well, like m'wife said—" At this point the *principessa* spoke up. "Do not worry yourself. You are very lucky to have such luck. The prince has everything—many properties—storerooms . . . everything! You will be provided."

I shook hands with the Southern couple and departed. As I was to move in the day after they left, I was a bit anxious about the timing and delivery from the prince's storerooms. Over the next ten days I called the *principessa* a couple of times and inquired about a rug, some lamps and kitchenware and always got the same effusive reassurances: "Not to worry—you will be provided."

And I was. I was provided with more damn flowers than I've ever seen in one room before, excepting a florist's shop. A building superintendent with a very tenuous grasp of English helped me with my bags to the apartment door; smiled, and said, "Many things—for you." So I unlocked the door in happy anticipation—and walked into a funeral parlor: dim, hushed, with a rather sickly smell of too many varieties of bloom. The only thing missing was a casket. The curtains on the great windows were open now but admitting very little light from the small piazza. I realized that on the ground floor I was at the bottom of a well, surrounded by grave and venerable buildings. One unlit table lamp stood on the floor, its cord too short to reach a socket. I didn't bother to move it but wound my way through flowerpots and vases to the bedroom. Either the fuse had not been replaced or there was a fault in the wiring. No light. The blind was closed. My shins found the bed. At least there was a bed.

A bed, a table lamp, one straight-backed chair, an eggbeater, a can opener, two plastic glasses and a cup with no handle. That was the inventory of my furnished apartment. This was to be the love nest that was to welcome Jessica. Seething, I groped my way round the bedroom in search of a telephone, prepared to blow the *principessa* out of the water. The telephone had been shut off. I sat in the one chair, still in my overcoat, staring at the dead ashes in the fireplace and contemplating suicide. Well, there was nothing for it but to go shopping—a lot of shopping. My faith in the *principessa* and the prince's storeroom was at very low ebb. As I was about to leave the apartment I noticed an envelope on the floor. Inside was a note bearing a coat of arms and signed by the *principessa*. In a flourishing hand was the one word "Welcome." I presume the floral offerings were in direct ratio to the missing furniture.

Somehow or other I managed to get the place furnished. After threatening to vacate, I did get a few pieces from the landlord, but that was only a beginning. I had one stroke of luck. Shopping one evening, I had a friendly man sidle up to me and say, "Shalom."

"Shalom."

"You are an American?"

"Well, actually, a Canadian."

"There are many Jews in Canada?"

"Quite a few—in the big cities."

"You are orthodox?"

"I'm not Jewish—my people came from Ireland—originally."

He looked puzzled. "But the beard—the yarmulke."

"Oh this isn't a yarmulke. It's a beanie—you know, what we call a beanie. I just grabbed it . . . an elephant stepped on my hat."

The puzzlement became cautious and he said warily and slowly, "Where . . . was . . . the . . . elephant?"

"On the set, in a film. I'm working in a film—with elephants. The wind came up and blew off my hat. . . . You know, a straw hat . . . a Panama. Ruined it. One of the elephants . . ." By this time I was more confused than he was. Stuttering, I tried to explain that I was not *on* the elephant but only watching; that I was working in the film *Cleopatra* . . .

That was the magic word that made everything clear. All Rome knew about *Cleopatra* and assumed everyone connected with it was slightly mad. My friend beamed at me, pointed an accusing finger and said, "You are an *artist!*"

"Well, I'm an actor—*attore.*"

"And what brings you to the ghetto?"

I didn't know I was in the old Roman ghetto. I'd explained to the hotel concierge that I had to do a wide variety of shopping. Where could I find linens and lamps, china and a sofa, kitchen stuff and and and—and not too expensive. (After all, I'd have to leave it all behind when I shook the dust.) And where would the shops be open late? So I ended up in the ghetto. My new friend simply adopted me, taking me from shop to shop and bargaining fiercely on my behalf. While I couldn't follow the spate of Italian, it was quite obvious what was going on, and I could catch the frequent references to "*attore*" and "*Cleopatra,*" which produced curious looks in my direction but seemed to have a softening effect on the merchants. I don't believe there was a single instance where I paid the asking price for anything we bought.

At the end of it all, I tried to pay him what I called a commission, but he wouldn't hear of it. He simply slapped me on the shoulder, said, "Give my love to Elizabeth Taylor," and disappeared into the night.

Tandy arrived from her school in Germany—a too-brief vacation. We went dancing together. And then Jess arrived. For a little while the sun shone even in the gloomiest weather. I even rediscovered my interest in Rome's glories by seeing them again through the eyes of those I loved. We all squatted together in the Piazza Margana. I never did make friends with that place, and remember very little about it now, except for the floral welcome, a persistent sore throat, and the matter of my pipes—not those in my throat but the ones habitually clenched between my teeth.

Despite constant gargling and cutting down on my smoking—an addiction I refuse to surrender unless I'm feeling really rotten—I could not get rid of that throat irritation. It would fade away only to come back again, and I decided that perhaps my pipes carried whatever infection was bothering me. Well, I would sterilize my pipes and see if that worked. I boiled a pot of water, dropped in my pipes and added half a bottle of Listerine for good measure. I let the whole simmer, filling the apartment with a reassuring medicinal odor. I put the pipes out to dry on the windowsill. They looked a bit wan: the black stems now gray, the briar bowls now bleached to an anemic color. Never mind, I was involved in a noble experiment. When the pipes were dry, I smoked one. The delicate aroma of my expensive tobacco (Turkish Latakia mixed with a mild Virginia) was quite obliterated by the overwhelming flavor of Listerine. How did I counter that? I had a further inventive inspiration. Suppose I sweetened the bowls with honey, then placed them on the hearth before the fire? Wood had pores hadn't it? After all, it had seemed to absorbed the Listerine. I built up the fire, applied the honey—a sticky business—placed the pipes on the hearth, had a big drink and went happily to bed.

The next morning, bleary-eyed, I stumbled into the sitting room to check on my beloved pipes. The fire was out, the pipes seemed to have disappeared, and unless I was hung over, the whole hearth seemed to be undulating. I knelt down. The hearth *was* undulating—under thousands of tiny ants. They weren't nicotine addicts but honey freaks. They totally obscured my pipes. After that I gave up on my home remedies—but that isn't the end of my pipe saga.

Several weeks later, with Jess and Tandy departed and nothing on the film schedule that involved me, I got the studio's permission to go to London for ten days. Blessed escape. When Joe Mank heard I was going, he collected half a dozen of his pipes and asked me to take them to Mr. Charles Fox on Old Bond Street.

"And who is Mr. Fox?"

"Best damn pipe shop in the whole world. I've been dealing with them for years. Try to bring them back with you."

"What do you want done?"

"Have them thoroughly cleaned and polished. They do a beautiful job—come out looking like new."

When I got to London I took myself off to Mr. Fox's establishment, explained the urgency of Joe's request, his undying admiration for Charles Fox and begged for their special consideration on behalf of an old and valued client. "We'll do our very best, sir, to convenience Mr. Mankiewicz." I then produced ten pipes—six of Joe's and four of my own. The gentleman behind the counter arranged them in a neat row, but his obliging manner turned to horror as he viewed the pipes. He picked up one of mine between his forefinger and thumb—holding it like a dead rat by its tail.

"This" he asked frostily, "is *Mr. Mankiewicz's pipe?*"

His tone was such that I thought I better employ my Walter Wanger equivocation technique. "I brought them all the way from Rome," I answered. The gentleman was not impressed; he simply moved a wastebasket out from under the counter with his foot and without so much as a by-your-leave dropped my pipe into it. *Thunk!* Then he picked up another, also mine, saying, "And this?" I nodded dumbly. *Thunk, thunk, thunk*—four times in all, and my pipes were disposed of. He then gave serious consideration to Joe's six remaining ones.

When I got back to Rome I told Joe the story, which I thought funny. Joe was outraged.

"You passed your filthy pipes off as *mine?*"

"Well, I'm not a customer, and as they were doing yours . . ."

"You can be put behind bars for that—fraudulent misrepresentation! You've ruined my reputation!"

"Oh come on Joe . . ."

"You devious little bastard!"

It was precisely this kind of complimentary exchange that was the basis of our long friendship, but Joe would not be soothed until he unwrapped his refurbished pipes. They were beautiful.

With the Piazza Margana apartment empty again I could no longer bear the gloom and moved to a penthouse on the Via Francesco Crispi. It was everything the Margana apartment had not been: top floor, flooded with light, and so cluttered with furniture you had to move sideways through the rooms. From the terrace in one direction there was a view of the Borghese Gardens, and in the other, across the street and beyond a high wall, the grounds of a monastery. Here there was a tennis court, and in idle moments—of which I had far too many—I could watch the monks play tennis. Despite their cassocks, they played with great verve, almost ferocity, grabbing up their gowns with one hand and racing to the net to smash a lobbed ball into their opponents' court. On one occasion I saw a priest, or perhaps he was a seminarian, lose his temper and hurl his racket against the wall. He immediately fell to his knees and crossed himself. I gave him my blessing. I knew the feeling well.

The owner of the Francesco Crispi apartment was, of course, a *baronessa*. She was anxious that we agree to continue the services of her maid, Tina, who lived in a tiny room beyond the kitchen. Tina must have been about fifty and looked like a large piece of unbaked dough, unsuccessfully belted in by an apron and topped with a faded blond fright wig. Her physical tribulations were endless and she was compelled to talk about them, demonstrating her symptoms with an accompanying vivid pantomine. I spoke no Italian and the gestures didn't help, so at the end of one of these vehement clinical descriptions there would be an embarrassed silence on my part. Tina would look at me in disappointment, shrug, and say, "*Povera* Tina." It became a sort of chorus.

When Jessica finally came back to Rome—for another too-short visit—Tina found a new audience. And very soon the expression "*Povera* Tina" became part of our vocabulary. If anything went wrong for one of us, the other would shake a mournful head and croon, "*Povera* Tina!" *Cleopatra* had given us a new family phrase, to join Father and his rubber bands.

THIRTY-
ONE

JOE MANK WAS WRITING parts for elephants. As writer-director he had to conceive and execute the whole magnificent spectacle of Cleopatra's entrance into the Roman Forum and her ceremonial greeting by Caesar. The only analogous situations I can think of would be staging a presidential inauguration combined with Macy's Thanksgiving Day parade—complete with balloons. Only in this case it was elephants, camels, cavalry, archers, snake dancers and a towering, slave-drawn pyramid with Queen Elizabeth Taylor perched near its peak. Once this huge procession got in motion, it had the forward momentum of a 200,000-ton oil tanker. To scream "Stop—go back" was not only a time-consuming disaster but a little like King Canute ordering the ocean to retreat, or Moses parting the Red Sea while worrying about whether the Israelites might get wet feet.

Altogether there was six thousand extras, all of whom had to be herded into place by a platoon of multilingual and eagle-eyed assistants, responsible not only for order in the ranks, but also for making sure that no waving hand sported a wristwatch and no eager face was wearing sunglasses. The logistics were mind-boggling.

Originally, this whole extravagant sequence had been

scheduled for shooting in the fall of 1961, but because of the weather, it had to be postponed again and again. A film company does not lightly order up six thousand extras unless it can count on sunlight or at least clear skies. Finally, it was decided to postpone the sequence to the spring—but it rains in the spring, too. And besides, the magnificent re-creation of the Forum had suffered through the winter months: paint peeled, plaster crumbled, scaffolding warped, and all this had to be repaired by an army of craftsmen. It took time.

The only serene creatures associated with this delay may have been the elephants. They had wintered over at company expense happily eating their own tonnage in elephant fodder while awaiting a break in the weather and the will of their mad masters. The studio had found it cheaper to engage and maintain an entire circus for five months than to try to contract for a variety of exotic animals at the last moment—which might well have been impossible anyway.

This is only one example of the kind of unusual expense to which the production of *Cleopatra* was subject. Two others that I remember were paper cups (paper cups!) and construction steel piping—the material used to build a framework when wood scaffolding won't stand the stress. I was told that the cost of paper cups for the entire production (remember those six thousand extras standing out in the sun for hours on end) amounted to one million lira or at the then current rate of exchange about $160,000. There was a well-founded suspicion that the Italian paper-cup impresario, his cousins, uncles, aunts and nephews all had very long arms reaching into *Cleopatra's* pockets.

As for the construction steel piping, the production's demand for it was so great that it caused a national shortage, infuriating Italian building contractors and provoking angry articles in the press. Every foot of the stuff required to build a re-creation of the Roman Forum and Cleopatra's vast Alexandrian palace at Anzio was *rented*—and the months slipped by.

On the morning of the actual shoot we had to go through makeup in relays. Almost the entire company was involved. I got in early to find the extras already assembled. Cinecittà was overwhelmed. There was to be a brief rehearsal involving elephants before the procession proper got under way. I've forgotten why. God knows we'd rehearsed it to a fare-thee-well. I was sitting in the makeup chair having my wig adjusted when Burton came in. He looked distinctly green about the gills. He was followed by a beautiful little French girl—perhaps five feet tall and weighing about a hundred pounds. I recognized her as one of the elephant riders, the one who was to sit on the head of the lead elephant. She was already in costume, which consisted of headdress, token bra, and not much more than a G-string. Beautiful and shapely she may have been, a perfect miniature, but on this particular morning she shared Richard's woebegone look and pallor. I had the unworthy thought that they might have shared one another's company and a bottle or two the night before and now shared monstrous hangovers. Richard was a boyo who got around.

The elephants were what old novels called "richly caparisoned," and their attendant mahouts were black men wearing ornate breech clouts and elaborate headdresses with long white plumes, making them seem about eight feet tall. They each held an ankus—a short, stout staff with a cruel iron hook at its end. Each elephant carried a pair of girls: one riding in relative security in a howdah, holding a basket from which she was supposed to scatter coins to the adoring crowd. The other was perched rather precariously on the elephant's head, being purely decorative. I watched our hung-over French girl being helped up onto the lead elephant, where she wobbled, looking extremely unhappy.

At the last moment a small change was made in the order of things. For some obscure reason, the scattering of coins hadn't worked and hard candies, rather like old-fashioned sour balls, were substituted instead. The elephants moved off, led by their mahouts, the howdah girls flung their candies, the crowd scrambled to pick them up but met some competition from the lead elephant, whose trunk shot out like a vacuum hose, snuffed up a couple of candies and tucked them into his mouth.

What happened next happened very quickly. The elephant increased his pace; the mahout tried to restrain him with a

quick jab from his ankus; the elephant stamped but was not
to be deterred; the mahout lost his headdress when the plumes
caught under his animal's trunk, temporarily blinding him; the
elephant reached ever forward in search of more candy, and
with its head lowered, the little French girl came cascading
down the outstretched trunk like a child on a chute.

She screamed as the rough hide removed the skin from
her buttocks with all the efficiency of a vegetable grater. Then
she threw up. At the same time, the mahout, deeply embarrassed by his loss of control, gave the elephant one poke too
many with his ankus, and it was the elephant's turn to scream.
It was a sort of prolonged and terrifying bellow that said quite
clearly, *"Don't doooo that!"* The crowd bent back on either side
like beach grass in a gale.

All of this might have been effective in a Keystone Kops
comedy, but it wasn't quite what Mankiewicz had in mind for
the splendid ceremonial of Cleopatra's entrance into Rome.
The French girl would have to be replaced, of course. She
couldn't sit down—on an elephant or anything else. They hur-
riedly found a replacement from among the circus's own company. The replacement wasn't as pretty or as petite as the
original, weighing perhaps an added forty pounds. However,
she was on familiar terms with "her" elephant, and I watched
her clamber nimbly up its trunk and onto its head with total
authority. The extras were reassured and herded back into
line; the business of scattering candies was cut, and the lineup
restored. Off they went again. All went well until the elephants approached the rostrum. Here sat Caesar on his throne
with the entire Roman Senate in ranks behind him. I, as the
Egyptian prime minister, was on his right. I've forgotten who
was on his left, but Burton as Mark Antony, looking very martial, prowled the edge of the rostrum waiting to make one of
his exhibitionist crowd-pleasing gestures. The script called for
Burton to sweep the girl from the head of the lead elephant,
kiss her soundly, and replace her on the succeeding elephant
in the parade. The procession was to continue without pause.
This business took nice timing and control.

Everything was going well as the spectacle approached the
reviewing stand: the elephants looked magnificent, the archers

shot their beribboned arrows into the air creating a rainbow of multicolored silk, the musicians played, the cavalry capered, the camels humped, and finally Cleopatra appeared on her pyramid drawn by dozens of straining, sweating slaves. The crowd went wild, roaring their approval. As the lead elephant drew level with the rostrum, Burton stepped smartly forward, seized the girl—and overcome by the unexpected weight, staggered backward and fell on his ass into a bed of azaleas. There was a wild threshing of arms and legs. It wasn't bravura, it was low comedy.

"Cut! . . . Back! Back! . . . We'll have to go back. . . ."

The procession ground to a halt, and so did the cameras— at which point the lead elephant relieved himself directly below Caesar's throne. It was an entirely unjustified critical comment. In a scene of this magnitude something is always bound to go wrong.

There are only two other episodes in the actual shooting of *Cleopatra* that I recall with any clarity. The first is my violent death at the hands of Roddy McDowall, who played Octavian. As an old and dear friend, Roddy has never stopped apologizing to me for this infamous act. In the climactic scene he stood high above me, carrying a spear. I was at the bottom of an incline, arms outstretched in fervent appeal, when Roddy threw his spear. I died—effectively I hope. That was the physical action of the scene. But it wasn't as simple as all that. Joe wanted the camera to *follow* the spear, see it actually strike Sosigines, see the blood spurt on impact, see me fall. None of this business of "man throws spear, cut to victim staggering with spear lodged in his chest." Oh no. This was going to be more vivid than that. However, not even Roddy, wonderful actor though he is, could guarantee that the actual spear he threw would find its precise target. We were at least thirty feet from one another. So there had to be one cut as the spear left Roddy's hand. Then, in turn, the camera would pick up a second spear in flight and follow it through to the end.

Now the special-effects people came into the picture, and mechanics took over. The second spear would be hollow and threaded onto piano wire—painted black, and invisible to the camera. Nobody would throw it. It would be launched by some sort of slingshot contraption and would travel down the wire at controlled speed and direction . . . so they said. I was to wear a steel breastplate covered by a vest of cork. The cork was supposed to hold the spear quivering in my chest. One end of the wire was to be anchored to my breastplate; the other, running through the spear, would be attached to the catapult. "Not to worry." All I had to do was keep tension on the wire—and act. Act?

"What about the blood?"

"Oh that's easy: blood capsule. Breaks on impact. Just don't move forward when you talk to Roddy . . . and keep your hands clear."

"Well, there's some movement when I throw my arms up."

"Okay—but *not* forward. We don't want the wire to go slack."

"What would happen if it did?"

"The spear could drop . . ."

"How far?"

"Depends."

"Look, fifteen inches below this wire is the jewel box—the steel only goes down as far as my navel. I don't want to end up a eunuch."

"Heh, heh, heh, . . ."

"Funny to you—but they're *my* balls."

I got dressed for the scene in something less than a merry mood: T-shirt, steel plate, cork vest (rather like a life preserver) and over all that my elaborate costume. I felt like a pouter pigeon about to have a nervous breakdown. Wardrobe didn't have such a thing as a metal cup protector.

Roddy had already been photographed hurling his spear into space, so it was just me and the catapult, the wire and the spear. I leaned back on my heels keeping the wire taut and launched into Sosigines' passionate appeal for peace—or whatever it was—and didn't even see the spear coming. It hit harder than I expected and there was no trick to falling on my knees and keeling over.

It had worked perfectly. Old Sausage Knees breathed his last and the actor would not have to sing soprano. We did *not* do a second take "for protection."

* * *

The barge she sat in, like a burnish'd throne
Burn'd on the water; the poop was beaten gold,
Purple the sails, and so perfumed that
The winds were lovesick with them.

So goes Shakespeare's description of Cleopatra's barge. I cannot swear that our facsimile was accurate but it was close enough in its magnificence. We were anchored alongside a jetty on the island of Ischia. I stood on the upper deck. Joe Mank and the camera were a deck below. The jetty was crowded with film crew and sightseers. Electric cables stretched across an intervening space of about twenty-five feet. I waved to Jessica, whose broad-brimmed sun hat marked her position in the crowd. She waved back. It was a beautiful day, June 28th, 1962, my last shot in the film. After ten months, the end—at least for me. Another month in Egypt lay ahead for the rest—filming the battle of Pharsalia.

I remember nothing about the scene we were shooting on the barge, only that I was there, and that as the hours dragged by I knew I would reach a moment when, for me at least, it would all be over. When it came, when Joe had said, "Cut!" I shouted down to him, "Is that it, Joe?" He looked down at the dock where the production manager, Doc Merman, stood. "Is Cronyn finished?" I saw Doc look at his watch. "He's been off salary for thirty seconds."

"Jessie," I screamed, "we're going home!" and spreading my cloak like a vampire bat, I dove over the side. It was a long way down and I very nearly didn't come up again. I hadn't anticipated the weight of my water-soaked costume. I couldn't even lift my arms above the surface, and I had to dog-paddle to the jetty where I was unceremoniously hauled out. As I stood there panting, dripping, one of the Italian hairdressers came racing over to me and started to comb my sodden wig. It was a ludicrous gesture—about on a par with my dive. But I didn't care. I was free.

THIRTY-
TWO

THE TYRONE GUTHRIE THEATER, or the "Miracle in Minnesota," as it was sometimes called, opened in the late spring of 1963. Jessica and I were the first members to be engaged for its acting company and so we were launched into one of the richest acting experiences of our lives.

The seed had been planted ten years earlier, when Tom Patterson of Stratford, Ontario, had the magnificently mad dream of creating a Shakespearean repertory theater in a town with a population of about sixteen thousand, noted principally for the manufacture of furniture and as a railway center. The sole connection with Shakespeare appeared to be the name Stratford and the River Avon which flowed through it.

Tom was an amazing man. Within a year, Sir Tyrone (Tony) Guthrie had agreed to direct the project, Alec Guinness and Irene Worth to head up the acting company, and Tanya Moiseiwitsch to design both the theater and the initial productions. Suddenly, the Stratford dream had all the promise of a Dickensian Christmas pudding and generated equal excitement and expectation. Somewhere in his book *First State* (subtitled *The Making of the Stratford Festival*) Tom says that Jess and I were the first financial contributors to the Festival from among the profession. I have no memory of that whatever, but hope it's true. Jessica and I were present for the laying of the corner-stone—which was actually little more than the blessing of a great muddy hole over which an enormous tent pavilion was to be raised.

In that tent, the Stratford Shakespeare Festival Company played its first season. I said to Tony, "If you're ever going to do this sort of thing again, will you please remember that Jessica and I want to be a part of it?"

Tony Guthrie was a man with a long memory. It must have been sometime in 1962 that we received a letter from him. "Doing it again . . . In Minn this time. . . . We'd like you to join us. . . . What plays would you like to do? The following have been suggested. . . ." After my ten months on the film of *Cleopatra*, this invitation was like a rainbow following a violent storm, and of course we said we'd be there.

Tony Guthrie was a born leader, and his zest in living, his exuberance were so life-affirming that they infected everyone around him. He didn't walk, he didn't fly, he *stalked* through the mists of the ordinary like some almost supernatural creature. If he were alive today and able to read this, he would say, "Oh, fucky-poo!" an epithet reserved for what he found either precious or grossly extravagant. "Oh fucky-poo!" with its contrary combination of gutter and nursery catches something of the ambivalence in his nature. For instance, he was a religious man who as a director never lost an opportunity to mock the clergy. Bishops were always falling down on stage, or bopping some other unfortunate prelate with their crosier.

And yet the dedication of a new theater under his direction was an occasion of religious ritual. When the formal dedication of the Guthrie Theater took place, presiding over the ceremony were three members of the clergy, a Lutheran pastor, a Catholic monsignor and a rabbi. A full church choir was in attendance, and the theater's acting company had been carefully coached by Tony in the responses and the hymns—"No sloppy enunciation, please."

Tony frequently played the headmaster, but this was leavened by a lovely sort of jubilation. Jessica tells a story of Tony's direction of some sort of rural pageant in England. He'd recruited many of the local townspeople to act as extras, and one scene required them all to lie down on the village green. Among all these prostrate huddled bodies came Tony moving with his exhortations, arranging the different groupings. At one point he stepped across the recumbent body of an elderly but ample lady, paused in mid stride, beamed down at her and said, "Isn't it fun getting up a play!" That anecdote is the essence of the Guthrie mystique.

Any physical description of Guthrie must start with his remarkable height. He was six feet five inches tall, and his wife, Judith, was not much shorter. There were those unkind enough to say that Tony had married his sister. In fact, Judith was a distant cousin. Watching them walk together, stalk together, was like seeing a pair of whooping cranes perambulating along some exotic shore. Tony's dress ranged from the conventional to the bizarre. He could look every inch the proper English knight in dinner jacket or a blue serge suit—providing he'd remembered to put on his socks—or he could be the total bohemian. It was in the latter costume that we, the company, most frequently saw him: navy blue sneakers, no socks, baggy flannels, nondescript shirt, a cardigan if it was chilly, and chilly or not a scarf flung around his neck and over one shoulder like some raffish academic insignia. Tony had the habit of hitching up his trousers. His belts never quite seemed to find secure purchase. The result was that after an active hour or two of rehearsal, his shirt would be out behind and gaping in front, providing a fine view of his belly button.

Sloppy he may have been in dress, but in speech, never. He had a horror of elisions. "My dear Hume, the word *to* has an *o* in it. I will not accept *t* apostrophe, as in 'T' be or not t' be' . . . so vulgar. Think of it as *t* double-*o* if you must." Tony's ear for language was impeccable, but he spent little time on examining the emotion behind it. In this he was the antithesis of a director like Harold Clurman, to whom every tremor in a character's psyche had to be explored for significance. If you questioned Tony, or differed with him in interpretation, he would often fall back on "But I don't like to fiddle with your interpretation. That's your business—providing it fits with the whole and doesn't contradict the text." Harold would never have settled for that, but then Harold was often at a loss to

stage a game of solitaire, and Tony could stage *anything*—the
bigger, the more complex, the more flamboyant, the better.
His directions to individual actors were sometimes inclined to
be puzzling. "Hume, do something giggly," or "Hume, that
was very nice, very neat and tidy—very *thoughtful* . . . but could
you manage to astonish me in the morning?" And with that,
rehearsal would be dismissed, and I would be sent home to
brood over what astonishment I might produce the following
morning that might be even vaguely appropriate for the character and the situation.

Nevertheless, lucky is the actor who can work for both a
Clurman and a Guthrie.

In Tony's book *A New Theatre,* under the chapter heading
of "The Actors Are Come Hither," I find these references to
our engagement:

> We began with two leading players. Hume Cronyn and
> Jessica Tandy offered their services for the season. . . .
> versatility was essential, . . . their names are well known;
> they would offer to our audience and, not less importantly,
> to other actors a certain reassurance that standards were
> likely to be high. . . . We all knew the Cronyns well enough
> to count on them as responsible leaders of the com-
> pany. . . . The morale of a theatre company is established
> and maintained by its leading actors.

While the above was written in retrospect, it was obvious from
the start that more was to be expected of us than just performance.

My own involvement started out in a far from auspicious
manner. It had been agreed that I was to play Harpagon in
The Miser, Dr. Tchebutykin in *The Three Sisters* and Willy Loman in *Death of a Salesman*—three walloping parts. Jessica's roles
were hardly less daunting: the Queen in *Hamlet,* Olga in *The
Three Sisters* and Linda Loman in *Salesman.* However, while
Jessica went about the job with her usual serenity, I made waves.

I had the bone of contention firmly between my teeth from
the day I arrived in Minneapolis. The production stage manager, Rex Partington, handed me a script of *The Miser* (the

Molière play that Larry O. had so encouragingly described as "funny as a baby's open grave") and it was an entirely different text from the one I'd been studying—and I'd been *studying*, with Larry's succinct dismissal ringing in my ears. It now appeared that I'd been studying the wrong script. There are various translations/adaptations of Molière's plays and I'd gone off on a holiday hugging the Miles Malleson version, to which I thought we'd all agreed—only to turn up for rehearsal and discover that the director, Douglas Campbell, had had a change of heart and opted for another version. I was horribly upset, although I must admit not entirely surprised. I'd been warned while I was away that another version of the play was under consideration, but I'd written what I thought was such a passionate and persuasive letter to Tony in defense of the Malleson version that I thought my choice (after all, I *was* playing the Miser) would prevail.

I took my first protestations to Dougie, who simply dismissed my reservations about his choice of text and said, "Malleson is too cute." I thought Malleson was funny and that Dougie's choice was turgid. I went away from that meeting feeling monumentally frustrated. There was nothing left for me to do but to appeal to the highest court—Sir Tyrone Guthrie—and if that didn't work and I held to my conviction, to withdraw from the production. Tony heard me out, then said, "Hume, if you *insist*, we'll do the Malleson, but we're not going to release you from your contract."

This placed me in a miserable dilemma. I could have my way but only at the expense of my director, who held opposite convictions. It could be a ghastly rehearsal experience for all concerned if I started out by imposing my will on the director and was proved wrong. Talk about company morale. . . . I backed down and we went into rehearsal with Campbell's choice. Thank God we did. Dougie was right and I had been wrong— dead wrong. What I had not taken into consideration was Dougie's approach to the play. He had conceived the production as a marvelous commedia dell'arte caper, rich in mime, dance, and outrageous business. In that last effort, I believe I was of considerable help to him, or at least an enthusiastic collaborator. But Dougie's inspired visions required a spare text, and no conflict between the verbal and the physical. That might have been harder to achieve with the Malleson.

Years later, seventeen to be exact, I was working with Douglas again at the Stratford Festival. Dougie and I were both members of the company and I was serving a brief sentence as a member of its board of governors as well. It was a year of upset and acrimonious debate—too complex and wearying to go into here. However, it roused passions, and at one public meeting of the Festival Foundation, which I was unable to attend, my authoritative opinion on the controversy was quoted. Dougie, who held opposite views from mine (I can remember neither now), rose from his seat in the packed auditorium and in his magnificent actor's voice boomed, "Hume Cronyn has been known to be wrong!"

Over the years I seem to have collected any number of depressing sobriquets. My friend Peter Stevens, at one time general manager of the Stratford Festival, used to refer to me as "Gloom Hume"; Peter Hall called me "Eeyore," after the complaining donkey in the Winnie the Pooh stories; Gielgud burst out at me one day in rehearsal with, "Oh Hume, you're such a worrier!" and Annie Bancroft, with whom I once served on the board of a now-defunct actors' organization, had precisely the same reaction when she shafted me with "My God, Hume, you can certainly think of all the objections!" In my one brief skirmish with psychotherapy, my analyst kept referring to my "free-floating anxiety." But I'm able to report that I had a marvelously happy time rehearsing and playing *The Miser*. Of all the things I've ever done, my performance as Harpagon probably came closer to achieving what I'd hoped for than anything else I've attempted. And it's entirely probable that my own collection of personal anxieties contributed to the portrait. Harpagon was suspicious, terrified, vulnerable, all too briefly ecstatic, and in a constant state of "free-floating anxiety." For him, money was the only security blanket. The latter doesn't seem to have been my problem, but instinctively I understood all the rest of it.

I did a lot of my preparatory study for *The Miser* on Children's Bay Cay—from the wrong script of course, but this didn't affect Harpagon's characteristics. I was making notes when I

saw the crab. We had a lot of them on the cay, of every variety
and hue, from the tiny, almost transparent ghost crabs that
scuttled along the tide line, to their giant cousins who attacked
our melons. I don't know just what variety this one was, not a
soldier or a hermit, but he had an olive black shell, white pincers tucked neatly beneath his body, and a gaudy orange trim
about other parts of him. He was trying to pretend he wasn't
visible. *"Go away, I'm not here."* I put out a cautious finger and
touched the back of his shell. *"How dare you!"* He immediately
sprang to attention, his multiple legs bowing under his saucer-
shaped body, his pincers immediately *en garde.* I reached for
a twig and flipped him over on his back. His under shell was
bright orange. He had a struggle getting right side up again,
but then darted toward me with the mandibles of his hugely
disproportioned claws spread wide. *"One more indignity of that
sort and I'll pinch the hell out of you!"*

But it was only a demonstration charge, no sooner started
than finished, and he began to creep backward. I waved my
right hand and he danced to my left; waved my left hand and
he scurried to my right; retreating a little every time but always threatening. *"You son of a bitch, what did I ever do to you?"*
In the desperate retreat to his burrow he went backward over
a stone, lost his balance and ended upside down again. He was
ludicrous, hostile, terrified.

And I suddenly realized that I'd found a physical image
for Harpagon. The terror, the threats, that evasive dancing
scuttle, those bowlegs, even the color scheme. When I got to
Minneapolis I took my little fantasy to Tanya, who needed no
help from me or any other actor when it came to designing a
costume—any costume. She is one of the greatest designers of
the theater world. She listened patiently and smiled. "We'll come
up with something," she said.

The something was brilliant: a sort of crushed, shabby purple velvet fez clamped onto a stringy gray wig (hair that hadn't
seen a comb in years); a knee-length gown—rather like those
worn by college graduates, originally black, but now green with
age; stained, knee-length pantaloons, patched stockings, some
sort of ill-matched vest; and most wonderful of all, beneath
the vest, an undershirt made up almost entirely of patches in

bright colors, so that when, in a paroxysm of despair over the loss of his fortune, Harpagon rent his clothes, what was exposed was the viscera—the color of his guts—the spilling entrails of the mortally wounded man. It was a beautifully designed costume. Now all I had to do was fill it–Hah!—find the movement and nail down the emotional substance that would give life to this grotesque.

It was the sort of part I revel in playing, as far away from the familiar and the personal—except in an emotional sense—as I could hope for. Harpagon was frightened and ludicrous in his fright. So am I—extreme in my anxieties and yet fully aware that I'm inclined to be ridiculous as I indulge them. Harpagon was someone in whom I could hide, and at the same time give vent to the wailing devils that sometimes possess me. Harpagon was also a clown. Clowns don't need stories, they need a situation, the more desperate, exaggerated and sometimes lyrical, the better. Hilarity and poignance: what a divine mixture. The image of Jimmy Savo singing "River stay way from my door" and the frantic pantomime that accompanied it—"Don't come up any higher, I'm so all alone" (one could almost swear he was going to have to swim offstage)—is something that I'll never forget. Or another endearing clown, Emmett Kelly, sweeping up the spotlight that pinned him to the circus ring, sweeping and sweeping while that circle of light grew smaller and smaller until he finally swept himself into darkness and oblivion. It was a metaphor that ranks with Samuel Beckett's equally unforgettable lines, "I can't go on, I can't go on. . . . I'll go on." Or there was Red Skelton (whom my children insisted on calling Red Skeleton) as a television announcer advertising the virtues of "Guzzler's Gin" and becoming increasingly potted as he demonstrated his enjoyment of the product, "so smooooth." Marcel Marceau catching butterflies. Bill Irwin, confronting himself with wild surmise on a television screen. And Grock the legendary clown, who went to a doctor to complain about his chronic depression. The hearty doctor failed to recognize his patient without his circus makeup but urged him to cheer up, keep his bowels open, and laugh more often . . . "Go and see Grock." Then came the patient's melancholy reply, "But Doctor, I *am* Grock."

And so are we all: Grocks, Kellys, Irwins, Savos and "Skeletons," singing our bright little songs in the face of nuclear holocaust, a poisoned atmosphere, AIDS, drugs, and murder in the streets. It takes more than a smirk to offset the front-page anguish of the daily newspaper. It takes identification, delighted recognition—and the belly laugh that originates in the heart.

So when Tom Prideaux in *Life* magazine called *The Miser* "easily the most entertaining U.S. production of Molière ever given" it was rewarding. Much of that entertainment was provided by Zoe Caldwell as Frosine, the matchmaker. What a joy it was to work with her. What a joy to be at the Guthrie.

Jessica and I spent two seasons there, the opening one in '63 and two years later, in '65. In that time we appeared in eight plays between us, all classics, and in between in '64, I played in the Burton *Hamlet* directed by Gielgud. So I had three years in a row of the best material any actor can hope for. Since that time—twenty-five years ago now—Jess and I have had some very happy and successful experiences both on and off Broadway, but as I said at the beginning of this chapter, nothing that compared in richness with the Guthrie experience and working with Tony—"the Flying G." As for the company! "We few, we happy few, we band of brothers" (and sisters) . . . I've named only two of them, Jessica and Zoe, not through oversight, but because there were so many wonderful and talented people involved on both sides of that thrust stage that if I were to enter into a roll call, it would not only become tedious but certainly in the process I would neglect the contribution of some friend I admired. It was the *Company* that counted.

In talking about life in the theater, Tony Guthrie once called it a "strange, amusing, perilous journey." Do note the "amusing"—he was proud to entertain. And in speaking of the purpose to which he felt the theater was consecrated, he said, "It is to show mankind to himself, and thereby to show to man, God's image."

Amen, and *requiescat in pace*.

THIRTY-
THREE

THE GUTHRIE THEATER's very first production in 1963 had been
Hamlet. Tony had asked me how I'd like to play Polonius, and
I told him in no uncertain terms that I would *not*, having only
just recovered from playing what Joe Mank had described as
"an Egyptian Polonius"—Old Sausage Knees. Now, less than a
year later, there was a cable from John Gielgud asking me if I
would join him and Richard Burton in a Broadway production of *Hamlet,* to play—of course—Polonius. The cable arrived in Minneapolis toward the end of our first season. I
showed it to Jessie.

"But of course you must do it."

"Why?"

"*Why?*" It's a marvelous part . . . and with John and
Richard. . . ."

"Look, I've seen *Hamlet* six or seven times: Barrymore's,
Gielgud's, Evans's, Breen's, Grizzard's, Olivier's. . . . I've even
played it myself—after a fashion—and I cannot remember one
single Polonius. All I remember is a fatuous and prolix old
man approaching senility. . . . To hell with it. Besides,
I'm tired."

"But it's perfect for you."

"Thanks a lot. If I'm as prolix as all that, I don't need further rehearsal."

"You're mad."

"Possibly—but I'll just send a polite reply saying I'm committed elsewhere—that I have a conflict."

"Most actors would give their eyeteeth to be in this production. And you adore John. I think you're crazy."

"You've already said that. . . ."

I had a conflict all right. I had one with my wife, who rarely, rarely, urges me to do anything for which I lack an appetite. It was a strange reversal of roles. I had urged Jess to play Miss Collins in *Portrait of a Madonna,* Agnes in *The Fourposter* and Miss Graves in *Now I Lay Me Down to Sleep,* and perhaps in one or two others. Now, she would give me no peace. She was passionate on the subject and finally resorted to outright insult.

I cabled to Johnny G. saying I would be delighted to join his company. We were to go into rehearsal in January of 1964.

In writing about this particular production of *Hamlet,* it's important to winnow the wheat from the chaff. Chaff first.

The entire undertaking was enveloped in the mystique of the Burton-Taylor romance. It was a replay of the hysteria that had existed throughout the world press during the latter half of the filming of *Cleopatra* in Rome. It was inescapable. Never mind about the film *Cleopatra* or the play *Hamlet*: what were the lovers Richard and Elizabeth up to? The play was to rehearse and open in Toronto, and it was there that the newspaper caption "Dickenliz" first appeared. The public interest in the Dickenliz phenomenon seemed unquenchable. Poor old Shakespeare didn't stand a chance—at least not when it came to publicity. The hullabaloo continued throughout the Toronto and Boston engagements and on into New York. In each of those three cities, I remember at least one incident that was illustrative of the general madness.

With Elizabeth in Toronto to hold Richard's hand throughout rehearsals, the pressure from press and particularly the photographers (Richard called them the "Canadian paparazzi") was enormous. There came a point when Dickenliz would have sold their souls for a couple of days of peace, quiet, and solitude. Since I knew them better than anyone else in the

company and, as a Canadian, was on my home turf, I undertook to find them a bolt hole. I couldn't have done it alone.
My niece Katie Grass and her husband, Ruliff, together with
their friends Tony and Lou-Ann Cassels, arranged to spirit
them away for a weekend at Lake Simcoe. The preparations
were all very cloak-and-dagger. Rully was to pick up Elizabeth,
Katie was to pick up Richard, and we would all meet at my
apartment for what was ostensibly a supper party. After a decent interval, Elizabeth would leave with the Cassels, Richard
would leave with Katie, and at some trysting point or other
the cars would meet, exchange passengers, and Dickenliz would
be on their way to the lake. There, in February, they could
actually leave their borrowed cottage and take a walk together
without photographers popping out of the bushes to harass
them. A few weeks later I was to be party to a similar charade.
Again there was to be the business of switching cars and indi-
rect routes, but this time the destination was the Toronto Airport. Somehow or other we managed to get the cars, separately,
out onto the runway so there was no exposure to the terminal
crowds where—short of whiskers, wigs, bandages and smoked
glasses—an appearance would have inevitably led to recognition. As it was, the cover was blown when they reached Montreal. On March 15th, 1964, Elizabeth and Richard were married
in their suite at the Ritz Carlton Hotel. The ceremony was
performed by a Unitarian minister. Quebec law did not require either blood tests or a license.

Representative Michael Feighan of Ohio had called the
Burton-Taylor relationship "a public outrage" and urged the
revocation of Richard's visa on the grounds of moral turpi-
tude. Now that they were Mr. and Mrs. Burton it might have
been expected that all the furor would fade away. Not a bit of
it. If anything, it grew worse. The *Hamlet* company's move from
Toronto to Boston by chartered jet ended with a nightmare
reception at Logan Airport. Crowds broke through the police
barriers and surrounded the aircraft. The company couldn't
disembark. The combined forces of police and airport person-
nel were inadequate to control the mob—and a mob it had
become. After a considerable delay, the plane was towed from
the runway into an empty hangar, but even there the most

persistent and manic of the fans and a good number of press managed to get inside.

Two limousines were brought into the hangar. The first to leave was a decoy. The second carried Dickenliz off to the Copley Plaza Hotel. There the crowd was even bigger and more unruly. Press photographs taken in the lobby show a shoulder-to-shoulder mass of people with a grim-looking Burton (he kept saying, "I told them—I told them") with his arm around an uncharacteristically terrified Elizabeth, attempting to make their way to the elevators. It was bedlam. Once they were safely in their suite, a doctor was summoned, and he ordered a sedated Elizabeth to bed.

Weeks later, long after the play had opened in New York, Richard asked Jess and me to join him and Elizabeth for something to eat between the matinee and evening performances. I've never forgotten that limousine ride. It was the only time in my life that I remember being frightened by a crowd. We walked down the theater alley out onto 45th Street to be faced by about two thousand people. Vehicular traffic was at a standstill. A great roar went up when Elizabeth and Richard appeared. Mounted police kept a passage open across the sidewalk between the alley and the open door of the limo. But it was still a gauntlet of snatching hands, cheers, jeers ("Liz is a baaad girl") and waving autograph books. To have paused to sign one would have been fatal. Elizabeth, Jessica and Richard climbed into the back of the car, I got in front with the driver. Suddenly, on the opposite side of the windshield appeared two grinning gargoyle faces—upside down. A couple of teenagers had managed to get onto the roof of the limousine and were hanging there, not three feet from me, peering inside between the windshield wipers.

Doors locked and windows tightly closed, we moved at snail's pace out from the curb into a sardine can of humanity. Even with mounted police clearing the way, it wasn't easy, and God forbid that anyone should get bumped, let alone run over.

Jess's memory of that ride—as vivid as my own—is of a sweet, smiling Elizabeth, waving like royalty while silently mouthing, "Fuck you—and you—and you, dear." This was not Elizabeth's usual style with her public. But in this instance she'd simply had it. Usually, she was charming, patient and polite to a degree I thought remarkable, but the *Hamlet* episodes were as bad as anything she'd endured during the making of *Cleopatra*—and there, paparazzi had literally been chased out of the trees surrounding her house, from where they had a clear view of bedrooms and bathrooms upstairs.

That was the chaff, the stressful atmosphere that befogged company life offstage—particularly that of our Hamlet, Richard Burton.

But there *was* a play, there were rehearsals and openings, and reviews (some of them very contentious), and problems aplenty. The only one we seemed to escape was at the box office. This production of *Hamlet* was to break every known record in terms of its length of run and in box-office receipts. I wish I could say this was Shakespeare's triumph or the collective effort of a hardworking company, or even a discriminating audience starved for classical theater and an opportunity to see a production of one of the greatest plays of all time. Sadly, it was none of the above, but rather a triumph of publicity and curiosity.

The "concept" of this particular production, jointly agreed to, I believe, by John and Richard, was not simply that it be in modern dress, but that it be in the form of a final rehearsal—before the actors got into costume or the set had been put up. They hoped to catch the excitement that sometimes prevails when you see a play *before* the company has had to cope with period costume, before they have made an elaborate setting their own living space, and before either one of the above distracts an audience from exercising its own imagination to create a stage reality. I remember seeing two great plays in this fashion: they were final rehearsal run-throughs of Arthur Miller's *Death of a Salesman* and Thornton Wilder's *Our Town*, and they were unforgettable. I saw them both again later, garnished with sets and costumes, but was less impressed by the essence of either play. There was a truer "illusion of the first time" in those final rehearsals than in the final production—at least for me. Consequently I was persuaded that John's concept had validity—not that I gave it much thought. Perhaps I should have done, because in this case it really didn't work.

If tights, cross garters, togas, or buskins can be distracting, so can sneakers and blue jeans when worn with a sword belt. Clothes no less than manners should conform to a play's language and period. Attempts to free a play from the trappings of its time usually fail, except in those cases where another period is substituted that is analogous in style and does not contradict the text. However, my job was to act, to bring Polonius to life, and leave "concept" to others. It's one of the glories of being an actor that you can put on a large pair of blinkers and concentrate on just one problem—your own part— while the poor director has to worry about every detail in the totality. If I sound dogmatic on this point, perhaps it's because I've had no little experience in doing both, even sometimes— in an excess of hubris—attempting both together. That doesn't work either.

William Redfield, a delightful man as well as a very good actor, played Guildenstern in this production of *Hamlet,* and wrote a book about it called *Letters from an Actor.* It is the best book I've ever read on the rehearsal progress of a single production: full of wit, insight, informed opinion, and the agonies of an unhappy actor—much of that unhappiness masked by self-mockery and affection for his fellow company members. If there is a bias in Billy's book, it may be that he mistook Guildenstern for Hamlet in regard to the former character's importance to the play as a whole. Every actor—even though he may have only two lines—should look on his own contribution to the play as having the significance of Hamlet, whether justified or not. The trouble comes with expectation. A director cannot be expected to give the time and attention to Guildenstern (or Polonius) that he must give to Hamlet.

Billy was not happy in this production, and he had a great deal of company. Sometimes I felt I was the only member of the cast who was reasonably content. Oh, I had my anxieties (I would be lost without them), but whether by luck or management, I hit on an interpretation of the character that seemed to work. In my storm with Jessica over the character of Polonius, she'd likened him to Winston Churchill. I didn't buy that at all. Polonius may have had Churchill's authority, but as an image, he seemed to me dead wrong. Dean Acheson or even Neville Chamberlain came closer to the mark for me. These images, particularly the former, made my selection of "rehearsal clothes" fairly easy. I wore a dark gray business suit with a very faint chalk stripe; shirt and tie, of course; a vest with a watch chain; my reading glasses hung around my neck; conservative black shoes; and I carried a cane. I hoped to establish an impression of formality together with something vaguely old-fashioned.

So much for the physical; but what about the far more significant aspects of the inner man? It is easy to write Polonius off as a "tedious old fool" as Hamlet does; or again as "a wretched, rash, intruding fool." But are those descriptions accurate? One of the most deceptive traps an actor can fall into is to accept another character's description of the character he is playing. The describer is frequently prejudiced, and almost inevitably subjective. Polonius is certainly "tedious," "old" and "intruding." But a "fool"? Never. As with Brutus, the elements are mixed in him. There's a lovely irony in the fact that this man Polonius, whose most famous speech idealizes character, prudence, forbearance, modesty, thrift, and half a dozen other virtues, is the same man who uses his daughter little better than a pimp might. He is a master of connivance (listen to his cynical advice to Reynaldo), and his true view of humanity is summed up with "'twere a thing a little soiled i' the working." Does that mean that Polonius is an out-and-out hypocrite? Not at all. I think he fervently believes in his high-minded advice to his son, Laertes. But Polonius is a believer in the precept that says, "Don't do as I say, but as I do." That's what makes him such a fascinatingly contradictory character. Polonius, don't forget, has served both king and state through two administrations. He is a prime minister. Such a man may on occasion prove a bumbling bore, but is not likely to lack political expertise or ambition.

Lady Macbeth, in speaking of her husband, says, "Art not without ambition, but without the illness should attend it." No such lack afflicted Polonius. He had the "illness" down to a fine art, and would no doubt have termed it practical politics, and shrugged off any suggestion of deviousness. Having baited a trap with his daughter to discover Hamlet's intention, and put a prayer book in her hand (nice touch, that), he justifies his action to King Claudius with this observation:

> "Tis too much proved!—that with devotion's visage
> And pious action we do sugar o'er
> The devil himself."

What an inspired rationalization for a dirty bit of business! Polonius's humanity is indeed soiled in the working.

It was this complex character that I carried into rehearsal with me. Like Billy Redfield, I had read everything I could lay my hands on relating to *Hamlet*. However, reading doesn't make a performance for any actor, it can only stimulate and challenge, like a good tennis opponent. You have to master your own strokes all by yourself, with, you hope, the coaching of a director—and in this instance I had one of the very best.

John Gielgud probably knows more about *Hamlet* than any actor alive. However, I cannot tell you how intimidating it is to rehearse a play when the director knows every word of the play without reference to the text. And therein lay part of our company's problems. American actors in general do not have the classical background of the best of the English actors, and the occasional gulf between our company and our director was I think largely attributable to the company's inexperience.

Redfield wrote, unhappily: "Gielgud talks little, rehearses even less. Many of the people grow uneasy, myself included. It's all too smooth, too relaxed, too easily approved. We break too early. We take too many 'fives.' Every five will get us ten. . . . Obviously John places sublime faith in the actor's ability to work things out on his own." If John as actor could work things out on his own, why couldn't we? If John as actor could adapt *immediately* to an acceptable piece of direction, what was wrong with us? The answer is fairly obvious: most of us lacked his skills. As for John's silences, his apparent distaste for "talk" and his preference for "Let's push on shall we?" here are two instances of direction to Burton (as reported by Billy) that strike me as pithy and about as helpful "talk" or direction as an actor could hope for.

"Have a care as to your playfulness. It's splendid that you have such humor and wit and quickness in the part, but the long lines of Hamlet must be sad. If you frolic too much too often you may not be able to stop the laughter later on. No, don't scowl—you're going to make them laugh quite a bit, have no fear. But if you make them laugh too much and you can't stop them, you will have won their stomachs while losing their hearts. 'Look to it.' "

Now that strikes me as pretty good talk, and to the point. And here again is another piece to Burton.

"Have a care as to shouting. You shout brilliantly; both you and Larry Olivier do—two splendid cornets. I am a violin, I'm afraid, not too good at shouting. But these hunting calls you do so well can be tiresome when sounded too often. Don't overuse it. It's a wonderful weapon but it's your *last* weapon. Use it only when all else fails."

And here's a piece of direction given to me, and again cribbed from Billy's account.

"My dear fellow, when you say to Claudius 'What do you think of me?' you simply must say 'What do you think of *me*.' You must emphasize the word *me*."

And Redfield adds his own comment:

Cronyn finds this inflection baffling, since his intelligence indicates the reading to be "What to you *think* of me?" When he asked Gielgud for an explanation, Sir John shook his head. "I can't give you one," he said. "Just read it that way."

And read it that way I did. Sometimes I know when I'm in the presence of my betters. Also, when I *thought* about it, considered the context in which the question was asked as well as Polonius's sense of self-importance—his hunger for approval by his king—the reading seemed right to me. John has a near-infallible ear. I argue all too easily and often when I have a conviction, but not when the director is Gielgud and it's a matter of the music of words.

Billy writes, "The personal conviction of the individual actor is what finally persuades an audience." I don't think that's an absolute, but there's a considerable measure of truth in it. But what if the actor's conviction is in conflict with that of the director? In extreme cases they would best wave goodbye to one another—especially if there is no playwright around to arbitrate and speak passionately of his conception of the character. Who can say with total authority what Shakespeare had in mind for *Hamlet*? Perhaps Richard Burbage, presumably with Shakespeare at his elbow (and playing the Ghost in the same production), could have spoken with authority, but he's long gone, and over the past four hundred years it's been up to the conviction of the actor at bat. No interpretation of *Hamlet* can satisfy everyone. Gielgud had his, and Burton a somewhat different one—"more modern," he felt—yet both actors had immense respect for one another. Richard hoped to learn from John; John felt that Richard's gifts, his very lyric Welshness, his vigor, sensibility, beautiful voice—and yes, his modernity—would make for an exciting and contemporaneous Hamlet. Both actor and actor-director wanted to work with one another, and yet, and yet . . .

To an extraordinary extent the play *Hamlet, Prince of Denmark* is the character of Hamlet alone. He is the sun around which the other characters revolve. So there's little wonder that the director's first and foremost concern must be given to that character and the actor playing it. As I've said, I'm not sure that Billy or the rest of the company appreciated that fact. We were all in desperate need of John's attention. The production was awkward, the wardrobe gave trouble, and the bare stage, surrounded by the brick walls of the theater, was as distracting as an unnecessarily elaborate set might have been. The production did not jell. Richard was brilliant but uneven, and the rest of us uneven and less than brilliantly supportive.

As Polonius, I never felt any lack in John's attention to me. My principal concern was that I not be too "cute," too adorable in mannerism—in short, that I not be *too* funny. There are marvelous comic aspects to the character of Polonius, but they are *there*, Shakespeare provided them. The actor adds more at his peril. Having run a sword through Polonius's guts, Hamlet says, "Thou find'st to be too busy is some danger." That might be addressed to the actor who plays Polonius as well.

Every actor goes into rehearsal hoping that his director will turn out to be God, that he can do no wrong, and that somehow he will annoint his actors with a magical balm of inspiration and capability. They expect him to lead them into some promised land where they will finally be recognized as multi-talented or at the very least "brilliant." When it comes to this sort of faith, I am not merely heretic but downright agnostic. Directors can be obtuse, blind, abusive, insensitive and *wrong*. I know, I've been one. If there is an actor's prayer to be addressed to his Godlike director it might run "Dear Father, may you be kind, patient, long-suffering, inspired, and above all may you have reliable taste and judgment; for I, your not-too-humble servant, am extremely vulnerable and in dire need of your blessing."

Afterthought. "Oh, yes, and may you have the gift of communication, so that even after having said the same thing to me ten times without result, you will be prepared to try an eleventh—if necessary, in Swahili."

Of course, John had certain idiosyncrasies as a director that were easy to mock, but the mockery was exercised with great affection. For one thing, he believed in trial and error (what else are rehearsals for?) and he moved so quickly—particularly in the matter of staging a scene—that the actors sometimes felt they were caught in a blender. John also didn't hesitate to read a line for an actor or to demonstrate a move he thought might be helpful. This is a practice some American actors find reprehensible, even downright insulting. Not me, I like it. Some streak of arrogance in my makeup will allow me to say, "Oh, I see what you mean; now I'll do it—only better." Communication needs all the help it can get, either verbal or physical.

One day I sat in my dressing room while John struggled to stage a scene involving Claudius and his courtiers. One of these, Voltemand, was played by Phil Coolidge, an accom-

plished, bony-faced New Englander of considerable experience. Things weren't going well. The stage picture would not
come right. I could hear every shuffle and word of dialogue
from onstage through the dressing room p.a. system. John's
voice rose above the rest and acquired a certain frantic note.
"No, no, no! It's terrible—quite terrible. . . . Coolidge, wear
a hat!" I nearly fell out of my chair with laughter at this wonderful non sequitur. It was pure Gielgud.

We opened in Toronto to a vast variety of reviews—most
of them bad. The two most influential critics of that city, Herbert Whitaker of *The Globe and Mail* and Nathan Cohen of *The
Star,* headed their reviews respectively as follows: "Burton dis-
appointing in long-awaited unadorned *Hamlet.*" Nathan was
more concise, calling it simply an "unmitigated disaster." You
can imagine what effect such judgments had on a company
that was already insecure. On the morning that these notices
appeared our producer, Alex Cohen (as he quickly pointed
out, no relative to Nathan), called the company together and
gave one of the very best speeches I've heard from a manager
in his unhappy position. Alex was very frank, very realistic
and funny—no mean trick in that black crepe-hung atmosphere. He pointed out that we still had six weeks ahead (the
Toronto and Boston runs and the previews in New York) before we would have to face the music from the Broadway critics, so "Let's push on, shall we?" as John G. so frequently put
it. We applauded him gratefully.

One area in which the Toronto reviews had no effect whatever was at the box office. The O'Keefe Centre has, as I remember, 3,200 seats; Billy referred to it unaffectionately as
"the most beautifully decorated aeroplane hangar in the world."
It is an impossible space for any play, but there were warm
bottoms on all those seats for every performance. "Dickenliz"
again.

In New York, the reviews were, again, mixed, but this time
they were far more favorable. We had improved. And there
were moments in Burton's playing of Hamlet when I felt that
rare *frisson* of excitement at greatness.

Personally, I came out of this production of *Hamlet* rather
well. Over a long period of years I've been nominated for a

Tony six times, but only with Polonius did I manage to win. (Jessica has been nominated an equal number of times but has won on three occasions—a statistic whose significance I don't wish to examine too closely.)

As for working with Gielgud, I can only say that if John were to cable me tomorrow asking me to join him in Samarkand to play Peter Pan, I'd pack immediately.

* * *

I cannot let the *Hamlet* production go by without mentioning one other person whose name does not appear in the program. Malcolm Wells and I worked together for the first time in this play. We have now worked together for twenty-six years, and I would be lost without him. Malcolm was and is my dresser. This is a job which is poorly understood even by theater professionals. The least of its responsibilities is handling the actor's wardrobe. A good dresser—and Malcolm is the best—becomes an intimate friend, confidant, confessor, psychologist, keeper of terrible secrets, and knows just when to refuse you a much-needed drink. Added to all that, Malcolm is kind, patient, extraordinarily sympathetic and just occasionally tyrannical. Long ago I gave up speaking of *my* dressing room; clearly it is *his*.

When I have been suicidal, Malcolm has rallied me; when I have been ill, Malcolm has nursed me. This extraordinary man is among other things a registered nurse, a considerable philosopher, and in the war of 1941–45 he held the highest rank obtainable by a noncommissioned officer: regimental sergeant major—and don't you forget it! When I lost one eye in 1969 and before I'd adjusted to the blur (I was on tour), Malcolm cooked for me, shopped for me and, offstage, led me around like a puppy on a string—a habit that continues long after my recovery. His only peer is Wilhelmina Reavis, who outranks Malcolm by ten years, having "dressed" Jessica for thirty-six years.

This kind of relationship between actor and dresser seems to have gone out of fashion as the theater has changed and dwindled, but these remarkable people, Willie and Malcolm, have earned not only our undying gratitude but the infinite respect of every backstage crew and management wherever we may have played. One final quote from *Hamlet*'s Polonius seems appropriate:

> "Those friends thou hast, and their adoption tried,
> Grapple them to thy soul with hoops of steel."

Only in this instance, the sentiment is far more than unction. Willie and Malcolm, Malcolm and Willie, we salute you.

THIRTY-
FOUR

ON FEBRUARY THE SECOND, 1965, Jessica and I appeared at the White House at the invitation of President and Mrs. Johnson in something called "Hear America Speaking." It was not my title, I hasten to add, and was a rather pretentious misnomer for the collage of materials I'd pasted together.

The whole thing had started with a telephone call I'd received on Children's Bay Cay in January. We'd retreated to the island to recover. The year 1964 had been one of too many things after another: *Hamlet* for me; the Spoleto Festival for Jess; *The Physicists* for both of us, and for good measure I had produced a play (together with Lewis Allen and Roger Stevens) called *Slow Dance on the Killing Ground*.

Neither *The Physicists* nor *Slow Dance* really "worked," which is professional-theater–speak for a production that doesn't return a nickel to its investors, but I was proud to have been associated with both of them. *The Physicists* was written by Friedrich Dürrenmatt, directed by the formidable Peter Brook, and had a wonderful cast, and William Hanley, who wrote *Slow Dance*, is an exceedingly talented writer. Neither play lasted more than two months on Broadway. Unfortunately, the shortness of a run bears no direct ratio to the degree of exhaustion it can generate—it's more likely to be the other way about. So, there we were on the island; away from mail and telephones, excepting one call a day from the Nassau out-island operator that gave us some minimal link with our children—or relayed matters of extreme urgency. I hated that daily call, resented it too. Ship-to-shore telephones are temperamental devices, easily upset by weather conditions, mechanical difficulties, and party-line interruptions. What's more, the whole world is listening—or at least that part of it on your radio frequency—so watch your language.

On that particular morning, I was monitoring the beast and waiting for the operator to reach Z.F.X. (our call letters) on her schedule. A German freighter kept up a plaintive but unanswered call: "S.S. *Lorelei* calling Nassau Marine, come in please." The freighter had no business using our frequency and was being ignored by the out-island operator. Doubtless, after a bit, the German would grow discouraged and switch channels—perhaps even find the right one. On the schedule ahead of me someone was ordering groceries, a long and tedious business. Between bursts of static I could catch fragments of the list as the voice droned on: ". . . twenty pounds of flour; two cases orange soda; ten pounds white sugar; one plastic clothesline, you carry clothespins?"

"S. S. *Lorelei* calling Nassau Marine." A voice that I recognized as that of an American charter-boat captain whom I knew cut in with an abrupt: "You're on the wrong channel, Bud."

The grocery list continued. "How about nylon then. . . . Oh, about thirty feet . . . and make it four dozen pins. . . ."

Suddenly the out-island operator's voice broke in. "All stations stand by—stand by please. Calling Z.F.X. Z.F.X., come in please."

I pushed the button on my transmitter. "This is Z.F.X. Good morning."

"Z.F.X., we have an urgent call for Mr. Cronyn from the States."

My heart sank. "Urgent call" spelled trouble. "Go ahead operator, this is Mr. Cronyn."

"Nassau Marine, Nassau Marine, this is *Lorelei*, S.S. *Lorelei*, please come in."

"Listen Buster, give it a rest. Switch! Switch! You're suppose to be using sixteen."

"Operator . . . Operator, this is Z.F.X. You have a call for me. . . ."

I couldn't catch her next few words. At one moment she would be loud and clear and at the next there would be only a distorted whisper, but I thought I heard her say, ". . . from the White House in Washington, D.C. Stand by while I connect you."

The White House!? There must be some mistake. I didn't know anybody at the White House. Then it hit me. Of course. My old friend Roger Stevens, head of the Kennedy Center for the Performing Arts—someone had told me that Roger had an office in the bowels of the White House. What could Roger want?

"Z.F.X. go ahead please."

The next voice I heard was not Roger's; it was that of a lady with a pronounced Texas accent.

"Mr. Cronyn? Mah name is Bess Abel, ah am Mrs. Johnson's secret'ry. Mrs. Johnson an' the pres'dent have asked me—"

"Nassau Marine, Nassau Marine, Nassau Marine! This is S. S. *Lorelei* calling. S. S. *Lorelei* calling Nassau Marine . . . *please* come in."

"Listen you stupid kraut I've told you—you're using the wrong frequency. Now get the hell off. You're buggering up the whole system."

"All stations, all stations, *please stand by* . . . Z.F.X., are you there?

"I'm here."

"Go ahead Washington."

"Mr. Cronyn?"

"I'm sorry, Mrs. Abel, we're having some problems here. Would you mind repeating what you said?"

"Ah sayed the pres'dent an' Mrs. Johnson would lak yew an' Miss Tandy to come to the White House on February the second to entertain them an' their guests."

My relationship with the radiotelephone has never been good. It is filled with mistrust and is likely to induce panic. Under these circumstances I am inclined to shout, as though by lung power alone I could reach my oh-so-distant caller. In this particular instance I was screaming. Jessica came from the other end of the house and put a soothing hand on my shoulder. We both heard what followed—or at least I heard (between bursts of static) and Jess picked up the gist from my near hysterical arguments, reservations and lies. I explained to Mrs. Abel that while we were greatly honored by the invitation, we had no hip-pocket act, no "turn," no party piece; in short, nothing suitable that we could produce on such short notice. It was already mid-January. February 2nd was just around the corner. Mrs. Abel heard me out with patience and tact and said, "Ah'm sure you'll think of somethin'."

I'd heard this line before and have heard it since. It has all the charm of a death knell. I didn't want to "think of somethin' "—I just wanted to put on a diving mask and disappear into the silent and serene waters of another world. In desperation I told a whopping lie. "But Mrs. Abel, we have guests arriving from England. I'm not sure I can even reach them. They're somewhere in the mid Atlantic now."

There was a short pause. Then Bess Abel said: "Mr. Cronyn, don't yew think yo' guests would understan' if yew explained to them that yew an' Miss Tandy had to leave fo' a few days t' entertain the pres'dent of the United States and Mrs. Johnson?"

It was said with gentle restraint, slowly, and in that soft Texas drawl, and it made me feel like a dirty little boy who might better deserve having his lying mouth washed out with soap. Mrs. Abel wasn't going to take any form of no for an answer. From behind me Jess whispered, "The Iron Butterfly."

"Mrs. Abel, can I talk to Miss Tandy about this and call you back?"

"Why certainly—an' yew enjoy yo' holiday, y'heah?"

I sat there stunned, as the aggrieved voice of the man whose shopping order had been interrupted came back onto the circuit: "Three quarts of Myers rum, a dozen rolls of toilet paper . . ." I switched off.

Jessica said, "We're going to have to do it, you know."

"Do it? Do it! Do *what*?"

She patted my shoulder reassuringly. "You'll think of something."

There was nothing else for it; we had to pick up and fly back to New York. I wondered who they *really* wanted? Who turned them down? And what excuses did *they* find? What in God's name were we to do—what "something"? As luck would have it we were between apartments, with all our worldly goods, including my books, in storage. I prayed that I might find Joe Mankiewicz in New York and that he would permit me the run of his library. But what could I find as a centerpiece, what would be appropriate to the occasion?

I was not comforted to learn that the dinner was to be a state occasion given by the president for the entire cabinet, the entire Supreme Court, and a representative number of university presidents, publishers, editors, business tycoons and other ladies and gentlemen of national influence—hardly a typical audience to be found on West 45th Street. I've never been so nervous in my life and never expect to be again.

> Charge once more then, and be dumb!
> Let the victors, when they come,
> When the forts of folly fall,
> Find thy body by the wall.

So I finally decided to "charge" with a piece from President Johnson's recent State of the Union Address—sometimes referred to as "The Great Society Speech"—as a springboard. At least it wouldn't offend our hosts. But what were we to use to buttress it?

One anxiety-ridden day I realized that within the past twelve months Winston Churchill, T. S. Eliot and Sean O'Casey had all died. There was at least a topical if tenuous link there—so I exploited it. And we ended up with the nice irony of a program entitled "Hear America Speaking," which consisted largely of lines composed by two Englishmen and an Irishman, and read by an Englishwoman and a Canadian. Jessica did finish with an American poem: "The Ballad of Lost Objects" by Phyllis McGinley. It's an amusing poem with a recurring line, "Where in the world did the children vanish?" and was apt in that the last of the Johnson children had just left the nest.

We flew to Washington on February 1st and did a rehearsal run through on the following afternoon. I remember nothing about it except that the word *whore* appeared in one of my selections. It's a perfectly respectable word and was used in a perfectly respectable context, but it precipitated a hurried huddle among the White House advisers who were seeing what we were up to. (I hadn't submitted a script beforehand—there was no time.) I was asked to cut the word or to find a substitute. What substitute? Tart? Prostitute? *Fille de joie?* I refused to cut or change the word, preferring to eliminate the selection. They were a nervously apprehensive group—at least we had that in common.

I'm sure it was a very good dinner, but I had no appetite and only went through the motions of eating. Over coffee, President Johnson made a speech, proposed toasts, and was replied to in turn by Vice-President Hubert Humphrey, Speaker of the House John McCormack, and Chief Justice Earl Warren. I kept looking at my watch and worrying about whether our program would be too long. The audience was already being treated to a surfeit of words.

Finally, we adjourned to the East Room, where a small stage had been set up. It held two lecterns with reading lamps and our scripts. The wings were curtained off and Jess and I cowered there waiting for the audience to settle itself and for the marine officer to say the dreaded "Now"—at which point we would be "on" and God be with us both.

First, however, came Mrs. Johnson's introduction. It was charming, and she'd *learned* it, which I found impressive. I particularly liked the moment when she spoke of our work in Minneapolis but "dried" on the name of the theater. Nothing fazed, she turned to the vice-president and said, "Hubert, what is the name of that theater in your state?"

"The Guthrie Theater, Lady Bird."

I found that little hiccup immensely reassuring. All at once this intimidating occasion seemed like a family affair.

I remember nothing at all about the performance/reading except that the audience seemed to be held and that we plowed on.

Jessica and I had agreed that at the end there was bound to be applause—out of politeness if nothing else—and that we must be careful not to appear to milk it. "*One* bow and let's get the hell off."

When the moment came, we took our bow, retreated to the wings and stood there holding one another's icy hands. The applause continued. We waited. Suddenly our harassed-looking marine officer reappeared and said, "Miss Tandy—Mr. Cronyn—you've *got* to go back on. The president and Mrs. Johnson are waiting for you." So on we went and there indeed they were, standing, waiting, at the edge of the stage. Behind them, two by two, like couples waiting entry to the ark, stood many others. We shook hands murmuring "thank you," "thank you," in turn. It was an extremely graceful gesture on behalf of such a distinguished audience. If, God forbid, a bomb had struck the White House that night, the United States would have been left without a government, because its principal authorities were—as Bess Abel had said they would be—all present.

It was over! The East Room was empty except for Jay Carmody, dean of the Washington drama critics at that time. I was sitting on the edge of the stage dying for a drink. Jay was standing on the floor below me, asking questions about our choice of material—as well he might. Suddenly, in mid sentence, he stuttered and his eyes went over my head. I turned to discover what had caught his attention and immediately scrambled to my feet. It was the president, with McGeorge Bundy by his side. I've never thought of Lyndon Johnson as being psychic, but the first words out of his mouth were, "Mr. Cronyn, wouldn't you like a drink?" He went on to thank me, and to excuse himself, as he and Mr. Bundy had "a few matters to discuss." He looked gray, pouch-eyed, exhausted, and it was already close to midnight.

I think I'd rather be an actor—even a very nervous one—than president of the United States.

THIRTY-
FIVE

IT WAS EARLY IN 1965 that the "sea eagle"—an osprey probably—perched on the top of our radio mast at Children's Bay
Cay. He must have had a magnificent view; pretty much the
same view that I'd first had from the joewood tree eighteen
years earlier, when I'd set foot on the island for the very first
time, cut my way up the hill with a machete, clambered up the
tree and said to myself, "We'll put the house here."

Had the sea eagle deigned to look down at his immediate
surroundings on shore rather than scanning the sea for fish,
he would have seen my dream become reality. Five buildings;
groves of coconut palms, great masses of color from the plantings of hibiscus, oleander and bougainvillea; wharves, jetties,
boats bobbing at anchor off the home beach; and with his incredible eyesight he might have even counted the fruit on the
trees in the orchard: mangoes, bananas, grapefruit, limes, oranges, papaya . . .

I had not seen the osprey myself. Will Nixon had told me
of the bird's appearance, but in such a hangdog and depressed manner that I asked what troubled him.

"It's bad luck," he answered. He looked away, his tongue
exploring the inside of his cheek; his eyes dropped to his worn
sneakers. I waited, wondering. Will decided to kick away a

wandering soldier crab, then suddenly looked up and straight at me. "You goin' t' sell the cay?"

It was a moment I'd dreaded. Will had become a close friend—all of them had: Jacob, Carmen, Rev, Lucy, Big Rosie and those of their families whom we'd come to know. I'd made provision with the new owners, Jack and Dru Heinz, to keep them all on, but inevitably it would be different—better perhaps, but different.

It was true: we had sold Children's Bay Cay. The decision had been a long time coming. As Jess and I had grown ever busier, we were able to see less and less of the cay. In some recent years we'd only managed to spend three weeks there; and as the absences grew longer, the management responsibilities increased. And a serpent had crept into the garden in the shape of my passion to "improve." The commissioner's report to higher authority in Nassau spoke of Children's Bay as "the best-developed private island in the Exumas." But there was a price—not only a monetary one, but those endless "lawyer letters" of mine as Will called them, the sorting out of maintenance problems by long-distance telephone, and most difficult of all, the absolute requirement that we visit the cay whenever we had a week or so free. It became a duty. I would never, never fall out of love, but I wanted at least to look at other ladies.

One of these was East Africa: dusky, mysterious, perhaps even dangerous. And with a reputation for unsurpassing beauty. Of course it was just another fantasy, fed by the writings of Isak Dinesen, Hemingway, Alan Moorehead and Peter Hill Beard. The last named had just published a book called *The End of the Game.* The title had a double meaning and made me feel that if I was ever to explore my most recent dream, I'd better get about it quickly. I remember closing that book and thinking, I'm going to do it. But I also remembered my hawk-faced Uncle Edward who, despite his passion for fishing and the wilderness, was not a man to indulge daydreaming. He would have dismissed all the above as "romantic tosh."

Uncle Ed, as a young man, had seen service in the Boer War. For the rest of his life he wore a sort of leather stocking on his left forearm. It buckled on like a continuing series of broad wristwatch straps. I once dared ask him if he removed it when he went to bed and he answered tersely, "Only under special circumstances." I thought it better not to inquire just what those might be. As a boy, I found this arm appliance fascinating and I questioned him as to why it was necessary. Edward Cronyn's speech was staccato. He was a great man for thrift in all things including words, but I remember certain phrases. "Got tossed on my bum riding across the veldt . . . stroppy mount . . . silly bugger shied at his own shadow . . . smashed my arm to bits . . . remounted and wrapped the bridle around it . . . not entirely satisfactory . . . Brigade blacksmith did a better job—never mended properly though . . ."

When I asked him about Africa in general he said simply "wretched place," which was, I suspected, not an entirely objective judgment.

However, despite Uncle Ed, the other authorities prevailed, and I was determined to go. Of my other authorities, Dinesen and Hemingway were dead. Moorehead lived in Australia—and Peter Beard? Wherever he was I never expected to meet him. But I did eventually—in Africa—and in a very unexpected fashion.

For innocents the logistics of putting a full-scale safari together are mind-bending, so Jess and I used an excellent outfitting firm in Nairobi, Messrs. Ker, Downey and Selby. Of course if you don't insist on sleeping under canvas and being a self-contained unit, it can be done more simply and a good deal more cheaply. If you'll settle for staying at the various government lodges within the game parks—many of them very comfortable—you can travel between them by car or bush plane or join a group and go by bus. Then, however, you're at the mercy of a tour guide, the will of the majority, and in all probability a very tight schedule. Jess and I—and Bob Whitehead, who was coming with us—wanted none of that. We wanted freedom. I, in particular, wanted it. I even hesitated about taking a camera. Too many hours in too many beautiful wilderness places have been cramped for me by worrying about the photographs and squinting at the exposure meter. On the other hand, we wanted a record. We made an extravagant compromise. We would try to find a professional film cameraman to go along with us and I would commit myself to keeping a daily journal.

Over the past sixty years I've kept only two or three journals, and I'm not sorry. To sit down at the end of a wonderfully exhausting day and have to scribble—before it all fades away—is not my idea of fun. I'd rather have a drink and laugh over the day's triumphs or disasters than have to put it all down on paper. Reading my African journal now does not fill me with the echoing delight that my memory does. Memory can be a judicious editor, omitting trial and tribulation. It can also be a terrible liar—but I think I prefer the lies to recorded anxieties. Rereading my journal I discover that at one point I had a miserable and prolonged stomach upset; Jessica caught the flu; our supplies failed to catch up with us; our film stock ran out; there was no report from the photographic lab in London—were we sending them anything but blank film? Our mail had been sent to Mombasa and we were a thousand miles away. Were the children all right? . . . I don't *remember* any of that.

What I remember is the grandeur and contrast of the country—where you could travel from the snow-covered peaks of Mount Kilimanjaro or Mount Kenya to seemingly barren desert in no time at all; where teeming wildlife and endless movement could dissolve into total rest—a stillness and silence as comforting as the womb; where the starlit canopy of night might be as quiet as the grave or broken only by the hiss and crackle of your own safe campfire. There was time to watch and marvel, to think of things usually unthought about, to touch the face of nature and even, perhaps, to hear the voice of God.

All that on a bustling safari, with its trucks and Land Rovers and attendant crew of drivers, spotters, cook, tent "boys" and the rest of them? Yes, all that and more. We didn't *have* to do anything. Stay in camp and sleep if we liked. Or follow a usual routine—but not a compulsive one. Awakened in the dark by a silent figure bearing a hot cup of tea—hoarfrost on the grass and glad of your ski jacket. Out for an early-morning scout, the campfire still burning, headlights on in the Land

Rover and a delicious smell of frying bacon from the cook tent. Have a look round, perhaps come on a pride of lions still feasting over a night's kill; approach, with caution, a buffalo still bedded down in high grass and not at all happy about the intrusion; mark where the game is, watch the sun come up and go back to camp for a big breakfast.

Or sleep in. Have breakfast first. Start the whole thing later—perhaps as late as eight o'clock. You won't stay out beyond eleven; the game will all be lying up in the shade by then and you'll be dripping with sweat. Lunch behind a net covering the open side of the dining tent, and to your sleeping tent afterward to snooze or read through the heat of the day. Out again about four to see what you can see: perhaps a gerenuk, one of the most graceful of all antelopes, standing on his hind legs to browse on the tender shoots at the top of a bush. The Land Rover will not frighten him, whereas a man on foot would send him scampering. He may turn from the bush, still on his hind legs, and stare at you, his forelegs bent, the posture being that of a trick dog begging.

Perhaps it will be a pair of cheetahs hunting, or a group of crowned crane looking very regal even while searching for insects in the grass. Across the plain there will be herds of zebra or wildebeest, their outlines distorted by the heat waves. Standing on a giant anthill you may see a topi doing a precarious balancing act. He has yellow stockings, blue-black haunches and delicate twisted horns curving backward. He stands as still as stone watching you—a living African monument on a pedestal. And Simon's camera records it.

Officially, Simon Trevor was our cameraman, but he proved to be much more than that: friend, counselor, and ultimate authority on wildlife. For some years he'd been a park warden, and there was little about East Africa, its people and its animals that he did not know. Much of his film of our safaris is breathtaking. How, with a hand-held camera, he managed to follow and focus on the flights of flamingoes, eagles, and indeed anything that moved, with such precision and smoothness, was amazing. He also had an uncanny sense of just where and when an animal might move. Wildlife photography can be an intuitive art as well as a skill—and it takes enormous patience. We frequently spent four to six hours with just one animal or one group of animals. Simon seemed to know precisely where to place the car, from which quarter the wind was blowing—even when I could have sworn there was not so much as a zephyr—and in just which direction the game was likely to move. Juggling all this information, not to mention the position of the sun and how it was likely to affect his photography, took some doing. Fortunately, our "white hunters," who were in total charge of our safaris and who were ultimately responsible for our safety, our camps' operation and our various expeditions, all seemed to recognize Simon's talent and were content to let him arrange matters, providing we did not leave the cars and walk. Walking was strictly forbidden.

I had not anticipated this restriction, and bridled at it. On arrival at our very first campsite in the Masai-Mara Reserve, our tents were to be pitched beneath some towering fever trees. They reminded me of California eucalyptus. Before even getting out of the car, I spotted several giraffe on the horizon and announced that I was going to walk toward them. I was stiff and sticky from a long hot ride over abominable roads and great clouds of red dust that we had generated along the way. It was late afternoon of a beautiful day in the African spring of December. The grass was green, the towering fever trees threw long shadows; it would take time to pitch the tents, and there were the giraffe against the horizon. I wanted to stretch my legs. Our hunter, John Fletcher, a very nice, reasonable man, said, "Better not." Not walk? Why, for God's sake? "It's against the rules."

"You mean we can't walk at all?"

John looked unhappy, then said, "You can walk around here—" gesturing to the campsite "—in circles."

"You've got to be kidding. . . . I want to get closer to them." I pointed to the distant herd of giraffe.

John seemed pained. It was the very first day of our first safari. Finally he relented. "Very well, you can walk for two hundred yards in that direction—then straight back the way you came. Under no circumstances go near the bush," and he indicated a patch of thick scrub to our left. "I'm sorry, but I have to think of your safety—and my license."

Bob Whitehead and I set off. Jessica sat in the shade. We walked our two hundred yards, then three—and four and finally turned around out of guilt and headed back to camp. We seemed to have got no closer to the giraffe; distance across these rolling plains and in this clear-as-crystal light can be very deceiving.

The following morning we discovered a reason for John's concern about walking. We woke up just after dawn. There was some sort of disturbance outside our tent—a medley of excitable voices speaking Swahili. I looked outside and saw the backs of three Masai *morani* (warriors) complete with shields and spears, bead necklaces and red ochre makeup, following John toward his tent. The Masai in the middle appeared to be bleeding badly; rivulets of bright blood flowed from his scalp and down his back. I nipped back into my tent and put on trousers. When I came out, John was emerging from his tent carrying a metal box with a broad red cross on its cover. The bleeding Masai had had a canvas camp stool shoved under him. I walked over.

"What happened?"

"Leopard. . . . Here, hold this." I took the end of the bandage while John fished a pair of surgical scissors from the first aid kit. The worst wound appeared to be on the left upper arm, where a strip of flesh about two inches wide and ten inches long hung below the Masai's elbow like a torn shirt sleeve. John swabbed it with disinfectant, which must have hurt like hell, but the young *moran* didn't even wince. We pulled the torn skin back into place and bound it tightly with gauze. There was blood over everything.

"We'll have to get him to the park warden at Keekarok where they can sew him up. Going to delay us a bit this morning I'm afraid."

We drove to Keekarok; I shared the back seat with the patient while Jess and Robert sat in front with John. It was a long drive. I kept waiting for the *moran* to pass out. Nothing like it; he seemed utterly impervious to his wounds, to us, to the bouncing car, and to the flies that—even at thirty miles an hour—swarmed in clusters around his wounds and the caked blood.

Once he'd been turned over to the warden, another black man, who spoke fluent English, the patient was led away, but the warden lingered to gossip.

"What's going to happen to him?" I asked.

"Fine of fifty shillings . . . that may teach him not to mess with my leopards."

I noted that possessive "my." "You mean *he* provoked the attack?"

"Of course he did. He'll swear that the leopard dropped on him from a tree, but that's rubbish. A leopard won't choose to attack a man unless he's starving or wounded. Silly bugger tried to spear him—showing off for his friends."

I saw the patient once again about a week later. They'd shaved his head. His scalp was marked by ugly black scabs and the flies were still around him. He seemed reasonably content.

*   *   *

Jessica and I had left New York for Nairobi on December 9th, 1965. We broke the trip in London where I had to set up lab arrangements for processing our film. In this Timothy Burrill was a great help. Poor Timothy; for the next three months he was busy sending me cables that always arrived late or not at all.

From London we flew to Rome, where we picked up Bob Whitehead. Robert had just lost his first wife, Virginia, to cancer and was a vulnerable man. He needed a new world more than we did. (Our first safari was composed of three clients: Jessica and I and Robert; later I went on a second with Elia Kazan and Barbara Loden, Jessica having gone back to London to spend some time with her family there.)

I have no intention of burdening the reader with an itinerary of African names or a travelogue. Suffice it to say that in the near three months I spent in Africa, I visited about a dozen game parks throughout Kenya and Tanzania. Among the better known were the Masai-Mara Reserve, Serengeti, Lake Manyara, Amboselli, the Ngorongoro Crater, both East and West Tsavo, Samburu, Lake Nakura, Mount Kenya, and a couple of others whose names now escape me even if the images haven't.

*   *   *

My journal begins in London.

Saw *Ivanov* this evening. Had supper with John Gielgud afterward. John's comment on the African venture: "Most interesting I imagine, but what does one *do* in the evenings?" Flora and fauna are something less than a passion with him. A friend of John's kept turtles, and while away asked John to keep an eye on them. The turtles died. The following crisis dialogue was reported:

"John, you've killed my turtles!"

"Oh nonsense, Martin—I don't even know how they work."

Went to Colour Film Services for further education and made arrangements with them. I can see the lab reports reaching us by native runner and cleft stick. All we have to do is get the film "out of the bush" into Nairobi, out of Nairobi into the English customs, out of customs to Colour Film Services, Ltd., and then run the whole gamut backwards.

*   *   *

Sixty degrees in Nairobi and it's obviously been raining. Immigration asked how long we expected to stay. Jess said five weeks, I said ten and Bob said four. Bob turned to me and said, "We better get organized." The inspector apparently considered this remark as a criticism of their procedures and shot back, "You certainly should—just try getting into Canada or the States, then you'll appreciate this." Welcome to Kenya! Customs were amiable and perfunctory.

We were met by our "hunter," John Fletcher. Perfect casting. Safari boots, knee socks, brown knee-shorts and an open khaki shirt. Early thirties I'd guess, with a strong face, very blue eyes and a nose which looks as though it might have suffered a break. Whitehead has nicknamed him

H.C. as Jimmie Luton in *Big Fish, Little Fish*, 1961

Below, Jason Robards, Jr., George Grizzard, and H.C. in *Big Fish, Little Fish*, 1961

H.C. with Laurence Olivier in
The Moon and Sixpence, for
NBC-TV, 1959

Below, H.C. and Elizabeth Taylor being directed by Joseph L.
Mankiewicz in *Cleopatra,* 1961

Friedman-Abeles

Above, H.C. and Robert Shaw
in Dürenmatt's *The Physicists*,
1964

J.T. and H.C. in *The Physicists*,
1964

Friedman-Abeles

H.C. making up for Harpagon
at the Guthrie Theater, 1963
(J.T. in mirror)

H.C. as Harpagon in Molière's
The Miser, Mark Taper Forum,
1968 (played originally at the
Guthrie Theater, 1963 and
1965)

Rehearsal with Zoe Caldwell:
Harpagon and Frosine, Guthrie
Theater, 1963

H.C. as Polonius, 1964

Below, modern-dress *Hamlet,* 1964. *Left to right:* William Redfield as
Guildenstern, Clement Fowler as Rosencrantz, Richard Burton as
Hamlet, H.C. as Polonius.

Simon Trevor

Above, Lake Manyara, Kenya, 1966

J.T., H.C., and lion, Kenya

H.C. with Masai ladies and
    mirror

Simon Trevor

J.T. demonstrating lipstick
(note flies)

Simon Trevor

Simon Trevor

"Rust red elephants appearing suddenly and silently . . ."

"In wildness is the preservation of the world . . ."—Thoreau

Simon Trevor

"Young Wingate"—typical of those English types, usually sacrificed, that appear in films about the far-flung posts of Empire.

*   *   *

The guardian of a safari camp asked if we were interested in seeing herds of elephant from a particularly advantageous point. He didn't have to ask twice. We piled into his Land Rover. I sat beside him and noticed that he was wearing a sidearm. When questioned he muttered something laconic about poachers and bandits, a reply so obviously understated that it sounded alarming.

We climbed out of a valley to the top of a steep escarpment. Along its ridge was a barely discernible track studded with boulders; it was a bone-jarring ride, but worth it. The far side of the escarpment was almost precipitous but provided a sweeping view of the plain below. We bounced along with bush scraping each side of the car, until any vestige of track disappeared. We had to stop. There, far below us, were two herds of elephant, moving slowly, browsing as they traveled. It was like looking at miniatures, but the atmosphere was so clear we could see every detail. We watched the great animals push over trees, strip off the bark, and tear loose the limbs, stuffing bundles of foliage into their mouths. One enormous bull stood apart from the rest, his tusks reaching almost to the ground, his huge ears fanning gently while his trunk probed the air for scent of danger.

We must have stayed there for a couple of hours. When we decided to go back to camp, we had a difficult time turning the car around. There was simply no room to maneuver. Only inches forward, then inches back until we faced the way we'd come. Halfway back along the ridge we came around a turn and barely avoided smashing into a big boulder in the middle of the track. Most certainly it had not been there on our way out. It had been rolled into place to stop us. It did—with a jolt that threw me against the dashboard. I heard the guardian say softly, "Hello,

Hello," and his hand moved from the stick shift to hover over his pistol holster.

At that moment a wild man appeared out of the bush and stood in front of us, waving his arms and grinning broadly. He was dressed in nothing other than a colorful sarong, but he wore sandals. His bare torso was muscular and burned almost black, but this was obviously no African and he carried no weapon. I thought I heard him say, "Give us a lift, guv'nor?" and with that he was joined by an extraordinarily pretty girl wearing not much more than he was. Our guardian said, "Goddamn it, Peter, that's not funny!" The apparition was Peter Hill Beard: photographer, author, and one of my reasons for being in Africa. He and his beautiful companion had left their own vehicle farther down the track, having no taste (or perhaps too good judgment) for the rougher part of it that we'd crossed.

[Coming on Peter and his lady in this fashion was about as likely as meeting a Masai warrior carrying his spear and shield loping down Park Avenue. I was to see Peter again several times before leaving Africa and again later in New York, but sadly, like so many many other friends I've had, I've now lost sight of him. He was a romantic, passionate and knowledgeable adventurer, and I've met too few of such.]

* * *

There are areas of the Mara and Serengeti parks that look like the well-tended fairways of an expensive country club. The grass at this time of year is brilliantly green and short. The well-spaced acacias would complement the most gifted landscape architect. Even the kopjes, those sudden upthrustings of rock and massive boulders, are marvelously ornamental. There are birds everywhere, brilliant plumage and strange musical calls. The vistas are endless, finally falling away out of sight or ending in a range of ancient, gently rounded, violet hills. In the foreground, flowers in the grass and a herd of Thomson's gazelle frozen for a moment like figures in an Egyptian frieze then bounding away with a feeling more of gaiety than alarm.

Not a day has passed in which we haven't come across

a kill—sometimes two or three. The lion or the leopard may still be on it, or it may have passed down the line of precedent inheritors to the hyenas, jackals, vultures and maribou storks. The jackals are attractive little animals, alert, fox-faced and sometimes bold. Even the hyena has a certain grace, and I find none of the "mangy" quality in its appearance which cliché gives to it. But the blood and guts are there. There is nothing lyrical in the vulturine tug-of-war over a string of intestine. I saw three jackals tear a baby gazelle to pieces the day before yesterday. The one winning the head and one foreleg let us get within twenty feet for photographs. That whiteness in the grass is quite as likely to be sun-bleached bone as blossom.

That something the naturalists refer to as "the balance of nature" is not arrived at prettily, and "the fairway" is not as benign as it appears.

* * *

To really appreciate the herds you must see them from the air. We flew a long way over the park. An unforgettable sight. Literally as far as the eye could see in every direction, there were thousands of animals, zebra, wildebeest, gazelle, ostrich, eland. Simon, who was flying both lower and slower than we, reported counting thirty-five lions.

* * *

Late yesterday afternoon we watched a magnificent male lion climb a tree and sprawl, all four legs dangling, along a branch. Within fifteen minutes he was surrounded below by six vehicles: our two, a bus, and three private cars. He treated us all with wonderful contempt, staring distantly over our heads, eyes blinking against the flies and setting sun, watching first a herd of impala in one direction then elephant in another. I seemed to find the clatter of car starters, the cameras and giggles far more trying than he did. I found myself hoping he'd rouse himself to some sort of protest, snarl, or leap at one of the cars, as if to say "get the hell out of here and mind your own business." In fairness, I must admit that the situation was unusual. We've traveled for miles here without seeing another car or human, but this park is small and very popular.

* * *

Our campsite is near the lake on the edge of an acacia forest. In front of our tents a few small thorn trees, then a broad plain, a gray-green blur of forest beyond and finally the eastern wall of the Great Rift. The quiet is doubly quiet because of the cicadas and a medley of bird calls that seem quite unreal. The hard metallic note of the bush shrike, the bottle bird, the rollers, doves, the piercing scream of a fish eagle. I woke at five this morning. There was a leopard coughing somewhere close and a cacophony of bird sounds—strident at that hour. . . . At night you hear the grunt of lion and hippo, and too close by, the wail of hyena—very eerie, sinister and shivery.

* * *

We saw many elephant today, moving with extraordinary silent grace, through the forest with no sound other than a swish of grass or the rasp of thornbush along their sides. The ears swing wide, the trunk arcs up to scent us, there is a fleeting moment of still life then a slight change of course, the babies huddling close to their mothers, and they are gone.

* * *

Long after I have forgotten names or places I shall remember certain moments: a Masai woman leading Jessica by the hand to show her some sewing, a lion raising his head from the kill with blood on his beard, a pack of wild dogs—the most feared predator in Africa—appearing on the track in front of our car, standing, staring and wagging their tails, a secretary bird catching grasshoppers—and this particular evening on the edge of the lake.

The sun was well down and behind us. The light golden. Four reedbuck stood in the water, quite motionless. Reflections before, long shadows beyond. Close by, a herd of buffalo lay black and still in the shallows, every head and curving sweep of horn turned toward us. Suddenly a flight of egret took off from the grass, swept out over the water, banked sharply—a blinding of white wings—swung round and came back to rest where they'd started. Nothing else moved, and even in the car there was silence. Soon and suddenly it would be dark.

* * *

Today's big news was an attack by a rhino! Sex unknown. We were cutting through the brush in John's car, five of us, John, Jess, Bob, Sangau the game spotter and I. The track had run us into a dead end at a stream we couldn't cross. We veered off, making our own track through dense scrub. I heard Bob say, "Oh Jesus!"—there was a snorting, a flash of gray back, a jarring shock and the front of the car was lifted clear from the ground. The rhino got his horn hooked under our right front fender, and his disengagement took longer than the attack, but it was all over in a few seconds with only a line of wildly waving bush to mark the rhino's retreat. We drove to a clearing and examined the damage. These Toyotas are heavy and strongly built. There was nothing to see but a great scratch in the caked mud on the underside and an embossed ridge on the top. . . . That horn would go through a body as if it were cream cheese.

* * *

Elephants shuffled around our tents in the early A.M. I kept waiting for one of them to stumble over a guy rope bringing the tent down on our heads, but they don't stumble over anything, night or day. Sounds of clearing sinus, grass being cropped at the roots, chewing, chewing, chewing—stomach rumblings, and a long windy sigh of satisfaction.

* * *

Stopped in the road to take a pee. Drove on and in less than a hundred yards came across an ambling lioness, a magnificent animal of prime age and condition with very young cubs stashed away somewhere. She looked round and heavy with milk, the dugs prominent. She sauntered by and headed for the stream we'd just crossed. A lap or two of water and an effortless bound to the opposite bank. We raced back to the ford. By the time we caught up with her she was lying flat to the ground, rigidly still, in practically no cover at all—four-inch grass and a small thornbush to hide her head. A quarter of a mile away were a mixed herd of zebra and wildebeest. The wind was from them to her. Slowly, very slowly, feeding as they came, they were coming to water. We moved off at right angles. The lion paid no attention, her concentration on the herd absolute. The zebra stood, stared and went back to feeding. Very quietly, Simon got the camera on the roof mount. Then stood waiting in the hatch.

The next fifteen minutes were as tense as anything I ever remember. This was life and death in the balance. Two hundred yards, one hundred, two hundred feet. The lead zebra stallion saw something, there was no doubt about it. Ears cocked forward, he stared long and hard. My binoculars moved from one to the other. The herd came to a halt waiting for the stallion's decision. Was it a tawny rock or an anthill or something much more sinister? Not a muscle flickered on the lioness. The zebra appeared to relax. His tail flicked, his hide shivered the flies, and he looked behind at the herd as if to say, "You understand the problem?" He glanced again at the something then dropped his head as though to feed only to bring it up again with a jerk. Had the object moved? Another zebra joined him. Two pair of eyes are better than one. Another long, long, searching look—like two setters on point.

Unlike the zebras, the wildebeest seemed impatient and careless; they moved through the ranks crowding the leaders. Why the delay? Slowly the mixed herd moved on again and Simon nudged me with his foot. "They've had it." But I noticed that the two zebras made a small but critical detour. Soon they had passed the lioness and were down wind of her. That, I thought, will be the end of that. Zebras are skittish, and one can panic a herd because of the passing shadow of a vulture. I do not know why they didn't scent her. Some trick of the wind perhaps. The wildebeest came bumbling on, straight for the cover. At about forty yards (it looked like ten feet in my glasses, but they were shaking and I found them hard to focus), they turned down the bank to water, putting themselves at a terrible disadvantage. This would be it. Not at all; the lioness let the first animals drink. Up the bank they came again closer, ever closer. Then it happened. There was a magnificent arcing leap, a miss, and pandemonium. With the long, taut stride of a greyhound she was after them. And only feet apart. We lost sight of them all behind some bush, but there was an ominous cloud of dust in there. Simon pulled in the camera, started the car and we followed.

She'd missed. We finally found her lying up in the shade, still panting heavily. We followed her for seven hours. Twice she came to the car—once within ten feet—and examined us with quite objective and unconcerned curiosity. Near sunset we let her go back to her cubs. It was too late to follow further.

*   *   *

I had fallen asleep under a thorn tree. Simon's car woke me up. He got out while Jessica remained seated. "We have a passenger," she called. I walked over. She had a baby zebra cradled in her lap. They'd found it just a few minutes before, lying in the sun with two vultures standing by and no sign of the mother. It seemed quite unharmed but very weak and probably not more than a day old—a piece of the umbilical cord was still attached. There may be some malformation of the front hooves or some internal injury, but none of us is sufficiently expert to know. We pour a little water down its throat and take it back to camp. I cut up Jess's bathing cap and tried to make a bottle nipple, but a piece of chamois proved more successful. The formula was a mixture of very weak powdered milk, warm water and sugar. By evening the patient's ears had perked up. The breathing was regular, it had lost all fear of us and

was taking a few staggering steps. It has been named Ezekiel by Jess (found alone in the wilderness?) and will spend
the night in Simon's tent wrapped up in his sleeping bag.

* * *

Ezekiel died about midmorning. I suppose we didn't
do anything right—not even the christening, as *he* turned
out to be a *she*. This business of trying to save newborn
wild animals is almost impossible. We've been through it
before. . . . When the mother leaves its young, the por-
tents are almost always ominous. It's a pity, she was a beautiful little animal, not more than about twenty pounds, with
huge dark eyes, ridiculously long lashes and a silky coat.

* * *

Tsavo is red and its elephants are red. The roads, long
gashes of bleeding earth, and those rust-red elephants appearing suddenly and silently from the green of riverine
forest are what I remember best. The country as a whole
seems more arid than in the parks to the west. Vehicles
travel in a self-enveloping cloud of dust, and there is much
of the thorn scrub found at Samburu. This harshness is
compounded by the devastation caused by elephant—nearly
as many trees splintered, uprooted and flat to the ground
as are left standing—and by long, black inverted rivers of
lava, snaking across the plains like gargantuan mole runs.

* * *

When the light had gone Simon led me out of the car
and on foot to within sixty feet of the one remaining bull
and his cow. We crouched in the shrubbery at the edge of
the pool and watched a small drama of family reunion—at
least I suppose it was such.

African elephants loom large in the distance. Nearby,
they are overwhelming, like the prehistoric re-creations at
the American Museum of Natural History. These two were
alternately drinking and spraying themselves with water,
changing from rust red to lead black before our eyes as

they washed away the dust and caked mud of the Tsavo wallows. Whatever they heard, we didn't hear, but suddenly they turned their backs to us and waited. Another bull and cow appeared from the bush beyond them. The newcomers stopped. Four trunks searched the air, then slowly, the thirsty ones came on. The bulls met first, very slowly, like freight cars at a coupling. There was an audible clicking of tusks as they came forehead to forehead, then a mutual and delicate exploration by trunk. These intertwined, touched mouth and eyes, curled round the ivory and caressed the head. It was not merely recognition but undoubted affection as well. We have seen this too with lions and cheetah, not just between mates or mother and child but between almost all members of the same pride or family group. It was not until the newcomers had drunk and wandered to within forty feet of our cover that the bull saw us or saw something—their eyesight is very bad. Ears wide, he stared long and hard, his trunk probing the wind—which was strong toward us or we wouldn't have been there. He moved forward. Simon hissed, "Get going," and I, trying to be half as light-footed as the elephant, tiptoeing carefully back through the bush, tripped, sprawled, dropped the camera I should never have brought with me and the elephant screamed. It's a real scream and terrifying, a mixture of outrage and fury. Simon tells me the charge was only "a demonstration" and not more than a dozen feet. I wouldn't know. I didn't even try to pick up the camera, which Simon recovered later, but scrambled to the car and its very alarmed driver in quite graceless retreat. I've watched animals give way on confrontation and they generally manage it with an air of nonchalance as though implying "I didn't much want to stay here anyway"—but not me!

* * *

[From a letter to Jessica in London. February 11th, 1966]
Driving back to our camp about 8:30 (pitch dark, and strictly against the rules), we saw in our headlights hundreds of pairs of eyes pelting down the road toward us. The wil-

debeest are all calving and are constantly harried by hyenas. Rather an ugly business. We hear both all night long. The lowing of the wildebeest, the sudden drumming of hooves as they bolt, and that whole repertory of hyena calls.

I don't know that our driver could have done anything about it. Perhaps he should have switched off his lights. The car was at a standstill when the wildebeest hit us. He was going all out and the realization of what was going to happen was as close as I ever want to come to facing a charge. A sickening, head-on smash. Flying glass, radiator fragments and a quivering animal on the road in front of us. Quite dead—blood pouring from nose and mouth, one broken horn and horribly protruding teeth.

I suppose it took less than four minutes for us to get back to camp, change cars, pick up half a dozen of the crew and return to the scene. Three hyenas were on the carcass and had eaten into the stomach.

I hadn't realized that fresh meat was such an all important item to the boys—I mean "crew." I hate that "boys" argot. Our hunter says meat is one of a safari outfitter's most persuasive recruiting agents. The photographic safari can hardly be popular. Well, we now have fresh meat. The animal was skinned, cut up, hung, and the very few remnants disposed of before we went to bed.

My flashlight revealed eight hyenas waiting on the outskirts of camp, and they serenaded us to sleep.

* * *

So, there you have it, a glimpse at any rate. Jess and I have been very fortunate in a shared sense of wonderment—whether it be around a coral reef, on a mountaintop, beside a multi-colored sea, in primeval forest, or our own garden. And animals, fish and birds have given us great delight. As Thoreau said: "In wildness is the preservation of the world"—and our own souls' preservation as well.

THIRTY-
SIX

AN ACTOR SHOULD END by talking to actors.

In an editorial from *American Theatre* of December 1988, Peter Zeisler (not an actor, but a man who has spent his life working in the theater) writes a piece called "The Courageous Act." I quote one sentence: "The art and craft of acting is so personal, the process of developing a performance so mysterious and intuitive, that writing about the art of acting is extraordinarily difficult." Right on! How do I set about it then? What has helped me?

When I find myself in trouble as an actor, which is not infrequently, I believe I open up my little grab bag of basic maxims, scrabble around inside it, and hope to come up with just one truth that may put me back on the right road. There are no absolutes, of course. Because I choose one road to heaven, why should I suggest that your road won't get you there? All I can offer the young actor are the thoughts that I've filed away over the years—opening the bag and letting the maxims, aphorisms, subject headings, whatever they should be called, come out helter-skelter. I put them down as they appear to me under shorthand headings—which may even be helpful if someone wishes to take a second look at them.

TRAINING. I believe that it is desirable to have it. You can of course get by—even prosper—without it, but if your schooling gives you no more than a rudimentary sense of your instrument—the control of your body, voice, the power of your imagination, perhaps even a peek into your own soul—then you've made a fortunate start.

TALENT. It is indispensable, but it is not rare. Do not cripple yourself by comparing your gifts with those of others. There will always be people whose talent seems so much greater than your own. Some people seem to be touched by the finger of God. I have seen young actors who had a magnificent physical instrument, great beauty, intelligence, a lively imagination, a vibrant voice and a passion for the work, totally eclipsed by someone whose gifts were far more modest. Talent is essential, but its initial degree is not important. It grows and grows in some and withers away in others. What is important is what you do with whatever portion you have.

CHARACTER. If the tortoise and the hare fable has any validity, and if the race is not always to the swift, who wins then? Perhaps it goes to the survivors; perhaps it's a matter of "character." I'm not talking about a character in the play, but about the character of the actor, something I can't define, since it is necessarily different for each personality. Whatever its components, its sum total must be able to exercise "the slow dead heave of the will"; to insist on discipline, courage, imagination, perseverance, and a host of other qualities that add up to just plain hard work.

A pinch of humor might be included in any recipe, to prevent what is serious from becoming solemn. I offer a quotation from the *New York Times* obituary of Rex Harrison, an enormously skillful actor whose range far exceeded his brilliance in *My Fair Lady*:

> Serious but unpretentious about his work, the actor once said: "There's always a struggle, a striving for something bigger than yourself in all forms of art. And even if you don't achieve greatness—even if you fail, which we all

must—everything you do in your work is somehow connected with your attitude toward life, your deepest secret feelings."

THE CHARACTER YOU PLAY (as opposed to your own). It is the keystone to all our work. Understand that and you're more than halfway home. It has its roots in your own character, experience and personality. Then you must apply "the magic if." *If* I was in this situation (given you by the playwright) how would *I* react? *If* I was that person (drawn by the playwright) how would *he* react?

TECHNIQUE. This is a word grossly misunderstood. In common usage among the profession, it would seem to imply mere mechanical proficiency. The actor moves well, uses his voice well, knows his lines and doesn't bump into the furniture, and so on. I prefer my own definition: "The actor's technique is that *personal* and *private* means by which he gets the best out of himself."

The means must embrace voice and movement of course, but far more important, they must tap into that reservoir of emotional memory that the actor lends to the character he plays, giving it a rich inner life.

"EFFECTIVE MEMORY." I don't remember who coined this phrase. Perhaps it was Stanislavski. For me, it means the ability to go back into your own experience and to dredge up— even from an unwilling subconscious—those emotional states that are applicable to the character you're playing. Sometimes it's painful, occasionally unreliable, but it's an absolute necessity—this time I can't avoid the word *absolute*—and, I suspect, a process as old as the use of the spoken word.

In cultivating effective memory, the actor learns to monitor his own feelings as he experiences them. There's something rather shameful about that activity. It's bad enough to have to go back and paw through your emotional guts, but to have to learn to record your traumas as they happen, to file them away, no matter how hateful, is asking a bit much. Instinct prompts us to forget what's disagreeable, and yet here you are stockpiling something you desperately want to exorcise.

Not long ago my sister K died after a too-long and too-painful illness. I had literally prayed that she might be allowed to die. And then it had happened. After the first numbing shock of the news, I sneaked away by myself and wept. No sooner had I done so than some familiar but loathsome inner voice started its shrieking whisper: "Watch it; remember it; you may have to use it. Exactly what are you crying for? You got what you wanted, didn't you? What are you doing about your tears? What are your hands doing? Do you feel sick?" And so it goes until you long to scream back, "For Christ's sake, shut up, get lost, drop dead yourself!" But out of hideous habit I answered the questions and made some discoveries.

I was not crying for my sister at all. I was crying for me. At that moment I didn't give a damn about her pain, her terrible depressions, only my own sense of loss. Yes, I got what I wanted, but both too late and too soon. My tears? I had a handkerchief, but I used the heel of my hand. My hands? I kept running them through my hair like a man with a bad headache (a gesture that I've always considered cliché). Did I feel sick? Hell no, but in a rage, absolutely furious with God and the injustice of my sister's miserable ending.

I don't think I've ever imagined what a large part rage can play in grief. Perhaps I would have played Shylock better if I'd had that on file. And so it goes—at least with this actor.

KIRCHOFF'S LAW OF RADIATION. This first came to my unwilling attention at the age of about fourteen, when I was an uninterested observer in a physics class. The law states that "the best absorbers are the best emitters." I can even remember the experiment that proved the law, which is extraordinary, as my concentration on the problems posed by physics, chemistry and mathematics was sadly limited.

"The best absorbers are the best emitters." Actors are in the business of emitting—of giving out—and you can't give out what you haven't taken in.

FORM AND CONTENT. They are requirements of any artist in any medium; dual considerations that are inescapable.

I've touched on them above under "technique." To offer all form and no content may provide a dazzling but lifeless display of skills. To offer all content but without form, you may as well play to your navel as to an audience. You won't reach them.

I've seen actors so drunk on emotional content—usually of the more self-indulgent variety—and so innocent of form that they couldn't be heard in the third row, and actors whose movement so contradicted their emotion that the audience was bewildered.

READING. Every actor's experience has its limitations. What you haven't experienced you must live vicariously, or through the imagination. As an actor your very first act is to read the play; then read it again and again. Your second may be to embrace the character you are playing; to know him intimately, understand him, sympathize with him even if you find him repugnant or a bore. It is in this phase that "the magic if" comes into play. Then you must read again—anything and everything that may stimulate your imagination and interpretation. For instance, if you have to play Shakespeare (if you're lucky enough to get the opportunity), I think it's madness not to go to a library and dig out a variorum of the play. These are gold mines of information, frequently annotated with comment on performance and interpretation; they are not merely dry-as-dust comparisons of the differences in text between quartos and folios.

I can hear some young actor say, "I'm not interested in all that academic crap—I'm just going to do it *my* way." That's great if you're certain-sure what your way is; but why not give yourself a choice, consider alternatives? Then, possibly, you'll *know* what your way is. That is until such time as your director, the audience, or the interpretation of your fellow actors tells you you've got it all wrong.

FLEXIBILITY. And so what do you do when you discover you've got it all wrong? You change—fast! You may flounder around for a while, but you make big changes, not tiny ones. This facility, this courage, is a divine asset to the actor. "Oh, you want me to do it that way? . . . Right. Here goes." And to start with, until you've made the change your own, you may make an ass of yourself. Never mind. "On, on, on!" You never get everything your own way. The whole process is one of inevitable compromise. You are not alone in producing your baby. It is always a collaboration.

ON LEARNING LINES AND COPYING OTHER ACTORS. Two utterly unrelated subjects, but touched on here because very inexperienced actors ask about both.

Ideally, I think, you would learn the words only in rehearsal—suiting "the word to the action"—but this is impractical in our theater (it is impossible in films and television) and can be damn irritating to those of your fellow actors who have done their homework and are far ahead of you in preparation. I try to find a happy medium, holding the book until I have at least a rough blocking and then sweating out the memorization.

Yes, but how?

Actors learn by very different methods. Some lucky ones seem to have a near-photographic memory and appear to do it visually. For others it's oral, a matter of speaking the line over and over again. Or it's aural, hearing a line over and over again. For the majority it's a combination of all three.

In 1977 and through 1979, Jessica and I played in a two-character play called *The Gin Game.* Mike Nichols directed. He was not only brilliant and supportive, he is a very good friend. But during the early days of rehearsal his presence embarrassed us. We could not learn the words. The script required us to play fourteen games of gin rummy, all of them different and yet fiendishly similar. Panic took over—*Dear God, is this game number seven or have I skipped to nine?* I begged Mike to stay at home until we'd mastered this nightmare problem. He'd have none of that. The harder we tried, the worse it got. One day Mike said laconically, "You'll never get it with clenched heads. Give yourselves a crib. Write it out—the sticky parts— on the tabletop. No one can see. Just let your eyes slip over the top of your cards to find out where you are."

I thought this idea professionally outrageous. A *crib,* for God's sake? However, we did as he suggested—and inside a couple of days the problem had disappeared. We no longer needed the crib. Mike had handed us a security blanket that resolved what was largely a psychological problem.

Actors can develop a mind lock that inhibits learning anything. I've tried tape recorders, writing out difficult speeches in longhand (sometimes helpful), endless cuing from some poor put-upon assistant stage manager, drink, don't-give-a-damn pills, but despite any combination of these, I can feel my muscular tension increase and hear the despair in that small evil inner voice that whispers, "You're never going to learn it."

What seems to work best for me is a combination of saying the words *out loud*—and walking. My unprovable theory is that saying the words aloud employs both oral and aural sensibilities, and that the walking discharges an inhibiting physical tension. Of course you have to be careful about *where* you walk. Fifth Avenue is not a good choice; neither is Greenwich Village. You may draw some very alarmed stares. I favor vast parking lots where the only hazard is a zealous attendant who may suspect you of casing the cars with a view to theft. The best spot in New York City is, of course, Central Park, providing it's a weekday and during business hours, when normal people are decently occupied. Best of all is a deserted country road, but that's no help if you're in a town. Your bathroom is a last resort.

Copying another actor is not to be recommended—unless of course you're an understudy and the stage manager requires it. Stealing, on the other hand, should be encouraged. What the singer Tony Bennett calls "sweet thievery." Watching other actors, good actors, can open hidden doors of possibility. Their examples can resolve the "how to" of execution in a way that no amount of verbal direction or erudite discussion by the playwright can illuminate. The trick is to make the stolen idea yours: to remove the serial number and hallmark of the original and make it truly your own. If you can do that, you're exonerated from theft; you've simply borrowed an inspiration.

AWARENESS. I lost one eye in 1969. After getting out of the hospital, my first social occasion was having a drink with the distinguished architect Max Abramovitz. He waved me to a sofa and I sat down, leaned forward to place my drink on the coffee table, let go the glass and missed the table by a good four inches. It was embarrassing: all that good liquor and ice on Max's carpet. With only one eye, I'd lost depth perception. At fifty-eight I had to learn to make certain adjustments that a baby makes automatically. I used to wander around the garden practicing—standing at different distances from a bush and trying with one sure movement to pluck off a leaf. I left some bushes nearly defoliated. It was an object lesson in awareness, one that had grown rusty from disuse.

As a young actor I used to practice awareness: of dress, of mannerism, of painting and sculpture, of the furnishing of a room, but most particularly of people. I would set out with the sole purpose of people-watching; of sitting in a waiting room or restaurant, just to watch. (Producers' offices, doctors' offices—including the dentist—subways at rush hour, Grand Central terminal, were all rich fields of discovery.) Anywhere people are under stress, you'll find the gamut of emotions, frequently masquerading as normal, don't-give-a-damn behavior.

It's fascinating work—beats bird-watching.

DEVIL AND ANGEL. "When playing a devil, look for the angel in him; when playing an angel, look for the devil." I've said it before, but it's worth repeating. None of us is one color. It's the contradictions that rivet attention. Perhaps it's the gentle voice and impeccable manners of an absolute shit that fascinate, or the gross stupidity and drunken boorishness of an essentially good man. Try to avoid the immediately obvious. Don't billboard your character. Let an audience discover it. Always look for counterpoint to what you have decided are strong characteristics.

More than forty years ago I appeared in a film called *Brute Force*. It was a story about prisons and prison brutality, and in it, as I've recounted earlier, I played a miserably sadistic prison guard called Captain Munsey—a total horror. The colors were all primary. Together with Jules Dassin, the director, I tried to find the counterpoint. We made him soft-spoken, a lover of classical music, and inoffensive in demeanor. In one nightmarish scene Munsey gave a prisoner a dreadful going-over in his office with a piece of rubber hose. He went about the business very calmly, methodically, while the "Liebestod" came from the record player in the background. This was counterpoint with a vengeance and might have produced derisive laughter. It didn't. And for some years after I was followed down the streets by kids who would chant "Yah, yah, yah, Captain Munsey!" which had been one of the prisoners' catcalls. In a perverse fashion, it did say something about the impression left by the character.

LAUGHTER AND TEARS. While you must always be faithful to the playwright's text, beware those parenthetical directions that go "(*He laughs*)" or "(*She cries*)." They are what the playright heard as he created the situation and are probably appropriate—but not always. Sometimes it is a directly opposite reaction that is most telling. Again, it is the impact of contradiction. The most affecting crying scenes I've seen on a stage are always those when the character is trying desperately *not* to cry. When faced with a shower of tears, the audience is likely to turn off the faucet.

"A PASSIONATE EMOTION ALWAYS OUTLIVES ITS USEFULNESS." What the hell does this untidy little maxim mean? Well, suppose you are faced with a situation so terrifying or so infuriating that your body produces a rush of adrenaline, either to help protect you or to arm you for attack; and then suppose it turns out to be a false alarm and the cause is immediately removed. That doesn't stop the adrenaline. Its effects wear off slowly. You are lucky if you don't turn dead white, feel weak at the knees, and, in extreme cases, vomit. And so it is with all extreme emotion. You can just drop a previous color because the succeeding one is totally different. There is always a conflict, and that conflict, that change, shifting of gears, holds great riches for both the actor and his audience.

BODY LANGUAGE. It conveys at least as much as the words and frequently makes words superfluous. This is just one reason why an actor must maintain a truly responsive physical instrument. That entails constant exercise, practice and acute observation. Observation of others of course, but also observation of one's own performance. How many times have I sat down and crossed my legs? How many times have I stuck my hands in my pockets? How often have I used that gesture? What are my hands saying? Am I the right shape for the age or health of my character? How does *he* walk? And on and on, down to the details of how your character (not you) holds a teacup, carries a cane or sword, manages her bustle, uses her fan, gets rid of the tails of his coat when he sits down, wears his hat, shakes hands. For period pieces one must learn a whole new language. And of course the same principal of control and selection holds true for the use of one's voice and speech.

On a personal note, I have always been more successful with my body than my voice. Despite good teachers (and a few terrible ones), I've never acquired the vocal range and flexibility that a first-rate actor should possess. Why? There's nothing wrong with the instrument. I'm not battling a speech impediment or a tin ear. "The fault, dear Brutus, is not in our stars,/But in ourselves, that we are underlings." Or to put it in less highfalutin terms, I have not practiced what I preach: constant vocal exercise. Please consider doing what I say, not what I do or should have done.

Again, I can hear that same imaginary young actor who challenged me under the heading of "Reading" say, "How do you expect me to remember all this stuff, all your preachments or maxims, or whatever you call them? Besides, I'm never going to have to manage a bustle!" And my answer is, "Peace." I don't expect you to remember any of them. You'll come on them all in your own time and in your own fashion—if you stick with it. I have been in your shoes: so intimidated by so much advice that I felt like the centipede being questioned by the toad, who

> Said "Pray, which leg goes after which?"
> That worked her mind to such a pitch,
> She lay distracted in a ditch,
> Considering how to run.

DON'T ASK "HOW?"—ASK "WHY?" If you understand *why* a character is behaving as he/she does in any given situation, you will be well on your way to discovering *how* he/she behaves. If your first consideration becomes *how* ("How do I do this effectively?"), you may end up in a blind alley—being effective perhaps, but at the expense of the playwright's intention and the truth of the character you're playing.

ANALYSIS PARALYSIS. It is a pernicious affliction of the student actor.

> Myself when young did eagerly frequent
> Doctor and saint, and heard great argument
> About it and about: but evermore
> Came out by the same door where in I went.

Omar Khayyám offers no solutions as to whether your character stands or sits, roars or whimpers, is furiously active or stony still—and sometimes the director is less helpful than you hoped he'd be. So just *do* it. Do whatever your intuition prompts. You may very well get it wrong—whatever "it" may be—but have a go and then another and another. Beware the quicksand of overintellectualization. You must "act" even in total repose. Don't suffer the fate of the centipede.

Learning any craft is so full of confusions and seeming contradictions that of course you don't know what comes first or last; but if even one of my notes seems persuasive, you might make it your own and then the whole lot will have served their purpose. I should also warn you that I haven't quite finished.

THE ACTOR'S ENERGY. It is hard to define. It is not Shakespeare's "robustious periwig-pated fellow" tearing a passion to tatters. It is not bellowing, or some wild thrashing about of arms and legs. It is not acrobatics (though some familiarity with such can serve an actor well). It's more like some invisible emanation that sweeps through the auditorium, demanding an audience's total attention. It is a life force which must be ever-present but *carefully controlled,* and I suspect that its source is a simple fierce concentration.

As an occasional teacher and director, I've tried to demonstrate this energy by two different means. I may suddenly break off whatever I'm saying or doing and follow an imaginary insect across a tabletop. I have to see what's not there. The others can see nothing. But they watch. *What the hell is he doing? Is it a spider—a cockroach—a particularly rude piece of graffiti—what?* It's rare that anyone will even ask until my concentration is broken and they are released.

Another trick I've used with underenergized actors, even in a small rehearsal space, is to insist that they speak to the balcony, that they project. This is a physical requirement rather than a mental one. There's something about the exercise of the diaphragm that energizes the whole system—and I am not speaking of shouting. Even in film, where much dialogue is recorded in a near whisper, these *controlled* applications of mental and physical energy are vital.

I have emphasized control. The essential energy must always be there, but an audience should always feel that there's more where that came from, that indeed there is a powerful reserve. Never go to the top of your scream, but always push to the limit of your concentration. . . .

STILLNESS. If your character has nowhere to go, you can't improve on stillness; if your character has nothing to say, you can't improve on silence. A concentrated stillness onstage can demand attention like little else. I assume that you, the actor, are listening—not just hearing, but listening; or that if you are alone, that you are thinking. Listening and thinking are both very positive actions; and knowing the action, the intention, of your character at every moment in the play is a must.

When Harold Clurman was directing and came upon a complex or muddy passage in the play, he would frequently ask the actor to divide the blank page opposite the text into three columns. The first was headed "Action"; the second, "Activity"; and the third, "Mood." The last meant emotional coloration. The second, physical activity—if any. The first, and most important, which generally held the key to the other two, was the character's intention. What is he trying to do? The shorthand answer almost always started with the word "To . . ." as in "to defend himself"; "to hide"; "to impress"; "to persuade"; "to withdraw"; "to wound"; and so on.

Let's take a simplistic example. The scene is that of a parent helping a child with homework. Reading across the page from left to right the actor might scribble under *Action*: "to encourage"; under *Activity*: "adjusting the reading lamp"; and under *Mood*: "boredom"—which may very well be what the reader is feeling right now. However, note that the first and third, "to encourage" and "boredom," produce an interesting character conflict that you may have overlooked. It can be a clarifying exercise and can sometimes dispel that vacuum of confusion that at one point or other besets every actor in rehearsal and leaves him in despair, muttering: "I don't know what the hell this is all about."

FURNITURE. Make friends with it. It has a bigger part than yours. It's onstage longer. Inanimate it may seem, but it can give you a nasty bite if you get careless.

I can remember that lovely actress Sara Allgood playing in something by O'Casey. We were on the same bill together. Sara would appear onstage before the half hour, her hair wrapped up in gauze preparatory to putting on her wig. She would prowl around the stage making minor adjustments; shifting the footstool a few inches this way or that; opening the drawer a crack so it would be less likely to stick, trying out door knobs, etc. Then she would retire to her dressing room to finish her makeup. Shortly after this, a conscientious stage manager would come onstage, close the drawer, put the footstool back on its marks, tidy up the sofa cushions that Sara had so carefully arranged to support her back, and go off to make the call.

At "five minutes," Sara would come back on again just to reassure herself, only to discover that her little adjustments had all been corrected. She would clutch at her wig in anguish, and in a fine Irish brogue exclaim, "Someone in this theater is tryin' to destroy me!"

RHYTHM. Every good play, every scene and speech, has its particular music. It's played in concert with others, and the director is both concert master and conductor, but you have to do without him once the curtain is up. It's necessary to learn the score. I have seen the dismay on the faces of actors when faced with a very long speech. They may understand and feel the emotional content but are overcome by the problem of form, of execution. Try to think of it in musical terms. Where are the rests?—and are you putting them in where they don't belong, so that the ones that count lose their impact? Is this passage of sentences *adagio,* so that the words seem almost to overlap? Is this *piano*? Could that be *fortissimo*? Is this a trill, is that *largo*?

I am a dismal student of music. At boarding school I had to choose between a bath and piano lessons. We were allowed two proper baths a week (six tubs for sixty boys) and my as- signed bath hours conflicted with my scheduled piano prac- tice. There were even fewer pianos than bathtubs. As no one seemed able to resolve this conflict, I opted for cleanliness rather than a musical education.

I made one further abortive attempt to learn something about music when I was at McGill. I took private singing les- sons. My teacher was an imperious lady named Mrs. Archibald with an affection for Wagner. She had a great pile of white hair, precariously held in place with tortoise-shell combs, and a generous, heaving bosom. I kept waiting for the agitation of the latter to bring down her hair, revealing an antique Brun- nehilde. Disappointingly, it never happened.

As a singer, I could not be said to have held promise, ex- cept perhaps in a wetlands chorus. I had all the talent of a frog. To this day I cannot easily hold a tune. Jessica swears I sing everything, including "God Save the Queen," to the air of "Onward Christian Soldiers." I remember Mrs. Archibald for her valiant efforts on my behalf, and for one maxim which I treasure because it is such terrible advice when applied to the actor. Mrs. Archibald was fond of saying, "The vowels are your friends, cling to them; the consonants, your servants, dismiss them!"

The actor who dismisses consonants may well send his au- dience out to buy hearing aids or at least to demand a refund.

So, beware of maxims, including those that I have to offer. "Let your own discretion be your tutor." And as I've allowed myself that one quotation only from Hamlet's advice to the players (Act 3, Scene 2), go ahead and learn it, if you haven't already done so. Shakespeare says it all so much more beautifully and succinctly than anyone else.

While I feel I've hardly begun, I'm going to end with a poem by Christopher Logue. I've used it before in this book, but it bears repeating, and is my ultimate maxim.

> Come to the edge.
> We might fall.
> Come to the edge.
> It's too high!
> COME TO THE EDGE!
> So they came
> and he pushed
>
> and they flew.

POSTSCRIPT

A letter to Susan Cooper:

Dear Sue,

What else shall I tell you? What else do you want to know? You nagged me into writing this book and here it is—up to 1966. But I have to go back to work now; that is, I have to stop talking and start acting again. The prospect terrifies me. Will I remember how? I haven't stepped on a stage in over three years. I don't count films: that's piecework and doesn't demand the same sustained concentration. I've heard it said that acting is like swimming or riding a bicycle, you can't forget, but that's not true. I've *seen* actors forget. They disappear into another medium for a few years only to come back to the stage and drive in the wrong gear; sometimes, God help us, even in the wrong lane. It happened to me after my stint at M.G.M. in the good bad old days. You asked me about those. It was on your list, and I've obliged as best I could, but there

410

are a lot of items I haven't reached: *Hadrian VII,* the loss of my eye, *A Delicate Balance,* performing in the Soviet Union, my gunpoint confrontation with art thieves, *The Gin Game, Foxfire, Cocoon,* and so forth and so on—on and on . . .

Well, maybe—someday—perhaps and if. For the present I shall just have to remain vertical, remember the words and get to rehearsal on time.

Love,
Hume

BIOGRAPHY OF HUME CRONYN

November 1990

(Extract from *The Biographical Encyclopaedia & Who's Who of the American Theatre.* James T. White & Co., 1700 State Highway Three, Clifton, N.J.)

CRONYN, HUME. Actor, director, writer. b. July 18, 1911. London, Ontario, Can., to Hume Blake and Frances Amelia (Labatt) Cronyn. Grad. Ridley Coll., St. Catherines, Ontario, 1930; studied at McGill Univ., 1930–31; studied acting under auspices of N.Y. Sch. of the Theatre; with Harold Kreutzberg, Mozarteum Salzburg, Aust., Summers 1932, 1933; and at AADA, 1932–34. Hon. LL.D. U. Western Ontario, London, Canada 1974. Hon. Doctor of Humane Letters, Fordham U. 1985. Order of Canada, November 8, 1988; Married to Jessica Tandy, actress, Sept. 27, 1942; one son, one daughter, one step-daughter. Member of AEA (Councillor, 1962); SAG (Director 1946); SSD&C (Founder-Governor); ASCAP; WGA; AFTRA; The Dramatists Guild; Past Director, Society Stage Directors & Choreographers; Past Director, The Screen Actors Guild; Past Council Member, The Actors' Equity Association (2 terms); Director, Theatre Development Fund; Trustee, The American Academy of Dramatic Arts; Past Council Member, Yale University School of Drama; Past Member, Board of Directors, Guthrie Theater Foundation and Board of Governors, Stratford Festival, Canada. Author of various short stories and magazine articles; Coauthor of play, *Foxfire,* screenplay,

412

The Dollmaker, and *Dinner at the Homesick Restaurant* (1983). Business address: 63-23 Carlton Street, Rego Park, N. Y. 11374.

Theater. While a student at McGill Univ., Mr. Cronyn appeared with the Montreal Repertory Th. and the McGill Player's Club in productions which included *The Adding Machine, Dr. Faustus, From Morn to Midnight, The Road to Rome, Alice in Wonderland,* and the *Red and White Revue* (1930–31).

He made his professional debut with Cochran's Stock Co. in *Up Pops the Devil* (Natl., Washington, D.C., Spring 1931); joined R. Porterfield's Barter Th. Co. as production director and played Austin Lowe in *The Second Man,* Dr. Haggett in *The Late Christopher Bean,* Jim Hipper in *He Knew Dillinger* (later entitled *Hipper's Holiday*), and Doke Odum in *Mountain Ivy* (Summer 1934). His first appearance on Broadway was as a Janitor and understudy to Burgess Meredith in the role of Jim Hipper in *Hipper's Holiday* (Maxine Elliott's Th., Oct. 18, 1934); subsequently joined the Jitney Touring Players, appearing as Stingo and Sir Charles Marlowe in *She Stoops to Conquer* and as Gideon Bloodgood in *The Streets of New York* (Mar.–Sept. 1935).

He played Erwin Trowbridge in the national (touring) production of *Three Men on a Horse* (Oct. 1935–June 1936); succeeded (Sept. 1936) Garson Kanin as Green in *Boy Meets Girl* (Cort, N.Y.C., Nov. 27, 1935), and played it on tour; appeared as Elkus and understudied Burgess Meredith in the role of Van Van Dorn in *High Tor* (Martin Beck Th., N.Y.C., Jan. 9, 1937); succeeded (Aug. 1937) Eddie Albert as Leo Davis in *Room Service* (Cort, May 19, 1937), continuing in the role on tour.

He appeared as Abe Sherman in *There's Always a Breeze* (Windsor, N.Y.C., Mar. 2, 1938); Steve in *Escape This Night* (44 St. Th., Apr. 22, 1938); Harry Quill in *Off to Buffalo* (Ethel Barrymore Th., Feb. 21, 1939); and played two seasons with the Lakewood Th. (Skowhegan, Me.) in roles which included Hutchens Stubbs in *Susan and God,* Toby Cartwright in *Ways and Means,* George Davies in *We Were Dancing* from *Tonight at 8:30,* Francis O'Connor in *Shadow and Substance,* Christy Dudgeon in *The Devil's Disciple,* Lloyd Lloyd in *Kiss the Boys Goodbye,* Judas in *Family Portrait,* The Stage Manager in *Our Town,* Denis Dillon in *The White Steed,* Karl Baumer in *Margin for Error,* and Joe Bonaparte in *Golden Boy* (May–Sept. 1939; May–Sept. 1940).

He played Andrei Prozoroff in *The Three Sisters* (Longacre, N.Y.C., Oct. 14, 1939); Peter Mason in *The Weak Link* (John Golden Th., Mar. 4, 1940; Lee Tatnall in the Group Th. production of *Retreat to Pleasure* (Belasco, Dec. 17, 1940); produced and appeared in a revue

for the Canadian Active Service Canteen (May 1941); played Joe Bonaparte in *Golden Boy* (Bucks County Playhouse, New Hope, Pa., July
1941); played Harley L. Miller in *Mr. Big* (Lyceum, N.Y.C., Sept. 30,
1941); for the USO, produced *Junior Miss* (Jan. 1942); co-produced
and appeared in a USO revue, *It's All Yours* (Mar. 1942); appeared
as Tommy Turner in an Actor's Laboratory Th. production of *The
Male Animal,* which toured military installations in Calif. (May 1944);
and in a vaudeville sketch in Canada for the Victory Loan (Oct. 1944).

Mr. Cronyn directed an Actors' Laboratory Th. production of
Portrait of a Madonna (Las Palmas Th., Los Angeles, Calif., Summer
1946); played Jodine Decker in *The Survivors* (Playhouse, N.Y.C., Jan.
19, 1948); the title role in an ANTA touring production of *Hamlet*
(Mar.–May 1949); directed *Now I Lay Me Down to Sleep* (Stanford
Univ., Calif., July 1949) and in N.Y.C. (Broadhurst, Mar. 2, 1950);
appeared in *The Little Blue Light* (Brattle Th., Cambridge, Mass., Aug.
1950); directed *Hilda Crane* (Coronet, N.Y.C., Nov. 1, 1950); and
played Michael in *The Fourposter* (Ethel Barrymore Th., Oct. 24, 1951).

With Norman Lloyd, he staged the initial Phoenix Th. (N.Y.C.)
production, *Madam, Will You Walk,* in which he played Dr. Brightlee
(Phoenix, Dec. 1, 1953); with his wife, Jessica Tandy, appeared in
concert readings, titled *Face to Face,* on a cross-country tour (Sept.–
Dec. 1954); played Michael in *The Fourposter* (N.Y. City Ctr., Jan. 5,
1955); played Curtis and Bennett Honey in *The Honeys* (Longacre,
Apr. 28, 1955); Julian in *A Day by the Sea* (ANTA, Sept. 26, 1955);
and Oliver Walling in a touring production of *The Man in the Dog
Suit* (June–Sept. 1957).

Mr. Cronyn directed *The Egghead* (Ethel Barrymore Th., N.Y.C.,
Oct. 9, 1957); directed and toured with Miss Tandy in *Triple Play,* a
bill of three one-act plays and a monologue, in which he appeared
as the Doctor in *Portrait of a Madonna,* Jerry in *A Pound on Demand,*
John Jo Mulligan in *Bedtime Story,* and as "Professor" Ivan Ivanovitch
Nyukhin in the monologue *Some Comments on the Harmful Effects of
Tobacco* (Summer 1958); appeared as Oliver Walling in *The Man in
the Dog Suit* (Coronet, N.Y.C., Oct. 30, 1958); directed and repeated
his roles in *Triple Play* (Playhouse, Apr. 15, 1959); and appeared as
Jimmie Luton in *Big Fish, Little Fish* (ANTA, N.Y.C., Mar. 15, 1961;
Duke of York's, London, Sept. 18, 1962).

He appeared with the Minnesota Theater Co. (Tyrone Guthrie
Th., Minneapolis, Minn.), in its first season, as Harpagon in *The Miser* (May 8, 1963); Tchebutykin in *The Three Sisters* (June 1963); and
Willie Loman in *Death of a Salesman* (July 16, 1963). He played Polonius in Richard Burton's *Hamlet* (Lunt-Fontanne, N.Y.C., Apr. 9,

1964; Newton in *The Physicists* (Martin Beck Th., Oct. 7, 1964); and produced *Slow Dance on the Killing Ground* (Plymouth, Dec. 1, 1964). On February 2, 1965, together with his wife, Jessica Tandy, appeared at the White House, Washington, D.C., at request of the President and Mrs. Johnson in *Hear America Speaking*. Appeared in title role of *Richard III* (May 10, 1965), as Yepihodov in *The Cherry Orchard* (June 15, 1965) and as Harpagon in *The Miser* (Sept. 7, 1965) at The Tyrone Guthrie Theater's third season, Minneapolis, Minn.; appeared as Tobias in *A Delicate Balance* (Martin Beck Th., Sept. 22, 1966); U.S. Tour (Jan. 17, 1967). Revival *The Miser* (Mark Taper Forum, L.A., Mar. 15, 1968).

Played Frederick William Rolfe in *Hadrian VII* with the Stratford National Theatre Co. of Canada in Stratford, Ont. (Aug. 5, 1969) and in National Tour (Sept. 4, 1969); played Capt. Queeg in *Caine Mutiny Court Martial* (Ahmanson Th., Los Angeles, Calif., Nov. 30, 1971); appeared in *Promenade All* pre-Broadway tour (Jan. 31, 1972) at Alvin Th., N.Y.C. (Apr. 16, 1972); Summer Tour (Aug. 14, 1972) and Winter Tour (Jan. 24, 1973); portrayed Krapp in *Krapp's Last Tape*, Willie in *Happy Days* and The Player in *Act Without Words I* in a limited engagement with his wife, Jessica Tandy, as part of a Samuel Beckett Festival at the Forum of Lincoln Center (Nov. 20, 1972); appeared in title role of *Krapp's Last Tape* at the St. Lawrence Theatre Center, Toronto, Canada, Arena Stage, Washington, D.C. and universities in the East (Sept. 4, 1973).

Appeared as Verner Conklin and Sir Hugo Latymer in the double bill of *Noel Coward in Two Keys*, pre-Broadway Tour (Dec. 22, 1973) and at Ethel Barrymore Th., N.Y.C. (Feb. 28, 1974); National Tour (Feb. 17, 1975). With his wife performed in *Many Faces of Love*, a limited "concert recital" tour (Oct. 7, 1974 and Oct. 11, 1975), appearing also at the Tyrone Guthrie Th. (Nov. 23, 1975) and Seattle Repertory Th. (Dec. 2, 1975).

Played Shylock in *Merchant of Venice* and Bottom in *A Midsummer Night's Dream* in Stratford Festival 1976, Stratford, Ont., Canada (June 7–Oct. 10, 1976); "Many Faces of Love," Theatre London, London, Ont. (Oct. 28, 1976) and continued on tour (Nov. 15, 1976).

Coproduced with Mike Nichols and performed in *The Gin Game*, (Pulitzer Prize–winning play of 1978) as Weller Martin with his wife, Jessica Tandy, at the Long Wharf Theater, New Haven, Conn. (June 1977), and at The Golden Theater, N.Y.C. (Oct. 6, 1977), continuing in the role on tour in the U.S., Toronto, London, England, and the U.S.S.R. (Oct. 1978 to Dec. 1979).

Coauthored with Susan Cooper and played in *Foxfire*, as Hector

Nations, with his wife, Jessica Tandy, at the Stratford Festival, Stratford, Ont., Canada (Aug. 7–Oct. 12, 1980) and at The Guthrie Theater, Minneapolis, Mn. (Sept. 5–Nov. 21, 1981); and at the Ethel Barrymore Theater, N.Y.C. (Nov. 11, 1982–May 15, 1983).

Appeared in world premiere of *Traveler in the Dark* as Everett at the American Repertory Theater, Loeb Drama Center, Cambridge, Mass. (Feb. 3–Mar. 17, 1984). Again played in a limited run of *Foxfire* as Hector Nations, with his wife, Jessica Tandy, at the Ahmanson Theater, Los Angeles (Nov. 26, 1985–Jan. 11, 1986). Played General Sir Edmund Milne in *The Petition* with his wife, Jessica Tandy, at the Golden Theater, N.Y.C. (Apr. 24, 1986–June 29, 1986).

Films. Mr. Cronyn made his debut as Herbie Hawkins in *Shadow of a Doubt* (U, 1943); subsequently appeared in *The Cross of Lorraine* (MGM, 1943); *The Seventh Cross* (MGM, 1944); *Main Street After Dark* (MGM, 1944); *Lifeboat* (Fox, 1944); *A Letter for Evie* (MGM, 1945); *The Sailor Takes a Wife* (MGM, 1945); *The Green Years* (MGM, 1946); *The Ziegfeld Follies* (MGM, 1946); as Dr. Robert Oppenheimer in *Beginning of the End* (MGM, 1947); *Brute Force* (U, 1947); *The Bride Goes Wild* (MGM, 1948); wrote the screenplay treatments for *Rope* (WB, 1948) and *Under Capricorn* (WB, 1949); appeared in *Top o' the Morning* (Par., 1949); *People Will Talk* (Fox, 1951); *Crowded Paradise* (Tudor, 1956); as Louis Howe in *Sunrise at Campobello* (WB, 1960); *Cleopatra* (Fox, 1963); *Gaily Gaily* (Mirisch-Simkoe 1968, Dir. Norman Jewison); *The Arrangement* (Athena Prod. 1968, Dir. Elia Kazan); *There Was a Crooked Man* (Warner Bros.–Seven Arts 1969, Dir. J. L. Mankiewicz); *Conrack* (20th C. Fox 1973, Dir. Martin Ritt); *Parallax View* (Par. 1973, Dir. Alan Pakula); *Honky Tonk Freeway* (Kendon Films, Inc. 1980, Dir. John Schlesinger); *Rollover* (IPC Films 1981, Dir. Alan Pakula); *Garp* (WB 1981, Dir. George Roy Hill); *Impulse* (ABC 1983, Dir. Graham Baker); *Brewster's Millions* (Universal 1984, Dr. Walter Hill); *Cocoon* (Fox-Zanuck/Brown Prod. 1984, Dir. Ron Howard); *Batteries Not Included* (Universal, 1986, Dir. Matthew Robbins); *Cocoon: The Return* (20th C. Fox 1988, Dir. Dan Petrie).

Television. Mr. Cronyn's first appearance was as Ned Ferrar in *Her Master's Voice* (NBC, 1939). He produced and directed *Portrait of a Madonna* (Actors' Studio ABC, Sept. 26, 1948); produced and appeared with Jessica Tandy in their own series, *The Marriage,* on radio and television (NBC, 1953, 1954). He appeared seven times on *Omnibus* (CBS); three times on the *Ed Sullivan Show* (CBS); played Michael in *The Fourposter* (NBC, 1955); performed in *The Great Adventure*

(CBS, 1956); *The Confidence Man* (NBC, 1956); *The Big Wave* (NBC, 1956); *The $5 Bill* (CBS, 1957); *Member of the Family* (CBS, 1957); *The Bridge of San Luis Rey* (Dupont Show of the Month, CBS, Jan. 1958); *The Moon and Sixpence* (NBC, Oct. 30, 1959); *A Doll's House* (NBC, Nov. 15, 1959); *Juno and the Paycock* (Play of the Week, WNTA, 1960); the *John F. Kennedy Memorial Broadcast* (NBC, 1963); and played Polonius in *Hamlet* (Electronovision, Fall 1964); "Many Faces of Love" (CBC, Canada, Mar. 1977); *The Gin Game* (RKO General, 1979). Coauthor with Susan Cooper of *The Dollmaker* (IPC Films for ABC, 1985) a three-hour teleplay. Appeared with Jessica Tandy in *Foxfire*, teleplay on CBS, Dec. 13, 1987. *Day One* (CBS, 1988); *Age Old Friends* (HBO) 1988/89.

Awards. Mr. Cronyn was nominated for an Academy (Oscar) Award (1944) for his performance in *The Seventh Cross.* He and his wife received the Comoedia Matinee Club's Award (1952) for their performances in *The Fourposter.* He received the Barter Theater Award (1961) "for outstanding contribution to the theater"; was nominated for the Antoinette Perry (Tony) Award (1961) and received the Delia Austria medal from the N. Y. Drama League (1961) for his performance as Jimmie Luton in *Big Fish, Little Fish;* received the Antoinette Perry (Tony) Award and won the Variety N. Y. Drama Critics Poll (1964) for his performance as Polonius in *Hamlet.* Received the American Academy of Dramatic Arts Ninth Annual Award for Achievement for Alumni (Dec. 1964).

Was nominated for the Antoinette Perry (Tony) Award (1967) and received the Herald Theater Award for his performance as Tobias in *A Delicate Balance.* Received the Los Angeles Drama Critics Circle Award for best actor in *Caine Mutiny Court Martial* (1972); received Fourth Annual Straw Hat Award for best director 1972 for direction of *Promenade All.* Received Obie Award for 1972–73 for outstanding achievement in the Off-Broadway Theater for distinguished performance in *Krapp's Last Tape.*

Recipient of Brandeis University Creative Arts Award, April 19, 1978, receiving Theater Arts Medal for a lifetime of distinguished achievement. Nominated by Drama Desk 1977–78 for outstanding actor, and for Antoinette Perry (Tony) Award for best actor in *The Gin Game,* 1979. Recipient of Los Angeles Critics' Award for performance in *The Gin Game.*

Elected to Theater Hall of Fame 1979 in recognition of outstanding contributions to American Theater. Received National Press Club

Award 1979; Received 1983 Common Wealth Award for dramatic arts.

With Susan Cooper, received 1985 Christopher Award and Writers Guild Award for screenplay *Dollmaker,* an ABC teleplay; as well as the 1985 Humanitas Prize for achievement in television.

Was nominated for the Antoinette Perry (Tony) Award 1986 for his performance as Edmund in *The Petition.* Honoree of 1986 Kennedy Center Honors.

Recipient of Alley Theater Award (Houston) March 22, 1987, in recognition of significant contributions to the theater arts. Received the Franklin Haven Sargent Award from the American Academy of Dramatic Arts in recognition as a distinguished alumnus for the quality of acting. May 1, 1988.

On February 1, 1989, the Academy of Television Arts & Sciences paid tribute to Mr. Cronyn and Miss Tandy for 50 years of television performances.

On October 26, 1989, together with his wife, Jessica Tandy, received the Arnold Gingrich Arts & Business Council 1989 Encore Award for extraordinary achievement in the arts, and on May 8, 1990, New Dramatists paid tribute to them.

Recipient of the 1990 National Medal of Arts awarded by the President of the United States at the White House on September 10, 1990, in special recognition of outstanding contribution to the excellence, growth, support and availability of the arts in the United States.

Received the 1990 Emmy award for outstanding lead actor in a miniseries or special in *Age Old Friends* from the Academy of Television Arts & Sciences and the 1990 ACE Award from the National Academy of Cable Programming.

INDEX

419